American Ballads
and
Folk Songs

COLLECTED AND COMPILED BY

JOHN A. LOMAX

Honorary Consultant in American Folk Song
and Curator of the Folk Song Archives of
the Library of Congress

AND

ALAN LOMAX

WITH A FOREWORD BY
GEORGE LYMAN KITTREDGE
Harvard University

New York·The Macmillan Company·Mcmliii

To the Mother who sang many of these songs into the lives of Shirley, John, Jr., Alan, and Bess Brown, in grateful and loving memory, we dedicate this book.

FOREWORD

PROFESSOR LOMAX needs no introduction. His "Cowboy Songs," published years and years ago, won forthwith a classic rank among books of folk-poetry—in whatever sense controversialists may choose to interpret that much-vexed term. But, though introduction is superfluous, a word of greeting may not be out of place. Lomax has never flagged in his zeal as a collector, and his success has been proportionate with his energy. Of late, too, he has enjoyed the assistance of his son, and their combined activities have greatly increased our knowledge of the subject. In the volume now offered to the friendly reader there is much that is novel; yet the old familiar fields are not neglected. Here, then, is a book of songs that illustrates many phases of our strangely multifarious life and manners. There is something for every mood and for every intelligent taste. And the whole thing is intensely American and has been contrived by a man who knows what he is about and is in vital contact with the materials that he has so skilfully brought together. *Caveat emptor* is a good book-buying motto nowadays, but in this case the buyer may take his chances without trepidation.

G. L. KITTREDGE

ACKNOWLEDGMENT

WHEN I went first to college in Texas I carried in my trunk, along with my pistol and other implements of personal warfare, a little manuscript roll of cowboy songs. My father's farm and small ranch was located on the Chisholm Trail, over which many thousand Longhorn cattle were driven to Dodge City, Kansas; sometimes on to Montana and the Dakotas. Especially at night when lying awake, I had heard the cowboys sing to the cattle "bedded down" near our home. These songs and others like them were also current among a number of neighbor boys, older than myself, who each spring went on the round-up and afterwards trailed a herd of cattle to a Northern market. They brought new songs back with them for the entertainment of their friends.

On one occasion I exhibited my store of cowboy songs to a somewhat startled Texas English professor. I was told politely that they had no value. So I put them away until I became, years afterwards, a student in Harvard. There, during a course in American literature taught by Professor Barrett Wendell, I was encouraged to believe that the songs were worth preserving. In order to aid my work in collecting, he and Professor George Lyman Kittredge sent out to many newspapers of the country a letter asking that all types of folk songs be forwarded to me. Later on, after I had been appointed a Traveling Sheldon Fellow "to investigate American folk songs," Professors Wendell and Kittredge were joined in a second appeal to the public by Dean L. B. R. Briggs and Professor Fred N. Robinson. Such sponsorship resulted, during the three years I held the Sheldon fellowship, in the accumulation of a great mass of material.

Two books of cowboy songs were issued from material secured principally in Texas, Oklahoma, New Mexico, Arizona, Colorado,

Acknowledgment

Wyoming, and other states where I visited and recorded tunes in saloons and on remote ranches. Several thousand pages of unused manuscript were filed away. The present book is a direct outgrowth of the collection which was then made under Harvard patronage.

Whatever its fortune, it goes to a public whose interest in folk material is much greater than in 1910, when *Cowboy Songs* was published. At that time no publisher would print the cowboy song music, except a few illustrative examples. Records of this music had been made on wax cylinders, which, alas! have crumbled with age. However, the music then set down and printed, long unnoticed, is now often heard over the radio. It has been said that the song "Home on the Range" was the most popular tune of the first half of 1933. The music for that song was obtained twenty-three years ago from the Negro proprietor of a low drinking and gambling dive in the slum district of San Antonio. It remained safely buried in *Cowboy Songs* for nearly a quarter of a century. The publication of this volume is, therefore, largely due to the unflagging interest of two men. So long as Professor Barrett Wendell lived, he gave my work his cordial support, and through the resulting association I, in turn, gave him my everlasting affection. To me, as well as to all who collect folk songs, or who write of this literature, Professor Kittredge is ready with advice, help, and, when needed, forceful admonition. These words are set down in grateful recognition and appreciation.

Many other people have helped to make this book possible. Entitled perhaps to first mention is Miss Mary Gresham, a competent musician and teacher of Washington, who transcribed from aluminum, wax, and celluloid records made this summer much of the Negro music in this book, and, in addition, other songs from singing and from rough manuscript notation. Edward Neighbors Waters, Assistant in the Music Division, Library of Congress, wrote out the music for approximately fifty songs, principally from singing. Other members of the Music Division, notably Carl Engel, its Chief, Oliver Strunk, Assistant Chief, and Frank Megill, Assistant, were constantly courteous

[xii]

and helpful. None of the faults of the book or responsibilities growing out of it, however, are chargeable to these persons.

To Mrs. Janice Reed Lit of Haverford, Pennsylvania, whose helpfulness in many ways has been constant since the book was first definitely planned; to Professors Howard W. Odum, Guy Johnson, and A. P. Hudson, all of the University of North Carolina, that is, along with near-by Duke University, the folk song collecting center of the South; to Professor Arthur G. Brodeur of the University of California; to Professor Joseph W. Clokey of Pomona College; to Frank Dobie of the University of Texas; to Professor E. C. Beck, Central State Teachers College, Mt. Pleasant, Michigan; to Louise and Cletus Oakley of Brown University; to Professor Lucy Lockwood Hazard of Mills College; to "Slim" Critchlow, Forest Ranger and soloist for the Utah Buckaroos; to Dean L. B. R. Briggs of Harvard University; to Professors Josiah Combs and Newton Gaines of Texas Christian University; to Professor George E. Hastings of the University of Arkansas; to Sigmund Spaeth, New York City; to Professor George Pullen Jackson, Vanderbilt University; to Sam P. Bayard, State College, Pennsylvania; to Mr. H. H. Fuson, Harlan, Kentucky; to Mr. and Mrs. Oscar Callaway, Comanche, Texas; to Carl Sandburg, Harbert, Michigan; to Professor and Mrs. Harold William Thompson, New York State College for Teachers; to Miss Dorothy Scarborough, Columbia University; to Major and Mrs. Isaac Spalding, Washington, D. C.; to Professor H. M. Belden, University of Missouri; to John A. Lomax, Jr.; to Miss Martha Harrold, Memphis, Tennessee; to John Lang Sinclair, New York City; to Shirley Lomax Mansell and Bess Brown Lomax, Lubbock, Texas— to all these, special thanks are due for special favors.

Along with these in point of service I must place that group of Negro "boys" who this summer, cheerfully and with such manifest friendliness, gave up for the time their crap and card games, their prayer meetings, their much needed Sunday and evening rest, in order to sing for Alan and me—that group whose real names we omit

[xiii]

Acknowledgment

for no other reason than to print the substituted picturesque nicknames. Those black "boys" of Texas, Louisiana, Mississippi, and Tennessee by their singing removed any doubt we may have had that Negro folk songs are without a rival in the United States. To Iron Head, Clear Rock, Chin Shooter, Lead Belly, Mexico, Black Samson, Lightnin', Can't Make It, Butter Ball, Ing Shing, Scrap Iron, Bowlegs, Tight Eyes, Double Head, Bull Face, Log Wagon, Creepin' Jesus, Long Distance, Burn Down, Steam Shovel, Rat, Black Rider, Barrel House, Spark Plug, to two "girls," Dink and Bat, and others who helped without giving their names, and to many another among the thousands we saw, in happy memory tinged with sadness, I offer grateful thanks.

As this book represents twenty-five years of desultory collecting, I cannot but fail to omit to mention names that should be included in the list to whom is also due, and who herewith receive, my gratitude:

Miss Virginia Brown, Dallas, Texas; Joanna Colcord, author of *Roll and Go;* Professor John H. Cox, University of West Virginia; Professor Frank Davidson, Indiana University; Captain A. E. Dingle, West Bermuda; Professor Horace A. Eaton, Syracuse University; Professor Milton Ellis, University of Maine; Captain R. J. Flanagan, Manager of Central State Farm, Texas; Colonel Frederick Stuart Greene, Commissioner of Public Works, Albany, New York; Judge Louis B. Hart, Buffalo, New York; Harvard University Press, Cambridge, Massachusetts; Superintendent R. L. Himes, General Manager Louisiana prison system; Captain H. J. Jackson, Manager Darrington State Farm, Texas; George Milburn, formerly of the University of Oklahoma; Professor and Mrs. George M. Miller, University of Idaho; Bertha K. Millette, Washington, D. C.; John J. Niles, co-author *Songs My Mother Never Taught Me;* Miss Mary Elizabeth Barnicle, New York University; Professor L. W. Payne, University of Texas; F. E. Peyton, Greenwich, Connecticut; Miss Louise Pound, University of Nebraska; Allen Prothro, Chattanooga, Tennessee; Augustus H. Shearer, Buffalo, New York; Frank Shay, author of

Acknowledgment

Drawn from the Wood, Provincetown, Massachusetts; Peter Smith, publisher, New York; Manager O. G. Tann, Parchman, Mississippi; Professor W. H. Thomas, College Station, Texas; Henry Trevelyan, Wiergate, Texas; Professor R. P. Utter, University of California; R. V. Utter, Clayton, Missouri; John T. Vance, Library of Congress; Stewart Edward White; Professor Newman I. White, Duke University; Owen Wister, Bryn Mawr, Pennsylvania; Professor Homer E. Woodbridge, Wesleyan University, Middletown, Connecticut; Miss Louise Wyman, author of *Lonesome Tunes;* Miss Jean Thomas, author of *Devil's Ditties,* Ashland, Kentucky.

J. A. L.

CONTENTS

Contents

[xviii]

Contents

[xix]

Contents

Contents

Contents

Contents

[xxiii]

Contents

INTRODUCTION

The sun is sorta sinkin', an' the road is clear,
An' the wind is singin' ballads that I got to hear.

—BERTON BRALEY

RECENTLY a professor of music from Oxford University said in a public lecture at Bryn Mawr College: "Since America has no peasant class, there are, of course, no American folk songs." Twenty years ago his statement might have gone without serious challenge. But the results flowing from the teaching of Professor George Lyman Kittredge of Harvard and his many torch bearers and co-workers would offer contrary evidence.

Robert W. Gordon, for several years Curator of Folk Songs in the Library of Congress, holds both that American folk-song examples are greater in number, and also that folk-song production is more active in America than in any other country that is preserving this form of literature. Likewise he asserts that ballad making will continue, and that we shall always have the folk to preserve them. Mr. Gordon speaks not only as a scholar but as an experienced and successful collector. The books of Professors Howard W. Odum, Guy Johnson, and A. P. Hudson of the University of North Carolina; of Newman I. White, Duke University; Louise Pound, University of Nebraska; Dorothy Scarborough, Columbia University; George Pullen Jackson, Vanderbilt University; Jean Thomas and H. H. Fuson, Kentucky; Joanna Colcord and Fannie Eckstorm, Maine; Frank Dobie and the Texas Folk-Lore Society; Cecil Sharp; Carl Sandburg, Michigan; Louise Wyman, Kentucky; and others perhaps not less worthy, all serious studies of our own native folk-song product, also appear as witnesses for the defense.

Since the publication of *Cowboy Songs* in 1910 the interest in

[xxv]

American balladry has increased enormously, as is shown by the more than one hundred ballad books in the Library of Congress, issued since that year. This number does not include the smaller collections of quasi-folk songs put out by radio singers and other minstrels.

At Round Top, Virginia, during the past summer newspapers report that 20,000 people attended a three-day Folk Festival. Kentucky also has an organization, the American Folk Song Society at Ashland, with an annual meeting for the preservation of folk tunes and folk dances. At the University of Idaho, Professor George Miller includes in his course in the English ballad a study of the American product. Professor Harold Thompson at the New York State College for Teachers, and Miss Mary Elizabeth Barnicle at New York University, do the same. Professor Frank Dobie talks and teaches folk lore and folk song the year round at the University of Texas, as does Professor John Lee Brooks at Southern Methodist University, Dallas, Texas. Other instances abound of the growing interest in what the Modern Language Association calls "popular literature," and a special section each year hears learned discussions on topics falling in this category.

*   *   *   *   *

An editorial writer in the New York *Evening Post* recently stated: "As with folk tales and dialect tales, we need reassurance that ballad singing is not dying. . . . There probably always will be uninstructed souls enough—sometimes whole communities of them—to keep alive these things that are closest to the heart of man. For all their crudeness, traditional songs are interesting for breathing the mind of the ignorant, and as 'a voice from secret places, silent places and old times long dead.'"

Although the spread of machine civilization is rapidly making it hard to find folk singers, ballads are yet sung in this country. What we may by courtesy call ballads are being made. The Boll Weevil came a-visiting from Mexico thirty years ago. He had not long settled in the South before the Texas Negro made a song about him that grew in length as the Boll Weevil journeyed on eastward by easy stages to the Atlantic Ocean. And the Negroes named their song "De Ballit of de Boll Weevil." "Billy Marie," "Bugger Burns," "Stagolee," "De Titanic," "Frankie and Albert," widely sung songs of tragedy, are known to be of recent composition. Only this summer a Negro on a large cotton plantation we visited, misunderstanding our request for "made-up" songs, composed a satire on the overseer. This song, "Po' Farmer," was greeted with shouts of approval when the author sang it that night at the plantation schoolhouse. It is the type of song that may grow into a genuine ballad.

The cowboy, the miner, the tramp, the lumberjack, the Forty-niner, the soldier, the sailor, the plantation Negro (as also his sophisticated city cousin), the sailor on the Great Lakes, and even the boatman in the early days of the Erie Canal, all have "made-up" songs describing their experiences or detailing situations religious, tragic, sentimental, humorous, and at times didactic. The frontier has been beaten back to the accompaniment of singing; and there are yet eddies where such songs are created.

A life of isolation, without books or newspapers or telephone or radio, breeds songs and ballads. The gamut of human experience has been portrayed through this unrecorded (at least until recently) literature of the people. These people had no literary conventions to uphold. But they were lonely or sad or glad, and they sought diversion. A complete anthology of American folk songs would cover many thousand pages. Moreover, by the time the collection was brought together and published, a revision would immediately be necessary. New songs spring up, and almost every version of a current song shows interesting changes.*

In *American Ballads and Folk Songs* the purpose is to present the

---

* Robert W. Gordon has 300 versions of "Frankie and Albert." An industrious private collector has brought together more than half a thousand stanzas of "Mademoiselle of Armentières." "The Old Chisholm Trail," a cowboy song, is an epic of a thousand stanzas.

best examples of the most noteworthy types, words and tunes. We offer a composite photograph of what we and others, in field and forest, on mountain and plain, by the roadside and in the cabin, on big cane or cotton plantations and in prison camp, have set down of the songs of the people—isolated groups, interested only in an art which they could immediately enjoy, and thus an art that reflected and made interesting their own customs, dramas, and dreams. Grimm has said that the folk song composes itself. Its music comes straight from the heart of the people, and its idioms reveal their daily habits of speech. Furthermore, the individual author is so unimportant that he usually is lost sight of altogether. In the spirit of this theory the first line of a cowboy song runs: "My name is nothin' extry, so that I will not tell." The examples given herein measure up in some degree, we hope, to accepted definitions of folk literature.

We are offering these songs for what the tunes may be worth as music, and what the words may be worth as literature. Literature has been defined as whatever in written speech has an abiding human interest. In this sense some folk songs, however fragile in thought and rough in phraseology, have won their way to recognition. The Negro's ability to portray an emotional situation or to picture an incident in a few graphic and powerful one-syllable words is almost without parallel. The texts of the folk songs offer illustrations. Already even the recently known music of the cowboy songs is found in themes of standard musical composition. The influence of Negro music has been growing for many years. Folk-song radio programs attest the widespread popularity of this music. American folk music does have widespread human interest. With each song printed we offer our choice of the tunes current in various sections. Except in the case of "Alabama Bound," the tune is given entire, without mixture with a tune current elsewhere. With the words the treatment is different. Numbers of the songs are composites; that is, we have brought together what seem the best stanzas, or even lines, from widely separated sources. No one person probably has ever sung entirely a number of the songs, as herein printed; but all the words given have been sung by some people.

We justify the use of the composite ballad—the stringing together of the best stanzas, no matter where found—partly by an experience in collecting the "Ballad of the Erie Canal." Some years ago, at Union College, Schenectady, New York, the late Professor E. E. Hale gave us a single stanza of the song. Later a Rio Grande cattleman sent another stanza; still another came from Montana, and a fourth from a correspondent in Chicago. Some time afterward a Seattle lawyer sent three additional stanzas along with the refrain, and also the music as he sang the song while working as a towpath boy out of Buffalo from 1871 to 1877. Only recently, we found in the library of Allegheny College at Meadville, Pennsylvania, a final stanza. The eight stanzas and the refrain as herein printed, coming from six widely separated sources, seem to belong together. Necessarily the arrangement is ours.

This folk poem is thus to some extent literary. But if we had printed each version separately? The reader, instead of being presented with a humorous picture of the dangers of life on the Erie Canal, would have been informed that a man in Seattle, one in Montana, one in Chicago, one on the banks of the Rio Grande, and a professor in a New York college, all had poor memories and had known at one time, whether at first hand or through the telling of another person, about the Erie Canal and its song. In the same way we could have printed several hundred pages of the variants of "Frankie and Albert" or the "Levee Camp Holler." Only a few persons would be interested in comparing these variants, but we should have had the satisfaction of knowing that we had followed a very ancient scholarly convention. Instead, we have made this a collection of composites of what seemed to be the most freshly interesting stanzas that have been sung to the various songs. Out of the jumbled and disconnected stanzas of Negro work songs and Blues, we have selected a group that present, for instance, some connected theme.

Recordings of these and other Negro songs, made during June, July, and August of the present year, on big cotton plantations and lumber camps in Texas, in farm prison camps in Texas, Louisiana, and Mississippi, and in the two state prisons of Tennessee, seem worthy of special comment. All the singing was done by Negroes, principally by men. Our purpose was to find the Negro who had had the least contact with jazz, the radio, and with the white man. Both on the farms and in the lumber camps the proportion of whites to Negroes was approximately 100 to 1. In the prison farm camps, however, the conditions were practically ideal. Here the Negro prisoners were segregated, often guarded by Negro trusties, with no social or other contacts with the whites, except for occasional official relations. The convicts heard only the idiom of their own race. Many—often of greatest influence—were "lifers" who had been confined in the penitentiary, a few as long as fifty years. They still sang the songs they had brought into confinement, and these songs had been entirely in the keeping of the black man. Examples of the findings in such environments are included in the Negro section. Being naturally imitative, the Negro's singing, under the influence of the idiom and custom of his white neighbors, is unconsciously yet surely changed by white influences. He is apt to sing as he thinks the whites wish him to sing, and, as a result, he quickly abandons the musical nuances that make his music what it is.

A Negro cook in Houston, Texas, was heard to sing,

> "Niggers gittin' mo' like white folks,
> Mo' like white folks every day.
> Niggers learnin' Greek and Latin,
> Niggers wearin' silk and satin—
> Niggers gittin' mo' like white folks every day."

"Learnin' Greek and Latin," daily association with the whites, and modern education prove disastrous to the Negro's folk singing, destroying much of the quaint, innate beauty of his songs. Moreover, with most of the Southern Negro ministers and teachers urging their followers to abandon the old songs, a flood of jazz and of tawdry gospel hymns comes in. A black giant in the Nashville penitentiary resolutely refused to sing an entirely innocuous levee camp work song since he was a Hardshell Baptist and his church regarded such melodies as "Devil's songs" or "sinful songs."

Such opposition was found everywhere. Two days spent at a largely attended college for Negroes, where the approval of the president and the teacher of music was readily obtained, proved almost futile. Our object was soon known all over the campus. The students met our requests evasively, though from the dormitories floated snatches of many songs for which we were searching. In cities such as New Orleans, Nashville, and Memphis (even Beale Street) jazz * reigns happily and completely in the barrel-house regions. Only long and patient search could unearth the old tunes.

Seventy-five years ago a gentleman from Delaware wrote:

"We must look to their non-religious songs for the purest specimens of Negro minstrelsy . . . I have stood for more than an hour, often listening to them [black stevedores in Philadelphia and Baltimore] as they hoisted and lowered the hogsheads and boxes of their cargoes; one man taking the burden of the song (and the slack rope) and the others striking in with the chorus." There was nothing religious in their songs. "Quite the reverse—but generally rather innocent and proper in their language, and strangely attractive in their music." This group singing had passed away, "to be heard only . . . in out of the way places where opportunities for respectable persons to hear them are rather few. . . . In parts of the South 'fiddle sings,' 'devil songs,' 'corn songs,' 'jig-tunes,' and what not, are common. . . . It is often no easy matter to persuade them to sing their old songs, even as a curiosity, such is the sense of dignity that has come with freedom."

Happily for our purpose, we hope, it was mainly for the non-reli-

* Krehbiel called jazz the debased offspring of Negro songs.

gious songs among the Negroes that the search of the past summer was made. And the songs of black labor—gang singing of Negroes working in groups—that we found are the type which will receive special attention in the pages which follow.

Krehbiel said, "The truest, the most intimate folk music, is that produced by suffering." The songs of the Negro prisoners in convict camps furnished confirmation of this theory. Only one song is recalled that reflected unrestrained abandon to joyous emotions.* In the Blues, humorous verses often are put into tunes doleful or broodingly sad. Even the throbbing chants of labor, swaying with energy and rhythmic power, are colored with pathos. Was it the forbidding iron bars, the stripes, the clank of occasional shackles, the cruel-looking black bullwhip four feet long, which in some places hung in plain sight inside the door of the main hall—was it such surroundings that made the songs seem sad?

And yet the sadness, the melancholy, did not, it is believed, grow out of brutal treatment. The men were well fed and their sleeping quarters looked comfortable. In most places they worked hard, but the early "All quiet" † permitted sufficient hours of sleep. The visitors were given every freedom, and no case of cruelty was noted. The melancholy in the prison songs comes doubtless from the Negro's desire, as one said, "to git away f'om here. I jis' don' nachly like dis place." Black Samson, huge and kindly-looking (he was a double murderer), said, "Boss, do you think dem songs of mine will help me any up dere in Washington?" Songs that have been brought into the prison become colored with this gloomy note. The Negro makes a model prisoner, as one guard said, easy to control, but in his singing he abandons himself to a brooding hopelessness, as though freedom were beyond reach.

* "My Yellow Gal."
† A line from a prison Blues:
"Gonna tell my baby when I gits back home
Been down here where de lights burn all night long."
(Burning the lights all night is a necessary precaution in all prison farm dormitories.)

The experience was unforgettable. Eager, black, excited faces, swaying bodies, the ring of metal to mark the beat of the song, tones such as can come only from untrained voices—free, wild, resonant— joined in singing some semibarbaric tune in words rough and crude, sometimes direct and forceful, the total effect often thrillingly beautiful. While all around sat other men, alert and watchful, with guns in their hands! Yes, we agree that much of folk music grows out of suffering, if the songs of prison life only be considered. This note of sadness voices the Negro convict's intense and constant longing for freedom, home, and "Rosie."

Consistency in printing Negro dialect and grammar was not found possible in a book which contains Negro compositions from every Southern state. When we attempted to spell the words as the Negro singer pronounces them, with the same faithfulness with which the machine recorded the tunes he sang, we soon found that in one sentence he would, for example, pronounce "the" correctly and in the next sentence call it "de," "th'," "dee" or, possibly, "deh"; "going to" becomes "goin'," "gwine," "gwinter," "gonna," "gonter," etc. The Carolina and Virginia Negro pronounces many words far differently from the Negro of Louisiana and Mississippi. In some instances, following Odum and Johnson, whose work in Negro folk song is outstanding, we retain the precise form of the word as it comes to us. Negroes of education who sang some of these songs, dropped, perhaps unconsciously, into the idiom of the song as they in turn had heard it from a person lacking formal education. We have tried, in general, to establish a norm, having in mind always the reader who is unacquainted with the Negro's distinctive and often beautifully expressive dialect. Much that we have heard, if written out precisely as it sounded, would be unintelligible to the average reader. In the Negro songs, for instance, the *r* ending a word and the long *i* are generally to be pronounced as "ah" or "uh"; final consonants are to be slurred or dropped entirely, if one is to arrive at an approximation of Negro pronunciation.

These three characteristics of Negro dialect make rhyming easy. "Bolt," for instance, may be rhymed with "floor" because they are pronounced "bo'" and "flo'." There are many other examples of vowel rhyming in the Negro sections of this book, which will not seem rhymes at all to the reader; but, when they come from the lips of the folk-singers, these rhymes do not attract notice until one attempts to write them down.

It is true of Negro folk-songs in general and of Negro work-songs in particular that the tune and its mood and rhythm are more important to the singer than the words. The Negro laborer, swinging his pick, fits the first phrases that occur to him into the rhythm of the pick-points. When they are written out, these phrases often seem jumbled and disconnected, just as a page of *Ulysses* is at first confusing to an unprepared reader. Occasionally, however, these jumbled phrases fit themselves into sentences, and, since the mind of the un-self-conscious singer turns most readily to those things in his experience which are most important to him, and which he knows the best, these sentences are often terse and epic summaries of his important life relations. Professor White, in his excellent and scholarly book *Folk-Songs of the American Negro*, quotes a verse that is typical of this stark truthfulness, "All a nigger wants is fat meat and sundown," a phrase which we have often heard in various forms on the lips of unsophisticated Negroes.

In giving ample space to the songs of the Negro, who has, in our judgment, created the most distinctive of folk songs—the most interesting, the most appealing, and the greatest in quantity—we may have put into too narrow limits songs of other types, such as the songs of the Great Lakes, the soldier, and the sailor, and the numerous quasi-ballads of Pennsylvania and the Middle West. Although much of the material represents actual field work, a considerable portion we "went and took" from indulgent and generous correspondents and, by permission, from collections already in print. The previous collectors in turn picked up the songs somewhere. The real author or authors remain unknown. In fact, all compilers are guilty of a species of thievery. As Garrick once wrote:

Poets and Painters, who from Nature draw
Their best and richest stores, have made this law:
That each should neighbourly assist his brother,
And steal with decency from one another.

"This law is still in force," adds Mr. Carl Engel of the Library of Congress in one of his delightful essays. Even Homer stole, and a modern poet adds that when Homer was accused of theft " 'E winked back—the same as us!"

Worse than thieves are ballad collectors, for when they capture and imprison in cold type a folk song, at the same time they kill it. Its change and growth are not so likely to continue after a fixed model for comparison exists. In this instance a Mergenthaler commits murder.

There is thus an element of sadness in imprisoning a folk song in type. For the song at once becomes adult; it grows no more. The printed form becomes a standard, and a fixed standard. So long as the song is passed from one to another by "word of mouth," its material is fluid, frequent changes occurring both in the words and in the music. Growth in length and change in phrase flourish best in freedom of remote mountain coves, the melancholy loneliness of wind-swept plains, the silence of river bottom regions, the quiet of far-away forest ranges, the monotonous dreariness of life in a prison camp.

* * * * *

The songs in this book (we hope it will be found a singing book) represent the personal choice of the compilers from a large mass of material from which other legitimate and defensible choices might have been made. Necessarily, environment, poetic and musical judgment have been the controlling factors. Believing some recently recorded Negro Spirituals are new to the public, we include them instead of reprinting others, well known and widely popular. In a very few instances songs are printed that have little apparent reason for appearing in this book. Easily recognizable even by the casual reader, there is no attempt at deception. It should be added, however, that at least to one of the compilers, either in tunes or in words, the choice of these songs could be defended. In the main, then, this collection represents what seems to the compilers the best among the available indigenous or semi-indigenous folk product, both words and tunes, found thus far in the United States, omitting only Indian songs.

Lack of space forces the exclusion of the Spanish traditional ballads that have been preserved by the peons of Mexico and their descendants in Texas, Arizona, New Mexico, and California. We have excluded, also, the beautiful English ballads that it has been America's artistic good fortune to inherit. The bald fact is that the characters that animate these ballads lived, died, and had most of their folk-stature before they came to this country. These folk histories have, it is true, gone through some changes in the hill country and more particularly among the Negroes, but in the main these have been minor changes and have not reflected, except in idiom and dialect, much of the social history of this country. A notable exception to this general statement is the version of "Barbara Allen" which we recorded from the singing of a Negro convict this past summer. He mounted "Bobby," as he familiarly called her, on a buckskin pony and sent her to her burying ground in the sands of the Arizona desert attended by six pretty maidens. At another place in the song he shipped her corpse out of the depot at Dallas, Texas, while her relatives and friends were "squallin' an' holl'in' " in an access of grief.

The student of folk music will undoubtedly find many survivals of English ballad and dance tunes in our collection, but only when the song has had such a wide popularity among the folk or has grown so extensively by accretion in this country that it is quite safe to say it is an indigenous folk song. "Weevily Wheat" has been enjoyed at play parties in backwoods districts in every part of the country. "Rye Whisky," which set out in life as "The Waggoner Lad," has grown and changed until it is nearly unrecognizable, except as to air, as a survival of English folk song.

We know that Sam Hall was an English bad man who came to his bad end on an English gallows, and that the ballad about this bad man is of definite English origin. But once near San Francisco we heard a group of good fellows * roar it out with such joyous abandon that we could not deny the public their version and tune. Then, too, we have so often sung "Captain Kidd" that it seems American. Of the Mexican and Creole folk songs we need only say that the characters and emotions which animate them are obviously drawn out the experience of American folk.

* * * * *

The music for the songs was obtained from several sources:

1. Wax records.

2. Aluminum and celluloid records. (Recording of the three types was by the compilers.)

3. Singing by different members of the Lomax family, through lines of ancestry reaching Virginia, South Carolina, Alabama, Mississippi, and Texas. More than forty songs are included to which they furnished tunes and words.

4. From published collections, acknowledgment for which is given elsewhere, and from contributions sent in. Included in this collection are several songs without musical text, in the hope that the tunes will be sent in by interested readers. It may well be that some have been already in print. Their intrinsic interest as folk, or at least semi-folk, literature forbids their exclusion from a book which is intended to appeal more to the general reader than to the meticulous student of the ballad.

No lover of folk songs who hears the untutored ballad singer render them fails to realize that the music is more vital for the total effect

* The Adventure Campfire Club, led by Professor Arthur Brodeur.

than the words. Therefore, whenever obtainable, along with the words, the melody, only, is printed. Few, if any, musicians would write identical harmonization to these tunes; so it seems simpler to omit any harmonization whatever. After all, even differences in noting down the tunes would probably arise should two musicians transcribe the same tune from a record. Those who wish to work from the original records and give their own interpretations of them will find this music in the Library of Congress on permanent aluminum and celluloid discs which reveal with fidelity what was sung into the microphone of our recording machine.

JOHN A. LOMAX
ALAN LOMAX

Washington. D. C.

This book provides the student of folk music with a collection of songs for interesting and valuable study. The field of Negro music covered is particularly noteworthy in that it includes a phase inadequately covered in the other books on the subject: the Negro work songs. There is, perhaps, in the work songs a more natural, spontaneous expression with less "white" influence than in any other type of the Negro song.

Since the effectiveness of any folk song is largely dependent on the understanding and interpretive powers of the performer, the most effective approach to the study of Negro folk music is to hear, either at first hand or by means of records, the Negro sing his songs. In the study of the written versions of these songs, one must keep in mind the limitations of all music notation. The inadequacy of music notation becomes increasingly apparent when working with Negro songs. Any attempt to transcribe the songs of the Negro into conventional notation is attended by many difficulties, and in some respects is an impossible task. First of all, the Negro does not sing in accordance with conventional pitch, and his songs must be "reduced," as it were, to conventional pitch; secondly, there is no way of expressing those indefinable variations of pitch and intonation which are fundamental characteristics of Negro singing. In the preparation of the present volume, there was the added difficulty of transcribing the songs from recordings—recordings made under all sorts of conditions, indoors and outdoors.

In dealing with the "chants," the only way of expressing them on paper was to write them in free chant form, without measure signature. It is not to be assumed, however, that they are not rhythmical. They are *very* rhythmical, but it is a free, natural, flowing rhythm without regular accents, which cannot be confined between bars in conventional measures.

The unavoidable inaccuracies which occur in the written form of these songs should not detract from their value to the serious student. They will be of no importance if he familiarizes himself with Negro music as sung by the Negro. It is, in fact, impossible to justly appreciate or understand the songs of the Southern Negroes without having heard them singing at their work—using as a relief from the daily hardships the most primitive medium of emotional expression: *music*.

MARY E. GRESHAM

Washington. D. C.

I

WORKING ON THE RAILROAD

"Take a mule an' a track jack
Fer to line dis track back."

JOHN HENRY*

"Taking a long chance on the weather, my guide, Manny Campbell, and I made the trip of three miles from Edisto to Fenwick [Island] in a rowboat. . . . Suddenly a stiff, cold wind came from the north, and a few moments later the rain began to fall in torrents. . . . Manny and I took refuge in a two-room cabin where two women and several children were sitting around an open fire trying to keep warm. . . . With the help of Manny, I soon got one of the women to 'talk some ol' storee.' This good fortune did not last long. George White, husband of the story teller, came in from the field wet and disgusted, dampening the spirit of the party. There was too much rain, the rain was going to rot the potatoes, the cabbage and lettuce were going to ruin, the whole damned island was a hell of a place. . . . After his temper had cooled a little, his wife reminded him that it would be a good idea for him to row down to Bennett's Point for some supplies.

" 'We got grits, enty?' said White. 'We can git along till tomorrow.'

"His wife was silent for a few minutes, then again suggested the great need of food for the family.

" 'Great Gawd!' growled George, 'go out in dis wedder? Not me, I got enough o' boats for a w'ile.' He launched into a story of a rowboat trip. . . . He had rowed all day and half the night. . . .

" 'My hands ain' got over it yet. . . . W'en I got here my hands was gripped to dem oar. . . . I couldn' even turn dem oar a-loose. Dey had to take 'em out o' my hands for me.'

*Story made from Carl Sandburg's *Songbag*, from Professor Guy Johnson's *John Henry*, and from various Negro singers in Southern penitentiaries.

[3]

" 'T'ink of ol' John Henry,' said his wife. 'If he could die wid dat hammer in his hand, you ought not to fuss about rowin' two mile to git us somethin' to eat.'

" 'Dat's all right,' replied George, 'but I ain't a-gwine a-die wid no oar in my hand if I can help it!'

"At the mention of John Henry my spirits went up considerably. I had only been waiting for an auspicious moment to bring him in myself. When the laughter over George's drollery had subsided, I professed an interested ignorance about John Henry. Getting up from his box-seat he began to tell how he had heard about John Henry. . . . As his story progressed, George grew more and more eloquent. He stood behind the dining table, wet slouch hat hanging down over one eye, acting out the story as he went. . . .

" 'It was de flesh ag'in de steam,' he concluded. 'De flesh ag'in de steam.'

"Manny seemed thrilled but saddened by the tale. It was his introduction to John Henry, and White's telling made a deep impression on him. He encouraged the narrator with frequent interjections such as 'Dat's right' and 'Lawd-Jeesus!' At the climax he had stared wide-eyed for several seconds.

"John Henry was a magic wand. George White was more than pleased with himself. He consented to 'talk ol' storee,' and later I saw him in his boat pulling for Bennett's Point.

"Crossing back to Edisto Island was not exactly a pleasure. Wind and tide were against us, and the cold rain soaked us. . . . Manny cast apprehensive glances over his shoulder. . . .

" 'Going to make it?' I asked.

" 'Yas-suh! I jus' been study about dat John Henry. If dat man could beat de steam, I t'ink I bring dis ol' boat back to dat landin' all right. If I don't, I'll die wid dese oar in my han'.'

"Thus does the story of John Henry, half a century after its origin, continue to capture the imagination of those who hear it for the first time." *

* From *John Henry*, by Guy B. Johnson (Chapel Hill, N.C.: University of North Carolina Press, 1929).

[4]

John   Hen - ry   was   a   li - 'l   ba - by,   uh-huh,Set-tin'

on   his   ma - ma's knee,oh,yeh,Said:"De Big Bend Tunnel on de

C.   and   O.   road   Gon - na   cause   de   death   of

me,Lawd,Lawd,Gon - na   cause   de   death   of   me."

John Henry was a li'l baby, uh-huh,*
Sittin' on his mama's knee, oh, yeah,*
Said: "De Big Bend Tunnel on de C. & O. road
Gonna cause de death of me,
Lawd, Lawd, gonna cause de death of me."

John Henry, he had a woman,
Her name was Mary Magdalene,
She would go to de tunnel and sing for John,
Jes' to hear John Henry's hammer ring,
Lawd, Lawd, jes' to hear John Henry's hammer ring.

John Henry had a li'l woman,
Her name was Lucy Ann,
John Henry took sick an' had to go to bed,
Lucy Ann drove steel like a man,
Lawd, Lawd, Lucy Ann drove steel like a man.

* The syllables "uh-huh" and "oh, yeah" are to be repeated in each stanza.

Cap'n says to John Henry,
"Gonna bring me a steam drill 'round,
Gonna take dat steam drill out on de job,
Gonna whop dat steel on down,
Lawd, Lawd, gonna whop dat steel on down."

John Henry tol' his cap'n,
Lightnin' was in his eye:
"Cap'n, bet yo' las' red cent on me,
Fo' I'll beat it to de bottom or I'll die,
Lawd, Lawd, I'll beat it to de bottom or I'll die."

Sun shine hot an' burnin',
Wer'n't no breeze a-tall,
Sweat ran down like water down a hill,
Dat day John Henry let his hammer fall,
Lawd, Lawd, dat day John Henry let his hammer fall.

John Henry went to de tunnel,
An' dey put him in de lead to drive;
De rock so tall an' John Henry so small,
Dat he lied down his hammer an' he cried,
Lawd, Lawd, dat he lied down his hammer an' he cried.

John Henry started on de right hand,
De steam drill started on de lef'—
"Before I'd let dis steam drill beat me down,
I'd hammer my fool self to death,
Lawd, Lawd, I'd hammer my fool self to death."

White man tol' John Henry,
"Nigger, damn yo' soul,
You might beat dis steam an' drill of mine,
When de rocks in dis mountain turn to gol',
Lawd, Lawd, when de rocks in dis mountain turn to gol'."

John Henry said to his shaker,
"Nigger, why don' you sing?
I'm throwin' twelve poun's from my hips on down,
Jes' listen to de col' steel ring,
Lawd, Lawd, jes' listen to de col' steel ring."

Oh, de captain said to John Henry,
"I b'lieve this mountain's sinkin' in."
John Henry said to his captain, oh my!
"Ain' nothin' but my hammer suckin' win',
Lawd, Lawd, ain' nothin' but my hammer suckin' win'."

John Henry tol' his shaker,
"Shaker, you better pray,
For, if I miss dis six-foot steel,
Tomorrow'll be yo' buryin' day,
Lawd, Lawd, tomorrow'll be yo' buryin' day."

John Henry tol' his captain,
"Looka yonder what I see—
Yo' drill's done broke an' yo' hole's done choke,
An' you cain' drive steel like me,
Lawd, Lawd, an' you cain' drive steel like me."

De man dat invented de steam drill,
Thought he was mighty fine.
John Henry drove his fifteen feet,
An' de steam drill only made nine,
Lawd, Lawd, an' de steam drill only made nine.

De hammer dat John Henry swung,
It weighed over nine pound;
He broke a rib in his lef'-han' side,
An' his intrels fell on de groun',
Lawd, Lawd, an' his intrels fell on de groun'.

[7]

John Henry was hammerin' on de mountain,
An' his hammer was strikin' fire,
He drove so hard till he broke his pore heart,
An' he lied down his hammer an' he died,
Lawd, Lawd, he lied down his hammer an' he died.

All de womens in de Wes',
When dey heared of John Henry's death,
Stood in de rain, flagged de eas'-boun' train,
Goin' where John Henry fell dead,
Lawd, Lawd, goin' where John Henry fell dead.

John Henry's lil mother,
She was all dressed in red,
She jumped in bed, covered up her head,
Said she didn' know her son was dead,
Lawd, Lawd, didn' know her son was dead.

John Henry had a pretty lil woman,
An' de dress she wo' was blue,
An' de las' words she said to him:
"John Henry, I've been true to you,
Lawd, Lawd, John Henry, I've been true to you."

"Oh, who's gonna shoe yo' lil feetses,
An' who's gonna glub yo' han's,
An' who's gonna kiss yo' rosy, rosy lips,
An' who's gonna be yo' man,
Lawd, Lawd, an' who's gonna be yo' man?"

"Oh, my mama's gonna shoe my lil feetses,
An' my papa's gonna glub my lil han's,
An' my sister's gonna kiss my rosy, rosy lips,
An' I don' need no man,
Lawd, Lawd, an' I don' need no man."

[8]

Dey took John Henry to de graveyard,
An' dey buried him in de san',
An' every locomotive come roarin' by,
Says, "Dere lays a steel-drivin' man,
Lawd, Lawd, dere lays a steel-drivin' man." *

JOHN HENRY
[A Variant]

"Here is a song you may not know. I learned it from a white man
who said he learned it from Negroes. As it stands it is too perfect for a
Negro song, but, to me, it bears the earmarks of Negro origin, and
the same holds true of the tune—which I wish I could transmit." †

John Henry was a steel drivin' man
And he drove at the head of his squad.
One day the head of his hammer come off
And he laid down his hammer and he died, by God,
Yes, he laid down his hammer and he died.

John Henry's wife came out of the east
And she come all dressed in blue,
Looked down at her pretty little feet—
And I wish my wife was true, by God,
Yes, I wish my wife was true.

John Henry's wife came out of the east,
And she come all dressed in red,
Looked down at her pretty little feet—
And I wish my wife was dead, by God,
Yes, I wish my wife was dead.

Now Rattler was a good coon dog,
But as blind as he could be,

* This stanza and the two preceding are quoted from Odum and Johnson's *Negro Workaday Songs*.
† R. V. Utter, R.F.D. No. 1, Clayton, Mo.

Treed fou'teen possums up an old gum stump,
And I thought old Rattler could see, by God,
Yes, I thought old Rattler could see.

Went up on the mountain,
And I thought he'd treed a coon,
But when I got close to where the old dog was,
Old Rattler was a-barkin' at the moon, by God,
Yes, old Rattler was a-barkin' at the moon.

STEEL LAYING HOLLER

Rochelle Harris, Chattanooga, Tennessee, went without his supper
to record this chant for us. Once he had been the foreman of a steel-
laying gang whose job it was to unload rails from a flat-car and then
place them in position on the ties. The first qualification in the South
for a foreman of this sort is that he have a good voice and a fine sense
of rhythm, along with the ability to improvise. A regulation railroad
iron weighs nearly two tons, and it takes fourteen good stout men to
handle it safely and easily. To keep these men working together so
that none of them would strain himself unduly or get in the way of the
falling rail, then, Rochelle chanted the following directions and in the
tenderest manner imaginable. Note the frequently occurring "nows."

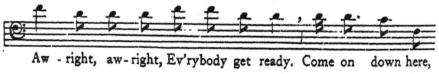

Aw - right, aw - right, Ev'rybody get ready. Come on down here,

Come on, boys. Bow down. Aw-right, up high, Aw-right, thow'way.

Aw-right, let's move on down 'n' get a-noth-er one.

Aw-right, bow down. Awright, head high, thow 'way. Aw-right, boys,

da's aw-right now, Move on down ag'in. Bow down. Up high Thow'way.

Come on down here, boys. Come on down now. Come on now.

Now, boys, Now stop. An' I want you to list-en at me now.
(Spoken) When I git this las' one, I'm goin' home to Ju-lie

I'm gon-na tell you a sad warn-ing now.
And tell her what I have made by this hard la-bor.

Bow down ea - - - sy, boys, head high, boys, thow it a-way.

Awright, awright.

Ev'rybody get ready.

Come on down here, come on, boys. *(The men group themselves at the end of the rail.)*

Bow down. *(They bend over and lay hold of the rail.)*

Awright, up high. *(They lift the rail up to chest level.)*
Awright, throw 'way. *(They push it away, off the car.)*

Awright, le's move on down 'n' git another one.
Awright, bow down.
Awright, head high,
Throw 'way.

Awright, da's awright now.
Move on down ag'in.
Bow down.
Up high.
Throw 'way.

Come on down here, boys, come on down now, come on now.
Now, boys, now, stop.
An' I want you to listen at me, now.
I'm gonna tell you a sad warnin' now. (Don' git hurt.)
Bow down ea—sy, boys.
Head high, boys.
Throw it away.

Come on down here, boys, come on down now, come on now.
Now, boys, now, stop.
When I git dis las' one,
I'm goin' home to Julie an' tell her what I have made by dis hard
     labor.
Bow down ea—sy, boys.
Head high, boys.
Throw it away!

THE HEAVY–HIPTED WOMAN

A Tie-Tamping Song

Quit yo' long-time talk-in' 'bout yo' heav-y- hipt-ed woman, She done

gone, Oh, babe, She done gone. Quit yo' long-time talk-in' 'bout yo'

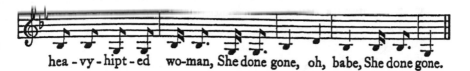

hea - vy - hipt - ed wo-man, She done gone, oh, babe, She done gone.

Quit yo' long-time talkin' 'bout yo' heavy-hipted woman,
She done gone, oh, babe, she done gone.
Quit yo' long-time talkin' 'bout yo' heavy-hipted woman,
She done gone, oh, babe, she done gone.

Got my learnin' from a coal-black nigger,
In de mines, oh, babe, in de mines.

My woman, she keeps on a-grumblin',
'Bout a new pair o' shoes, oh, babe, 'bout a new pair o' shoes.

I gave her five silver dollars,
Jus' to buy some tans, oh, babe, jus' to buy some tans.

She come back a-whoopin' an a-holl'in',
Wid a pair o' brogans, oh, babe, wid a pair o' brogans.

Got a bulldog weighin' nine hunderd,
In my back yard, oh, babe, in my back yard.

When you hear my bulldog barkin',
Somebody's 'roun', oh, babe, somebody's 'roun'.

When he barks, he ro' like thunder,
All under de groun', oh, babe, all under de groun'.

When you hear my pistol shootin',
'Nother man's dead, oh, babe, 'nother man's dead.

When you hear dat peafowl holl'in',
Sign o' rain, oh, babe, sign o' rain.

When you hear dat blue goose holler,
Gwineta tu'n col', oh, babe, gwineta tu'n col'.

When I cross dat wide ol' mountain,
I'll be free, oh, babe, den I'll be free.

Take my houn' dog an' give it to my brother,
Tell him I'm gone, oh, babe, tell him I'm gone.

You may look till yo' eye runs water,
I won' be back, oh, babe, I won' be back.

TIE-SHUFFLING CHANT

Black Samson, having refused to sing anything that had to do with
"worl'ly" and thus sinful matters, objected not at all to this work
song. He furnished the air and, along with other Negro convicts in
Texas, Louisiana, Mississippi, and Tennessee, the verses.

"Tie-shuffling" is the lining or straightening out of a railroad track.
To understand the work-rhythm that forms this chant it will be necessary to describe Henry Trevelyan's section gang as it worked to tune.

Henry, the foreman, stooped over and squinted off down the shining
rail; then stood up and bawled out directions to his gang in the im-
possibly technical language of the railroad. They, with heavy wooden
bars on their shoulders, trotted off down the track, jammed their lining
bars down under the rail on the inner side, and braced against them.
One of their number, a handsome yellow man, when he was sure that

they were ready to heave, threw back his head and sang. On the first and next to the last beat of every verse, each man threw his weight against his bar; the refrain was repeated until Henry, who had kept his eye to the rail meanwhile, shouted his directions about the next "johnnyhead." At that signal the song was broken off, the gang stopped heaving, and the whole scene was repeated a few yards on down the track. The accented syllables represent the concerted movements of the gang against their lining bars.

LEADER: Ho, boys, is you right?
GANG: I done got right.
LEADER: Ef I could I sholy would,
Stan' on de rock where Moses stood.
Chorus: Ho, boys, cancha line 'em,
Ho, boys, cancha line 'em,

Ho, boys, cancha line 'em?
See Eloise go linin' track.

The following stanzas are a few among the many couplets of this
widely current song of the Negro section gangs.

Ol' Moses stood on de Red Sea shore,
Smote de water wid a two-by-four. (*Chorus.*)

Way down yonder in de holler o' de fiel',
Angels workin' on de chariot wheel.

Mary, Marthy, Luke, an' John,
All dem 'ciples dead an' gone.

I got a woman on Jennielee Square,
Ef you would die easy, lemme ketch you dere.*

The reason I stay wid my cap'n so long,
Ever' mornin' gimme bisquits to rear back on.

Little Evaline settin' in de shade,
Figurin' on de money I done made.

July de red bug, July de fly,
Ef Augus' ain' a hot month, Lawdy, I pray to die.

You keep on talkin' 'bout join-'er-ahead,†
Never said nothin' 'bout my hog an' bread.

Went to de mountain, to de tip-top,
See my baby do de Eagle-Rock.

Jack de rabbit, Jack de bear,
Cain' you move it jes' a hair?

* This stanza and the two following are quoted from Odum and Johnson's *Negro Workaday Songs*
(Chapel Hill, N.C.: University of North Carolina Press, 1926).
† Pronounced "jonny head."

All I hate 'bout linin' track,
Dese ol' bars 'bout to break my back.

Jes' lemme tell you what de cap'n done,
Looked at his watch an' he looked at de sun.

Chorus:
'Ho, boys, you cain' quit,
Ho, boys, it ain' time,
Ho, ho, you cain' quit,
Sun ain' gone down yit.

TIE-TAMPING CHANT

Rochelle Harris, after a shovel had been found for him, stood before the microphone, tapped the cement floor, and sang, just as if he were out on some railroad line, under the hot sun, packing in gravel around a tie. The accents in the music and text represent the blows of the tamper or the shovel.

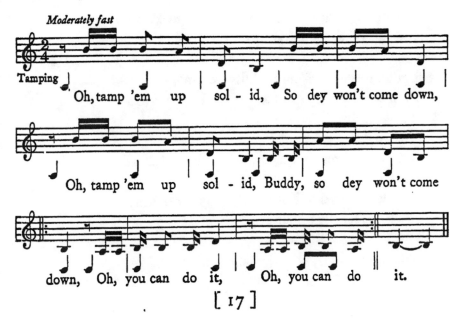

Oh, tamp 'em up sol - id, So dey won't come down,

Oh, tamp 'em up sol - id, Buddy, so dey won't come

down, Oh, you can do it, Oh, you can do it.

Chorus:

Oh, tamp 'em up solid,
So dey won' come down,
Oh, tamp 'em up solid,
Buddy, so dey won' come down,

Refrain:

Oh, you can do it,
Oh, you can do it, . . .

This last line is to be repeated as long as it is necessary to keep tamping at the same place.

The stanzas that can be and are used in this chant, follow. They sing to the same tune as the chorus.

Ef I'd 'a' knowed dat my cap'n was blin',
I wouldn' went to work till de clock struck half-pas' nine.

Oh, de cap'n done learnt me how to make a day—
Jes' rap on de railin' an' pass de time away.

I got a new way o' tampin' dat de cap'n don' lak,
I kin tamp 'em up solid an' never ben' my back.

You fool de cap'n, an' I fool de straw,
But de gen'l road manager, he gonna fool us all.

Oh, de ol' folks tell us dat de right will win;
We're on an eight-hour system, an' de cap'n works us ten.

Mary got a baby, an' I know it ain' mine,
I b'lieve it is de cap'n's 'cause he goes dere all de time.

"Pay day tomorrow." "How do you know?"
"Cap'n tol' de water-boy, an' de water-boy tol' me so."

*   *   *

T.P.* an' de Morgan runnin' side by side,
T.P. tol' de Morgan, "Don' let no hobo ride."

T.P. an' de Morgan runnin' side by side,
T.P. throwed water, water in de Morgan's eye.

*   *   *

Mattie, when you marry, git a railroad man.
Ev'y day be Sunday, an' a dollar be in yo' han'.

Mattie an' de baby was a-layin' in de bed,
Mattie's got a fever, an' de baby's got an achin' in de head.

Oh, Mattie an' de baby jes' a-layin' in de shade,
A-waitin' for yo' dollar, an' you ain' got nary one cent.

Shake, shake, Mattie, shake, a-rattle an' a-roll,
Oh, shake, shake, Mattie, Mattie want to win my gol'.

*   *   *

Godamighty made a monkey, Godamighty made a whale,
Godamighty made a 'gator wid hickies all over his tail,

All over his tail,
All over his tail, etc.

* The Texas & Pacific and the Morgan railroads run through Louisiana, where some verses of this song were recorded.

GOOD–BY, PRETTY MAMA
[A Variant of the Tie-Tamping Chant]

I'm gonna take those shoes I bought you,

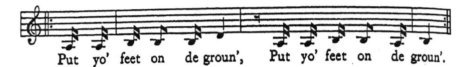

Put yo' feet on de groun', Put yo' feet on de groun'.

I'm gonna take those shoes I bought you,
Put yo' feet on de groun',
Put yo' feet on de groun'.

I'm gonna leave you jes' like I foun' you,
All out an' down,
All out an' down.

I ain' gonna buy you nothin' else,
When I go to town,
When I go to town.

PADDY WORKS ON THE ERIE *

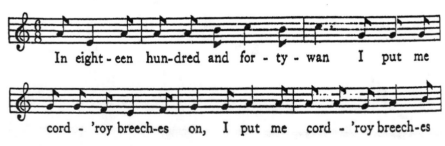

In eight-een hun-dred and for-ty-wan I put me

cord-'roy breech-es on, I put me cord-'roy breech-es

* Old newspaper clipping. Cf. Carl Sandburg's *American Songbag*, pp. 356–357.

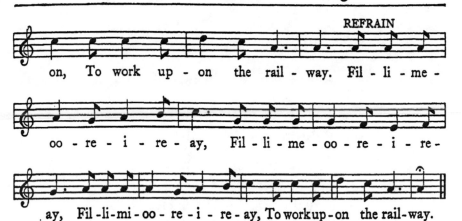

on, To work up-on the rail-way. Fil-li-me-oo-re-i-re-ay, Fil-li-me-oo-re-i-re-ay, Fil-li-mi-oo-re-i-re-ay, To work up-on the rail-way.

In eighteen hundred and forty-wan
I put me cord'roy breeches on,
I put me cord'roy breeches on,
To work upon the railway.

Refrain:
        Fil-i-me-oo-re-i-re-ay,
        Fil-i-me-oo-re-i-re-ay,
        Fil-i-me-oo-re-i-re-ay,
        To work upon the railway.

In eighteen hundred and forty-two,
I left the ould world for the new,
Bad cess to the luck that brought me through,
To work upon the railway.

When we left Ireland to come here,
And spend our latter days in cheer,
Our bosses they did drink strong beer,
And Pat worked on the railway.

Our contractor's name it was Tom King,
He kept a store to rob the men,

A Yankee clerk with ink and pen,
To cheat Pat on the railroad.

It's "Pat, do this" and "Pat, do that,"
Without a stocking or cravat,
And nothing but an old straw hat,
While Pat works on the railroad.

One Monday morning to our surprise,
Just half an hour before sunrise,
The dirty divil went to the skies,
And Pat worked on the railroad.

And when Pat lays him down to sleep,
The wiry bugs around him creep,
And divil a bit can poor Pat sleep,
While he works on the railroad.

In eighteen hundred and forty-three,
'Twas then I met sweet Biddy Magee,
And an illygant wife she's been to me,
While workin' on the railway.

In eighteen hundred and forty-six,
The gang pelted me with stones and bricks.
Oh, I was in a hell of a fix,
While workin' on the railroad.

In eighteen hundred and forty-seven,
Sweet Biddy Magee, she went to heaven,
If she left one child, she left eleven,
To work upon the railway.

In eighteen hundred and forty-eight,
I learned to take my whisky straight,
'Tis an illygant drink and can't be bate,
For working on the railway.

MIKE *

Section men a-workin' there all side by side;
Section men a-shirkin', as the hot sun fried.

Chorus:
　　Damn be the President,
　　My name's Mike,
　　I got a hand in it,
　　I drive the spike.

Mike he come from Tipperary, his name's O'Burke.
Fought like he was stewed, but didn't fight to work.

A-levelin' up the road bed ain't no fun,
Nor a-drivin' down the spikes in the boilin' sun.

Heat boils down, and shakes along the blazing rails,
Hangs around your head until your mind nearly fails.

Shovel in the ground when he hoists the tie;
Supper time a-comin' in the sweet by 'n' by.

Mike was pilin' ties near the ditch by the road
Out among the jimpson where the boys ain't mowed.

He picked up a crosstie without much vim,
Blacksnake wiggles up between his pants and him.

Mike lit out for Oklahoma, ain't come back,
Showed no hesitation as he tore down the track.

Caught up with a special, an' he hollered like a man,
"Bedad, if you can't run, let me *ahead wot can.*"

* From the Belden Collection, Harvard University. Sent by J. Brown.

THE GILA MONSTER ROUTE*

The lingering sunset across the plain,
Kissed the rear-end door of an east-bound train,
And shone on a passing track close by,
Where a dingbat sat on a rotten tie.

He was ditched by a shack and a cruel fate.
The con high-balled, and the manifest freight
Pulled out on the stem behind the mail,
And she hit the ball on a sanded rail.

As she pulled away in the falling night,
He could see the gleam of her red tail-light.
Then the moon arose and the stars came out—
He was ditched on the Gila Monster Route.

Nothing in sight but sand and space;
No chance for a gink to feed his face,
Not even a shack to beg for a lump,
Or a hen-house to frisk for a single gump.

As he gazed far out on the solitude,
He dropped his head and began to brood;
He thought of the time he lost his mate
In a hostile burg on the Nickel Plate.

They had mooched the stem and threw their feet,
And speared four-bits on which to eat;
But deprived themselves of their daily bread,
And sluffed their coin for "dago red."

Down by the track in the jungle's glade,
On the cool green grass, in the tules' shade,
They shed their coats and ditched their shoes
And tanked up full of that colored booze.

* Written for the *Railroad Man's Magazine*, by L. F. Post and Glenn Norton.

Then they took a flop with their skins plumb full,
And they did not hear the harnessed bull,
Till he shook them out of their boozy nap,
With a husky voice and a loaded sap.

They were charged with "vag," for they had no kale,
And the judge said, "Sixty days in jail."
But the John had a "bindle"—a workers' plea—
So they gave him a floater and set him free.

They had turned him up, but ditched his mate,
So he grabbed the guts of an east-bound freight,
He slung his form on a rusty rod,
Till he heard the shack say, "Hit the sod!"

The John piled off, he was in the ditch,
With two switch-lamps and a rusty switch,
A poor old seedy, half-starved bo,
On a hostile pike, without a show.

From away off somewhere in the dark
Came the sharp, short note of a coyote's bark.
The bo looked round and quickly rose,
And shook the dust from his threadbare clothes.

Off in the west through the moonlit night,
He saw the gleam of a big headlight—
An east-bound stock-train hummed the rail;
She was due at the switch to clear the mail.

As she drew up close, the head-end shack
Threw the switch to the passing-track,
The stock rolled in and off the main,
And the line was clear for the west-bound train.

When she hove in sight far up the track,
She was working steam, with her brake-shoes slack.
She hollered once at the whistle-post,
Then she flitted by like a frightened ghost.

He could hear the roar of the big six-wheel,
And her driver's pound on the polished steel,
And the screech of her flanges on the rail,
As she beat it west o'er the desert trail.

The John got busy and took the risk,
He climbed aboard and began to frisk,
He reached up high and began to feel,
For the end-door pin—then he cracked the seal.

'Twas a double-decked stock-car filled with sheep—
Old John crawled in and went to sleep.
She whistled twice and high-balled out,
They were off—down the Gila Monster Route.

HALLELUJAH, BUM AGAIN

"The song was found scribbled on the wall of a Kansas City jail where an old hobo, known as 'One-Finger Ellis,' had spent the night, recovering from an overdose of rotgut whisky." George Milburn in his *Hobo's Hornbook* (published by Ives Washburn, New York) quotes the following version of the famous hobo song and gives its source in the above note.

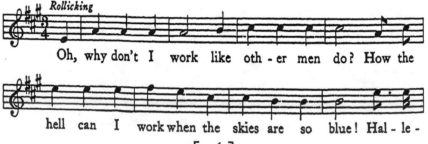

Rollicking

Oh, why don't I work like oth - er men do? How the
hell can I work when the skies are so blue! Hal - le -

lu - jah! I'm   a   bum, Hal - le - lu - jah! Bum   a - gain, Hal - le -

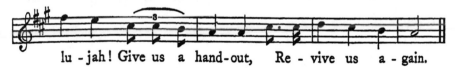

lu - jah! Give us   a   hand-out,   Re - vive us   a - gain.

Oh, why don't I work like other men do?
How the hell can I work when the skies are so blue?

Chorus:

    Hallelujah, I'm a bum!
    Hallelujah, bum again,
    Hallelujah, give 's a handout,
    Revive us again.

If I was to work and save all I earn,
I could buy me a bar and have money to burn.

Oh, the winter is over and we're all out of jail;
We are tired of walking and hungry as hell.

Oh, I ride box cars and I ride fast mails,
When it's cold in the winter I sleep in the jails.

I passed by a saloon and I hear someone snore,
And I found the bartender asleep on the floor.

I stayed there and drank till a fly-mug came in,
And he put me to sleep with a sap on the chin.

Next morning in court I was still in a haze,
When the judge looked at me, he said, "Thirty days."

Some day a long train will run over my head,
And the sawbones will say, "Old One-Finger's dead."

Additional Stanzas

When the springtime does come, oh, won't we have fun?
We'll throw up our jobs and go on the bum.

Oh, springtime has come, and I'm just out of jail,
Ain't got no money, it all went for bail.

I came to a house and I knocked at the door,
And the old lady says, "I have saw you before.

"Why don't you work like other men do?"
"How the hell we going to work when there ain't no work to do?"

TEN THOUSAND MILES FROM HOME

With a steady swing

Chorus:
Watch her an' catch her an' jump her ju - - ber - ju, Re - lease the brakes and let 'er go, The bums will ride— her through. Don't stop for wa - ter, Just catch it on the fly, Will I get Ho - ly Mo - - ses On the Penn - syl - van - - ia line!

[28]

A *

Chorus:
Watch her and catch her
And jump her juberju,
Release the brakes and let her go,
The bums will ride her through.

Chorus:
Don't stop for water,
Just catch it on the fly,
Will I get Holy Moses,
On the Pennsylvania line!

Get out, get out, you dirty bum,
You're on the Nashville train,
Ten thousand miles away from home,
Riding an old freight train.

or

Ten thousand miles away from home
My heart was filled with pain.

B †

Standing on the platform,
Smoking a cheap cigar,
A-listening for the next freight train
To catch an empty car,

My pocketbook was empty,
My heart was full of pain,
Ten thousand miles away from home,
A-bumming the railroad train.

* As sung by a seventy-one-year-old ex-jailbird, a one-legged, "retired" Negro in New Orleans.
† Kentucky mountain version. From H. H. Fuson's *Songs of the Kentucky Highlands*.

And I was cold and hungry,
And had not a bite to eat;
I laid me down to take a nap
And rest my weary feet.

Then I walked up to a kind miss,
And asked for a bite to eat,
A little piece of cornbread
And a little piece of meat.

She threw her arms around me:
"I love you as a friend,
But if I gave you this to eat
You'd bum 'round here again."

"Kind miss, kind miss,
Don't talk to me so rough,
You think that I'm a old hobo,
Because I look so tough."

She took me in her kitchen,
She treated me nice and kind;
She got me in the notion
Of bumming all the time.

And as I left the kitchen
And went down to the town,
I heard a double-header blow,
And thought she was western bound.

I walked down on the sidetrack
And stopped at the railroad shop;
And heard an agent tell a man
The train it would not stop.

My heart began to flutter
And I began to sing,
"Ten thousand miles away from home,
A-bummin' a railroad train."

I pulled my cap down over my eyes
And walked on down the tracks;
Then I caught a sleeping-car,
And never did look back.

I got off at Danville,
Got struck on a Danville girl;
You bet your life she was out of sight,
She wore those Danville curls.

She wore her hat on the back of her head,
Like high-tone people do.
And the very next train comes down this line,
I'll bid that girl adieu.

THE WRECK ON THE C. & O.

OR

THE DEATH OF JACK HINTON *

"The ballad and the facts agree as follows: (1) The F.F.V., train
No. 4, running east on the C. & O. Railroad, was wrecked near Hinton
(Virginia) by a landslide. (2) The regular engineer, George Alley,
was killed. (3) The fireman saved his life by jumping from the
engine." *

* From Professor J. H. Cox's *Folk-Songs of the South* (Cambridge, Mass.: Harvard University Press, 1925).

A-long came the F. F. V., the fast-est on - - the line,

Run - ning o'er the C. and O. road, twenty

min - utes be - hind the time; Run - ning in - to

Sew - ell yard, was quar-tered on the line,

A-waiting for strict ord - ers and in the cab to ride.

CHORUS

Many a man's been murd-ered by the rail - road, rail-

road, rail-road; Many a man's been murd-ered by the

rail - road, And laid in his lone - some grave.

Along came the F.F.V., the fastest on the line,
Running o'er the C. & O. Road, twenty minutes behind the time;

Running into Sewell yard, was quartered on the line,
A-waiting for strict orders and in the cab to ride.

Chorus:.
Many a man has been murdered by the railroad, railroad, railroad,
Many a man has been murdered by the railroad,
And laid in his lonesome grave.

And when she blew for Hinton, her engineer was there,
George Alley was his name, with bright and wavery hair;
His fireman, Jack Dixon, was standing by his side,
A-waiting for strict orders and in the cab to ride.

George Alley's mother came to him with a basket on her arm,
She handed him a letter, saying: "Be careful how you run;
And if you run your engine right, you'll get there just on time,
For many a man has lost his life in trying to make lost time."

George Alley said: "Dear mother, your letter I'll take heed.
I know my engine is all right and I know that she will speed;
So o'er this road I mean to run with speed unknown to all,
And when I blow for Clifton Forge, they'll surely hear my call."

George Alley said to his fireman, "Jack, a little extra steam;
I intend to run old No. 4 the fastest ever seen;
So o'er this road I mean to fly like angel's wings unfold,
And when I blow for the Big Bend Tunnel, they'll surely hear my call."

George Alley said to his fireman, "Jack, a rock ahead I see,
And I know that death is lurking there for to grab both you and me;
So from this cab, dear Jack, you leap, your darling life to save,
For I want you to be an engineer while I'm sleeping in my grave."

[33]

"Oh, no, dear George! that will not do, I want to die with you."
"Oh, no, no, dear Jack; that will not be, I'll die for you and me."
So from the cab dear Jack did leap, ol' New River was running high,
And he kissed the hand of his darling George as No. 4 flew by.

So up the road she dashed; against the rock she crashed;
The engine turning over and the coaches they came last;
George Alley's head in the firebox lay, while the burning flames
    rolled o'er:
"I'm glad I was born an engineer, to die on the C. & O. Road."

George Alley's mother came to him and in sorrow she did sigh,
When she looked upon her darling boy and saw that he must die.
"Too late, too late, dear mother! my doom is almost o'er,
And I know that God will let me in when I reach that golden shore."

The doctor said, "Dear George, O darling boy, keep still;
Your life may yet be spared, if it be God's precious will."
"Oh, no, dear Doc, that cannot be, I want to die so free,
I want to die on the engine I love, 143."

The people came from miles around this engineer to see.
George Alley said, "God bless you, friends, I am sure you will find
    me here."
His face and head all covered with blood, his eyes you could not see,
And as he died he cried aloud, "Oh, nearer, my God, to thee."

NACHUL–BORN EASMAN *

According to Henry Trevelyan, section gang foreman for the Wier
Lumber Company of Wiergate, Texas, this is the original "Casey
Jones," that he heard when he went to work on the Illinois Central
line that runs through Canton, Mississippi.

* An "easman" is a "hustler," that is, a man who wanders from town to town living off women,
often other men's wives.

"Name printed on de tail of his shirt,
Nachul-born easman, don' have to work."

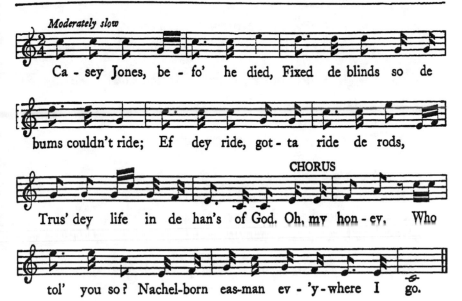

Casey Jones, befo' he died,
Fixed de blinds so de bums couldn' ride;
"Ef dey ride, gotta ride de rods,
Trus' dey life in de han's of God."

Chorus:

    Oh, my honey, who tol' you so?
    Nachul-born easman, ev'ywhere I go.

Casey Jones was a li'l' behin',
He thought prob'ly he could make de time,
Got up in his engine, an' he walked about,
Gave three loud whistles an'-a he pulled out.

Right-hand side dey was a-wavin' of flags,
Wavin' of flags to save Casey's life,
Casey blowed de whistle an' he never look back,
Never stopped a-runnin' till he jumped de track,

Oh, my baby, till he jumped de track,
Never stopped a-runnin' till he jumped de track.

On de right-hand side was a tuzzle switch,
On de left-hand side was a ten-foot ditch,
Fireman looked out, got ready to jump,
Two locomotives here, bound to bump.

Number 3 got within a mile of the place,
Number 4 stared him straight in de face,
Casey tol' his fireman to keep his seat and ride,
"It's a double-track * road, we're runnin' side by side."

When Casey's wife heard dat Casey was dead,
She was in de kitchen, makin' up bread,
She says, "Go to bed, chilluns, an' hol' yo' breath,
You'll all get a pension at yo' daddy's death."

Casey called up his wife and son,
Willed them an engine, had never been run.
When Casey's son did come of age,
Says, "Daddy's done willed me a narrow gauge."

CASEY JONES

In 1910 O. L. Miller, mayor of Canton, Mississippi, wrote to the senior editor of this collection as follows: "Wallis Sanders is the composer of the popular song 'Casey Jones.' Casey was running between Memphis and Canton when he was killed fourteen miles north of Canton. He was a great favorite with the roundhouse men as well as all who came in contact with him. The darkey, Wallis Sanders, made the song in his own way . . . will get to singing this song

* According to Trevelyan, Casey was drunk at the time of his famous wreck and so saw a double track where there was only a single line.

now and add words that suit Casey's railroad life just as well as
the original does. I read your letter to Wallis and he said, 'Boss, is
there anything in it?' I told him no money but lots of fame, and he
said, 'What dat, Boss?' . . . I was for forty years foreman of the
railroad shops here."

Twenty-three years later we went to Canton to find Wallis Sanders.
He was dead. Mayor Miller was dead. But his married daughter
took us to see an old Negro whom she had known in the roundhouse
ever since she was a little girl—Wallis Sanders' close friend, Cornelius Steen.

Cornelius Steen, seventy years old, retired after nearly forty years
of coal heaving in the old roundhouse at Canton, told us this story
about the origin of "Casey Jones." While visiting in Kansas City
many years ago, he had heard the song "Jimmie Jones" (of which the
only verse he could remember is quoted below) sung by a strolling
street guitarist. He brought the tune and some of the verses back with
him to Canton and to the roundhouse where he worked. "Wash"
Sanders, who also worked as a coal heaver, heard the song, liked it,
and made it his own by adding verses that described the wreck in
which poor old Jimmie Jones was killed. When sufficiently in his
cups, he could sing on for a long time and never repeat a stanza.
Some time after, Casey Jones, who had a regular run as an engineer
between Memphis and Canton, and whom Steen said he knew well
and saw often, was killed in the now famous wreck. Sanders then
changed the words "Jimmie Jones" to "Casey Jones." Later it was
picked up by some traveling vaudevillians and revamped to make the
popularly known song, "Casey Jones."

The following is the only verse of "Jimmie Jones" that Cornelius
Steen could remember:

> On a Sunday mornin' it begins to rain,
> 'Round de curve spied a passenger train,
> On the pilot lay po' Jimmie Jones,
> He's a good ol' porter, but he's dead an' gone,

Dead an' gone, dead an' gone,
Kase he's been on de cholly * so long.

Slowly—almost in a speaking voice

On a Sun - day morn - in' it be - gins to rain,

Round de curve spied a pas-sen-ger train, On de pilot lay po'

Jim - mie Jones, He's a good ol' port - er, but he's

dead an' gone, Dead an' gone, Dead an' gone,

Kase he's been on de chol - ly so long.

And here are the verses that the old man could remember long dead
Wallis Sanders singing:

> On a Sunday mornin' it begins to rain,
> 'Round the curve spied a passenger train,
> Under de cab lay po' Casey Jones,
> He's a good engineer, but he's dead an' gone,
> Dead an' gone, dead an' gone,
> Kase he's been on de cholly so long.

* "On de cholly" is equivalent to "out on the hog," or "on the bum."

Casey Jones was a good engineer,
Tol' his fireman not to have no fear,
All I want's a lil water an' coal,
Peep out de cab an' see de drivers roll,
Oh, see de drivers roll, see de drivers roll,
Peep out de cab an' see de drivers roll.

On a Sunday mornin' it begins to rain,
'Round de curve come a passenger train,
Tol' his fireman he'd better jump,
Kase dose two locomotives is boun' to bump,
Boun' to bump, boun' to bump,
Kase dose two locomotives is boun' to bump.

But although "Casey Jones" may have originated as Cornelius Steen
says that it did, it had its roots in an old ballad tradition—

"There's many a man killed on the railroad,
And laid in his lonesome grave."

The following scraps, whether they were fathered by "Casey Jones"
or whether "Casey Jones" is only one among many similar ballads,
attest to the vigorousness of this tradition.

THE WRECK OF THE SIX-WHEEL DRIVER *

Joseph Mickel was a good engineer,
Told his fireman, well, oh, not to fear.
All he wanted was to keep her good and hot.
Says, "We'll make Paris 'bout four o'clock."
Says, "We'll make Paris 'bout four o'clock."

* Contributed by H. M. Harris, who learned it in 1906 from a Negro working in the cotton field.

When we got within a mile of the place,
Number One stared us all in the face.
The conductor pulled out his watch
And he mumbled and said,
"We may make it, but we'll all be dead.
All be dead, oh, we'll all be dead,
We may make it but we'll all be dead,
For I've been on the Charley so long."

As the two locomotives was about to bump,
The fireman prepared for to make his jump.
The engineer blowed the whistle
And the fireman bawled,
"Please, Mr. Conductor, won't you save us all,
Save us all, oh, save us all,
Please, Mr. Conductor, won't you save us all?
For I've been on the Charley so long."

Oh, you ought to been there for to have seen the sight,
Screaming and yelling, both colored and white.
Some were crippled, and some were *lame;*
But the six-wheel driver had to bear the blame.
Ain't it a pity, oh, ain't it a shame
That the six-wheel driver had to bear the blame?
For I've been on the Charley so long.

OL' JOHN BROWN

Passenger train stood in the shed,
'Twas a drizzling rain, and clouds o'erhead,
Up on the engine was ol' John Brown,
He was a good ol' frien', but he done broke down.

Little more steam an' a little more coal,
Put your head out the window and see the drivers roll,
Ol' John Brown, his back's most broke,
But he must shovel coal to make the engine smoke.

CHARLEY SNYDER

A ballad sung by the Negroes along the Ohio River.

Charley Snyder was a good engineer,
He told his firemen he had nothing to fear,
All he needed was water and coal,
Put your head out the window, see the drivers roll,
    See the drivers roll,
    See the drivers roll,
Put your head out the window, see the drivers roll.

On Sunday morning it began to rain,
When around the bend came a passenger train,
On the bumpers was-a hobo John,
He's a good old hobo, but he's dead and gone,
    He's dead and gone,
    He's dead and gone,
He's a good old hobo, but he's dead and gone.

Jay Gould's daughter said before she died,
"Father, fix the 'blinds' so the bums can't ride,
If ride they must, let them ride the rod,
Let them put their trust in the hands of God,
    In the hands of God,
    In the hands of God,
Let them put their trust in the hands of God."

Jay Gould's daughter said before she died,
"There's just one more road o'er which I'd like to ride."
"Tell me, daughter, what can it be?"
"It's in southern California on the Santa Fe,
    On the Santa Fe,
    On the Santa Fe.
It's in southern California on the Santa Fe."

Hurry up, engine, and hurry up, train,
Missie gwine to ride over the road again,
Swift as lightning and smooth as glass,
Darkey, take your hat off when the train goes past,
    When the train goes past,
    When the train goes past,
Darkey, take your hat off when the train goes past.

II

THE LEVEE CAMP

"All de nigger is lookin' for is fat meat an' sundown."—From White's *Folk Songs of the American Negro.*

SHACK BULLY HOLLER

"Early in de mornin', Charley Diamon's levee camp, long about three, four clock, you can hear Mr. Isum Lorantz (killed mo' men up an' down de Mississippi dan de influenzy) knockin' on de ding-dong wid his nigger punchin' 44. Nigger by de name o' L. W. Simmons hollers way down end o' de quarters."—HENRY TREVELYAN, former levee worker, Wingate, lower Tunno.

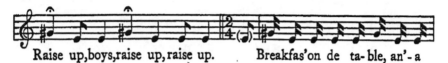

Raise up,boys,raise up,raise up. Breakfas'on de ta-ble, an'-a

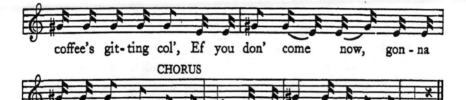

coffee's git-ting col', Ef you don' come now, gon-na

CHORUS

throw it out-do's. Ain-cha gwine, ain-cha gwine, boys, ain-cha gwine?

Who dat knockin' on de fo'-day dong?
Mus' be Isum Lorantz, 'cause he don' knock long.

Den Mr. Isum Lorantz spoke up his own se'f, says,

Raise up, boys, raise up, raise up—
Breakfas' on de table, coffee's gettin' col',
Ef you don' come now, goin' throw it outdo's.
Aincha gwine, aincha gwine, boys, aincha gwine?

Den ol' shack bully Simmons 'gin to holler same way.

[45]

Ol' nigger Shakleton in bed yit,
Here I am smokin' my third cigaritt.

Refrain:

Aincha gwine, aincha gwine, boys, aincha gwine?

Spoken

Come an' see what you got on yo' breakfas' table:

Ram, ham, chicken, an' mutton;
Ef you don' come now, you won' git nuttin'.

Here come a toad frog, got grea' big eyes.
Good God-a'mighty, dese niggers won' rise.

This ain' no place to collar no nod,
White folks wants you on de lumber yard.

White man call you, you come all right;
Nigger man call you, you want to fight.

Little bell call you, big bell warn you.
Ef you don' come now, I'm gonna break in on you.

Aincha gwine, aincha gwine, boys, aincha gwine?

REASON I STAY ON JOB SO LONG*

*The words and air are quoted from Odum and Johnson's *Negro Workaday Songs* (University of North Carolina Press).

Reason I stay on job so long,
Lawd, dey gimme flamdonies
An' coffee strong.

Reason I love my captain so,
'Cause I ast him for a dollar,
Lawd, he give me fo'.

Reason why I love Boleen,
She keeps my house
An' shanty clean.

Why I like Roberta so,
She rolls her jelly
Like she rolls her dough.

GWINETER HARNESS IN DE MORNIN' SOON

A levee camp song, sung by Dink, a "colored lady" from the banks of the Mississippi River.

Chorus: Gwine to har-ness in the morn-ing soon, soon, Gwine to har-ness in the morn-ing soon. Stanza: Cap-'n, Cap-'n, what time o' day? Bil-ly done hol-ler for his oats and hay.

Baby, baby, you don't know
De way you treat me I bound to go.

Chorus:
    Gwineter harness in de morning soon, soon,
    Gwineter harness in de morning soon.

Skinner, skinner, you know yo' rules,
Den go to de stable an' curry yo' mule.

Captain, captain, what time o' day?—
Billy done holler for his oats and hay.

Billy wuz fat and Queen wuz lean,
But I swear, by God, was a wheelin' team.

Look here, Capt'n, whut Billy done done,
He done sot down on de wagon tongue.

Went to de towel to wipe my face,
Couldn't see nothin' but trimmin' an' lace.

Well, I hear mighty rumblin' up in de sky,
Mus' be my Lord go passin' by.

Hollered at ol' Beck and she wouldn't gee,
Hit her on the head wid de singletree.

Went uptown, goin' to buy me a rope,
Goin' to whip Miss Sally till she "buzzard lope."

Well, capt'n, capt'n, you mus' be blin';
Look at yo' watch! See, ain't it quittin' time?

Every time de dang-dong ring,*
Ise got him by de head an' Ise gone ag'in.

Ringin' de dong don't worry me,
Ef I don't want t' work, God knows Ise free!

LEVEE CAMP "HOLLER"

This song is the workday of a Negro behind a team of mules.
Wherever the scrapers pile up dirt on the levees of the Southern
rivers this song rises from the dust and heat. It voices the day-long
reflections, the recurrent experiences and conflicts of the Negro mule-
skinner. We have never heard a stanza that made any mention of religious matters, for it is a devil's song and good church members do not
dare be heard singing it. Black Samson, whom we found breaking rocks
in the Nashville State Penitentiary, admitted that he knew the song
and had once sung it; but, since he had joined the church and had
turned away from the world, he no longer dared to sing it. All our
arguments were in vain. The prison chaplain protested that he would
make it all right with the Lord. But Black Samson replied that he was
a Hard-shell Baptist and that, according to their way of thinking, he
would be in danger of hell-fire if he sang such a song. At last, however, when the warden had especially urged him to sing, he stepped
in front of our microphone and, much to our surprise, when he had
made sure that his words were being recorded, said: "It's sho hard
lines dat a poor nigger's got to sing a worl'ly song, when he's tryin' to
be sancrified; but de warden's ast me, so I guess I'll have to." And he
did. But he had registered his protest before the Lord on an aluminum
plate, now filed in the Library of Congress at Washington.

The air was recorded from the singing of a prisoner at Angola,
Louisiana. The words come from levee camps in the far South.

* Dang-dong, or dong, is the bell that calls to work.

[49]

We git up in de mornin' so dog-gone soon,
Cain' see nothin' but de stars an' moon.
    Um—m, cain' see nothin' but de stars an' moon.

I looked all over de whole corral,
An' I couldn't fin' a mule wid his shoulder well.
    Um—m, etc.

Runnin' all aroun' de whole corral, Lawdy-Lawdy-Lawd,
Tryin' to git de harness on Queen an' Sal.

Way down on de river an' I couldn' see,
Couldn' hear nothin', Lawdy-Lawd, but "Whoa-haw-gee."

"Cap'n, cap'n, ol' Nell is sick."
"God damn ol' Nell, put de harness on Dick."

My name is Ron, I wuks in de san', oh, my Lawd,
I'd ruther be a nigger dan a po'-white man.

Cap'n, cap'n, what's de matter wid you?
Ef you got any Battle-Ax, please, suh, give me a chew.

Oh, Lawd, dat been my woman cry, eh Lawd,
Go way, Eadie, quit worryin' my min'.

Lawd, a brown-skin woman wear my watch an' chain,
But a jet-black woman, um-m Lawd, cain' call my name.

Lawd, a brown-skin woman get anything I got,
But a jet-black woman cain' come in my back yard.

I heared a mighty rumblin' down 'bout de water trough,
Mus' been de skinner whoppin' hell out de walkin' boss.

Cap'n got a 44 an' he try to play bad,
Take it dis mornin' ef he make me mad.

Cap'n, cap'n, will you sen' me some water?
Ain' had none since dis long mornin'.

Lawd, de cap'n call me an' I answered, "Suh."
"Ef you ain' gonna work, what you come here fuh?"

This time, this time another year,
I may be rollin', but it won' be here.

Cap'n, cap'n, doncha think it's mighty hard?
Work me all day on 'lasses an' lard, oh; Lawd.

I ask de cap'n what time o' day,
He look at me, an' he walk away.

I'd ruther be a nigger an' plow ol' Beck,
Dan a white hill-billy wid a long red neck.

I got a clock in my stomach an' a watch in my head,
I'm a-gettin' superstitious 'bout my hog an' bread.

I look at de sun an' de sun look high,
I look down on de boss-man an' he look so sly.

"Boss man, boss man, cain' you gimme my time?"
An' de boss man say, "One day behin'."

"Boss man, boss man, cain' you gimme one dime?"
An' de boss man say, "One dime behin'."

Ask Cap'n George did his money come,
Said, "De river too foggy, de boat won' run."

Well, if I had my weight in lime,
I'd whip my cap'n till he wen' stone blin'.

He don' like whisky, but he jes' drink a can.
Oh, I'd ruther be a nigger dan a po'-white man.

You cain' do me like you did po' Shine,
Take Shine's money, but you cain' take mine.

Cap'n, cap'n, you mus' be cross,
Six clock in hell 'fo' you knock off.

SHOT MY PISTOL IN DE HEART OF TOWN *

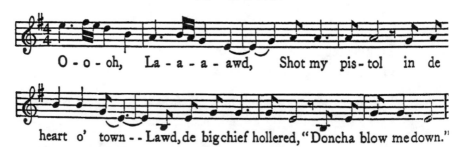

O - o - oh, La - a - a - awd, Shot my pis-tol in de

heart o' town - - Lawd, de big chief hollered, "Doncha blow me down."

* Words and music from Odum and Johnson's *Negro Workaday Songs* (University of North Carolina Press).

Oh, Lawd,
Shot my pistol
In de heart of town.
Lawd, de big chief hollered,
"Doncha blow me down."

"Oh, Lawd,
Which-a-way
Did de po' gal go?"
"She lef' here runnin'
Is all I know."

"Oh, Lawd,
Which-a-way
Do de Red River run?"
"Lawd, it run eas' and wes'
Like de risin' sun."

Oh, Lawd,
Jes' two cards
In de deck I love,
Lawd, de Jack o' diamonds
An' de ace o' clubs.

Oh, Lawd,
Stopped here to play
Jes' one mo' game.
Lawd, Jack o' diamonds
Petered on my han'.

III

SONGS FROM SOUTHERN CHAIN GANGS

"Them niggers is always hollerin' out in the fields, but I never paid 'em no min' enough to know what they sing about."

Thirty men in stripes are "flat-weeding" a ditch; every hoe strikes the ground at the same instant. The driver walks his horse behind them, shotgun across the pommel of his saddle. Guards, black trusties, ready and eager to shoot down any man who makes a break for freedom—if one kills his man, it may mean a pardon or a parole—pace behind the gang. The sun stands hot and burning overhead and the bodies of the men sway easily to the swing of their arms and the rhythm of the work. Presently some big buck with a warm, powerful voice throws back his head and begins "Rosie," "Stewball," or "Great God-a'mighty." At the chorus the gang joins in with a full-throated response, and the voices blend into a strange harmony where, perhaps, no voice is on pitch. Thus the song is begun, and thus it goes on through the "long, hot, summer day"; first one leader and then another takes it up and sings his favorite stanzas, with the probable addition of some comment on the cruelty of the sun, the captain, his woman, or his "grea' long time." "While de blood's runnin' warm," some one of the men will shout out in a rhythmic interjection, "Talk it to time, now!" or "It's hard, boys, it's hard," or "Tell 'em about it!" —just as there are frequent exclamations during a Negro sermon.

No stanza is ever sung in the same way as another. The Negroes play with the melody and the rhythm, vary them, keep silent, burst out suddenly, and impose a great variety of ornament and original deviation upon the pattern of the tune. But the whole is dominated and swept along by the heavy rhythm of the hoes. It is in this way that the songs should be sung. Get the "wham!—wham!—wham!" of the big splay feet, the axes, the hoes, firmly and heavily in mind. Open your mouth and shout the songs. They are not gentle or sedate or subtle. They are the work-songs of driven, despairing men, who sing about their troubles to be rid of them.

When you think I'm laughin',
I'm laughin' to keep from cryin'.

[57]

AIN' NO MO' CANE ON DE BRAZIS*

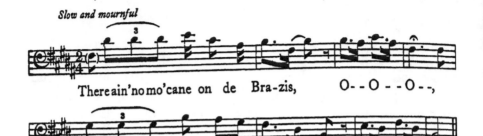

Slow and mournful

There ain' no mo' cane on de Bra-zis, O--O--O--,

Done groun' it all in mo-lazz - is, O-O--O--.

It ain' no mo' cane on de Brazis,

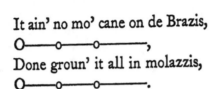

Done groun' it all in molazzis,

Better git yo' overcoat ready,
Well, it's comin' up a norther.

Well, de captain standin' an' lookin' an' cryin',
Well, it's gittin' so col', my row's behin'.

Cap'n, doncha do me like you did po' Shine,
Drive dat bully till he went stone-blin'.

Cap'n, cap'n, you mus' be blin',
Keep on holl'in' an' I'm almos' flyin'.

One o' dese mornin's, an' it won' be long,
You gonna call me an' I'll be gone.

Ninety-nine years so jumpin' long,
To be here rollin' an' cain' go home.

* From the Central State Farm near Houston, Texas; sung by Mexico, Lightnin', and Dave Tippin.

Ef I had a sentence like ninety-nine years,
All de dogs on de Brazis won' keep me here.

I b'lieve I'll go to de Brazis line,
Ef I leave you here, gonna think I's flyin'.

B'lieve I'll do like ol' Riley,
Ol' Riley walked de Brazis.

Well, de dog-sergeant got worried an' couldn' go,
Ol' Rattler went to howlin' 'cause de tracks too ol'.

Oughta come on de river in 1904,
You could fin' a dead man on every turn row.

Oughta come on de river in 1910,
Dey was drivin' de women des like de men.

Wake up, dead man, an' help me drive my row,
Wake up, dead man, an' help me drive my row.

Some in de buildin' an' some on de farm,
Some in de graveyard, some goin' home.

I looked at my Ol' Hannah,* an' she's turnin' red,
I looked at my podner an' he's almos' dead.

Wake up, lifetime, hold up yo' head,
Well, you may get a pardon an' you may drop dead.

Well, I wonder what's de matter, somepin' mus' be wrong,
We're still here rollin', Shorty George done gone. †

Go down, Ol' Hannah, doncha rise no mo',
Ef you rise any mo' bring judgment day.

* The sun, which gets hot in South Texas.
† See page 199 for note on Shorty George.

BLACK BETTY

Black Betty is not another Frankie, nor yet a two-timing woman that a man can moan his blues about. She is the whip that was and is used in some Southern prisons. A convict on the Darrington State Farm in Texas, where, by the way, whipping has been practically discontinued, laughed at Black Betty and mimicked her conversation in the following song.

Marked rhythm

O Lawd, Black Bet - ty, Bam - ba - lam, O

Lawd, Black Bet - ty, Bam - ba - lam, Black

Bet - ty had a ba - by, Bam - ba - lam, Black

Bet - ty had a ba - by, Bam - ba - lam.

Oh, Lawd, Black Betty,
Bam-ba-lamb,
Oh, Lawd, Black Betty,
Bambalamb,
Black Betty had a baby,
Bambalamb,
Black Betty had a baby,
Bambalamb.

Oh, Lawd, Black Betty,
Bam-ba-lamb,
Oh, Lawd, Black Betty,
Bam-ba-lamb,
It de cap'n's baby,
Bam-ba-lamb,
It de cap'n's baby,
Bam-ba-lamb.

Oh, Lawd, Black Betty,
Bambalamb,
Oh, Lawd, Black Betty,
Bambalamb,
But she didn' feed de baby,
Bambalamb,
But she didn' feed de baby,
Bambalamb.

Oh, Lawd, Black Betty,
Bambalamb,
Oh, Lawd, Black Betty,
Bambalamb,
Black Betty, where'd you come from?
Bambalamb,
Black Betty, where'd you come from?
Bambalamb.

THE HAMMER SONG

This work chant is to the same air as "Black Betty."

Oh, my hammer,
Hammer ring,
Oh, my hammer,
Hammer ring,

[61]

Ringin' on de buildin',
Hammer ring,
Ringin' on de buildin',
Hammer ring,
Doncha hear dat hammer?
Hammer ring,
Doncha hear dat hammer?
Hammer ring,
She's ringin' like jedgment,
Hammer ring,
She's ringin' like jedgment,
Hammer ring.
Oh, Lawd, dat hammer,
Hammer ring,
Oh, Lawd, dat hammer,
Hammer ring.

ROSIE

The authorities of the Mississippi State Farm occasionally allow the Negro men to entertain their feminine visitors as they please. Rosie, we think, is the prison counterpart of Mademoiselle from Armentières, who comforted so many American soldiers during the last war. At any rate she has been immortalized in what is, perhaps, the most stirring of all prison work songs. This song, shouted out all day long under the "hot boiling sun" of Parchman, Mississippi, filled full of a fierce and bitter despair, can be compared in its effect on the hearer only with that famous English broadside, "Sam Hall." A group of convicts at Camp No. 1 of the Mississippi State Farm sang it for us late one evening after they had come in from a day's work in the fields, and what they sang is essentially unreproducible; for along with the singing one must hear the beat of their hoes on the hard ground, the shouted exclamations at intervals in the song—"Talk it to time,

[62]

now!" "Explain it to 'em!" "Dat's all right, now!" Over all throbs the strange, wild harmony, as you see the somber iron bars, groups of men in striped clothes, guards lolling and listening, gun on knee.

Ain' but de one thing I done wrong,

Ain' but de one thing I done wrong, Ain' but de one thing I done wrong, Stayed in Miss'-ip-pi jes' a day too long, Day too long, Law-dy, day too long, — — — Stayed in Miss'ip-pi jes' a day too long. Oh, Ros-ie, O-ho, Oh, Ros-ie, Oh, Lawd, gal! Oh, Ros-ie, O-ho, Oh, Ros-ie, Oh, Lawd, Gal!

Ain' but de one thing I done wrong,
Ain' but de one thing I done wrong,
Ain' but de one thing I done wrong,
Stayed in Mis'sippi jes' a day too long,

[63]

Day too long, Lawdy, day too.long,
Stayed in Mis'sippi jes' a day too long.

Chorus:

    O Rosie, oho,
    O Rosie, oh, Lawd, gal.
    O Rosie, oho,
    O Rosie, oh, Lawd, gal.

I'm in trouble down on de farm,
I'm in trouble down on de farm,
I'm in trouble down on de farm,
I'm in trouble, Lawdy, all day long,
All day long, honey, all day long,
I'm in trouble, honey, all day long.

Chorus:

    O Rosie, oho,
    O Rosie, oh, Lawd, gal.
    O Rosie, oho,
    O Rosie, oh, Lawd, gal.

Think I'll jump in forty foot of water,
Over my head, Lawdy, over my head.

You needn' worry, you kin take yo' time,
Kin give me ninety an' still have nine [*years*].

Oh, I wonder who got de sergeant
Down on me, Lawdy, down on me.

Some ol' snitcher mus' got de sergeant
Down on me, Lawdy, down on me.

Ef I don' kill him, I'm gonna fix him so
He won' be snitchin' on me no mo'.

      *   *   *

Lil baby Franklin wasn' but nine days ol',
Stuck his finger in a crawfish hole;

Crawfish back back an' he wunk one eye,
"Lil baby Franklin, you is born to die."

* * *

Ain' but de one thing worries my min',
My cheatin' woman an' my grea' long time.

She says she loves me, but I b'lieve she's lyin',
Haan' been to see me in a grea' long time.

Well, this keepin' Rosie sho is hard,
Dress she wo' it cos' a dollar a yard.

Wake up, Rosie, an' turn up yo' clo'es,
May be de las' time, I don't know.

I don' wan' ev'ything I see,
Jes' want dat lil bit you promised me.

If they mistreat me, tell you what I'll do,
I'll cut dis steel an' bring it home to you.

Come an' git me an' a-take me home,
Dese lifetime devils, dey won' let me 'lone.

Well, I come in here wid a hundred years,
Tree fall on me, I don' bit mo' keer.

Axes a-walkin', chipses a-talkin',
All day long, honey, all day long.

    O Rosie, oho,
    O Rosie, oh, Lawd, gal.

OL' RATTLER

Mose Platt ("spells it P-L-A-W-P [P-L-A-double T], jes' lak you plait a whip"), alias Big Foot Rock, tells how he ran away from prison upon a time, how "ol' Rattler, de fastes' an' de smellin'es' bleedhoun' in de South" trailed and treed him.

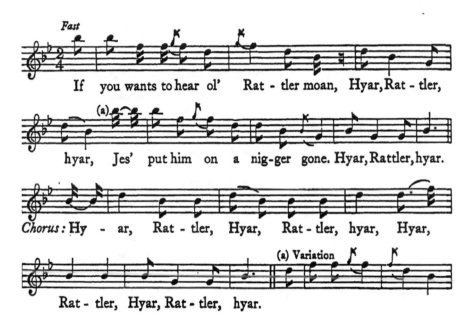

Ef you wants to hear ol' Rattler moan,
Heah, Rattler, heah,
Jes' put him on a nigger gone,
Heah, Rattler, heah.

Refrain:
Heah, Rattler,
Heah, Rattler, heah,
Heah, Rattler,
Heah, Rattler, heah.

B'lieve to my soul dere's a nigger gone,
Heah, Rattler, heah,
He went right down through dat corn,
Heah, Rattler, heah.

He cross right 'cross dat ol' foot log,
I b'lieve to my soul da's a nigger dog.

I think I hear a horn blow,
Ef I trip dis time, I'll trip no mo'.

You got to ride, ride, oui avail,
Ol' Rock's walkin' de Brazos.

Got a baby here, got a baby there,
Gonna take my baby to the worl'y fair.

Dey tell me one, dey tell me two,
Now ef you stay on de groun' Rattler'll sho ketch you.

Ol' Rattler jumped a cottontail,
Run dat fool off de trail.

I wouldn' stop ef I see myse'f dyin',
I'm on my way to de long-leaf pine.

Now I run till I'm almos' blin',
I'm on my way to de long-leaf pine.

I didn' have no time to make no thimpathee,
My nighes' route was up a tree.

I had a face all full of frowns,
You won' never ketch me on de groun'.

Now, hol' on, boys, let's stop an' see,
Dey got Big Foot Rock settin' in a tree.

STEWBALL

Skew Ball was an Irish race horse of broadside fame. The song came over to America and was turned into a work song by the slaves as some of the quoted stanzas will testify. And now Skew Ball has become "Stewball" and his race is sung in the prisons of Louisiana, Texas, Mississippi, and Tennessee. It is the most widely known of the chain-gang songs in the states we visited, and by far the most constant as to tune and words.

The following stanza illustrates the way Stewball is sung by a gang of Negro workmen in the fields. The accents mark the hoe or ax blows.

LEADER	CHORUS
Way out in	Unh-h'unh—
Californy,	Unh-hunh—
Where ol' Stewball	Unh-hunh—
Was born,	Was born—
All de jockeys	Unh-hunh—
In de country	Unh-hunh—
Said he blew there	Unh-hunh—
In a storm,	In a storm—
In a storm, man,	Unh-hunh—
In a storm.	In a storm.

Way out in, Uh-huh, Cal - i - for - ny, Uh-huh, Where ole

Stew - ball, Uh - huh, was born, Was born, All de

jock-eys, Uh-huh, In de coun-try, Uh-huh, Said he

blew there, Uh-huh, In a storm, In a storm, In a

storm, man, Uh-huh, In a storm, In a storm.

Ol' Stewball was a fas' hoss. I wish he was mine.
He never drunk water, but always drunk wine,
Drunk wine, man; drunk wine. *(Chorus, etc.; also for each follow-ing stanza.)*

Ol' Stewball was a white horse befo' dey painted him red.
But he winned a great forchun jes' befo' he fell dead,
Fell dead, man; fell dead.

Well, his bridle was silver an' his saddle was gol',
An' de price on his blanket hasn't never been tol',
Been tol', man; been tol'.

There's a big day in Dallas: doncha wish you was there?
You could bet yo' las' dolluh on dat iron-gray mare,
Gray mare, man; gray mare.

There's a big bell on a tassel for dem hosses to run,
Young ladies, young gen'lemun, from Baltimo' come,
Mo' come, man; mo' come.

Ol' Missus bet millions an' Massa bet poun's,
Dat ol' Stewball could beat Molly on any ol' groun',
Ol' groun', man; ol' groun'.

Young mistah, kind massa, I am ristin' my life,
Jes' to win a great forchun for you an' yo' wife,
Yo' wife, man; yo' wife.

The kittledrum was a-bangin' an' the word was given "Run";
Ol' Stewball was tremblin' like a crim'nal to be hung,
To be hung, man; to be hung.

When de hosses was saddled an' de word was given "Go,"
Ol' Stewball, he shot like an arrow from a bow,
From a bow, man; from a bow.

De ol' folks, dey hollered, an' de young folks, dey bawl;
But de lil chillun des a-look-a-look-a-look at de noble Stewball,
Stewball, man; Stewball.

Ef you had-a been dere at de firs' runnin' 'roun',
You a-swore by yo' life dat dey never tech groun',
Tech groun', man; tech groun'.

Molly was a-climbin' dat great big long lane,
An' she said to her rider, "Caincha slack dat lef' rein?"
Lef' rein, man; lef' rein.

Ol' Stewball was a-ramblin' up dat nine-mile-high hill;
His jockey looked behin' him an' he spied ol' Wil' * Bill,
Wil' Bill, man; Wil' Bill.

De races, dey ended, an' de judges played de band,
An' ol' Stewball beat Molly back to de gran' stan',
Gran' stan', man; gran' stan'.

Me an' my husband offa gamblin': I'm fixin' my bed.
My chillun stark naked: they is cryin', "Mo' bread."
Mo' bread, man; mo' bread.

* Wild.

[70]

I shot dice in Cuby an' I played cards in Spain,
Never was no money loser, till I learnt dat skin game,
Skin game, man; skin game.

Gwine to build me a castle on de mountain so high,
So's I can see ol' Stewball as he passes by,
Passes by, man; passes by.

"Good mornin', young lady." "How you feelin', young man?"
"I hope you cos' money: I ain' got no small change."
Small change, man; small change.

Dat peafowl done holler, an' dat turkle dove done moan.
I'm a po' boy in trouble an' a long way from my home,
From my home, man, from my home.

DE MIDNIGHT SPECIAL

Two prisoners are leaning against a barred window, their minds
heavy and listless with the monotony of days and endless, unsatisfied
desires. Eager to notice anything that will break through their narrow
horizon, hedged in by bars, guns, curses, day-long rolling in the fields,
they comment and let their imaginations play upon the few passers-by.

Sung in prisons all over the South, this song is probably of white
origin.

Well, you wake up in de mornin',
Hear de ding-dong ring,
Go marchin' to de table,
See de same damn thing.
Well, it's on-a one table,
Knife-a, fork, an'-a pan,
An', ef you say anything about it,
You're in trouble wid de man.

Chorus:

    Let de Midnight Special shine its light on you:
    Let de Midnight Special shine its ever-lovin' light on you.

"Well, yonder comes Dr. Melton."
"How in de worl' do you know?"
"Well, dey give me a tablet
The day befo'."
"Well, dey never was a doctor,
Travel through by lan',
Dat could cure de fever
On a convict man."

"Yonder comes Bud Russell."
"How in de worl' do you know?"
"Tell him by his big hat
An' his 44.
He walked into de jail-house
Wid a gang o' chains in his han's;
I heard him tell de captain,
'I'm de transfer man.'"

"Ef you go to Houston,*
You better walk right,
You better not stagger,
You better not fight.
Or Sheriff Benson *
Will arrest you,
He will carry you down.
Ef de juris find you guilty,
You'll be penitentiary bound."

"Yonder comes li'l Rosie."
"How in the worl' do you know?"
"I can tell her by her apron

---

* The song "Midnight Special" is widely current in the South. Instead of Houston, the singer may substitute the name of whatever town he was arrested in, and instead of Benson the name of the sheriff who arrested him.

An' de dress she wo'.
Umbereller on her shoulder,
Piece o' paper in her han',
Well, I heard her tell de captain,
'I want my man.' "

"Lord, Thelma say she love me;
But I b'lieve she tol' a lie,
'Cause she hasn' been to see me since de las' July.
She brought me lil coffee,
She brought me lil tea,
She brought me nearly ev'thing
But de jail-house key."

"Looky, looky yonder,
What in de worl' do I see?
Well, dat brown-skin woman,
Comin' after me.
She wore a mother hubbard
Jes' like a mournin' gown;
Trimmin' on her apron,
Lawd God, how it do hang down!"

"T. K. Erwin went to Austin
Wid a paper in his hands
To get de intermediate sentence
Passed on de convict man.
He hand de paper to de gov'nor,
And dere it stood.
I know she gonna sign it,
'Cause she said she would." *

"I'm gwine away to leave you,
An' my time ain' long.

*This verse, however, is not current outside of Texas.

De man is gonna call me,
An' I'm goin' home.
Then I'll be done all my grievin',
Whoopin', holl'in, an'-a cryin';
Then I'll be done all my studyin'
'Bout my great long time."

"Well, de biscuits on de table,
Jus' as hard as any rock.
Ef you try to swallow dem,
Break a convict's heart."
"My mother wrote a letter,
My mother wrote a card,—
'Ef you want to come to see us,
You'll have to ride de rods.' "

LONG GONE

In the introduction to W. C. Handy's *Blues* there is a story about the escape of a Negro prisoner, one Long John Green. It seems that the county had recently acquired a pack of bloodhounds and the sheriff wanted to try them out. Long John Green, in jail at the time, was chosen to make trail, since he was famous for the way he could get over the ground. They gave John halfway round the courthouse for a start and then unleashed the pack. On his first lap John crawled through a barrel, got the hounds off the scent and then he was "long gone." Whether or not Lightnin', who sang us the following song, knew the above story, it is hard to say: his own evidence would be worth very little.

The accents mark the ax-blows of a group of four men, who are chopping down a tree.

[75]

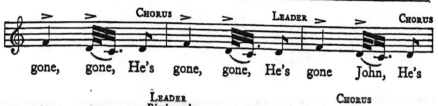

LEADER	CHORUS
Wid his di'mond blade,	Wid his di'mond blade,
Got it in his han',	Got it in his han',
Gonna hew out de live oaks,	Gonna hew out de live oaks,
Dat are in dis lan'.	Dat are in dis lan'.

Refrain

He's long gone,	He's long gone,
He's Long John,	He's Long John,
He's gone, gone,	He's gone, gone,
Like a turkey through de corn,	Like a turkey through de corn,
Wid his long clo'es on,	Wid his long clo'es on,
He's gone, gone,	He's gone, gone,
He's gone John,	He's gone John,
He's long gone.	He's long gone.

Stanzas

NOTE: It is effective to sing stanzas two, three, and four, stanzas five and six, stanzas seven, eight, and nine, and stanzas ten, eleven, and twelve as groups without injecting the chorus. Then roar out the refrain after each group of stanzas. This is the way the song is actually sung by the Negroes when they are chopping down a tree. It is well to note that the ax-blow, and thus the most heavily stressed syllable, is the accented syllable that stands nearest to the end of each line.

Ef I had a-listened
What Rosie said,
I'd a-been sleepin'
In a-Rosie's bed.

But-a I wouldn' listen;
Got to runnin' aroun',
An' de firs' thing I knew,
I was jail-house boun'.

Well, I got in de jail,
Wid my mouf poked out;
Now I'm in de pen,
An' I cain' get out.

Well-a, John made
A pair of shoes;
Funnies' shoes
Dat was ever seen;

Had a heel in front
An' a heel behin';
Well, you couldn' tell where
Dat boy was a-gwine.

Well-a, come on, honey,
Lemme shet dat do'.
Well, de dogs is a-comin'
An' I got to go.

Well-a, hear dat sergeant,
Jus' a-huffin' an' a-blowin';
Well, I b'lieve I hear
Ol' Rattler moanin'.

Well, I crossed dat Brazos
In de mornin' dew;

Well, I leave you, sergeant,
An' de captain too.

Well-a, good mornin', Mary;
How do you do?
Well, I crossed dat river
Jus' to see you.

All dis summer
Won' call no mo'.
Ef I call nex' summer,
Den I'm gone come mo'.

He's long gone,
He's Long John,
He's gone, gone,
Like a turkey through de corn,

Wid his long clo'es on,
He's gone, gone,
He's gone John,
He's long gone.

GREAT GOD–A'MIGHTY

Lightnin', "a blue-black, bad nigger," was leading a song that described the days when convicts were leased by the state to owners of large cotton plantations, sometimes to be driven under the lash until they fell from exhaustion, many, according to rumor, dying from sunstroke amid the sun-baked rows of cotton and cane in "dem long hot summer days." The song pictures what went on in the minds of a gang of field workers, one of whom was about to be punished. Even outside in the adjacent iron-barred dormitory the chatter and clamor of two hundred black convicts was stilled into awed and reminiscent

[79]

silence as the song swept on, growing in power toward the end, while Lightnin's eyes blazed, and he sang, "Great Godamighty!"

He's a-chop-pin' in de new groun', He's a-chop-pin' in de

new groun', He's a - chop - pin' in de

new groun', Great God a' - migh - ty.

The accented words mark the recurrent ax or hoe strokes.

The stanzas have this form—

He's a-choppin' in de new groun',
He's a-choppin' in de new groun',
He's a-choppin' in de new groun',
Great Godamighty. (*Refrain that is repeated after every stanza.*)

Verses

He's choppin' Charley,

He's a-choppin' jes' to fool you,

He's a pool-doo fooler,

Well, I got a crane wing;

Well, my pardner's got de same thing;

My blade is order made;

Where did you order it from?

It's o'dered from Dallas;

Got a number one blady;

Did you hear dat sergeant?

He's a-ridin' an' a-squabblin';

Well, I wonder what's de matter?

Yonder come de cap'n;

Better go to drivin';

Ridin' like he's angry;

Lord, I'm in trouble;

Ridin' in a hurry;

Better go to rollin'.

Well, he's got his bull-whup;

Cowhide in his other han';

Well, I wonder what's de matter;

It's gonna be trouble;

If you don't go to drivin';

Well, de captain went to talkin',

An' de bullies went to walkin';

Bully went to pleadin';

I'm a number one driver;

Cap'n, let me off, suh;

Woncha 'low me a chance, suh?

Bully, low down yo britches;

Put it off no longer;

The bully went to holl'in';

An' de cap'n hollered, "Hold him";

Cancha hear th' bully squallin'?

Cancha hear th' bully screamin'?

Oh, I better git to rollin';

Oh, my blady;

My blady's on fire; *

Jes' a-rockin' in de timber;

It's a-burnin' down, suh.

JUMPIN' JUDY

Allen Prothro from Chattanooga, Tennessee, sang "Jumpin' Judy."
The only definition we heard last summer of the peculiar adjective
"jumping" as applied to the Julie or Judy, who is famous throughout
Southern prison camps, is the way men work when driven in the fields
by an angry captain. For a further reference see stanza 13 of the "Tie
Tamping Chant."

* Ax-blade, moving fast.

[82]

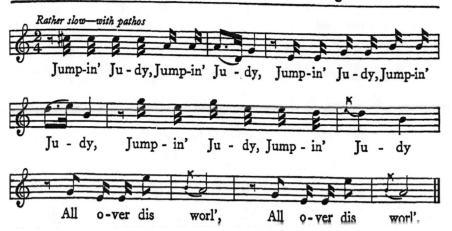

Rather slow—with pathos

Jump-in' Ju - dy, Jump-in' Ju - dy, Jump-in' Ju - dy, Jump-in'

Ju - dy, Jump - in' Ju - dy, Jump - in' Ju - dy

All o-ver dis worl', All o-ver dis worl'.

Jumpin' Judy, jumpin' Judy, hanh!
Jumpin' Judy, jumpin' Judy, hanh!
Jumpin' Judy, jumpin' Judy, hanh!
All over dis worl', hanh, all over dis worl', hanh! *

Well, you kick an' stomp an' beat me,
Well, you kick an' stomp an' beat me,
Well, you kick an' stomp an' beat me,
Da's all I know, da's all I know.

Yonder come my cap'n,
Yonder come my cap'n,
Yonder come my cap'n,
Who has been gone so long, who has been gone so long.

Gonna tell him how you treat me,
Gonna tell him how you treat me,
Gonna tell him how you treat me,
So you better git gone, so you better git gone.

He got a 44,
He got a 44,

* Each following stanza should contain all the stressed words.

He got a 44,
In-a his right han', in-a his right han'.

Gonna take dis ol' hammer,
Gonna take dis ol' hammer,
Give it back to jumpin' Judy,
An' tell her I'm gone, suh, an' tell her I'm gone.

Ef she asks you was I runnin',
Ef she asks you was I runnin',
Ef she asks you was I runnin',
You can tell I's flyin', you can tell I's flyin'.

Tell 'er I crossed de St. John's River,*
Tell 'er I crossed de St. John's River,
Tell 'er I crossed de St. John's River,
Wid my head hung down, wid my head hung down.

GOIN' HOME

A Pick Song

This song comes from the State Farm at Parchman, Mississippi. The "hanhs" represent the violent exhalations of breath that occur when the point of the pick sinks into the earth.

Moderately fast and well marked rhythm

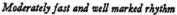

Ev - ry - where   I —   hanh—   Where   I   look   this

morn - in' —   hanh —   Ev - ry - - where   I —   hanh —

---

*Across the St. Johns River in Florida, it is said, fugitive slaves found refuge among the Seminoles. We recorded this verse in both Mississippi and Tennessee from the singing of uneducated Negroes for whom it could hardly have retained its original meaning.

Where I look this morn - in' —— hanh— Look like

rain — hanh— My Lord, looks like rain— hanh.

Everywhere I—hanh!
Where I look this mornin'—hanh!
Everywhere I hanh!
Where I look this mornin'—hanh!
Looks like rain—my Lawd!
Looks like rain—hanh!

The stanzas that follow can be fitted to the same form:

Got a rainbow * tied all around my shoulder,
Ain' gonna rain, my Lawd, ain' gonna rain.

I done walk till, walk till my feet's gone to rollin'.
Jes' like a wheel, my Lawd, jes' like a wheel.

I done hammered, hammered all over this ol' county,
My las' time, my Lawd, my las' time.

Ev'y mail day, mail day I git a letter,
"My Son, come home, my Lawd, son, come home."

My baby sister, sister keeps on a-writin',
"Buddy, come home, my Lawd, buddy, come home."

I cain' read her, read her letter for cryin',
My time's so long, my Lawd, my time's so long.

* "Rainbow," the arc of a swinging pick, probably going so fast that it becomes red-hot.

[85]

Dat ol' letter, letter read 'bout dyin',
My tears run down, my Lawd, my tears run down.

Jes' wait till I make these few days I started,
I'm goin' home, my Lawd, I'm goin' home.

I ain' got no, got no ready-made money,
I cain' go home, my Lawd, I cain' go home.

I'm gonna write me, one mo' letter to de gov'nor,
'Bout my time, my Lawd, 'bout my time.

By and by, buddy, we'll all get a pardon,
Get to go home, my Lawd, get to go home.

Doncha hear yo', hear yo' mother callin',
"Run, son, run, my Lawd, run, son, run"?

I'm gonna break right, break right pas' dat shooter.
I'm goin' home, my Lawd, I'm goin' home.

IV

NEGRO BAD MEN

"One preacher even described Christ as a man who would 'stand no foolin' wid.' 'Jesus such a great man, no one lak him. Lord, he could pop a lion's head off jes' lak he wus fryin'-size chicken, an' could take a piece o' mountain top and throw it across the world.' "—From *Negro Workaday Songs*, by Odum and Johnson.

BAD MAN BALLAD*

Moderately fast

Late las' night I was a - ma - kin' my rounds,

Met my wo - man an' I blowed her down,

Went on home an' I went to bed,

Put my hand can - non right un - der my head.

Late las' night I was a-makin' my rounds,
Met my woman an' I blowed her down,
Went on home an' I went to bed,
Put my hand cannon right under my head.

Early nex' mornin' 'bout de risin' o' de sun,
I gets up-a for to make-a my run.
I made a good run but I made it too slow,
Got overtaken in Mexico.

*Words and air from a tongue-tied Negro convict at Parchman, Mississippi.

Standin' on de corno', readin' of a bill,
Up step a man name o' Bad Texas Bill:
"Look here, bully, ain' yo' name Lee Brown?
B'lieve you are de rascal shot yo' woman down."

"Yes, oh, yes," says. "This is him.
If you got a warrant, jes' read it to me."
He says: "You look like a fellow that knows what's bes'.
Come 'long wid me—you're under arres'."

When I was arrested, I was dressed in black;
Dey put me on a train, an' dey brought me back.
Dey boun' me down in de county jail;
Couldn' get a human for to go my bail.

Early nex' mornin' 'bout half pas' nine,
I spied ol' jedge drappin' down de line.
I heered ol' jailer when he cleared his th'oat,
"Nigger, git ready for de deestreec' cote."

Deestreec' cote is now regin,
Twelve big jurymen, twelve hones' men.
Five mo' minutes up step a man,
He was holdin' my verdic' in his right han'.

Verdic' read murder in de firs' degree.
I said, "O Lawd, have mercy on me."
I seed ol' jedge when he picked up his pen,
Say, "I don' think you'll ever kill a woman ag'in.

"This here killin' of women natchly got to stop,
I don't know whether to hang you er not.
Ninety-nine years on de hard, hard groun',
'Member de night you blowed de woman down."

Here I is, bowed down in shame,
I got a number instead of a name.

Here for de res' of my nachul life,
An' all I ever done is kill my wife.

* * *

I went up-a in Tennessee,
Two lil' womens got stuck on me,
One was name Sal and the other name Sue,
They was a-hustlin' an' I was too.

Oh, dey beat me up an' dey beat me down,
Oh, dey beat me up-a an' dey beat me down,
Oh, dey beat me up an' dey beat me down,
Betcha five dollars dey cain' beat me to town.

PO' LAZ'US (POOR LAZARUS) *

Moderately fast

High Sher-iff tol' de dep-u-ty—hanh—Go out an' bring me Laz'-us—hanh—High Sher-iff tol' de dep-u-ty—hanh— Go out an' bring me Laz'-us-hanh—Bring him dead or a-live, Lawd! Lawd! Bring him dead or a-live.

* Some of the verses of this ballad worksong we have taken from *Negro Workaday Songs*. The rest of the words and the tune were recorded in Southern prison camps.

High sheriff tol' de deputy, "Go out an' bring me Laz'us."
High sheriff tol' de deputy: "Go out an' bring me Laz'us.
Bring him dead or alive, Lawd, Lawd, bring him dead or alive."

Oh, bad man Laz'us done broke in de commissary winder,
Oh, bad man Laz'us done broke in de commissary winder,
He been paid off, Lawd, Lawd, he been paid off.

Oh, de deputy 'gin to wonder, where in de worl' he could fin' him;
Oh, de deputy 'gin to wonder, where in de worl' he could fin' him;
Well, I don' know, Lawd, Lawd, I jes' don' know.

Oh, dey found' po' Laz'us way out between two mountains,
Oh, dey found' po' Laz'us way out between two mountains,
An' dey blowed him down, Lawd, Lawd, an' dey blowed him down.

Ol' Laz'us tol' de deputy he had never been arrested,
Ol' Laz'us tol' de deputy he had never been arrested,
By no one man, Lawd, Lawd, by no one man.

So dey shot po' Laz'us, shot him wid a great big number,
Dey shot po' Laz'us, shot him wid a great big number,
Number 45, Lawd, Lawd, number 45.

An' dey taken po' Laz'us an' dey laid him on de commissary county,
Dey taken po' Laz'us an' dey laid him on de commissary county,
An' dey walked away, Lawd, Lawd, an' dey walked away.

Laz'us tol' de deputy, "Please gimme a cool drink o' water,
Laz'us tol' de deputy, "Please gimme a cool drink o' water,
Jes' befo' I die, Lawd, Lawd, jes' befo' I die."

Laz'us' sister run an' tol' her mother,
Laz'us' sister run an' tol' her mother,
Dat po' Laz'us dead, Lawd, Lawd, po' Laz'us dead.

Laz'us' mother, she laid down her sewin',
Laz'us' mother, she laid down her sewin',
'Bout de trouble, Lawd, Lawd, she had wid Laz'us.

Laz'us' mother she come a-screamin' an' a-cryin',
Laz'us' mother, she come a-screamin' an' a-cryin',
"Dat's my only son, Lawd, Lawd, dat's my only son."

STAGOLEE

"His real name was Stack Lee and he was the son of the Lee family of Memphis who owned a large line of steamers that ran up and down the Mississippi.". . . "He was a nigger what fired the engines of one of the Lee steamers.". . . "They was a steamer runnin' up an' down de Mississippi, name de Stacker Lee, an' he was one o' de roustabouts on dat steamer. So dey called him Stackerlee." Whoever he was, he was a bad man and he killed Billy Lyons, probably in Memphis some thirty or forty years ago. The A version presents the ballad as it was sung when the tale was new; the B version, the "Stagolee" that is sung in the honky-tonks and barrel-houses throughout Texas and Louisiana today. Ivy Joe White, barrel-house pianist extraordinary of Wiergate, Texas; Alexander Wells, "Little Alex" of the Louisiana State Prison at Angola; and Sullivan Rock, rounder and roustabout on the docks of New Orleans, furnished the words for the B version. Windy Billy of the Louisiana State Prison at Angola sang the air.

Version A—sent, February 9, 1910, by Miss Ella Scott Fisher, San Angelo, Texas: "This is all the verses I remember. The origin of this ballad, I have been told, was the shooting of Billy Lyons in a barroom on the Memphis levee, by Stack Lee. The song is sung by the Negroes on the levee while they are loading and unloading the river freighters, the words being composed by the singers. The characters were prominently known in Memphis, I was told, the unfortunate Stagalee belonging to the family of the owners of the Lee line of steamers, which are known on the Mississippi from Cairo to the Gulf. I give all this to you as it was given to me. The effect of the song with its minor refrain is weird, and the spoken interpolations add to the realism. It becomes immensely personal as you hear it, like a recital of something known or experienced by the singer."

In August, 1933, a visit to the Memphis levee district and the renowned Beale's Street region failed to uncover the tune of this text of "Stagalee" or any additional stanzas that would fit the particular rhythm. What echoes of "Stagalee" remained were badly mixed with the Blues and jazzed almost beyond recognition. A special inquiry among several thousand Negro convicts in Texas, Louisiana, Mississippi, and Tennessee was likewise fruitless.

[*Version A*]

'Twas a Christmas morning,
The hour was about ten,
When Stagalee shot Billy Lyons
And landed in the Jefferson pen.
        O Lordy, po' Stagalee!

Billy Lyons' old woman,
She was a terrible sinner,
She was home that Christmas mornin'
A-preparin' Billy's dinner.
        O Lordy, po' Stagalee!

Messenger boy came to the winder,
Then he knocked on the door,
An' he said, "Yer old man's lyin' there
Dead on the barroom floor."
        O Lordy, po' Stagalee!

[94]

[BILLY's OLD WOMAN:]
"Stagalee, O Stagalee,
What have you gone and done?
You've gone and shot my husband
With a forty-four gatlin' gun."
  O Lordy, etc.

[STAGALEE's FRIEND:]
"Stagalee, O Stagalee,
Why don't you cut and run?
For here comes the policeman,
And I think he's got a gun."
  O Lordy, etc.

[POLICEMAN, *a little scared of* STAGALEE:]
"Stagalee, O Stagalee,
I'm 'restin' you just for fun,
The officer jest wants you
To identify your gun."
  O Lordy, etc.

[STAGALEE *in jail:*]
"Jailer, O Jailer,
I jest can't sleep;
For the ghost of Billy Lyons
Round my bed does mourn and weep."
  O Lordy, etc.

[COUNSEL FOR THE DEFENSE:]
"Gentlemen of this jury,
You must let poor Stagalee go;
His poor and aged mammy
Is lyin' very low."
  O Lordy, etc.

[COUNSEL FOR THE PROSECUTION:]
"Gentlemen of this jury,
Wipe away your tears,
For Stagalee's aged mammy
Has been dead these 'leven years."
    O Lordy, etc.

Stagalee's old woman,
She hung around the jail,
And in three days she had him out
On a ten-thousand-dollar bail.
    O Lordy, po' Stagalee!

[*Version B*]

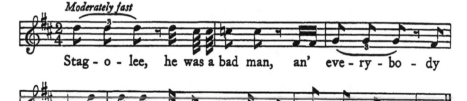

Stag-o-lee, he was a bad man, an' eve-ry-bo-dy knows He toted a stack-barreled blowgun an' a blue steel for-ty-fo'.

Stagolee, he was a bad man, an' ev'body know,
He toted a stack-barreled blow gun an' a blue steel 44.

Way down in New Orlean', called de Lyon club,
Ev'y step you walkin', you walkin' in Billy Lyon blood.

It was early one mornin' when I heard my little dog bark,
Stagolee and Billy Lyon was arg'in' in de dark.

Stagolee and Billy Lyon was gamblin' one night late,
Stagolee fell seven, Billy Lyon, he fell cotch eight.

Slowly Stack walked from de table, he said, "I can't let you go wid dat.
You win all of my money an' my milk-white Stetson hat."

Stagolee, he went walkin' right down dat I.C. track,
"I ain' gonna hurt you now, Billy, bet' not be here when I get back!"

Next day Stack went runnin' in de red-hot broilin' sun,
"Look in my chiffro drawer, Alberta, han' me my smokeless 41."

Alberta looked at Stack, said, "Babe, you all out of breath,
You look like you gonna be de cause of somebody's death."

Stack took out his Elgin, looked direc'ly at de time,
"I got an argument to settle wid dat bad man, Billy Lyon."

"Kiss me, good woman, you may not see me when I come back."
And Stack went runnin' up dat Great Northern track.

Well, he got outside in front of de barroom, an' he eased up to de door,
Billy Lyon had his 44 special, pacin' up an' down de floor.

Billy Lyon began to scream, "Stack, don't take my life,
I've got five lil helpless chilluns an' one po' pitiful wife."

He shot him three times in the forehead an' two times in de side,
Said, "I'm goin' keep on shootin' till Billy Lyon died."

Billy Lyon got glassy, an' he gapped an' hung his head,
Stack say, "I know by expression on his face dat Billy Lyon dead."

Mrs. Billy she went runnin' an' screamin': "Stack, I don' b'lieve it's so.
You an' my lil Billy been frien's since many long years ago."

Stagolee tol' Mrs. Billy, "Ef you don't b'lieve yo' man is dead,
Come to de barroom, see de hole I shot in his head."

Mrs. Lyon fell to her knees, an' she said to her oldes' son,
"When you git lil bit bigger, gonna buy you a 41."

"Mama, mama, oh, mama, you sho ain't talkin' to me,
He killed po' papa, now you gonna let him kill me."

It was early one mornin', Stagolee looked at de clouds an' say,
"Baby, it look mighty cloudy, it mus' be my jedgment day."

Chief Maloney tol' his deputies: "Git yo' rifles an' come wid me,
We got to arres' dat bad nigger, Stagolee."

Oh, de deputies took dey shiny badges, an' dey laid 'em on de shelf,
"Ef you wants dat nigger, go git him by yo' own damn self."

Slowly Chief Maloney, he walked to de barroom door,
Po' Stagolee was drunk an' layin' on de barroom floor.

Chief Maloney said to de bartender, "Who kin dat drunk man be?"
"Speak softly," said de bartender. "It's dat bad nigger Stagolee."

Chief Maloney touch Stack on de shoulder, say, "Stack, why don'
   you run?"
"I don't run, white folks, when I got my 41."

Stagolee, he tried to get up, staggered, pulled his pistol, could not
   get it out;
Chief Maloney pulled his pistol, shot de po' boy in de mouth.

Stagolee he went runnin' an' st'agglin' down Dumaine Street,
Boy, don' you know de blood was runnin' from his head down to
   his feet.

De jedge, he found Stack guilty, de clerk, he wrote it down,
Nex' col' winter mornin' Stack was Angola bound.

It was early one mornin', one bright summer day,
Chief Maloney 'ceived a wireless—Stack had runned away.

Chief Maloney got his men, an' he put dem roun' de town,
"Nex' time you see Stagolee, be sho to shoot him down."

* * *

De hangman put de mask on, tied his han's behin' his back,
Sprung de trap on Stagolee, but his neck refused to crack.

Hangman, he got frightened, he said: "Chief, you see how it be,
I cain' hang this man, you better let him go free."

Chief Maloney said to de hangman, "Befo' I'd let him go alive—"
He up wid his police special an' shot him six times in de side."

All de mans dey shouted, but de womens put on black an' mourned
Dat de good man Stagolee has laid down, died, an' gone.

Dey come a-slippin' an' a-slidin' up an' down de street,
In deir big mother hubbards an' deir stockin' feet.

He had a three-hundred-dollar funeral and a thousand-dollar hearse,
Satisfaction undertaker put him six feet under earth.

When de devil wife see Stack comin' she got up in a quirl,—
"Here come dat bad nigger an' he's jus' from de udder worl'."

All de devil' little chillun went sc'amblin' up de wall,
Say, "Catch him, pappa, befo' he kill us all."

Stack he tol' de devil, "Come on, le's have a lil fun,
You stick me wid yo' pitchfork an' I'll shoot you wid my 41."

Stagolee say, "Now, now, Mister Devil, ef me an' you gonna have
    some fun,
You play de cornet, Black Betty beat de drum."

Stagolee took de pitchfork an' he laid it on de shelf—
"Stand back, Tom Devil, I'm gonna rule Hell by myself."

OLD BILL*

Tell ol' Bill, be - fore he leaves home dis morn - in',

Tell ol' Bill, be - fore he leaves home dis eve - nin',

Tell ol' Bill be - fore he leaves home, to let dem down-town

coons a-lone. Dis morn - in', dis eve - nin', so soon.

Tell ol' Bill, before he leaves home dis mornin',
Tell ol' Bill, before he leaves home dis evenin',
Tell ol' Bill before he leaves home,
To let dem downtown coons alone
Dis mornin', dis evenin', so soon.

Bill left by de alley-gate, dis mornin',
Bill left by de alley-gate, dis evenin',
Bill left by de alley-gate, but he couldn't escape dat thirty-eight,
Dis mornin', dis evenin', so soon.

Bill's wife was a-makin' up bread, etc.,
When she got word that Bill was dead, etc.

Oh, no, dat cain' be so, etc.,
For Bill left home but an hour ago, etc.

* Tune and words from Carl Sandburg.

Oh, no, dat cannot be, etc.,
To shoot my husband in de first degree, etc.

Dey brought Bill home in de hurry-up wagon, etc.,
Dey brought Bill home with his toe-nails a-draggin', etc.

[*Another Version*] *

Oh, I was hungry from head to foot,
 Dis mornin', dis ebenin',
Oh, I was hungry from head to foot,
 Dis mornin', dis ebenin',
Oh, I was hungry from head to foot,
And I went to a place to get something to eat,
 Dis mornin', dis ebenin',
  So soon.

I bought me a doughnut and licked off the grease,
 Dis mornin', dis ebenin',
I bought me a doughnut and licked off the grease,
 Dis mornin', dis ebenin',
I bought me a doughnut and licked off the grease,
And gave the waiter a five-cent piece,
 Dis mornin', dis ebenin',
  So soon.

He looked at the nickel and he looked at me,
 Dis mornin', dis ebenin',
He looked at the nickel and he looked at me,
 Dis mornin', dis ebenin',
And he said, " 'Tain't good, and you can't fool me,"
 Dis mornin', dis ebenin',
  So soon.

* Sent by William E. Bolin, Ethical Culture School, Sixty-third Street and Central Park West, New York City.

"Dar's a hole in the middle, and it goes straight through,
  Dis mornin', dis ebenin',
Dar's a hole in the middle, and it goes straight through,
  Dis mornin', dis ebenin',
Dar's a hole in the middle, and it goes straight through."
Says I, "Dar's a hole in the doughnut, too,
  Dis mornin', dis ebenin',
    So soon."

I met a man a-walking on de track,
  Dis mornin', dis ebenin',
I met a man a-walking on de track,
  Dis mornin', dis ebenin',
I met a man a-walking on de track,
And he had a banjo, strapped on his back,
  Dis mornin', dis ebenin',
    So soon.

He stubbed his toe, and down he fell,
  Dis mornin', dis ebenin',
He stubbed his toe, and down he fell,
  Dis mornin', dis ebenin',
He stubbed his toe, and down he fell,
And he smashed the banjo all to hell,
  Dis mornin', dis ebenin',
    So soon.

FRANKIE AND ALBERT*

A

With great intensity

Fran-kie was a good wo-man, Ev-'ry-bo - - dy knows.

She spent a hundred dol - lars For to buy her man some

clothes. He was her man - - - but he done her wrong.

Frankie wuz a good woman,
Everybody knows,
She spent one hundred dollars
For to buy her man some clothes,
Oh, he wuz her man,
But he done her wrong.

Frankie went down to de corner,
Went there wid a can,
Ast de lovin' bartender:
"Has you seen my lovin' man?
He's my man,
But he's a-doin' me wrong."

Frankie went down to de corner,
Didn't go dere for fun,

---

*In 1909 the *A* version came from Texas sources. The *B* version is a composite of stanzas obtained from Connecticut, North Carolina, Mississippi, Illinois, Tennessee, and Texas. A study of the three hundred variants in the collection of Robert A. Gordon will yet, perhaps, call for a doctor's thesis. No one has ever heard precisely the same song sung by two individuals, unless they happened to be roommates.
Frankie, the heroine of this tragedy, yet lives, according to report, somewhat aloof to the curious only, in Seattle, Washington.

Underneath her raglin,
She had Albert's 41—
He was her man,
But she shot him down.

Frankie went down to de whore-house,
Rang de whore-house bell,
Says, "Tell me, is my lovin' Albert here?
Caze Frankie's gwine to raise some hell—
Oh, he's my man,
But he's a-doin' me wrong."

When Albert saw Frankie,
For the back door he did scoot,
But Frankie pulled dat forty-fo',
Went root-ta-toot-toot-ta-toot-toot—
En she shot him down,
Yes, she shot him down.

Well, when Frankie shot Albert,
He fell down on his knees,
Looked up at her and said,
"Oh, Frankie, please
Don't shoot me no mo', babe,
Don't shoot me no mo'.

"Oh, tu'n me over, doctor,
Tu'n me over slow,
Tu'n me over on my right-hand side
Caze de bullet is a-hurtin' me so."
He was her man,
But he's dead an' gone.

Frankie follered Albert to de graveyard,
Fell down on her knees.

"Speak one word, Albert,
An' git my heart some ease—
You wuz my man,
But you done me wrong."

Albert raise up in his grave,
To old Frankie he said,
"You bein' my lovin' woman,
Kindly put some cracked ice on my head—
I wuz yo' man,
But I done you wrong."

Now Frankie's layin' on old Albert's grave,
Tears rollin' down her face,
Says, "I've loved many a nigger son of a bitch,
But there's none can take Albert's place—
He wuz my man,
But he done me wrong."

En now it's rubber-tired carriages,
An' a rubber-tired hack,
Took old Albert to de graveyard
An' brought his mother back—
His soul's in hell,
His soul's in hell.

B

Sung by Lead Belly, "King of twelve-string guitar players of the world," Angola, Louisiana.

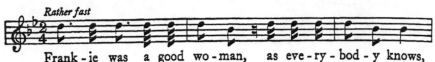

Frank - ie was a good wo - man, as eve - ry - bod - y knows,

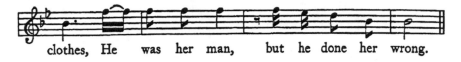

She did all the work a - round the house, and pressed her Al-bert's

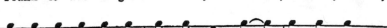

clothes, He was her man, but he done her wrong.

Frankie was a good woman,
As everybody knows,
She did all the work around the house
And pressed her Albert's clothes.
He was her man, but he done her wrong.

Albert was a yeller man,
Coal-black curly hair.
Everybody up in St. Louis
Thought he was a millionaire—
He was my son, and the only one.

Miss Frankie went to the barroom,
Called for a bottle of beer,
Says to the bartender:
"Has Mister Albert been here?
He is my man, and he's doin' me wrong."

Frankie and Albert were lovers,
Oh, my God, how they did love!
Just like sisters and brothers,
This whore and her turtle dove,
For he was her man, but she shot him down.

The bartender says to Miss Frankie:
"I cannot tell a lie;
Mister Albert was here about a minute ago
With a gal name Alkali.
He is your man, but he's doin' you wrong."

Little Frankie went down Broadway
With her razor in her hand,
Says: "Stand aside, you chippie.
I'm lookin' for my man,
He's a gamblin' man, won't treat me right."

Miss Frankie went up the stairway,
She didn't go for fun;
Underneath the ruffles of her petticoat,
She had a young Gatlin' gun.
He was her man an' he was doin' her wrong.

Miss Frankie opened the winder,
The gun she fired twice;
The second shot she fired,
She took Mister Albert's life—
He was her man, but he was doin' her wrong.

Well, when Frankie shot Albert,
First, he fell to his knees,
Then he looked up in her face,
Says, "Frankie, please don't shoot me no mo',
Please, babe, don't shoot me no mo'."

She shot three bullets in him,
He staggered to the door,
He gasped, "Oh, Frankie, you can't play 'round,
'Round this hop joint any more.
I was your man, but I done you wrong.

"Turn me over, Frankie,
Turn me over slow,
Turn me over easy on my left side
So my heart won't overflow
And kill me dead, and kill me dead."

Took po' Albert to the graveyard,
Stuck him in the ground,
Frankie, she was singin',
"I shot the sucker down—
He was my man, but he done me wrong."

The people says to Frankie,
"Little Frankie, why don't you run?
Yonder comes the Chief Police
With a smokeless 44 gun.
You killed your man, wouldn't treat you right."

"Well," says Miss Frankie,
"I don't care if I die,
Take and hang me to a telegraph pole,
Hang me good and high—
He was my man but he done me wrong."

Little Frankie went down Broadway
As far as she could see,
And all she could hear was a two-string bow,
Playing, "Nearer, My God, to Thee"—
All over the town, little Albert's dead.

Frankie went to Albert's mother,
Fell across her knees,
Said: "I'm sorry I killed your son,
Won't you excuse me, please?
He was my man, but he done me wrong."

"I will forgive you, Frankie,
I will forgive you not.
You sho shot Albert,
He's the only son I got,
He was my son, and the only one."

Frankie says to the sheriff,
"Well, what do you think it'll be?"
The sheriff said: "It looks like a case
Of murder in the first degree;
He was your man, but you shot him down."

It was not murder in the first degree,
It was not murder in the third,
A woman simply dropped her man
Like a hunter drops a bird.
He was her man, but she shot him down.

Frankie said to the sheriff,
"Oh, what do you think they'll do?"
"Strap you in the 'lectric chair,
'N' send thirty thousand volts through you.
Albert was your man, but you shot him down."

Passin' through the jail-house,
Went by Frankie's cell,
Asked her how she was feelin',
She said, "Go to Hell."
He was her man, but she shot him down.

Once more I saw Frankie,
She was sittin' in her chair,
Waitin' for to go an' meet her God,
With the sweat drippin' out her hair.
Albert was her man, but she shot him down.

Took Frankie to the graveyard
And stuck her in the ground,
Now all that's left of Frankie is
A wooden cross and mound.
He was her man—both dead and gone

Two little pieces of crape,
Hangin' on the door,
Show that lovin' Albert
Ain't lovin' Albert no more.
Frankie shot her man, what was doin' her wrong.

IDA RED *

I went down town one day in a lope;
Fool around till I stole a coat;
Den I come back and done my bes',
Fool around till I got de ves'.
Oh, weep! Oh, my Ida!
Fer over dat road Ise bound to go.

Dey carry me down to de jail-house do',
Where I never had been befo'.
The jailer come out wid a key in his han';
Say, "I jest got room fer one young man."
Oh, weep! Oh, my Ida!
Fer over dat road Ise bound to go.

Send little Ida down in town
To git somebody fer to go my boun',
But she come back wid a very sad tale,
"Cain't git nobody fer to go your bail."
Oh, weep! Oh, my Ida!
Fer over dat road Ise bound to go.

* From the Colorado River (Texas) bottoms.

Dey had me tied with a ball and chain,
Waitin' all ready fer de east-bound train;
And every station we pass by
Seem like I heard little Ida cry.
Oh, weep! Oh, my Ida!
Fer over dat road Ise bound to go.

If I had listened to whut Ida said,
I'd been sleepin' in Ida's bed;
But I pay no mind to my Ida Red,
An' now Ise sleepin' in a convict's bed.
Oh, weep! Oh, my Ida!
Fer over dat road Ise bound to go.

I wash my face and I comb my head,
Ise a mighty fool about Ida Red;
When I git out of dis old shack,
Tell little Ida Ise comin' back.
Oh, weep! Oh, my Ida!
Fer over dat road Ise bound to go.

BIG JIM *

Cold and chill is de winter wind,
Big Jim's dead an' gone.
Big Jim wuz my lovin' man;
Gawd! de years seem long, oh, long!
Long, oh, long are de years!

He wuz good and kind to me,
Jim wuz a grinder too,
But nothin' now won't bring him back,
Nothin' I can do.
Long, oh, long, are de years!

* From R. V. Utter, Vicksburg, Mississippi, through Professor R. P. Utter, University of California.

Listen to my story;
Seems like yesterday night
Jim went down to de hop house,
And that was the start of the fight.
Long are de years, yes, long!

Oh, my God, how I hate her!
An' I know she done it, too—
Cut his head mos' off'n his neck
An' whut fer he never knew.
Long, oh, long, are de years!

Big Jim's dead an' gone now;
Listen to my song.
Some day I'll be goin' too,
An' I hope it won't be long—
Long, long, long are de years!

DE BALLIT OF DE BOLL WEEVIL *

The farm-er took de bollweevil an' put him in de sand;

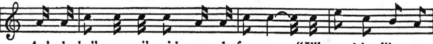

An' de boll-wee-vil said to de farm-er, "I'll stand it like a

man, for it is my home, For it is my home, home."

Oh, have you heard de lates',
De lates' of de songs?
It's about dem little Boll Weevils,

* Words from Texas and Mississippi; tune from Texas. Text largely collected in 1909.

Dey's picked up bofe feet an' gone
A-lookin' for a home,
Jes a-lookin' for a home.

De Boll Weevil is a little bug
F'um Mexico, dey say,
He come to try dis Texas soil
En thought he better stay,
A-lookin' for a home,
Jes a-lookin' for a home.

De nigger say to de Boll Weevil
"Whut makes yo' head so red?" *
"I's been wanderin' de whole worl' ovah
Till it's a wonder I ain't dead,
A-lookin' for a home,
Jes a-lookin' for a home."

First time I saw Mr. Boll Weevil,
He wuz on de western plain;
Next time I saw him,
He wuz ridin' on a Memphis train,
A-lookin' for a home,
Jes a-lookin' for a home.

De nex' time I saw him,
He was runnin' a spinnin' wheel;
De nex' time I saw him,
He was ridin' in an automobile,
A-lookin' for a home,
Jes a-lookin' for a home.

De fus' time I saw de Boll Weevil
He wuz settin' on de square,
De nex' time I saw de Boll Weevil

* The Negro must have his rhyme. He is thinking of the red-headed peckerwood.

[113]

He had all his family dere—
Dey's lookin' for a home,
Jes a-lookin' for a home.

Then the Farmer got angry,
Sent him up in a balloon;
"Good-by, Mr. Farmer;
I'll see you again next June.
A-lookin' for a home,
Jes a-lookin' for a home."

De Farmer took de Boll Weevil
An' buried him in hot san';
De Boll Weevil say to de Farmer,
"I'll stan' it like a man,
Fur it is my home,
It is my home."

Den de Farmer took de Boll Weevil
An' lef' him on de ice;
Says de Boll Weevil to de Farmer,
"Dis is mighty cool an' nice.
Oh, it is my home,
It is my home."

Mr. Farmer took little Weevil
And put him in Paris Green;
"Thank you, Mr. Farmer;
It's the best I ever seen.
It is my home,
It's jes my home."

Den de Farmer say to de Merchant:
"We's in an awful fix;
De Boll Weevil's et all de cotton up

An' lef' us only sticks.
We's got no home,
Oh, we's got no home."

Den de Merchant say to de Farmer,
"Whut do you tink o' dat?
Ef you kin kill de Boll Weevil
I'll give you a bran-new Stetson hat,
A Stetson hat,
Oh, a Stetson hat."

Oh, de Farmer say to de Merchant,
"I ain't made but only one bale,
An' befo' I bring yo' dat one
I'll fight an' go to jail,
I'll have a home,
I'll have a home."

De Sharpshooter say to de Boll Weevil,
"What you doin' in dis square?"
An' the Boll Weevil say to de Sharpshooter,
"Ise makin' my home in here,
Here in dis square,
Here in dis square."

Oh, de Boll Weevil say to de Dutchman,
"Jes' poison me ef yo' dare,
An' when yo' come to make yo' crop
I'll punch out every square,
When de sun gits hot,
When de sun gits hot."

De Boll Weevil say to de Farmer,
"You better lemme alone,
I've et up all yo' cotton

An' now I'll begin on de co'n,
I'll have a home,
I'll have a home."

Boll Weevil say to de Doctor,
"Better po' out all yo' pills,
When I git through wid de Farmer,
He cain't pay no doctor's bills.
He'll have no home,
He'll have no home."

Boll Weevil say to de Preacher,
"You better close yo' chu'ch do',
When I git through wid de Farmer,
He cain't pay de Preacher no mo',
Won't have no home,
Won't have no home."

De Merchant got half de cotton,
De Boll Weevil got de res';
Didn't leave de nigger's wife
But one old cotton dress.
And it's full of holes,
Oh, it's full of holes.

Rubber-tired buggy,
Decorated hack,
Took dem Boll Weevils to de graveyard,
An' ain't goin' bring 'em back.
Dey gone at las',
Oh, dey gone at las'.

Ef anybody axes you
Who wuz it writ dis song,
Tell 'em 'twuz a dark-skinned nigger

Wid a pair o' blue duckins on,
A-lookin' for a home,
Jes a-lookin' for a home.

BILL MARTIN AND ELLA SPEED

Lead Belly, self-acknowledged king of the twelve-string guitar, said that Bill Martin had shot po' Ella down in the street not long before he moved to Dallas, and that her sad death was already celebrated by the street musicians (of whom he was one). According to his own story, he helped to make up some of the loosely woven stanzas that tell the tale of Martin's jealousy. Each couplet is to be repeated twice except in the case of the four-line stanzas, which are to be sung as written. See "Alice B" in *The American Songbag*.

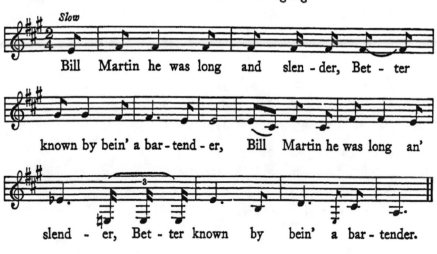

Bill Martin he was long and slen-der, Bet-ter known by bein' a bar-tend-er, Bill Martin he was long an' slend-er, Bet-ter known by bein' a bar-tender.

Bill Martin he was long an' slender,
Better known by bein' a bartender.
Bill Martin he was long an' slender,
Better known by bein' a bartender.

Bill Martin he was a man whut had a very small hand,
He worked ev'y night at de coffee stand.

[117]

He walked out for to borrow a gun,
Something Bill Martin had never done.

Ella Speed was downtown havin' her lovin' fun,
Long came Bill Martin wid his Colt 41.

De fust ball it entered in po' Ella's side,
De nex' ball entered in her breas',
De third ball it entered in her head;
Dat's de ball dat put po' Ella to bed.

All de young gals come a-runnin' an' cryin',
All de young gals come a-runnin' an' a-cryin',
"It ain' but de one thing worry de po' gal's min'—
She lef' her two lil boys behin'."

De deed dat Bill Martin done,
Jedge sentence: "You gonna be hung."

They taken Bill Martin to de freight depot,
An' de train come rollin' by,
He wave his han' at de woman dat he love
An' he hung down his head an' he cry.

All you young girls better take heed,
Don' you do like po' Ella Speed;
Some day you will go for to have a lil fun
An' a man will do you like Bill Martin done.

RAILROAD BILL *

That bad man of the ties, Railroad Bill, is a completely legendary character. It is interesting to note that he was killed or arrested by another Negro, after he had eluded the white officers of the law that set out after him.

* Text and tune are quoted from Odum and Johnson's *Negro Workaday Songs* (Chapel Hill, N.C.: University of North Carolina Press).

Firs' on ta - ble, nex' on de wall; Ol' corn

whis - ky cause of it all. It's dat bad Rail-road Bill.

Firs' on table, nex' on wall;
Ol' corn whisky cause of it all.
It's dat bad Railroad Bill.

Railroad Bill mighty bad man,
Shoot dem light out o' de brakeman's han'.
It's dat bad Railroad Bill.

Railroad Bill went out Wes',
Thought he had dem cowboys bes'.
It's dat bad Railroad Bill.

Railroad Bill, Railroad Bill,
He never work and he never will.
It's dat bad Railroad Bill.

Two policemen dressed in blue
Come down street in two an' two,
Wuz lookin' fer Railroad Bill.

Ol' McMillan had a special train,
When he got dere it was a shower of rain.
Wuz lookin' fer Railroad Bill.

Ev'body tol' him he better turn back;
Railroad Bill wuz goin' down de track,
Dat bad man Railroad Bill.

[119]

Railroad Bill wuz the worst ol' coon,
Killed McMillan by the light of de moon,
When wuz lookin' fer Railroad Bill.

Some one went home an' tol' my wife
All about—well, my pas' life.
It wuz dat bad Railroad Bill.

I went down on Number One,
Railroad Bill had jus' begun.
Wuz dat bad Railroad Bill.

I come up on Number Two,
Railroad Bill had jus' got through.
Dat bad Railroad Bill.

An' jus' as I caught dat Number Fo',
Somebody shot at me wid a fo'ty-fo',
Wuz dat bad Railroad Bill.

I went back on Number Five,
Goin' bring him back, dead or alive.
Wuz lookin' fer Railroad Bill.

I come back on Number Eight,
The folks say I wuz a minute too late.
Lookin' fer Railroad Bill.

When I come back on Number Nine,
Folks says, "You're jes' in time.
Lookin' for Railroad Bill."

When I got my men, they amounted to ten,
An' that's when I run po' Railroad Bill in.
An' that wuz the last of po' Railroad Bill.

V

WHITE DESPERADOES

"The night before he swung, he sang
To his mandolin."

WILLA CATHER

SPANISH JOHNNY *

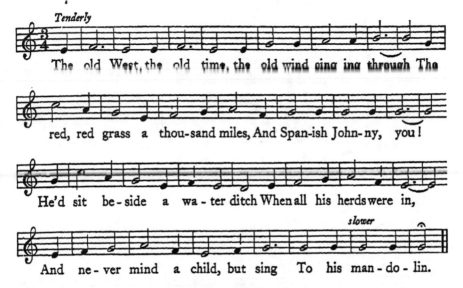

Tenderly

The old West, the old time, the old wind sing ing through The

red, red grass a thou-sand miles, And Span-ish John-ny, you!

He'd sit be-side a wa-ter ditch When all his herds were in,

slower

And ne-ver mind a child, but sing To his man-do-lin.

The old West, the old time,
The old wind singing through
The red, red grass a thousand miles,
And Spanish Johnny, you!
He'd sit beside a water ditch
When all his herds were in,
And never mind a child, but sing
To his mandolin.

* "The words are Willa Cather's; if you print them, of course, you'll have to get her permission.
The tune is a poor thing, but mine own. I liked the verse, and this is the way it sang itself
to me. A lot of people like it, and I used to like it myself; but I've sung it so often
now that it doesn't seem to mean much any more."—C. E. SCOGGINS, Sea Horse Hill,
Boulder, Colorado.

The big stars, the blue night,
The moon-enchanted lane,
The olive man who never spoke,
But sang the songs of Spain.
His talk with men was wicked talk,
To hear it was a sin,
But those were golden things he said,
To his mandolin.

The old songs, the old stars,
The world so golden then!
The hand so tender to a child
Had killed so many men.
He died a hard death long ago,
Before the Road came in.
The night before he swung, he sang
To his mandolin.

JOHN HARTY *

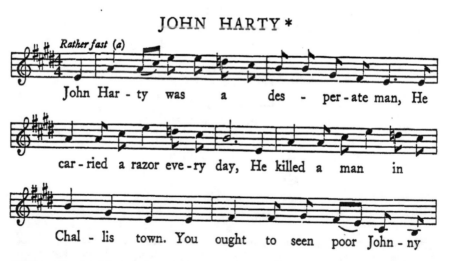

John Har - ty was a des - per - ate man, He
car - ried a razor eve - ry day, He killed a man in
Chal - lis town. You ought to seen poor John - ny

* Given to J. A. Lomax by J. H. Strickland of Idaho, who had it from Jeff Hamilton of Virginia, 1909. This song is usually sung as "John Hardy." See "John Henry," pp. 3ff.

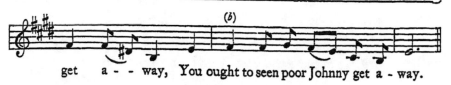

VARIATIONS

John Harty was a desperate man,
He carried a gun and a razor every day,
He killed a man in Challie town,
You ought to seen poor Johnny get away. (*Repeat.*)

John Harty went to this big, long town.
When he thought he was out of the way,
Up stepped a marshal and taken him by the hand,
Says, "Johnny, come and go with me." (*Repeat.*)

Johnny Harty had a father and mother,
He sent for them to go his bail.
No bail was allowed for murdering a man,
So they shoved Johnny Harty back in jail. (*Repeat.*)

Johnny Harty had a pretty little wife,
She was all dressed in blue,
She cried out with a loud little shout,
"Johnny, I've been true to you." (*Repeat.*)

Johnny Harty was standing in his cell,
With the tears running down each eye;
"I've been the death of many a poor man,
And now I'm ready to die.
O Lord, now I'm ready to die.

"I've been to the east, I've been to the west,
I've been this wide world round,
I've been to the river and been baptized,
So take me to my hanging ground,
O Lord, take me to my hanging ground."

SAM BASS

Each year thousands of visitors stop to visit the grave of Sam Bass at Round Rock, Texas. He was the most famous of Texas desperadoes, the Robin Hood of the Southwest.

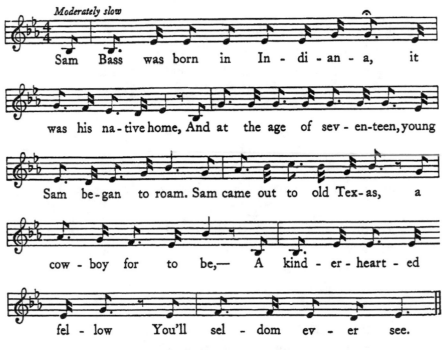

Sam Bass was born in Indiana, it was his native home,
And at the age of seventeen young Sam began to roam.
He came out to old Texas, a cowboy for to be—
A kinder-hearted feller you'll seldom ever see.

Sam used to deal in race stock, one called the Denton Mare,
He matched her in scrub races, and took her to the Fair.
Sam used to coin the money and spent it just as free,
He always drank good whisky wherever he might be.

Sam left the Collins ranch in the merry month of May
With a herd of Texas cattle the Black Hills for to see,
Sold out in Custer City and then got on a spree—
A harder set of cowboys you'll seldom ever see.

On their way back to Texas they robbed the U.P. train,
And then split up in couples and started out again.
Joe Collins and his partner were overtaken soon,
With all their hard-earned money they had to meet their doom.

Sam made it back to Texas all right side up with care,
Rode into the town of Denton with all his friends to share.
Sam's life was short in Texas; three robberies he did do,
He robbed all the mail, passenger and express cars too.

Sam had four companions—four bold and daring lads—
They were Richardson, Jackson, Joe Collins, and Old Dad;
Four more bold and daring cowboys the rangers never knew,
They whipped the Texas rangers and ran the boys in blue.

Sam had another companion, called Arkansas for short,
Was shot by a Texas ranger by name of Thomas Floyd;
Oh, Tom, he's a big six-footer and thinks he's mighty fly,
But I can tell you his racket—he's a dead-beat on the sly.

Jim Murphy was arrested, and then released on bail;
He jumped his bond at Tyler and then took the train for Terrill;
But Mayo Jones had posted Jim, and that was all a stall,
'Twas only a plan to capture Sam before the coming fall.

Sam met his fate at Round Rock, July the twenty-third,
They pierced poor Sam with rifle balls and emptied out his purse.
Poor Sam he is a corpse and six feet under clay,
And Jackson's in the bushes trying to get away.

Jim had borrowed Sam's good gold and didn't want to pay,
The only shot he saw was to give poor Sam away.
He sold out Sam and Barnes and left their friends to mourn—
Oh, what a scorching Jim will get when Gabriel blows his horn!

And so he sold out Sam and Barnes and left their friends to mourn,
Oh, what a scorching Jim will get when Gabriel blows his horn!
Perhaps he's got to heaven, there's none of us can tell [or say],
But if I'm right in my surmise he's gone right straight to hell [or the
other way].

JESSE JAMES

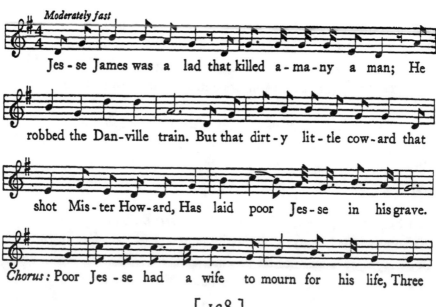

Moderately fast

Jes-se James was a lad that killed a-ma-ny a man; He
robbed the Dan-ville train. But that dirt-y lit-tle cow-ard that
shot Mis-ter How-ard, Has laid poor Jes-se in his grave.

Chorus: Poor Jes-se had a wife to mourn for his life, Three

chil - dren, they were brave. But that dirt - y lit - tle cow - ard that

shot Mis - ter How - ard, Has laid poor Jes - se in his grave.

[*Version A*]

Jesse James was a lad that killed a-many a man;
He robbed the Danville train.
But that dirty little coward that shot Mister Howard,
Has laid poor Jesse in his grave.

Chorus:

    Poor Jesse had a wife to mourn for his life,
    Three children, they were brave.
    But that dirty little coward that shot Mister Howard,
    Has laid poor Jesse in his grave.

It was Robert Ford, that dirty little coward,
I wonder how does he feel.
For he ate of Jesse's bread, and he slept in Jesse's bed,
Then laid poor Jesse in his grave.

Jesse was a man, a friend to the poor,
He never would see a man suffer pain;
And with his brother Frank he robbed the Chicago bank,
And stopped the Glendale train.

It was his brother Frank that robbed the Glendale bank,
And carried the money from the town;
It was in this very place that they had a little race,
For they shot Captain Sheets to the ground.

[129]

They went to the crossing not very far from there,
And there they did the same; ·
With the agent on his knees, he delivered up the keys
To the outlaws, Frank and Jesse James.

It was on a Wednesday night, the moon was shining bright,
They robbed the Glendale train;.
The people, they did say, for many miles away,
It was robbed by Frank and Jesse James.

It was on a Saturday night, Jesse was at home,
Talking with his family brave;
Robert Ford came along like a thief in the night
And laid poor Jesse in his grave.

The people held their breath when they heard of Jesse's death,
And wondered how he ever came to die;
It was one of the gang called little Robert Ford,
He shot poor Jesse on the sly.

Jesse went to his rest with his hand upon his breast;
The devil will be upon his knee.
He was born one day in the county of Clay
And came from a solitary race.

Jesse went down to the City of Hell,
Thinking for to do as he pleased;
But when Jesse come down to the City of Hell,
The Devil quickly had him on his knees.

This song was made by Billy Gashade,
As soon as the news did arrive;
He said there was no man with the law in his hand,
Who could take Jesse James when alive.

[*Version B*]

Jimmie Otis, a Negro convict on the State Farm at Angola, Louisiana, says that years ago in Kansas City he heard another "Jesse James" sung to the tune of "Casey Jones."

Living in Missouri wuz a bold, bad man,
His fame has settled down f'um Birmingham,
F'um Boston, Massachusetts, all around de state,
F'um Denver, Colorado, to de Golden Gate.

Chorus:
    Jesse James, we used to read of,
    Jesse James at his home at night,
    Jesse James, we used to read of—
    While de wind blows down de chimney we will shake with fright.

Jesse one evening at fo' o'clock,
Jesse polished up his rifle, put his trust in view.
He galloped out and said to brother Frank,
"We have to have some money out-a de Pittsfield bank."

Oh, Jesse got in town, it wuz four o'clock,
De cashier at de bank, he got an awful shock;
Jesse had him covered wid his forty-fo'.
"Oh, pass me half a million bones or mo'."

Jesse was at home de whole day long,
His wife has left him dere straightening up his home,
De do' bell did ring, Jesse said, "Walk in."
Up step forty members of dat outlaw band!—*Chorus.*

[131]

QUANTRELL *

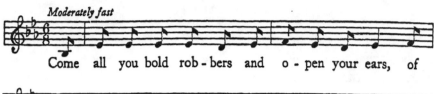

Moderately fast

Come all you bold rob-bers and o-pen your ears, of

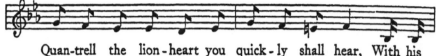

Quan-trell the lion-heart you quick-ly shall hear, With his

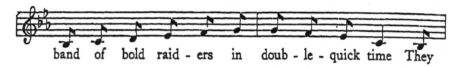

band of bold raid-ers in doub-le-quick time They

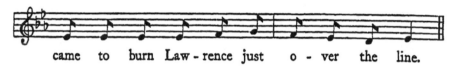

came to burn Law-rence just o-ver the line.

Come all ye bold robbers and open your ears,
Of Quantrell the lion-heart you quickly shall hear,
With his band of bold raiders in double-quick time
They came to burn Lawrence just over the line.

Chorus:

All routing and shouting and giving the yell,
Like so many demons just raised up from Hell,
The boys they were drunken with powder and wine,
And came to burn Lawrence just over the line.

They came to burn Lawrence, they came not to stay,
They rode in one morning at breaking of day,
Their guns were a-waving and horses a-foam,
And Quantrell a-riding his famous big roan.

* From singing of R. R. Critchlow (Slim Slocum), radio broadcasting station KSL, Salt Lake City, Utah

They came to burn Lawrence, they came not to stay.
Jim Lane he was up at the break of the day;
He saw them a-coming and got in a fright,
Then crawled in a corncrib to get out of sight.

Oh, Quantrell's a fighter, a bold-hearted boy,
A brave man or woman he'll never annoy,
He'd take from the wealthy and give to the poor,
For brave men there's never a bolt to his door.

SAM HALL *

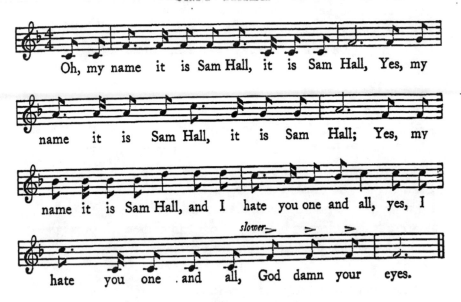

Oh, my name it is Sam Hall, it is Sam Hall, Yes, my
name it is Sam Hall, it is Sam Hall; Yes, my
name it is Sam Hall, and I hate you one and all, yes, I
hate you one and all, God damn your eyes.

Oh, my name it is Sam Hall, it is Sam Hall,
Yes, my name it is Sam Hall, it is Sam Hall;
Yes, my name it is Sam Hall, and I hate you one and all,
Yes, I hate you one and all, God damn your eyes.

* Tune and words from Professor Arthur D. Brodeur, as developed by that unique organization, "The Adventure Campfire Club," Berkeley, California. No other group can sing this song of a British bad man as does this happy company.

Oh, I killed a man, they say, so they say;
Yes, I killed a man, they say, so they say;
I beat him on the head, and I left him there for dead,
Yes, I left him there for dead, God damn his eyes.

Oh, the parson he did come, he did come,
Yes, the parson he did come, he did come;
And he looked so bloody glum, as he talked of Kingdom Come—
He can kiss my ruddy bum, God damn his eyes.

And the sheriff he came too, he came too;
Yes, the sheriff he came too, he came too;
Yes, the sheriff he came too, with his men all dressed in blue—
Lord, they were a bloody crew, God damn their eyes.

Now up the rope I go, up I go;
Yes, up the rope I go, up I go;
And those bastards down below, they'll say, "Sam, we told you so,"
They'll say, "Sam, we told you so," God damn their eyes.

I saw my Nellie dressed in blue, dressed in blue;
I saw my Nellie in the crowd, all dressed in blue:
Says my Nellie, dressed in blue: "Your triflin' days are through—
Now I know that you'll be true, God damn your eyes."

And now in heaven I dwell, in heaven I dwell,
Yes, now in heaven I dwell, in heaven I dwell;
Yes, now in heaven I dwell—Holy Christ! It is a sell—
All the whores are down in hell, God damn their eyes.

JIM HAGGERTY'S STORY

This long poem was written down by a convict in the Huntsville
Penitentiary who said that he learned it from a friend on the road.

In the shade of a tree, we two sat, him and me,
Where the Badger Hills slope to the rift,
While our ponies browsed around, reins a-dragging the ground.
Then he looked at me funny and laughed.

"Do you see that there town?" he inquired, pointing down
To some shacks sprawled about in the heat.
When I opined that I did, then he shifted his quid,
After drownding a tumblebug neat.

Then he looked at me square, "There's a man waitin' there,
That the sheep-men have hired to get me.
Are you game to go down to that jerk-water town
Just to see what the hell you will see?"

Then we rode down the hill, each a-puffin' a pill
To the shacks sprawled around in the heat,
And we stopped at a shack that was leanin' its back
'Gainst the side of the cowboys' retreat.

Just inside of the door, with one foot on the floor
And the other hist up on a rail,
Stood a big rawboned guy, with the oneriest eye
That I ever saw out of a jail.

By his side stood a girl, that sure looked like a pearl
That the Bible guy cast before swine.
She was pleadin' with him, her eyes all teary and dim,
As I high-signed the barkeep for mine.

Then the door swung again and my pal he stepped in,
And the look in his eyes was sure bad,
And the Big Guy, he wheeled, and the gal there, she squealed,
"Oh, for God's sake, don't shoot, Bill, that's Dad."

Now the thing that she saw was Bill reach for his draw,
When the guy she called Dad drew on Bill.
Dad was my pal, with his eyes on the gal,
And her eyes on his gun, standin' still.

Then the big raw-boned guy, with the onery eye,
Up and shot my pal dead in the door,
And right there Bill Baker went back to his Maker,
He won't take the advantage no more.

BILLY THE KID *

Billy was a bad man
And carried a big gun;
He was always after Greasers
And kept 'em on the run.

He shot one every morning
For to make his morning meal.
And let a white man sass him,
He was shore to feel his steel.

* From *Cowboy Songs* (New York: The Macmillan Company).

He kept folks in hot water,
And he stole from many a stage;
And when he was full of liquor
He was always in a rage.

But one day he met a man
Who was a whole lot badder.
And now he's dead,
And we ain't none the sadder.

BILLY THE KID *

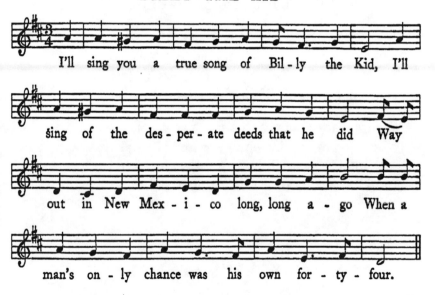

I'll sing you a true song of Bil-ly the Kid, I'll
sing of the des-per-ate deeds that he did Way
out in New Mex-i-co long, long a-go When a
man's on-ly chance was his own for-ty-four.

I'll sing you a true song of Billy the Kid,
I'll sing of the desperate deeds that he did,
Way out in New Mexico long, long ago,
When a man's only chance was his own 44.

*Victor record No. 20396.

[137]

When Billy the Kid was a very young lad,
In old Silver City he went to the bad;
Way out in the West with a gun in his hand
At the age of twelve years he first killed his man.

Fair Mexican maidens play guitars and sing
A song about Billy, their boy bandit king,
How ere his young manhood had reached its sad end
Had a notch on his pistol for twenty-one men.

'Twas on the same night when poor Billy died
He said to his friends: "I am not satisfied;
There are twenty-one men I have put bullets through
And Sheriff Pat Garrett must make twenty-two."

Now this is how Billy the Kid met his fate:
The bright moon was shining, the hour was late,
Shot down by Pat Garrett, who once was his friend,
The young outlaw's life had now come to its end.

There's many a man with a face fine and fair
Who starts out in life with a chance to be square,
But just like poor Billy he wanders astray
And loses his life in the very same way.

THE CRYDERVILLE JAIL *

C. E. Scoggins, a well known author of short stories, writes:
"Somewhat belatedly, I am sending you herewith the words—as
many as I know of them—and the melody for 'The Cryderville Jail.'

* A widely known jail song with various titles and differing texts. The tune appears
constant. Tune and three stanzas from C. E. Scoggins, Sea Horse Hill, Boulder, Colorado. Music
revised by Edward N. Waters, Music Division, Library of Congress. Remaining words from several
sources in Texas.

I am no musician, as you'll see; but I've tried to indicate the rhythm as I learned it from Dad Levins, of Omaha, who learned it sixty years ago as a small boy sitting on the sidewalk outside the jail in Cryderville —Kentucky, I think; or maybe it's West Virginia; I've never looked it up."

A story about the origin of the "Hard Times" song comes from

Old Dad Mor-ton has got us in jail, 'Tis hard.

Old Dad Mor-ton has got us in jail, Both

fa-ther and mo-ther re-fused his bail; 'Tis

hard! With the doors all locked and barred, With a

big log chain bound down to the floor, Damn their fool souls,

how could they do more? 'Tis hard times in the

Cry-der-ville jail, 'Tis hard times, I say.

Dr. S. Newton Gaines, now professor of physics in Texas Christian University, Fort Worth, Texas, in a letter dated 1911:

"The song was composed by Sam Houston, a white desperado and horse stealer, while he was in jail in Austin, Texas, in 1880. He was sentenced to twenty-five years in Huntsville. George Winn, then a colored boy of fourteen, heard him, and the song made a deep impression. George said, when he gave the song to me, that he had not thought of it in fifteen years. The tune is cynical but lively. George Winn is now in charge of the old Whipple place on the hill to the northeast of Austin, and lives there."

Then follow six four-line stanzas practically identical with those herewith printed. The Cryderville jail becomes, in Texas, Waco jail, Dallas jail, etc.

> Old Dad Morton has got us in jail,
> 'Tis hard!
> Old Dad Morton has got us in jail,
> Both father and mother refused his bail,
> 'Tis hard!
> With the doors all locked and barred,
> With a big log chain bound down to the floor,
> Damn their fool souls, how could they do more?
> 'Tis hard times in the Cryderville jail,
> 'Tis hard times, I say [or poor boys].

The new material in each verse consists of just two lines; the rest is all repeated as above.

> There's a big bull ring in the middle of the floor,
> And a damned old jailer to open the door.

> Your pockets he'll pick, your clothes he will sell,
> Your hands he will handcuff, Goddam him to Hell!

> It's both of my feet bound in the cell,
> My hands tied behind, Goddam him to Hell!

And here's to the cook, I wish he was dead,
It's old boiled beef and old corn bread.

The chuck they give us is beef and corn bread,
As old as Hell and as heavy as lead.

We pop it down in us within our cells,
Just like the pop from Heaven to Hell.

The coffee is rough, and the yard is full of hogs,
And we are guarded by two bulldogs.

No longer than yesterday I heard the Juller say,
He was feeding the prisoners at two dollars a day.

The times was so hard at such poor pay,
He couldn't feed 'em grub but two times a day.

Our bed it is made of old rotten rugs.
When we lay down, we are all covered with bugs;

And the bugs they swear if we don't give bail,
We are bound to get busy in the Tucson jail.

The nits and the lice, climb in the jist,
One fell down and hollered, "Jesus Christ!"

I said, "Mister Jailer, please lend me your knife,
For the lice and the bedbugs have threatened my life."

Old Judge Simpkins will read us the law,
The damndest fool judge you ever saw.

And here's to the lawyer, he'll come to your cell,
"Give me five dollars and I'll clear you in spite of Hell."

But your money they will get before they will rest;
Then say, "Plead guilty, for I think it is best."

There sits the jury, a devil of a crew,
They will look the poor prisoner through and through.

Your privileges they will take, your clothes they will sell,
Get drunk on the money, Goddam 'em to Hell.

And here's to the sheriff, I like to forgot,
He's the biggest old rascal we have in the lot.

And now I have come to the end of my song;
I'll leave it to the boys as I go along.

As to gamblin' and stealin', I never shall fail,
And I don't give a damn for lyin' in jail.

They'll send us away for a year or two,
For makin' a barrel of mountain dew.

PO' BOY *

Another fragment of "The Cryderville Jail."

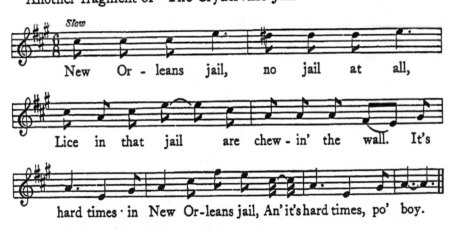

New Or-leans jail, no jail at all,
Lice in that jail are chew-in' the wall. It's
hard times · in New Or-leans jail, An' it's hard times, po' boy.

New Orleans jail, no jail at all,
Lice in that jail are chewin' the wall.

* Roy McDaniel, radio singer and former wanderer, furnished the words and air for this song.

Chorus:
It's hard times in New Orleans jail,
An' it's hard times, po' boy.

Mice in the kitchen a-makin' the bread,
Lice an' the chinches a-combin' my head.

An' it's hard times in New Orleans jail,
It's hard times, po' boy.

VI

SONGS FROM THE MOUNTAINS

"Every night when the sun goes in, I hang my head and mournful cry . . ."

DOWN IN THE VALLEY *

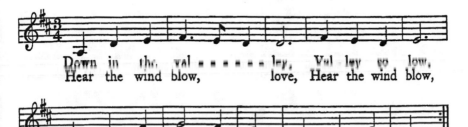

Down in the val - - - - - - ley, Val - ley so low,
Hear the wind blow, love, Hear the wind blow,

Hang yore head o - - - - ver, Hear the wind blow.

Down in the valley,
Valley so low,
Hang yore head over,
Hear the wind blow.
Hear the wind blow, love,
Hear the wind blow,
Hang yore head over,
Hear the wind blow.

If you don't love me,
Love whom you please,
But throw yore arms round me,
Give my heart ease.
Give my heart ease, dear,

* James Howard, a blind mountain fiddler of Harlan, Kentucky, supplied the tune and certain of
the verses for this song, and Harvey H. Fuson, also of Harlan, permitted the use of stanzas from
his Ballads of the Kentucky Highlands.

[147]

Give my heart ease,
Throw yore arms round me,
Give my heart ease.

Down in the valley
Walking between,
Telling our story,
Here's what it sings—
Roses of sunshine,
Vi'lets of dew,
Angels in heaven,
Knows I love you.

Build me a castle,
Forty feet high,
So I can see her
As she goes by.
As she goes by, dear,
As she goes by,
So I can see her,
As she goes by.

Bird in a cage, love,
Bird in a cage,
Dying for freedom,
Ever a slave.
Ever a slave, dear,
Ever a slave,
Dying for freedom,
Ever a slave.

Write me a letter;
Send it by mail;
And back it in care of

The Barbourville jail.
Barbourville jail, love,
Barbourville jail,
And back it in care of
The Barbourville jail.

EVERY NIGHT WHEN THE SUN GOES IN *

Ev - 'ry night when the sun goes in, ... Ev - 'ry
True love, don't weep,   true   love, don't mourn, True love, don't

night when the sun goes in, ... Ev - 'ry night when the sun goes
weep, true love, don't mourn, True love, don't weep nor   mourn for

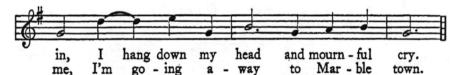

in,   I hang down my   head   and mourn - ful   cry.
me,   I'm   go - ing   a - way   to Mar - ble   town.

Every night when the sun goes in, (3)
I hang down my head and mournful cry.
True love, don't weep, true love, don't mourn,
True love, don't weep, true love, don't mourn,
True love, don't weep nor mourn for me,
I'm going away to Marble town.

I wish to the Lord that train would come, (3)
To take me back where I come from.
True love, don't weep, etc.

* Words and melody reprinted from the second volume of *English Folksongs of the Southern Appalachians*, collected by Cecil Sharp, edited by Maud Karpeles, by permission of the Oxford University Press.

It's once my apron hung down low, (3)
He'd follow me through both sleet and snow.
   True love, don't weep, etc.

It's now my apron's to my chin, (3)
He'll face my door and won't come in.
   True love, don't weep, etc.

I wish to the Lord my babe was born,
A-sitting upon his papa's knee,
And me, poor girl, was dead and gone,
And the green grass growing over me.
   True love, don't weep, etc.

THE ROVING GAMBLER *

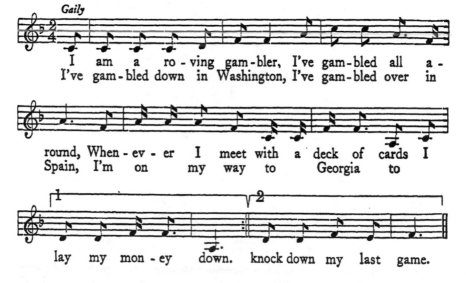

I am a ro-ving gam-bler, I've gam-bled all a-
I've gam-bled down in Washington, I've gam-bled over in

round, When-ev-er I meet with a deck of cards I
Spain, I'm on my way to Georgia to

lay my mon-ey down. knock down my last game.

* From the singing of Slim Critchlow and the Utah Buckaroos.

[150]

I am a roving gambler, I've gambled all around,
Whenever I meet with a deck of cards, I lay my money down.
I've gambled down in Washington, I've gambled over in Spain,
I'm on my way to Georgia to knock down my last game.

I had not been in Washington many more weeks than three,
Till I fell in love with a pretty little girl, and she fell in love with me;
She took me in her parlor, she cooled me with her fan,
She whispered low in her mother's ears, "I love this gambling man."

"Oh, daughter, oh, dear daughter, how could you treat me so,
To leave your dear old mother and with a gambler go?"
"Oh, mother, oh, dear mother, you know I love you well,
But the love I hold for this gambling man no human tongue can tell.

"I wouldn't marry a farmer, for he's always in the rain;
The man I want to marry is the gambling man who wears the big gold
    chain.
I wouldn't marry a doctor, he is always gone from home;
All I want is the gambling man, for he won't leave me alone.

"I wouldn't marry a railroad man, and this is the reason why,
I never seen a railroad man that wouldn't tell his wife a lie.
I hear the train a-coming, she's coming around the curve,
Whistling and a-blowing and straining every nerve.

"Oh, mother, oh, dear mother, I'll tell you if I can
If you ever see me coming back, I'll be with the gambling man."

I WISH I WAS A MOLE IN THE GROUND *

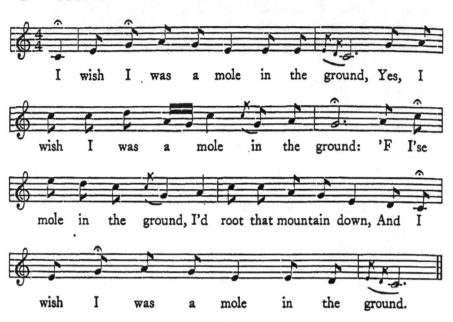

I wish I was a mole in the ground, Yes, I wish I was a mole in the ground: 'F I'se mole in the ground, I'd root that mountain down, And I wish I was a mole in the ground.

I wish I was a mole in the ground.
Yes, I wish I was a mole in the ground:
'F Ise a mole in the ground, I'd root that mountain down,
And I wish I was a mole in the ground.

Oh, Kimpy wants a nine-dollar shawl.
Yes, Kimpy wants a nine-dollar shawl:
When I come o'er the hill with a forty-dollar bill,
'Tis "Baby, where you been so long?"

I been in the pen so long.
Yes, I been in the pen so long:
I been in the pen with the rough and rowdy men.
'Tis "Baby, where you been so long?"

* As sung by Bascom Lamar Lunsford, "the Minstrel of the Appalachians," on a Brunswick record, No. 219 A. Sung first, perhaps, by a mountain moonshiner who had landed in jail.

I don't like a railroad man.
No, I don't like a railroad man:
'Cause a railroad man they'll kill you when he can,
And drink up your blood like wine.

I wish I was a lizard in the spring.
Yes, I wish I was a lizard in the spring:
'F Ise a lizard in the spring, I'd hear my darlin' sing,
An' I wish I was a lizard in the spring.

Come, Kimpy, let your hair roll down.
Kimpy, let your hair roll down;
Let your hair roll down and your bangs curl around,
Oh, Kimpy, let your hair roll down.

I wish I was a mole in the ground.
Yes, I wish I was a mole in the ground:
'F Ise a mole in the ground, I'd root that mountain down,
An' I wish I was a mole in the ground.

SUGAR BABE *

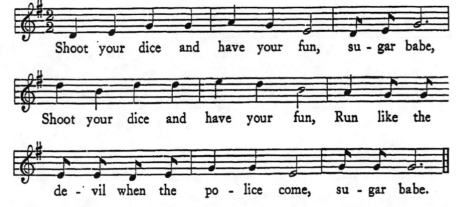

Shoot your dice and have your fun, su - gar babe,
Shoot your dice and have your fun, Run like the
de - vil when the po - lice come, su - gar babe.

* Words and melody reprinted from the second volume of *English Folk Songs of the Southern Appalachians*, collected by Cecil Sharp, edited by Maud Karpeles, by permission of the Oxford University Press.

[153]

Shoot your dice and have your fun, sugar babe,
Shoot your dice and have your fun,
Run like hell when the police come, sugar babe.

I got drunk and fell on the flo', sugar babe,
Good corn liquor and I want some mo', sugar babe.

I got drunk and reel against the wall, sugar babe,
Good corn liquor was the cause of it all, sugar babe.

I went fishin' an' I stayed all day, sugar babe,
Got a little sucker an' I saved it away, sugar babe.

Shoot your dice and roll 'em in the san', sugar babe,
I ain't a-goin' to work for no damn man, sugar babe.

Put yo' han' on yo' hip an' let yo' min' roll by, sugar babe,
'Cause your body's gonna swivel when you come to die, sugar babe.

WHEN I WAS SINGLE *

When I was sin - gle, went dressed all so, fine;

Now I am mar - ried, go rag - ged all the time.

CHORUS

I wish I was a sin - gle girl a - gain, O Lord,

don't I wish I was a sin - gle girl a - gain!

* Words and melody reprinted from the second volume of *English Folk Songs of the Southern Appalachians*, collected by Cecil Sharp, edited by Maud Karpeles, by permission of the Oxford University Press.

[*The Woman Speaks*]

When I was single, went dressed so fine;
Now I am married, go ragged all the time.

Chorus:
    I wish I was a single girl again,
    O Lord, don't I wish I was a single girl again!

When I was single, my shoes did creak;
Now I am married, my shoes they do leak.

Three little babies crying for bread,
With none to give them, I'd rather be dead.

Wash them and strip them and put them to bed,
Before your husband curses you and wishes them dead.

Wash their little feet and send them to school,
Along comes a drunkard and calls them a fool.

When I was single, I eat biscuit and pie;
Now I am married it's eat corn-bread or die.

When he comes in, it's a curse and a row,
Knocking down the children and pulling out my hair.

Dishes to wash and spring to go to;
When you are married, you've all to do.

Suppers to get, the cows to milk,
Them blame little children is all crying yet.

WHEN I WAS SINGLE

A

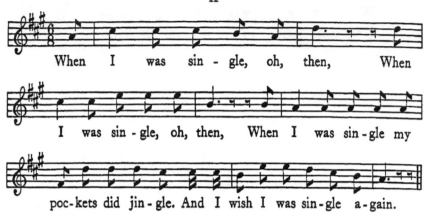

When I was sin-gle, oh, then, When

I was sin-gle, oh, then, When I was sin-gle my

poc-kets did jin-gle. And I wish I was sin-gle a-gain.

B *

With enthusiasm

When I was sin-gle, oh, then, oh, then, When

I was sin-gle, oh, then, When I was sin-gle my

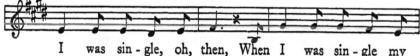

poc-kets did jin-gle, And I wish I was sin-gle a-gain.

[The Man Speaks]

When I was single, oh, then, oh, then,
When I was single, oh, then—
When I was single
My pockets did jingle,
And I wish I was single again.

* As sung by Roy McDaniel, the Yodeling Cowboy.

I married a wife, oh, then, oh, then,
I married a wife, oh, then—
I married a wife,
She's the plague of my life,
I wish I was single again.

My wife took sick, oh, then, oh, then,
My wife took sick, oh, then—
My wife took sick,
I went for the doctor right quick,
I wish I was single again.

My wife she died, oh, then, oh, then,
My wife she died, oh, then—
My wife she died,
Danged little cared I,
To think I was single again.

I married me another, oh, then, oh, then,
I married me another, oh, then—
I married me another,
She's the Devil's stepmother,
And I wish I was single again.

She beat me, she banged me, oh, then, oh, then,
She beat me, she banged me, oh, then—
She beat me, she banged me,
She swore she would hang me,
I wish I was single again.

She got the rope, oh, then, oh, then,
She got the rope, oh, then—
She got the rope,
And she greased it with soap,
And I wish I was single again.

The limb did break, oh, then, oh, then,
The limb did break, oh, then—
The limb did break,
My neck did escape,
And I wish I was single again.

Young men take warning from this, from this,
Young men take warning from this—
Be good to the first,
For the last is much worse,
And I wish I was single again.

DARLIN'*

"My brother, Frank Davidson, of Indiana University, was telling me of your visit to the University. He asked me to write you and give you some verse that he felt you might not have and would like.

"Five years ago I spent six weeks on a botany trip in the heart of the Great Smoky Mountains. Two mountaineer boys came to my camp and picked a 'gee-tar' and sang their ballads."

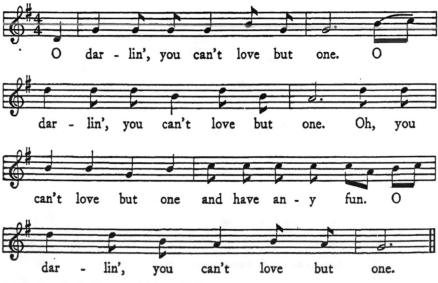

O dar - lin', you can't love but one. O
dar - lin', you can't love but one. Oh, you
can't love but one and have an - y fun. O
dar - lin', you can't love but one.

* From Joe H. Davidson, Patricksburg, Indiana.

O darlin', you can't love but one,
O darlin', you can't love but one,
Oh, you can't love but one and have any fun.
O darlin', you can't love but one.

O darlin', you can't love two,
O darlin', you can't love two,
Oh, you can't love two, and still to me be true.
O darlin', you can't love two.

O darlin', you can't love three,
O darlin', you can't love three,
Oh, you can't love three, and still be true to me.
O darlin', you can't love three.

O darlin', you can't love four,
O darlin', you can't love four,
Oh, you can't love four, and love me any more.
O darlin', you can't love four.

O darlin', you can't love five,
O darlin', you can't love five,
Oh, you can't love five, and get honey from the hive.
O darlin', you can't love five.

POLLY WILLIAMS *

"This ballad," writes Sam P. Bayard, "was composed in southwestern
Pennsylvania, and celebrates an occurrence of the year 1810. A man
of a wealthy family had seduced a country girl, and under pretense
of taking her to be married, he led her to a place called White Rocks
—near Uniontown, Fayette County, Pennsylvania,—where he threw

* From the collection of Sam P. Bayard, State College, Pennsylvania. Music as sung by Mrs.
Nancy White and Mrs. Annie Braden, Greene County, Pennsylvania.

[159]

her over a cliff and killed her. He was brought to trial, was acquitted and afterwards he married; but he was hated and persecuted wherever he went.

"The murder caused a tremendous sensation in the southwestern counties of Pennsylvania, and everyone can still tell the story, though few remember the song. Several songs were composed—both of the folk type and of the literary type. I have another folk ballad about this tragedy, which is longer and more detailed, but not complete. In the course of years, many legends—some of them being of a decidedly superstitious turn—have grown up about the career of the murderer after his acquittal and marriage.

"The victim's name was not Polly Williams; but for some reason, the composers of the songs chose this conventional name, and it is this name which is always used by those who tell the sad story."

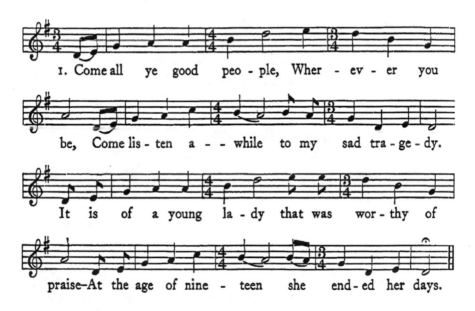

1. Come all ye good peo - ple, Wher - ev - er you be, Come lis - ten a - - while to my sad tra - ge - dy. It is of a young la - dy that was wor - thy of praise—At the age of nine - teen she end - ed her days.

Come all ye good people, wherever you be,
Come listen awhile to my sad tragedy.
It is of a young lady that was worthy of praise—
At the age of nineteen she ended her days.

Long time she'd been courted, as I have heard say,
And her lover to delude her took many a way.
For soon as he found that her love he had gained,
Her company he slighted, and her love he disdained.

And then to destroy her he contrived a plan:
To this mountain conveyed her, as I understand.
Oh, this innocent creature his mind did not know,
And in hopes to be married with this traitor did go.

And when to this mountain he did her convey,
Oh, he left her fair body for the varmints a prey.
She was cruelly treated and shamefully used
By this cruel tyrant—how could him excuse!

Which caused old and young to weep and to cry,
And to find out this traitor they each one did try.
He was apprehended, his cause to bewail—
Straightway he was conducted to Uniontown jail.

There by judge and by jury he was proven out clear,
And he now takes Polly Clayton, and he calls her his dear.
But, like a deceiver, he'll live in despair
Till the day of strict judgment when all must appear.

Oh, the judge and the jury they all will be there,
And with one accord the truth will declare.
Oh, the impartial Judge he will pass the decree,
And this cruel tyrant condemnèd will be.

Come all ye good people who saw this object,
Don't add nor diminish, deceive nor correct.
This honored young lady was found in a gore,
And her flesh by this traitor all mangled and tore.

Oh, it's every temptation is the future of some snare,
And of all such false lovers I would have you beware.
Oh, beware of false lovers who court in deceit,
Lest, like Polly Williams, it will prove your sad fate

To be brought by a lover to shame and disgrace.
And lose your sweet life in some wilderness place.
They will hug you and kiss you, and call you their own,
And when your back is turned they will leave you to mourn.

THE BEAR IN THE HILL*

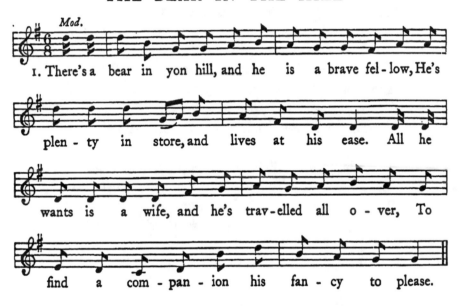

Mod.

1. There's a bear in yon hill, and he is a brave fel-low, He's
plen-ty in store, and lives at his ease. All he
wants is a wife, and he's trav-elled all o-ver, To
find a com-pan-ion his fan-cy to please.

There's a bear in yon hill, and he is a brave fellow,
He's plenty in store, and lives at his ease.
All he wants is a wife, and he's traveled all over,
To find a companion his fancy to please.

*From the collection of Sam P. Bayard, State College, Pennsylvania. The music as sung by James
T. Davis, Greene County, Pennsylvania.

As he was a-pattin', a-pattin' and a-blatin' [*sic*],
One day up the river he chanced for to meet—
As he was a-pattin', he met with a possum,
And kind, loving compliments had to her there.

"O dearest possum, where air you a-goin'?
It is a cold and blustery day.
If you'll go with me, oh, how I will love you!
I'll take you to my den, love, and there you may stay."

With all these kind compliments, possum lie grinning,
And then returned to her love and did say:
"Go to my uncle on the banks of the river,
And if he is willing, with you I'll agree."

So the bear and the possum they patted together
Till they retch' the bank of the river side.
He says, "Uncle Raccoon, I've been courting your possum,
And if you are willing, I'll make her my bride."

The match was struck up, all things were made ready,
This couple was jined in the very same day.
The wildcats and ground hogs were choosen for waiders [*sic*],
The priest was a painter,* I've heard people say.

THE LITTLE MOHEE †

Allegretto grazioso

As I went a-walk-ing all by the sea-shore, The
wind it did whis-tle, the wa-ter did roar.

* Or panther.   † Words and music from Loraine Wyman's *Lonesome Tunes*.

As I went a-walking all by the seashore,
The wind it did whistle, the water did roar.

As I sat amusing myself on the grass,
Oh, who did I spy but a young Indian lass!

She came and sat by me, took hold of my hand
And said, "You're a stranger and in a strange land.

"But if you will follow you're welcome to come
And dwell in the cottage where I call it my home."

The sun was fast sinking far over the sea,
As I wandered along with my little Mohee.

Together we wandered, together we roam,
Till I came to the little cottage where she called it her home.

She asked me to marry and offered her hand,
Saying, "My father's the chieftain all over this land.

"My father's a chieftain and ruler can be;
I'm his only daughter, my name is Mohee."

"Oh, no, my dear maiden, that never can be!
I have a dear sweetheart in my own countree.

"I will not forsake her, I know she loves me,
Her heart is as true as any Mohee."

It was early one morning, Monday morning in May,
I broke her poor heart by the words I did say.

"I'm going to leave you, so fare you well, my dear,
My ship's spreads are now spreading, over home I must steer."

The last time I saw her, she knelt on the strand.
Just as my boat passed her, she waved me her hand,

Saying, "When you get over with the girl that you love,
Oh, remember the Mohee in the cocoanut grove."

And when I had landed with the girl that I love,
Both friends and relations gathered round me once more.

I gazed all about me. Not one did I see
That really did compare with my little Mohee.

And the girl I had trusted had proved untrue to me,
So I says: "I'll turn my courses back over the sea.

"I'll turn my courses and backward I'll flee,
I'll go and spend my days with the little Mohee."

VII

COCAINE AND WHISKY

"This world is a bottle,
  Our life is a dram;
When the bottle is empty
  It ain't worth a damn."
    —*From Daca's New Door Bookstore,*
      Washington Square, New York City.

DRINK THAT ROT GUT*

Drink that rot gut, drink that rot gut,
Drink that red eye, boys;
It don't make a damn wherever we land,
We hit her up for joy.

We've lived in the saddle and ridden trail,
Drink old Jordan, boys,
We'll go whooping and yelling, we'll all go a-helling;
Drink her to our joy.

Whoop-ee! drink that rot gut, drink that red nose,
Whenever you get to town;
Drink it straight and swig it mighty,
Till the world goes round and round!

*From *Cowboy Songs* (Macmillan Company).

RYE WHISKY

With gusto

I'll eat when I'm hun-gry, I'll drink when I'm dry; If the
If the o-cean was whis-ky and I was a duck, I'd—

CHORUS

hard times don't kill me, I'll live till I die. Rye
dive to the bot-tom to get one sweet suck.

whis-ky, rye whis-ky, rye whis-ky I cry, If you

don't give me rye whis-ky I sure-ly will die.

I'll eat when I'm hungry,
I'll drink when I'm dry;
If the hard times don't kill me,
I'll lay down and die.

Chorus:
Rye whisky, rye whisky,
Rye whisky, I cry,
If you don't give me rye whisky,
I surely will die.

I'll tune up my fiddle,
And I'll rosin my bow,
I'll make myself welcome,
Wherever I go.

[170]

Beefsteak when I'm hungry,
  Red liquor when I'm dry,
Greenbacks when I'm hard up,
  And religion when I die.

They say I drink whisky,
  My money's my own,
All them that don't like me,
  Can leave me alone.

Sometimes I drink whisky,
  Sometimes I drink rum,
Sometimes I drink brandy,
  At other times none.

But if I get boozy,
  My whisky's my own,
And them that don't like me,
  Can leave me alone.

Jack o' diamonds, jack o' diamonds,
  I know you of old,
You've robbed my poor pockets
  Of silver and gold.

Oh, whisky, you villain,
  You've been my downfall,
You've kicked me, you've cuffed me—
  But I love you for all.

If the ocean was whisky,
  And I was a duck,
I'd dive to the bottom
  To get one sweet suck.

But the ocean ain't whisky
And I ain't a duck,
So we'll round up the cattle
And then we'll get drunk.

My foot's in my stirrup,
My bridle's in my hand,
I'm leaving sweet Lillie,
The fairest in the land.

Her parents don't like me,
They say I'm too poor;
They say I'm unworthy
To enter her door.

Sweet milk when I'm hungry,
Rye whisky when I'm dry,
If a tree don't fall on me,
I'll live till I die.

I'll buy my own whisky,
I'll make my own stew;
If I get drunk, madam,
It's nothing to you.

I'll drink my own whisky,
I'll drink my own wine;
Some ten thousand bottles
I've killed in my time.

I've no wife to quarrel
No babies to bawl;
The best way of living
Is no wife at all.

Way up on Clinch Mountain
  I wander alone;
I'm as drunk as the devil,
  Oh, let me alone.

You may boast of your knowledge
  En' brag of your sense,
'Twill all be forgotten
  A hundred years hence.

Negro Variant

In my little log cabin,
  Ever since I been born,
Dere ain't been no nothin'
  'Cept dat hard salt, parched corn;
But I know whar's a henhouse,
  De turkey he charve;
An' if ol' Mas'er don' kill me
  I cain't never starve.

Variant Chorus

Rye whisky, rye whisky,
  You're no friend to me;
You killed my poor daddy,
  Goddamn you, try me.

THE DRUNKARD'S DOOM *

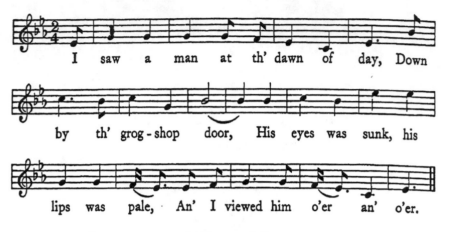

I saw a man at th' dawn of day, Down
by th' grog-shop door, His eyes was sunk, his
lips was pale, An' I viewed him o'er an' o'er.

I saw a man at the dawn of day,
    Down by the grogshop door,
His eyes was sunk, his lips was pale,
    An' I viewed him o'er an' o'er.

His oldest son stood by his side,
    An', weepin', murmurin', said:
"Father, mother is sick at home,
    An' sister cries for bread."

The drunkard rose an' staggered in,
    As he oft had done before,
An' to the landlord falterin' says:
    "Oh, give me one glass more."

He tuck the glass in his tremblin' hand
    An' drunk the bacchanal foul,
He drunk while his wife an' children starved
    An' his children has cried for bread.

* This version of a lugubrious temperance song is quoted from Vance Randolph's *The Ozarks* (New York: Vanguard Press, 1932). Carl Sandburg quotes another version in his *American Songbag.*

"O Gawd, forgive my husband dear,"
Th' dyin' woman said.
"Although he has been unkind to me,
  An' his children has cried for bread."

In just one year I passed that way,
  The hearse stood by the door,
I ask the cause, an' they tol' me
  That th' drunkard was no more.

I seen th' funeral a-passin' by,
  No wife nor children there,
For they had gone on long before
An' left this world of care.

LITTLE BROWN JUG

Me and my wife live all alone
In a little log hut we call our own;
She loves gin and I love rum,
And don't we have a lot of fun!

Chorus:

    Ha, ha, ha, you and me,
    Little brown jug, don't I love thee!
    Ha, ha, ha, you and me,
    Little brown jug, don't I love thee!

When I go toiling on the farm
I take the little jug under my arm;
Place it under a shady tree,
Little brown jug, 'tis you and me.

'Tis you that makes me friends and foes,
'Tis you that makes me wear old clothes;
But, seeing you're so near my nose,
Tip her up and down she goes.

If all the folks in Adam's race
Were gathered together in one place,
Then I'd prepare to shed a tear
Before I'd part from you, my dear.

If I'd a cow that gave such milk,
I'd dress her in the finest silk;
Feed her up on oats and hay,
And milk her twenty times a day.

I bought a cow from Farmer Jones,
And she was nothing but skin and bones;
I fed her up as fine as silk,
She jumped the fence and strained her milk.

And when I die don't bury me at all,
Just pickle my bones in alcohol;
Put a bottle o' booze at my head and feet
And then I know that I will keep.

The rose is red, my nose is too,
The violets blue and so are you;
And yet, I guess, before I stop,
We'd better take another drop.

ADIEU TO BON COUNTY *

1. It's a great sep - a - ra - tion my friends they have caused me, By
bear - ing their spite that my fa - vor was won; It's a
great sep - a - ra - tion, like - wise a vex - a - tion, And
they shall be sor - ry for what they have done. Eat,
drink, and be jol - ly, and care not for fol - ly, And
drownd a - way sor - row in a bot - tle of wine; Pass
it to the boys in full, flow - ing bump - ers, And
play on the fid - dle to pass a - way time!

* From the collection of Sam P. Bayard, State College, Pennsylvania. The music as sung by Allen G. Wayt, Marshall County, West Virginia.

It's a great separation my friends they have caused me,
By bearing their spite that my favor was won;
It's a great separation, likewise a vexation,
And they shall be sorry for what they have done.

Chorus:

Eat, drink, and be jolly, and care not for folly,
And drownd away sorrow in a bottle of wine;
Pass it to the boys in full, flowing bumpers,
And play on the fiddle to pass away time!

Adieu to Bon County, I'm bound for to leave you,
And seek my heart's fortune in some foreign land,
Where bottles and glasses is my greatest comfort
And when we do meet we'll jine heart and hand.

Farewell to my friends and my good old neighbors,
Likewise to the girl I'll never see more.
This world it is wide, and I'll spend it in pleasures—
I don't care for no one that don't care for me.

My fortune is small, so freely I own it,
What little I have it is all of my own.
I might have lived longer to enjoy it with pleasure,
If my poor friends had 'a' let me alone.

I have money a plenty to bear my expenses,
And when it's all gone I'll chop wood and get more.
When death it comes on me I'll freely go with it,
Pay up my last dues and go with it home.

GOOD OL' MOUNTAIN DEW*

Be - side a hill there is a still, Where the

smoke runs up to the sky; You can al-ways tell by the

whiff and the smell That the li - quor boys are nigh.

REFRAIN

That the li - quor boys are nigh, That the

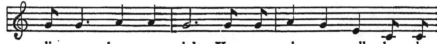

li - quor boys are nigh, You can al - ways tell by the

(LAST VERSE)

whiff and the smell, That the li - quor boys are nigh. We Do

Beside a hill there is a still,
Where the smoke runs up to the sky;
You can always tell by the whiff and the smell
That the liquor boys are nigh.

Refrain:
That the liquor boys are nigh,
That the liquor boys are nigh,

* "Often sung by certain good fellows in Buffalo," says Judge Louis B. Hart, who furnishes both words and tune.

You can always tell by the whiff and the smell,
That the liquor boys are nigh.

This mountain dew is made from grain,
    And mixed with water pure,
And the alcohol that it contains
    Will all your troubles cure.

Refrain:
        Will all your troubles cure,
        Will all your troubles cure,
        And the alcohol that it contains
        Will all your troubles cure.

All learned men who use the pen
    Have writ its praises high;
It fills the air with perfume rare
    Distilled with wheat and rye.

Refrain:
        Distilled with wheat and rye,
        Distilled with wheat and rye,
        It fills the air with perfume rare
        Distilled with wheat and rye.

Away with pills, 'twill cure the ills
    Of Pagan, Christian and Jew,
Off with your coat and wet your throat
    With the real old mountain dew.

Refrain:
        With the real old mountain dew,
        With the real old mountain dew,
        Off with your coat and wet your throat
        With the real old mountain dew.

[181]

So before we roll won't you have another bowl
Of the good old mountain dew?
Of the good old mountain dew?
Of the good old mountain dew?

Refrain:
Of the good old mountain dew?
Of the good old mountain dew?
So before we roll won't you have another bowl
Of the good old mountain dew?
WE DO.

LULU

With spirit

If you don't quit mon-keyin' with my Lu - lu, I'll
My Lu - lu had a ba - by, 'Twas

tell you what I'll do, I'll carve you up with my
born on Christ-mas Day, She washed its face in

Bowie knife And shoot you with my pis - tol,
bran - dy And called it Hen - ry

too, And shoot you with my pis - tol, too.
Clay, And called it Hen - ry Clay.

If you don't quit monkeying with my Lulu,
I'll tell you what I'll do,
I'll carve you up with my Bowie knife
And shoot you with my pistol, too,
And shoot you with my pistol, too.

My Lulu has a baby,
'Twas born on Christmas Day,
She washed its face in brandy
And called it Henry Clay,
And called it Henry Clay.

You know you couldn't gamble,
You ought to stayed at home
And picked up chips for your mamma,
And let the gamblers alone,
And let the gamblers alone.

I seen my Lulu in the springtime,
I seen her in the fall;
She wrote me a letter in the winter time,
Says, "Good-by, honey"—that's all,
Says, "Good-by, honey"—that's all.

My Lulu, she's a dandy,
She stands and drinks like a man,
She calls for gin and brandy,
And she doesn't give a damn,
And she doesn't give a damn.

I ain't goin' to work on the railroad,
I ain't goin' to lie in jail,
I'm goin' down to Cheyenne town
To live with my Lulu gal,
To live with my Lulu gal.

My Lulu hugged and kissed me,
She wrung my hand and cried;
She said I was the sweetest thing
That ever lived or died,
That ever lived or died.

Lulu had twin babies,
Born on Christmas Day,
She mashed one's head with a rollin' pin,
The other one got away,
The other one got away.

WILLIE THE WEEPER *

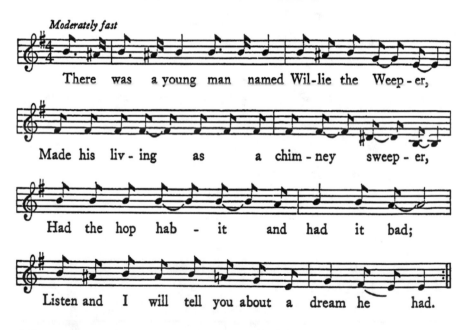

Moderately fast

There was a young man named Wil-lie the Weep-er,

Made his liv-ing as a chim-ney sweep-er,

Had the hop hab-it and had it bad;

Listen and I will tell you about a dream he had.

* The words as they floated around in Texas a quarter of a century ago; music from Frank Shay's *Drawn from the Wood* (New York: Macaulay Co.).

There was a young man named Willie the Weeper,
Made his living as a chimney sweeper,
Had the hop habit and had it bad;
Listen and I will tell you about a dream he had.

Went to the Chink's joint the other night,
Where he knew that the lights were always shining bright,
He called in the Chink and ordered a toy of hop,
Started in to smoking and thought that he never would stop.

He rolled and he smoked about a dozen pillo,
Said it drove away all the pains and ills;
Laying on his hip, he then fell asleep,
Dreamed that he was sailing on the ocean deep.

Started to playing poker when he left this land,
Won a million dollars on the very first hand.
Came to a place they call Siam,
He rubbed his nose and said, "I wonder where I am."

From the king of Siam he won a million more;
He then went to Monte Carlo, 'cause the king got sore,
While at Monte Carlo he played ro'lette,
Wins every penny and couldn't make a bet.

When he found that all the banks were broke
He bought a million dollars' worth of hops to smoke.
He said that he would lead a life from toil,
Bought a million dollars' worth of peanut oil.

Stabbed himself with an inchee gow,
Died with his head on a suee pow.
Willie awoke, his hops had vanished, his dreams were o'er,
He went to sweeping chimneys, as he did before.

HONEY, TAKE A WHIFF ON ME

The origin of this cheerful ditty of the dope-heads is doubtfu
At any rate the Southern barrel-house Negroes sing it and hav
made it their own. Verses 1–7 come from New York City, the othe
from the lips of Iron Head and Lead Belly. Most of the stanzas, :
we heard them in the prisons, are unprintable.

Whiff - a - ree an' a-whiff - o' rye, Gonna keep whiffin', boys

till I die. Ho, ho, hon-ey, take a whiff on me. Take a

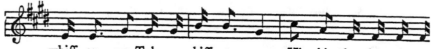

whiff on me, Take a whiff on me. Hi, hi, ba-by, take a

whiff on me. Ho, ho, hon-ey, take a whiff on me.

Oh, whiffaree an' a-whiffo-rye,
Gonna keep a-whiffin', boys, till I die.
Ho, ho, honey, take a whiff on me.

Chorus:

Take a whiff on me, take a whiff on me,
Hi, hi, baby, take a whiff on me,
Ho, ho, honey, take a whiff on me.

I went down to Mister Apperson's place,
Says to Mister Apperson, right to his face—
Ho, ho, honey, take a whiff on me—

"I ain' gonna buy coke here no mo',"
An' Mister Apperson slam de do'.
Ho, ho, honey, take a whiff on me.

Went to Mister Lehman's on a lope,
Sign in de window said, "No mo' coke."
Ho, ho, honey, take a whiff on me.

Well, I wake up in de mornin' by de city clock bell,
An' de niggers up town givin' cocaine hell,
Ho, ho, honey, take a whiff on me.

Goin' up State Street, comin' down Main,
Lookin' for a woman dat use cocaine,
Ho, ho, honey, take a whiff on me.

A yellow girl I do despise,
But a jut-black girl I can't deny,
Ho, ho, honey, take a whiff on me.

De blacker de berry, de sweeter de juice,
Takes a brown-skin woman for my pertickeler use.
Ho, ho, honey, take a whiff on me.

I'se got a nickel, you's got a dime,
You buy de coke an' I'll buy de wine.
Ho, ho, honey, take a whiff on me.

I chew my terbacker, I spit my juice,
I love my baby, till it ain' no use,
Ho, ho, honey, take a whiff on me.

Well, de cocaine habit is mighty bad,
It kill ev'body I know it to have had.
Ho, ho, honey, take a whiff on me.

Cocaine's for hosses an' not for men,
De doctors say it'll kill you, but dey don' say when.
Ho, ho, honey, take a whiff on me.

Chorus:
    Take a whiff on me, take a whiff on me,
    Hi, hi, baby, take a whiff on me,
    Ho, ho, honey, take a whiff on me.

VIII

THE BLUES*

"Takes a long freight train wid a red caboose to carry my blues away."

"When my heart struck sorrow de tears come a-rollin' down."

"Sometimes I jes' sings an' picks, an' sometimes I jes' sings an' thinks, an' sometimes I jes' sings. My blues ain't got no time, ain't got no place, don't mean nothin' to me an' nobody else. But good Lawd, I got de blues, can't be satisfied, got to sing. . . . When I gits 'bout half high as Georgia pine, 'bout forty wid de cleaver, an' 'bout half 'sleep, I sings slow blues, don't know what I'm singin', don't know what they mean. Still they has singin' feelin' an' I puts all sorts an' kinds together. . . .

"Hey, mama, hey, baby, you don't know my mind,
When you think I'm lovin' you, I'm leavin' you behin'.

Hey, mama, hey, baby, you don't know my mind,
When you think I'm laughin', laughin' to keep from cryin'."
—Left Wing Gordon, in Howard Odum's *Rainbow Round My Shoulder.*

* We are indebted to the books of Professor Newman I. White, Professor Howard Odum, and Professor Guy Johnson throughout this section.

CORNFIELD HOLLER

A lonely Negro man plowing out in some hot, silent river bottom, sings this way. It is in such music, we believe, that the "blues" had their origin. Any white person who is acquainted with the singing of untrained country Negroes in the South will tell you that "niggers are always hollerin' like that out in the fields."

Mournfully

Some - times I think my wo - man, she too
sweet to die. ——— Den some - times I
think she - ought to be buried alive. Some-times I think my
wo - man, she too sweet to die ———— Den
some - times I think she ought to be buried a - live.

Sometimes I think my woman, she too sweet to die,
Den sometimes I think she ought to be buried alive.

DIRTY MISTREATIN' WOMEN*

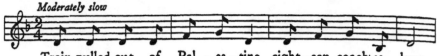

Train pulled out of Pal - es - tine, eight-een coach-es long.

All I want dat train to do—bring my Lu - lu home.

A dollar's roun' goes from han' to han',
Jes' de way dese women goes from man to man.

She drove me from her do', throwed ashes all in my face,
De way she mistreat me, she gonna drive me to my grave.

She cooked my breakfas' an' she th'owed it outdo's,
Had de nerve to ask me would a matchbox hol' my clo's.

Gwine lay my head on a railroad track,
Ef a train come along, gwine snatch it right back.

O ——, you don' do me no good,
I don' blame you, do de same thing ef I could.

Better stop yo' woman from smilin' in my face,
Ef she keeps on smilin', I'll be rollin' in yo' place.

O ——, you bet' leave my li'l girl 'lone,
She might mistreat you an' you swear she done you wrong.

Poor dog in de alley, jumpin' 'gainst de chain,
Got a high, high brown dat's doin' de same.

She change a dollar, give me a lovin' dime;
I'll see her when her trouble's jes' like mine.

* The air comes from a Negro boy in Wiergate, Texas.

I thought I'd tell you what a nigger woman do—
Have another man an' play sick on you.

DINK'S BLUES

A levee was being built along the Brazos River in Texas. The contractor had brought his mules and his mule-skinners with him from the Mississippi River. But he had neglected to provide one thing—women; and the men were raising Hell all over the bottom, with their midnight creeping, their fighting, and their razor play. It was a distinct hindrance to the progress of work on the levee. So it was that the contractor went to Memphis, hired a boatload of women, brought them down the river to the levee-camp, and turned them loose. It was not long before every man had a woman in his tent to wash his clothes, cook, draw water, cut firewood, and warm his bed. Dink was one of these women, and twenty-five years ago, after she had downed nearly a quart of gin, she sang these blues. The tune is lost.

Some folks say dat de worry blues ain' bad,
It's de wors' ol' feelin' I ever had.

Git you two three men, so one won't worry you min';
Don' they keep you worried and bothered all de time?

I wish to God eas'-boun' train would wreck,
Kill de engineer, break de fireman's neck.

I'm gwine to de river, set down on de groun',
Ef de blues overtake me, I'll jump overboard and drown.

Ef trouble was money, I'd be a millioneer,
Ef trouble was money, I'd be a millioneer.

My chuck grindin' every hole but mine,
My chuck grindin' every hole but mine.

Come de big *Kate Adam* wid headlight turn down de stream,
An' her sidewheel knockin', "Great-God-I-been-redeemed."

Ef I feels tomorrow like I feels today,
Stan' right here an' look ten-thousand miles away.

My mother tol' me when I was a chil',
'Bout de mens an' whisky would kill me after while.

Ef I gets drunk, wonder who's gwine carry me home,
Ef I gets drunk, wonder who's gwine carry me home.

I used to love you, but, oh, God damn you, now,
I used to love you, but, oh, God damn you, now.

De worry blues ain' nothin' but de heart disease,
De worry blues ain' nothin' but de heart disease.

Jes' as soon as de freight train make up in de yard,
Some poor woman got an achin' heart.

Tol' my mother not to weep an' mo'n—
I do de bes' I can, kase Ise a woman grown.

I flag de train an' it keep on easin' by,
I fold my arms, I hang my head an' cry.

When my heart struck sorrow, de tears come rollin' down,
When my heart struck sorrow, tears come rollin' down.

Worry now an' I won' be worry long,
Take a married woman to sing de worry song.

Ef I leave here walkin', it's chances I might ride,
Ef I leave here walkin', it's chances I might ride.

DINK'S SONG

Ef I had wings like Norah's dove,
I'd fly up the river to the man I love.
Fare thee well, O Honey, fare thee well.

Ise got a man, an' he's long and tall,
Moves his body like a cannon ball,
Fare thee well, O Honey, fare thee well.

One o' dese days, an' it won't be long,
Call my name an' I'll be gone.
Fare thee well, O Honey, fare thee well.

'Member one night, a-drizzlin' rain,
Roun' my heart I felt a pain.
Fare thee well, O Honey, fare thee well.

When I wo' my ap'ons low,
Couldn't keep you from my do'.
Fare thee well, O Honey, fare thee well.

Now I wears my ap'ons high,
Sca'cely ever see you passin' by.
Fare thee well, O Honey, fare thee well.

Now my ap'on's up to my chin,
You pass my do' an' you won' come in,
Fare thee well, O Honey, fare thee well.

Ef I had listened to whut my mama said,
I'd be at home in my mama's bed.
Fare thee well, O Honey, fare thee well.

WOMAN BLUE

"Great Gawd, I'm feelin' bad!
Ain' got de man I thought I had."
—From *The American Songbag*.

An eighteen-year-old black girl, in prison for murder, sang the tune and the first stanza of these blues.

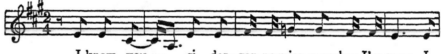
I know you —, ri - der, gon-na miss me when I'm gone, I

know you, ri - der, Gon-na miss me when I'm gone, Gon-na

miss yo' li'l ma-ma, ba - by, from roll - in' in yo' arms.

I know you, rider, gonna miss me when I'm gone,
I know you, rider, gonna miss me when I'm gone,
Gonna miss yo' li'l mama, baby, f'um rollin' in yo' arms.

I's goin' down de road where I get better care,
I's goin' down de road where I get better care,
I b'lieve I'll go, baby, I don' feel welcome here.

An' I laid right down an' tried to take my res',
An' I laid right down an' tried to take my res',
But my min' kep' ramblin' like wil' geese in de Wes'.

Did you ever wake up an' fin' yo' rider gone?
Did you ever wake up an' fin' yo' rider gone?
Put you on a wonder, wish you never had been bo'n.

I knows my baby, he's boun' to love me some,
I knows my baby, he's boun' to love me some,
He throws his arms aroun' me like a circle 'roun' de sun.

Jes' as sure as de birds fly in de sky above,
Jes' as sure as de birds fly in de sky above,
Life ain' worth livin', honey, ain' wid de man you love.

I'm goin' to de river, set down on a log,
I'm goin' to de river, set down on a log,
Ef I cain' be yo' woman, sho gonna be yo' dog.

Take me back, take me back, baby,
Take me back, take me back, baby,
I won' do nothin' you don' lak, baby.

I'll cut yo' wood, I'll make yo' fire,
I'll cut yo' wood, I'll make yo' fire,
I'll tote yo' water fum de Fresno bar.

De sun gwine shine in my back do' some day,
De sun gwine shine in my back do' some day,
De win' gwine rise, baby, an' blow my blues away.

GO WAY F'OM MAH WINDOW *

1. Go 'way f'om mah win - dow, Go
2. Go 'way in de spring - time, Come

'way f'om mah do', Go 'way f'om mah
back in de fall, Bring you

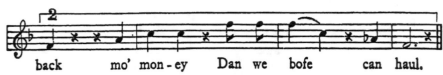

bed - side, Don' you tease me no mo'!

back mo' mon - ey Dan we bofe can haul.

Go way f'om mah window,
Go way f'om mah do',
Go way f'om mah bedside,
Don' you tease me no mo'.

Go way in de springtime,
Come back in de fall,
Bring you back mo' money,
Dan we bofe can haul.

MY LI'L JOHN HENRY

Iron Head, admittedly the "roughest nigger that ever walked the streets of Dallas," was sorry for the mighty John Henry.

* Carl Sandburg's *The American Songbag.*

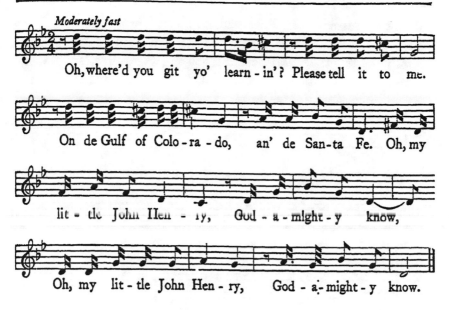

Moderately fast

Oh, where'd you git yo' learn-in'? Please tell it to me.

On de Gulf of Colo-ra-do, an' de San-ta Fe. Oh, my

lit-tle John Hen-ry, God-a-might-y know,

Oh, my lit-tle John Hen-ry, God-a-might-y know.

"Oh, where'd you git yo' learnin'? Please tell it to me."
"On de Gulf, Colorado, and de Santa Fe."

Oh, my li'l John Henry,
Godamighty know,
Oh, my li'l John Henry,
Godamighty know.

SHORTY GEORGE

Along by the Central State Prison near Sugarland, Texas, runs a narrow-gauge track, and down that track about sunset comes whistling a little gasoline motor car. It is on this train that the women who have come out for a Sunday with their men-folks leave the prison. "Case it's such a runty li'l train," the convicts have named it Shorty George, but they sing about it as if it were one of those favored men, like John Henry, who can get a woman by a crook of the finger.

Iron Head, in prison for life and not subject to reprieve or pardon, since he is classed as an "habitual criminal," broke down and cried while he sang "Shorty George." "My woman, she's sca'd to come to see me; she might as well be dead. So I gets res'less, an' I want to run away fum dis place. I jes' cain' hardly stan' to sing dat song."

Moderately slow and sorrowful

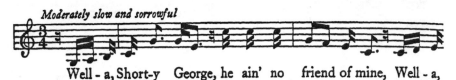

Well - a, Short-y George, he ain' no friend of mine, Well - a,

Short - y George, He ain' no friend of mine, Tak-en all

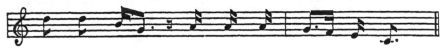

de wom - ens an' leave de mens be - hin'.

Note.—One of the very rare Negro tunes in triple time.

Well-a, Shorty George, he ain' no friend of mine,
Well-a, Shorty George, he ain' no friend of mine,
Taken all de womens an' leave de mens behin'.

Oh, when I get back to Dallas, gonna walk an' tell,
Dat de Fort Ben' bottom is a burnin' Hell.

My mama died when Ise a lad,
An' ev'y since, I been to de bad.

Well, my babe caught de Katy, I caught de Santa Fe,
Well, you cain' quit me, babe, cain' you see?

Well, I wen' to Galveston, work on de Mall'ry Line,
Babe, you cain' quit me, ain' no use you tryin'.

Got a letter fum my baby, "Come, at once, she's dyin' "—
She wasn' dead, she was slowly dyin'.

How kin you blame po' man f'um cryin',
When his babe ain' dead, but slowly dyin'?

Well, I followed her down to de buryin' groun',
You oughta heered me holler, when dey let her down.

I took my babe to de buryin' groun';
I never knowed I loved her, till de coffin soun'.

I wen' to de graveyard, peeped in my mama's face,
"Ain' it hard to see you, mama, in dis lonesome place?"

THE "CHOLLY"* BLUES

When I was out in West Texas, I was goin' f'um do' to do',
I was broke an' was hungry, didn' have no place to go,
An' da's de reason, baby, I jes' wants to know,
Kin I lay down here until day?
I'm a stranger in yo' town, ain' got no place to stay.

The Negro laborer, drifting from town to town and from job to job, makes his appeal for sympathy—and a soft bed. Perhaps, he plucks by the elbow some woman who passes him on the street, and begs her to take him home.

Mournfully

Broke an' hun - gry, rag - ged an' dir - ty too,

Broke an' hun - gry, rag - ged an' dir - ty too,

Jes' wants to know, ba - by, kin I go home wid you?

* Bummer; tramp.

Broke an' hungry, ragged an' dirty too,
Broke an' hungry, ragged an' dirty too,
Jes' wants to know, baby, kin I go home wid you?

Good ol' boy, honey, jes' ain' treated right,
Good ol' boy, honey, jes' ain' treated right,
Freezin' groun' was my foldin' bed las' night.

Well, my mama sick, baby, an' my papa dead,
Well, my mama sick, baby, an' my papa dead,
An' I ain' got nobody to pity po' me, po' me.

Big bell keeps a-ringin', lil bell fairly tone,
Big bell keeps a-ringin', lil bell fairly tone,
I'm a-lonely, lonely, lonely, an' a long ways f'um home.

Dey tell me de graveyard is a long ol' lonesome place,
Dey tell me de graveyard is a long ol' lonesome place,
Puts you six feet in de hard groun', throws clods all in yo' face.

Dig my grave, baby, wid a silver spade,
Dig my grave, baby, wid a silver spade,
An' let me down, pretty mama, wid a golden chain.

What makes you hol' yo' head so high?
What makes you hol' yo' head so high?
Any way you hol' it, baby, da's de way you gonna die.

I ain' good-lookin', ain' got no grea' long hair,
I ain' good-lookin', ain' got no grea' long hair,
But I got ways, pretty mama, dat take me everywhere.

When I go a-fishin', I take my hook an' line,
When I go a-fishin', I take my hook an' line,
But when I go a-courtin', I go wid a willin' min'.

I ain' no doctor, babe, ain' no doctor's son,
I ain' no doctor, babe, ain' no doctor's son,
But I kin cool yo' fever, babe, till de doctor come.

. . . .

Come on, babe, le's ease out on de edge o' town,
Come on, babe, le's ease out on de edge o' town,
Got a shack out dere, an' I know it won' break down.

. . . .

Don' min' marryin', babe, do, Lawd, settlin' down!
Don' min' marryin', babe, do, Lawd, oottlin' down!
Gwine pack my suitcase, babe, an' ride f'um town to town.

. . . .

I's tired of livin', pretty mama, I don' know what to do,
I's tired of livin', pretty mama, I don' know what to do,
You is tired of me, babe, an' I is tired of you.

I was settin' down here wond'rin',—would a matchbox hol' my clo'es,
I was settin' down here wond'rin',—would a matchbox hol' my clo'es,
Don' want no suitcase, pretty mama, on my lonesome road.

Down de road somewhere, down de road somewhere,
Down de road somewhere, down de road somewhere,
I'll fin' me a woman, babe, an' roam no' mo'.

FARE THEE WELL, BABE

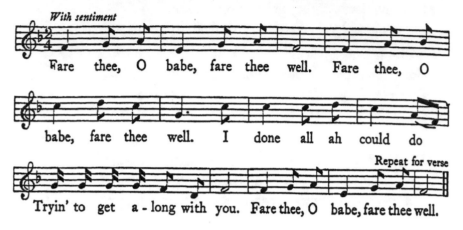

With sentiment

Fare thee, O babe, fare thee well. Fare thee, O

babe, fare thee well. I done all ah could do

Repeat for verse

Tryin' to get a - long with you. Fare thee, O babe, fare thee well.

Chorus:

Fare thee, O babe, fare thee well,
Fare thee, O babe, fare thee well,
I done all I could do,
Try'n' to git along with you.
So fare thee, O babe, fare thee well.

I love you, black gal, God knows I do,
I love f'um yo' head to yo' feet and clean th'ough,
So fare thee, O babe, fare thee well.

I love you, black gal, God knows I do,
'Fo' I'll be mistreated I'll kill myself an' you.
So fare thee, O babe, etc.

I'm packin' my trunk, my satchel, too,
Caze Ise a-gwine 'way jes' as far as I kin f'um you.

Dat eas'-boun' train done blowed an' gone,
An' Ise a-gwine too, jes' as sho' as you a' bo'n.

I been as good as a man could be,
But I done foun' out dat you jes' ain't true to me.

[204]

I done foun' out you don't want me 'roun',
Caze de meals dey ain't cooked, an' de bed ain't turned down.

I treats you right an' I treats you white,
But I jes' can't please yuh, try hard as I might.

You eats good grub, wears fine clo's, too;
Now what mo' in dis wide worl' kin a po' man do.

'Tain't no use to weep, no use to whine,
I done tol' you once, tol' you las', an' now Ise gwine.

You's a good gal when I fus' met you,
But now, ol' gal, done foun' out you jes' won' do.

I'm gwine somers, dunno where Ise gwine,
Ise gwine somewhere so's t' git you out my min'.

I love you, black gal, de people know,
Ise leavin' you, ol' gal, but it breaks m' heart to go.

ALABAMA–BOUND *

A barrel-house conversation. This song has been popular amongst both whites and blacks for several decades. We give the levee-camp version, as sung by Bowlegs, a prisoner at Parchman, Mississippi.

Slow and mournful. Well marked accents

1. I'm Al - a - bam - a   boun',   I'm Al - a - bam - a   boun',
2. Why don-cha be like me?   Why don-cha be like me?

Jes'   as   sho' as de train pull out
Drink yo' high - ten-sion whis - ky, babe, An' let   yo'

eas' to - day   I'm Al - a - bam - a   boun', Great
co-caine   be,   An' let yo' co-caine   be, Great

God - a - might - y, babe, I'm Al - a - bam - a   boun'.
God - a - might - y, babe, An' let   yo' co - caine be.

I'm Alabama-boun', (2)
Ef de train don' run, I got a mule to ride.
My home ain' here, (2)
Great Godamighty, babe,
My home ain' here.

Make me drunk ag'in, (2)
Ef you catch me gettin' sober, babe,

* We include in this version stanzas from Professor White's *Folk Songs of the American Negro*, from a collection made twenty years ago, and from the singing of prisoners in Texas, Louisiana, and Mississippi.

Make me drunk ag'in, I'm a windin' ball.
Great Godamighty, babe,
Don' deny my name.

If you married woman, you got no business here,
But if you are single, babe,
Let's buy some bottled beer, (2)
Great Godamighty, babe,
Let's buy some bottled beer.

Way down de road somewhere, (2)
I got a long, tall, teasin' brown,
Way down de road somewhere, (2)
Great Godamighty, babe,
Way down de road somewhere.

I tol' you once, you done been tol',
Takes a long, tall, brown-skin man
To satisfy my soul, (2)
Great Godamighty, babe,
To satisfy my soul.

She's long an' tall, an' she's thin an' slim,
She's got a hump on her back like a camel, babe,
She make a panther squall, (2)
Great Godamighty, babe,
She make a panther squall.

Her hair ain' curly, an' her eyes ain' blue,
Ef you don' want me, honey babe,
I don' want you, (2)
Great Godamighty, babe, ·
I don' want you.

Ef dat's yo' man, pin him to yo' side,
For if he mounts dis train, O babe,

Sho gonna let him ride. (2)
Great Godamighty, babe,
Sho gonna let him ride.

Ef you got a good woman, an' she won' treat you right,
You can knock 'er down, stomp on 'er, cut 'er head,
An' walk de streets all night, (2)
Great Godamighty, babe,
An' walk de streets all night.

Ef you got a good man, an' he won' treat you right,
Hit 'im in de head wid a burnin' lamp,
An' walk de streets all night, (2)
Great Godamighty, babe,
An' walk de streets all night.

*   *   *

Well, it's a dirty shame, (2)
To see dese woman spendin' money,
An' it's for cocaine, (2)
Great Godamighty, babe,
An' it's for cocaine.

Why doncha be like me? (2)
Drink yo high-tension whisky, babe,
An' let yo' cocaine be, (2)
Great Godamighty, babe,
An' let yo' cocaine be.

*   *   *

Doctor Cook's in town, (2)
Says, "De North Pole's too dog-gone col'.
I'm Alabama-bound, (2)
Great Godamighty, babe,
I'm Alabama-bound."

"Where was you, sister, when de Titanic wen' down?"
"On de back of my ol' gray mule,
Alabama-bound, (2)
Great Godamighty, babe,
Alabama-bound."

*   *   *

Oh, here I am, rap an' bottled beer,
Ef I happen to git drunk an' down,
Doncha leave me here, (2)
Great Godamighty, babe,
Doncha leave me here.

Ef dey don' nab me, 'fo' de sun goes down,
I swear to my Almighty God,
I'm Alabama-bound, (2)
Great Godamighty, babe,
I'm Alabama-bound.

I'm Alabama-bound, (2)
Ole George is good an' dead,
I'm Alabama-bound, (2)
Great Godamighty, babe,
I'm Alabama-bound.

Doncha leave me here, (2)
Ef you leave me, honey babe,
Leave me a dime for beer, (2)
Great Godamighty, babe,
Leave me a dime for beer.

I'm Alabama-bound, (2)
Jus' as sho as de train goes out eas' today,
I'm Alabama-bound, (2)
Great Godamighty, babe,
I'm Alabama-bound.

IX
CREOLE NEGROES

MICHIÉ PRÉVAL*

A satirical song of the Creole Negroes.

Mi - chié Pré - val li don - nin gran bal, Li fait

CHORUS

nèg' pa - yer pou sau - ter in pé. Dan - sé ca - lin - da, bou-

doum, bou-doum, Dan - sé ca - lin - da, bou - doum, bou-doum.

Michié Préval li donnin gran bal,
Li fé nèg payé pou sauter in pé.

Dans l'écui vie la yavé gran gala.
Mo cré soual la yé té bien étonné.

Michié Préval li té Capitaine bal,
Et so coché, Louis te maîtr' cérémonie.

Y'avé de négresse belles passé maîtresse,
Qui volé belbel dans l'ormoire momselle.

"Comment, Sazou, té volé mo cuilotte?"
"Non, no maîtr', mo di vous zes prend bottes."

* Words from Krehbiel's *Afro-American Folk-Songs*, tune from Allen, Ware, and Garrison's *Slave Songs of the United States.*

Ala maîtr' geole li trouvé si drole,
Li dit: "Moin aussi mo fé bal ici."

Yé prend maîtr' Préval yé metté le prison,
Pasque li donnin bal pou volé nous l'arzan.

Monsieur Préval gave a big ball; he made the darkies pay for their little hop.

The grand gala took place in a stable; I fancy the horses were greatly amazed.

M. Préval was Captain of the ball; his coachman, Louis, was Master of Ceremonies.

(He gave a supper to regale the darkies; his old music was enough to give one the colic!)

(Then the old jackass came in to dance; danced precisely as he reared, on his hind legs.)

There were Negresses there prettier than their mistresses; they had stolen all manner of fine things from the wardrobes of their young mistresses.

(Black and white both danced the bamboula; * never again will you see such a fine time.)

(Nancy Latiche to fill out her stockings put in the false calves of her madame.)

"Hów, now, Sazou, you stole my trousers?" "No, master, I took only your boots."

(And little Miss cried out: "See here, Negress, you stole my dress.")

It all seemed very droll to the keeper of the jail; he said, "I'll get up a dance for you here."

He took M. Préval and put him into the lock-up, because he gave a ball to steal our money.

* "The bamboula (a Creole Negro dance) is supposed to have been so called after the drum of bamboo which provided its musical stimulus."—Krehbiel in *Afro-American Folk-Songs.*

RÉMON *

Mo par - lé Ré - mon, Ré - mon, Li par - lé Si - mon, Si - mon, Li par - lé Ti - tine, Ti - tine, Li tom - bé dans cha-grin. O femme Rom - u - lus, O belle femme Rom - u - lus, Oh! O femme Rom - u - lus, O belle femme qui ça vou - lé mo fai.

Mo parlé Rémon, Rémon,
Li parlé Simon, Simon,
Li parlé Titine, Titine,
Li tombé dans chagrin.
O femme Romulus!
O belle femme Romulus!
O femme Romulus!
O belle femme qui ça voule mo fai!

* Quoted from Allen, Ware, and Garrison's *Slave Songs of the United States* (New York: Peter Smith, 1929).

CRIOLE CANDJO*

In zou' in zène Cri - ole Cand - jo, Belle pas - sé
blanc dan - dan là yo, Li té tout tans a - pé dire, —
"Vi - ni, za - mie, pou' nous rire."— "Non, Mi - ché,
m'pas 'ou - lé ri - re moin, Non, Mi - ché, m'pas 'ou - lé
ri - - re; Non, Mi - ché, m'pas 'ou - lé ri - re
moin, Non, Mi - ché, m'pas 'ou - lé ri - - re."

In zou' in zène Criole Candjo
Belle passe' blanc dan dan là yo,
Li te' tout tans ape' dire,
"Vini, zamie, pou' nous rire."
"Non, Miché, m' pas 'oule rire moin,
Non, Miché, m' pas 'oule rire."

Mo courri dan youn bois voisin,
Mais Criole la' prend même ci min,

*From H. E. Krehbiel's *Afro-American Folk Songs.*

Et tous tans li m' ape' dire,
"Vini, zamie, pou' nous rire."
"Non, Miché, m' pas 'oule rire moin,
Non, Miché, m' pas 'oule rire."

Mais li te' tant cicaé moi,
Pou li te' quitte' moin youn fois
Mo te' 'blize' pou' li dire,
"Oui, Miché, mo 'oule rire.
Oui, Miché, mo 'oule rire moin,
Oui, Miché, mo 'oule rire."

Zaut tous qu'ap'ès moin là-bàs
Si zaut te conne Candjo là,
Qui belle façon li pou' rire,
Dje' pini moin! zaut s're dire,
"Oui, Miché, mo 'oule rire moin,
Oui, Miché, mo 'oule rire."

Translation

One day one young Creole Candio,
Mo' fin-eh dan sho'-nuf white beau,
Kip all de time meckin' free,
"Swithawt, meck merrie wid me."
"Naw, sah, I dawn't want meck merrie, me,
Naw, sah, I dawn't want meck merrie."

I go teck walk in wood close by,
But Creole teck same road and try
All time, all time to meck free—
"Swithawt, meck merrie wid me."
"Naw, sah, I dawn't want meck merrie, me,
Naw, sah, I dawn't want meck merrie."

[217]

But him slide 'round and 'round dis chile,
Tell, jis fo' sheck 'im off li'l while,
Me, I was bleedze fo' say: "Shoo!
If I'll meck merrie wid you?
Oh, yass, I ziss leave meck merrie, me,
Yass, sah, I ziss leave meck merrie."

You-alls w'at laugh at me so well,
I wish you'd knowed dat Creole swell,
Wid all 'is swit, smilin' trick.
'Pon my soul! you'd done say, quick,
"Oh, yass, I ziss leave meck merrie, me.
Yass, sah, I ziss leave meck merrie."

UN, DEUX, TROIS*

A dance-song of the Creole Negroes.

Un, deux, trois, Car-o-line, qui fais com-me   ça, ma chère?

Un, deux, trois, Car-o-line, qui fais com-me   ça, ma chère?

Ma-man dit oui,   pa-pa dit non,   Ce-lui mo lais,

* From Dorothy Scarborough's *On the Trail of Negro Folk-Songs* (Cambridge, Mass.: Harvard University Press, 1925).

[218]

ce - lui   mo prends, Ma - man dit   oui,   pa - pa   dit non,

Ce - lui   mo   lais,   ce - lui   mo prends.

Un, deux, trois,
Caroline qui fais comme sa, ma chère?
Un, deux, trois,
Caroline qui fais comme sa, ma chère?
Maman dit oui, papa dit non,
Celui mo lais, celui mo prends.
Maman dit oui, papa dit non,
Celui mo lais, celui mo prends.

Translation

One, two, three,
Caroline, what is the matter with you, my dear?
One, two, three,
Caroline, what is the matter with you, my dear?
Mama says yes, papa says no.
It is he I wish, it is he I'll have.
Mama says yes, papa says no.
It is he I wish and he I'll have.

AURORE PRADERE*

"The Counjai evidently came under the personal observation of the lady who collected some secular Creole songs in St. Charles Parish, Louisiana, which found their way into *Slave Songs of the United States*. They were sung, she says, "to a simple sort of dance, a sort of minuet."

CHORUS

Au - rore Pra - dère, belle 'ti fille, Au - rore Pra - dère, belle 'ti fille, Au - rore Pra - dère, belle 'ti fille, C'est

FINE

li mo 'ou - lé, c'est li ma pren.

SOLO

Li pas man - dé robe mous - se - line, Li pas man - dé des bas bro - dé, Li pas mon - dé sou -

D.C.

liers prin - elle, C'est li mo 'ou - lé, c'est li ma pren.

Aurore Pradère, belle 'ti fille, (ter)
C'est li mo 'oulé, c'est li ma pren.

* We are indebted for this song to Dorothy Scarborough's *On the Trail of Negro Folk-Songs*, W. Allen, Ware, and Garrison's *Slave Songs of the United States*, and H. E. Krehbiel's *Afro-American Folk-Songs*.

Li pas mandé robe mousseline,
Li pas mandé des bas brodés,
Li pas mandé souliers prinelle;
C'est li mo 'oulé, c'est li ma pren.

Aurore Pradère, belle 'ti fille, (ter)
C'est li mo 'oulé, c'est li ma pren.
Ya moun qui dit li trop zolie;
Ya moun qui dit li pas polie;
Tout ça ya dit (Sia!) bin fou bin,
C'est li mo 'oulé, c'est li ma pren.

Translation

Aurore Pradère, pretty maid,
She's just what I want and her I'll have.
A muslin gown she does not choose,
She doesn't ask for 'broidered hose,
She doesn't want prunella shoes;
Oh, she's what I want and her I'll have.

Aurore Pradère, pretty maid,
She's what I want and her I'll have.
Some folks say she's too pretty quite;
Some folks say she's not polite,
All this they say—Psha-a-ah!
More fool am I!
For she's what I want and her I'll have.

Aurore Pradère, pretty maid,
She's what I want and her I'll have.
Some say she's going to the bad;
Some say her mama went mad;
All this they say—Psha-a-ah!
More fool am I!
For she's what I want and her I'll have.

OU SOM SOUROUCOU*

Ou Som Souroucou, qui ça ou gagnien, gagnien pou' boi' do l'eau?
—Mo mangé, mangé mais pou' boi' do l'eau—Mo mangé, mangé maïs
pou' boi' do l'eau.

Ou Som Souroucou, what's matter with you to drink so much water?
I ate corn and have to drink so much water.

* From Clara Gottschalk Peterson's *Creole Songs from New Orleans* (New Orleans: L. Gruenwald
& Co., 1909).

SALANGADOU *

A mother, who has lost her little girl, sings.

Salanga-dou-ou-ou, Salangadou-ou-ou,
Salanga-dou-ou, Salangadou,
Cote piti fille la ye,
Salangadou, Salangadou?

Salangadou,
Where is my little girl gone,
Salangadou?

* From Clara Gottschalk Peterson's *Creole Songs from New Orleans* (New Orleans: L. Gruenwald & Co.).

X

"REELS"

Songs "ob de Worl'ly Nigger"

FOLLER DE DRINKIN' GOU'D *

"One of my great-uncles, who was connected with the railroad movement, remembered that in the records of the Anti-Slavery Society there was a story of a peg-leg sailor, known as Peg-Leg Joe, who made a number of trips through the South and induced young Negroes to run away and escape. . . . The main scene of his activities was in the country north of Mobile, and the trail described in the song followed northward to the headwaters of the Tombigbee River, thence over the divide and down the Ohio River to Ohio . . . the peg-leg sailor would . . . teach this song to the young slaves and show them the mark of his natural left foot and the round hole made by his peg-leg. He would then go ahead of them northward and leave a print made with charcoal and mud of the outline of a human left foot and a round spot in place of the right foot. . . . Nothing more could be found relative to the man. . . . 'Drinkin' gou'd' is the Great Dipper. . . . 'The grea' big un,' the Ohio." *

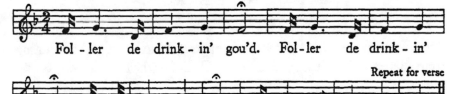

Fol-ler de drink-in' gou'd. Fol-ler de drink-in' gou'd. For de ol' man say, "Fol-ler de drink-in' gou'd."

Repeat for verse

When de sun come back,
When de firs' quail call,
Den de time is come—
Foller de drinkin' gou'd.

* H. B. Parks in Volume VII of the *Publications of the Texas Folk-Lore Society*.

Chorus:
  Foller de drinkin' gou'd,
  Foller de drinkin' gou'd;
  For de ol' man say,
  "Foller de drinkin' gou'd."

De riva's bank am a very good road,
De dead trees show de way;
Lef' foot, peg foot goin' on,
Foller de drinkin' gou'd. (*Chorus.*)

De river ends atween two hills,
Foller de drinkin' gou'd;
'Nother river on de other side,
Foller de drinkin' gou'd. (*Chorus.*)

Wha de little river
Meet de gre' big un,
De ol' man waits—
Foller de drinkin' gou'd. (*Chorus.*)

RUN, NIGGER, RUN!

George B. Elliott of the law department of the Atlantic Railroad Company wrote in 1911 from Wilmington, North Carolina, quoting from a letter he had just received from O. B. Smith, Henderson, North Carolina:

"Your card of inquiry for the words 'Run, Nigger, Run, the Patterroller Git You' came to-night and cheerful as the chirp of the cricket on the hearth. Jessie gave you Uncle Remus' version of recent hashed-up things since the War, before I had time to say anything, but I heard it in this wise before Uncle Remus was born:

"Just after the Nat Turner Insurrection in 1832 the Negroes were put under special restriction to home quarters, and patrolmen appointed to keep them in, and if caught without a written pass from owner they were dealt with severely then and there; hence the injunction to 'Run, Nigger, Run, the Patter-roller Git You' to the tune of 'Fire in the Mountains'—vigorous and lively with more pathos than ever 'Dixie' carried, which it antedated many years. The original words were:

> " 'The day is done, night comes down
> Ye are long ways from home—
> Oh, run, nigger, run, patter-roller git you.

> " 'Yaller gal look and trine keep you overtime,
> De bell done rung, overseer hallowing loud
> Oh, run, nigger, run—'

"Like everything of merit it has been plagiarized and burdened with outside inventions until it is hardly recognizable, but the 'Fire in the Mountains' still sticks."

Chorus Run, nig-ger, run, de pat-ter-roll-er catch you.
Run, nig-ger, run, it's al-mos' day. De nig-ger run, de
nig-ger flew, De nig-ger los' his Sun-day shoe.

Do, please, marster, don't ketch me,
Ketch dat nigger behin' dat tree;
He stole money en I stole none,
Put him in the calaboose des for fun!

Chorus:

 Oh, run, nigger, run! de patter-roller ketch you.
 Run, nigger, run! hit's almos' day!
 Oh, run, nigger, run! de patter-roller ketch you.
 Run, nigger, run! hit's almos' day!

Some folks say dat a nigger won't steal,
But I kotch one in my corn-fiel';
He run ter de eas', he run ter de wes',
He run he head in a hornet nes'!

De sun am set, dis nigger am free;
De yaller gals he goes to see;
I heard a man cry, "Run, doggone you,"
Run, nigger, run, patter-roller ketch you.

Wid eyes wide open and head hangin' down,
Like de rabbit before de houn',
Dis nigger streak it for de pasture;
Nigger run fast, white man run faster.

And ober de fence as slick as a eel
Dis nigger jumped all but his heel;
De white man ketch dat fast, you see,
And tied it tight aroun' de tree.

Dis nigger heard dat old whip crack,
But nebber stopped fur to look back;
I started home as straight as a bee
.And left my heel tied aroun' de tree.

My ol' Miss, she prommus me
Dat when she die, she set me free;
But she done dead dis many year ago,
En yer I'm hoein' de same ol' row!

I'm a-hoein' across, I'm a-hoein' aroun',
I'm a-cleanin' up some mo' new groun'.
Whar I lif' so hard, I lif' so free,
Dat my sins rise up in front er me!

But some er dese days my time will come,
I'll year dat bugle, I'll year dat drum,
I'll see dem armies a-marchin' along,
I'll lif' my head en jine der song—
I'll dine no mo' behin' dat tree,
W'en de angels flock fer to wait on me!

Polk Miller, Richmond, Virginia, who interpreted Negro songs successfully on the platform, contributed these stanzas:

I run down to de ribber, but I couldn't get across,
I jumped 'pon a hog and thought he was a hoss!

As I was goin' through the fiel'
A black snake bit me 'pon my heel,
Dat serpent he did 'ceive a shock,
For de nigger's heel's as hard as a rock.

As I was passin' Wright's old mill,
My team got balked at de foot o' de hill.
I hollered to de driver, "Dat won't do;
I must shove an' so mus' you."

PICK A BALE O' COTTON

Although no man has ever hand-picked more than eight hundred pounds of cotton a day, this Negro work song, that seems to be one of the survivors of the Civil War and slavery, speaks of a personal acquaintance, not only with one but with many men and women

[231]

who can pick a bale of cotton (which must weigh between thirteen and fifteen hundred pounds) in a day. Clear Rock; seventy-year-old water boy on the Central State Farm near Sugarland, Texas, shouted out the following song with as much vigor as if he could get up the next minute and pick a bale of cotton, and in a half-day.

Dat nigger fum Shiloh
Can pick a bale o' cotton,
Dat nigger fum Shiloh
Can pick a bale a day.

Chorus:
    A-pick a bale, a-pick a bale,
    Pick a bale o' cotton.
    A-pick a bale, a-pick a bale,
    Pick a bale a day.

Ol' Eli,
Pick a bale o' cotton,

Ol' Eli,
Pick a bale a day.

Ol' massa tol' de niggers,
Pick a bale o' cotton,
Ol' massa tol' de niggers,
Pick a bale a day.

I b'lieve to my soul,
I pick a bale o' cotton,
I b'lieve to my soul,
I pick a bale a day.

I had a little wife could
Pick a bale o' cotton,
I had a little wife could
Pick a bale a day.

HARD TO BE A NIGGER

Well, it makes no difference
  How you make out your time.
White man sho' to bring a
  Nigger out behin'.

Chorus:

  Ain't it hard? ain't it hard?
  Ain't it hard to be a nigger? nigger? nigger?
  Ain't it hard? ain't it hard?
  For you cain't get yo' money when it's due.

Lemme tell you, white man,
  Lemme tell you, honey,
Nigger makes de cotton,
  White folks gets de money.

[233]

Ef you work all de week
    An' work all de time,
White man sho' to bring a
    Nigger out behin'.

Ef a nigger gits 'rested,
    An' can't pay his fine,
They sho' sen' him out
    To the county gang.

Naught's a naught,
    Figger's a figger,
Figger fer de white man,
    Naught fer de nigger.

SHORTENIN' BREAD

Swinging

Two lit - tle nig - gers ly - in' in bed,

One of 'em sick an' de od - der mos' dead.

Call for de doc - tor an' de doc - tor said,

"Feed dem dar - kies on short' - nin' bread."

CHORUS

Mam-my's lit - tle ba - by loves short' - nin', short' - nin',

Mam-my's lit - tle ba - by loves short' - nin' bread.

Two little niggers lyin' in bed,
One of 'em sick an' de odder mos' dead.
Call for de doctor an' de doctor said,
"Feed dem darkies on shortenin' bread."

Chorus:

Mammy's little baby loves shortenin', shortenin',
Mammy's little baby loves shortenin' bread.

Or:

Shortenin' bread, shortenin' bread,
How I love shortenin' bread!

Or:

Shortenin', shortenin', shortenin' bread,
Don' my baby like shortenin' bread!

Stole de skillet, stole de led,
Stole dat gal makin' shortenin' bread.
Got six mon's fo' de skillet, got six mon's fo' de led;
I got six mon's fo' de gal makin' shortenin' bread, etc.

Went to de kitchen an' kicked off de led,
An' filled my pockets full o' shortenin' bread.
Shortenin' bread an' it baked thin,
Dat what it take to make 'em grin.

Put on de skillet, put on de led,
My lil baby wants shortenin' bread.

[235]

Two little niggers upstairs in bed,
One turned over an' to de odder said,

"How about dat shortenin' bread,
How about dat shortenin' bread?"
One lil nigger a-layin' in de bed,
His eyes shet an' still, like he been dead.

Two lil niggers a-layin' in de bed,
A-snorin' an' a-dreamin' of a table spread.
W'en de doctor come he simpully said,
"Feed dat boy some shortenin' bread."

T'other lil nigger sick in de bed,
W'en he hear tell o' shortenin' bread,
Popped up well, he dance an' sing,
He almos' cut de pigeon wing.

I do love liquor, an' I will take a dram,
I'd ruther be a nigger dan' a po' white man.

SANDY LAN'

Chorus: Big yam ta-ters in de san-dy lan', San-dy

bot - tom, san - dy lan'. Stanza: Sift your meal an'
Big buck nig-ger in de

save de bran, Mighty good liv-in' in de san-dy lan'.
san - dy lan', Raise big ta-ters in de san-dy lan'.
After each stanza the chorus may be repeated indefinitely.

[236]

Chorus:

> Big yam taters in de sandy lan',
> Sandy bottom, sandy lan',
> Big yam taters in de sandy lan',
> Sandy bottom, sandy lan'.

Sift your meal an' save de bran,
Mighty good livin' in de sandy lan'.

Big buck nigger in de sandy lan',
Raise big taters in de sandy lan'.

Big fat possum up-a 'simmon tree,
Make a big supper fer you an' me.

Hurry up boys in sandy lan',
Big fat possum up-a 'simmon tree,

We'll make our livin' in sandy lan',
Lot o' pretty gals in sandy lan'.

Right an' left in sandy lan',
On to de nex' in sandy lan'.

Dinah's got a wooden leg, so they say,
Shake that wooden leg, Dinah-o.

Sal's got meat skin laid away,
To grease that wooden leg, so they say.

PATTIN'

When musical instruments were rare among the plantation Negroes, they often made music for jig dancing by clapping their hands or slapping their thighs. The mouth with lips protruding often served as a substitute for the drum when intense emphasis was desired. Words sometimes were attached to these patting chants, just as words followed the mountain breakdown tunes. Two examples of Negro patting chants:

LITTLE GAL AT OUR HOUSE

To be declaimed not sung
Fast and steady

Pos-sum up de gum tree, Coo-ny in de hol-ler,

Lit-tle girl at our house, Fat as she can wal-ler.

Possum up de gum tree,
Coony in de holler,
Little gal at our house
Fat as she can waller.

RABBIT HASH

To be declaimed, not sung
Very rhythmical

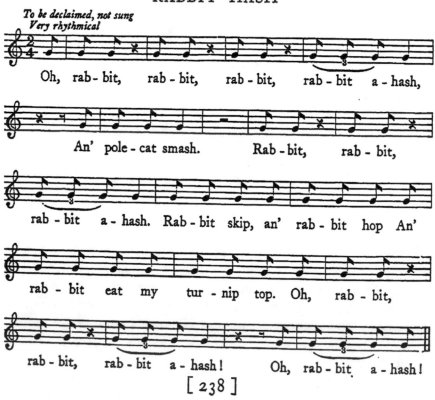

Oh, rab-bit, rab-bit, rab-bit, rab-bit a-hash,

An' pole-cat smash. Rab-bit, rab-bit,

rab-bit a-hash. Rab-bit skip, an' rab-bit hop An'

rab-bit eat my tur-nip top. Oh, rab-bit,

rab-bit, rab-bit a-hash! Oh, rab-bit a-hash!

[238]

Oh, rabbit, rabbit, rabbit,
Rabbit a-hash
An' polecat smash;
Rabbit, rabbit, rabbit a-hash.
Rabbit skip an'-a rabbit hop,
An' a-rabbit eat my turnip top.
Oh, rabbit, rabbit, rabbit, rabbit a-hash!
Oh, rabbit a-hash.

DA'S ALL RIGHT, BABY

Patting song by Clear Rock of the Central State Farm near Sugarland, Texas.

Da's all righ', hon - ey; Da's all righ', hon - ey. Way

up yon - der, dar - lin', 'Bove the sun, su - gar,

Girls all call me, hon - ey, Su - gar - plum.

Sho' 'nuff? Da's all righ', hon - ey; Da's all righ'.

Refrain for concluding stanza

Way up yonder, darlin',
'Bove the sun, sugar,

[239]

Girls all call me, honey,
Sugarplum. Sho' 'nuff?

Refrain:
> Da's all righ', honey;
> Da's all righ', baby.

Be careful, baby,
What you do, honey,
Yonder lil girl, honey,
Git you too. Sho' 'nuff?

I'm goin' tell you, honey,
De nachul fac', sugar,
Steal my woman, darlin',
'Ll bring her back. Sho' 'nuff?

Got a horse, sugar,
Buggy too, baby,
Horse's black, darlin',
Buggy's blue. Sho' 'nuff?

I'm goin' tell you, baby,
What to see, honey,
I'm goin' away, darlin',
Tennessee. Sho' 'nuff?

COTTON FIELD SONG *

Rac-coon an' a pos-sum, Rack-in' 'cross de prai-rie,

Rac-coon asked de pos-sum, Does she want to mar-ry?

* A composite. Tune from Mary Gresham.

Raccoon an' de possum,
　Rackin' 'cross de prairie,
Raccoon ask de possum—
　Does she want to marry?

Possum in a 'simmon tree,
　Raccoon on de groun',
Raccoon ask de possum
　To shake dem 'simmons down.

Well, I met a possum on de road
　An' ask him whar he's gwine.
He 'lowed it was his business,
　But it wasn't none o' mine.

Den I see Miss Rabbit,
　A-settin' in de brush,
All dressed up in her Sunday clothes,
　A-lookin' sweet and fresh.

Miss Rabbit am a gay young gal,
　She come to meet her beau;
Somepin's gwineter happen soon,
　Ef de preacher am too slow.

I met a rabbit in de road,
　I ast him whar he's gwine.
"I ain't got time to tell you now,
　De ol' gray houn's behin'."

"Say, Mister Rabbit,
　Your ears mighty thin."
"Yas, bless-a-God,
　They been a-splittin' de win'."

"Say, Mister Rabbit,
  Your fur mighty gray."
"Yes, bless-a-God,
  Seen a ha'nt 'fore day."

Hog an' a sheep,
  A-goin' to de paster,
Hog tol' de sheep,
  "Caincha trot a little faster?"

Thousand verses to my song,
  Hope I've sung 'em all.
'Fore I'd sing 'em all again,
  I'd see you all in hell.

DE GREY GOOSE

Iron Head grinned, very literally like the Devil, while he sang this saga of the grey goose. It has the feel of the Paul Bunyan tales and of Uncle Remus.

Well, las' Mon - day morn - in', Lawd, Lawd, Lawd, Well,
las' Mon - day morn - in', Lawd, Lawd, Lawd.

Well, las' Monday mornin',
Lawd, Lawd, Lawd,
Well, las' Monday mornin', ·
Lawd, Lawd, Lawd,
My daddy went a-huntin', etc.,

Huntin' for de grey goose, etc.,
An' he wen' to de big wood,
An' he took along his zulu,
An' de houn' dog he wen' too.
Houn' dog 'gin to whinin',
Long come a grey goose,
Well, up to his shoulder,
An' ram back de hammer,
An' pull on de trigger,
And de gun wen' boo loo,
Down he come a-fallin',
He was six weeks a-fallin',
An' he put him on de waggin,
An' he taken him to de white house.
Oh, yo' wife an' my wife,
They'll give a feather pickin';
He was six weeks a-pickin',
An' dey put him on a-cookin';
He was six weeks a-cookin',
An' dey put him on de table,
An' de fork couldn' stick him.
Well, dey throwed him in de hog-pen,
An' de hogs couldn' eat him,
Well, he broke de ol' sow's jawbone,
So dey taken him to de sawmill,
An' he broke de saws' teeth out,
An' de las' time I seed her,
She was flyin' 'cross de ocean,
Had a long string o' goslin's,
An' dey all went "Quonk, quonk,"
Lawd, Lawd, Lawd,
An' dey all went "Quonk, quonk,"
Lawd, Lawd, Lawd.

JULIE ANN JOHNSON

Lead Belly (Ledbetter) and his twelve-stringed guitar made it doubtful whether this was a dance tune or a work chant.

O Julie Ann Johnson,
Oho!
O Julie Ann Johnson,
Oho!

Gwineter catch dat train, boys,
Oho!
Gwineter catch dat train, boys,
Oho!

Gwineter fin' Julie,
Oho!
Gwineter fin' Julie,
Oho!

She gone to Dallas,
Oho!
She gone to Dallas,
Oho!

[244]

Gwineter hug my Julie,
Oho!
Gwineter hug my Julie,
Oho!

Lead Belly could go on at great length about Julie and his intentions toward her, but we shall leave the reader to improvise further according to his own fancy.

MY YALLOW GAL

As sung by Iron Head, an "habitual criminal," imprisoned on the Central State Farm near Sugarland, Texas. This is one of the few folk songs about women on the lips of Negro men that have any element of tenderness.

Oh! my dad-dy was a fool a-bout a yal-low gal,
Oh! my yal-low, yal-low, yal-low, yal-low, yal-low gal,

FINE

Oh! my dad-dy was a fool a-bout a yal-low gal.
Oh! my yal-low, yal-low, yal-low, yal-low, yal-low gal.

Oh! my yal-low, my yal-low, my yal-low gal,

D.C.

Oh! my yal-low, my yal-low, my yal-low gal.

Oh, my daddy was a fool about dat yallow gal,
Oh, my daddy was a fool about dat yallow gal.

[245]

Refrain:
> Oh, my yallow, my yallow, my yallow gal,
> Oh, my yallow, my yallow, my yallow gal,
> Oh, my yallow, my yallow, yallow, yallow gal,
> My yallow, yallow, yallow, yallow gal.

Alternate Refrains:
> My yallou, my yallou, my yallou gal, (2)
>
> My pretty, pretty, pretty, pretty yallow gal, (2)

Alternate Verses

God knows I'm a fool about a yallow gal, (2)

Got cold black hair, dat yallow gal, (2)

I walked to Milam County wid my yallow gal, (2)

Well, I walked and I talked wid my yallow gal, (2)

But I didn' get nothin' from my yallow gal, (2)

Well, I slep' all night wid my yallow gal, (2)

But I didn' get nothin' from my yallow gal, (2)

Well, I rolled and I tumbled wid my yallow gal, (2)

But I didn' get nothin' from my yallow gal, (2)

DE BLACK GAL

Oh, de white gal ride in a automobile,
Oh, de yaller gal try to do de same;
Oh, de black gal ride in a slow oxcart,
But she get dar jes' de same.

Oh, de white gal have a silk petticoat,
Oh, de yaller gal have de same;
Oh, de black gal have no petticoat a-tall,
But she git dar jes' de same.

Oh, de white gal ride in a parlor car,
Oh, de yaller gal try to do de same;
Oh, de black gal ride in de Jim Crow car,
But she git dar jes' de same.

Oh, de white gal have a high-heel shoe,
Oh, de yaller gal try to have de same;
Oh, de black gal have no shoe a-tall,
But she git dar jes' de same.

Oh, de white gal have a nice long ha'r,
Oh, de yaller gal try to have de same;
Oh, de black gal have a one-cent wig,
But he her ha'r jes' de same.

Oh, a white gal eats de cake an' pie,
Oh, de yaller gal try to do de same;
Oh, de black gal eats de ashy cake,
But she's eatin' jes' de same.

Oh, a white gal sleeps in a bed,
Oh, a yaller gal try to do de same;
Oh, a black gal sleeps on de flo',
But she's sleepin' jes' de same.

Oh, de white gal smell like sweet perfume,
Oh, de yaller gal try to smell de same;
Oh, de black gal smell like a billy goat,
But he her smell jes' de same.

[247]

XI

MINSTREL TYPES

"Git out yo' trombone, Rufus; we're goin' to raise a rukus tonight."

THE BALLAD OF DAVY CROCKETT *

Now, don't you want to know some-thing con-cern-in'
Where it was I come from and where I got my learnin'? Oh, the
world is made of mud out of the Miss-iss-ip-pi Riv-er! The
sun's a ball of fox fire, as well you may dis-ci-ver.

CHORUS

Take the la-dies out at night. They shine so bright They
make the world light When the moon is out of sight.

Now, don't you want to know something concernin'
Where it was I come from and where I got my learnin'?
Oh, the world is made of mud out o' the Mississippi River!
The sun's a ball of foxfire, as well you may disciver.

* From an article of Julia Beazley in Volume VI of the *Publications of the Texas Folk-Lore Society.*

Chorus:
>   Take the ladies out at night. They shine so bright,
>   They make the world light when the moon is out of sight.

And so one day as I was goin' a-spoonin'
I met Colonel Davy, and he was goin' a-coonin'.
Says I, "Where's your gun?" "I ain' got none."
"How you goin' kill a coon when you haven't got a gun?"

Says he, "Pompcalf, just follow after Davy,
And he'll soon show you how to grin a coon crazy."
I followed on a piece and thar sot a squirrel,
A-settin' on a log and a-eatin' sheep sorrel.

When Davy did that see, he looked around at me,
Saying, "All I want now is a brace agin your knee."
And thar I braced a great big sinner.
He grinned six times hard enough to git his dinner!

The critter on the log didn't seem to mind him—
Jest kep' a-settin' thar and wouldn't look behind him.
Then it was he said: "The critter must be dead.
See the bark a-flyin' all around the critter's head?"

I walked right up the truth to disciver.
Drot! It was a pine knot so hard it made me shiver.
Says he, "Pompcalf, don't you begin to laugh—
I'll pin back your ears and bite you half in half!"

I flung down my gun and all my ammunition,
Says I, "Davy Crockett, I can cool your ambition!"
He throwed back his head and he blowed like a steamer.
Says he, "Pompcalf, I'm a Tennessee screamer!"

Then we locked horns and we wallered in the thorns.
I never had such a fight since the hour I was born.
We fought a day and a night and then agreed to drop it.
I was purty badly whipped—and so was Davy Crockett.

I looked all around and found my head a-missin'—
He'd bit off my head and I had swallered hisn!
Then we did agree to let each other be;
I was too much for him, and he was too much for me.

RAISE A RUKUS TONIGHT

This song, probably of a minstrel origin, is one of the best known of all tunes among Negroes of the South. The verses are legion. The three verses quoted here were sung to us by a Negro boy, named Butterball, on the Smithers plantation near Huntsville, Texas. He was a runt, what the cowboys call, among cattle, "a dogie." And he sang for us, with scarcely a hesitation, some twenty stanzas of "Raise a Rukus," each an epigram that dealt with something good to eat, the whole a saga of the belly.

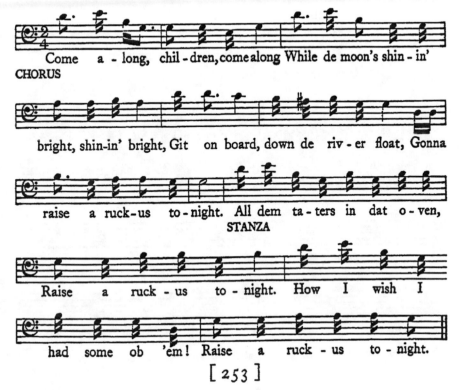

Come a - long, chil - dren, come along While de moon's shin - in'
CHORUS
bright, shin-in' bright, Git on board, down de riv - er float, Gonna
raise a ruck-us to - night. All dem ta - ters in dat o - ven,
STANZA
Raise a ruck - us to - night. How I wish I
had some ob 'em! Raise a ruck - us to - night.

[253]

Refrain:

Come along, chillun, come along,
While the moon's shinin' bright,
Git on board, down de river float,
We gonna raise a rukus tonight.

All dem taters in dat oven,
Raise a rukus tonight,
How I wish I had some ob 'em!
Raise a rukus tonight.

All dem peas in dat pot,
Raise a rukus tonight,
Look how many we have got,
Raise a rukus tonight.

All dem biscuits in dat pan,
Raise a rukus tonight,
Ef I don' git 'em, gonna raise some san',
Raise a rukus tonight.

WHEN DE GOOD LORD SETS YOU FREE*

A spiritual taken over by the "worl'ly." The changing and fluid chorus comes in at irregular intervals.

Big black nig - ger, ly - ing on de log,

Fin - ger on de trig - ger, eye on de hog,

* From different sources, principally students of Prairie View Normal (for Negroes), Texas.

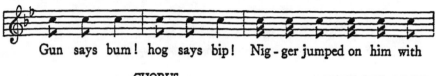

Gun says bum! hog says bip! Nig-ger jumped on him with

CHORUS

all his grip. Oh, mourner, you shall be free, Yes,

mourner, you shall be free, When de good Lord sets you free.

Big black nigger lying on the log,
Finger on trigger, eye on the hog.
Gun says bum! hog says bip!
Nigger jumped on him with all his grip.

Chorus:
    Got my pork chops,
    Good chitlins, big kidneys;
    Got the liver, too. You shall be free,
    When the good Lord sets you free.

Way down yonder 'bout Cedar Creek,
Niggers don't grow but 'leven feet;
They lay in the bed till it ain't no use,
Feet stick out like a chicken roost.

Chorus:
    Shout study, you shall be free,
    When the good Lord sets you free.

If you want to get to heben, I'll tell you how to do it:
Slick your feet in muttin suet,
When the devil gets at you with a red-hot hand,
Slip way over in the promised land!

Chorus:
> Talk about it, you shall be free,
> When the good Lord sets you free.

Went to the river to be baptize',
Stepped on a root and got capsize',
Water was deep, preacher was weak,
Nigger went to heben from the bottom of the creek!

If you want to see a preacher laugh,
Change a dollar and give him half;
Big black nigger, blacker 'n blackin' tar,
Tryin' to get to heben on a 'lectric car.

If you want t' see a rooster crow,
Th'ow some corn pone befo' yo do',
Take a stick in yo' right hand,
Knock him over in the promised land.

Nigger and rooster had a fight,
Rooster knocked the nigger clean out of sight.
Nigger said, "Mr. Rooster, that will be all right,
I'll meet you at the chicken roost tomorrow night,
With my cracker sack tomorrow night."

Kneelin' in de chicken house on my knees,
Thought I heard a chicken sneeze,
Sneeze so hard wid de whoopin' cough,
Sneezed his head and tail right off.

Chorus:
> Oh, mourner, you will be free,
> Yes, mourner, you will be free,
> When de good Lord sets you free.

Ain't no use for me workin' hard,
I got a gal in the white folk's yard,
Sift the flour and reach at the lard,
Wasn't for the bulldog I'd be in the yard.

Chorus:

    He might bite me, bad bulldog,
    In the morning when the good Lord sets me free.

Ol' Marse Jack come ridin' by.
"Say, Marse Jack, dat mule's gwine to die."
"Ef he die, I'll tan his skin,
An' if he don't, I'll ride him ag'in."

Peter Jackson, tall and black,
Hit Billy Chavers the finishing crack,
Jumped on de train and yanked de cord,
Now he's presented to an English Lord!

Chorus:

    Fightin' nigger! Den-a you shall be free,
    When de good Lord sets you free.

Nigger be a nigger whatever he do:
Tie red ribbon round the toe of his shoe,
Jerk his vest on over his coat,
Snatch his britches up round his throat.

Chorus:

    Singing high-stepper, you shall be free,
    When the good Lord sets you free.

I went down to hog-eye town,
Dey sot me down to table,
I eat so much of dat hog-eye grease,
Till de grease ran out my nable.

Chorus:
Run long home, Miss Hog-eye,
Singin' high-stepper, Lord, you shall be free.

God made bees, bees made honey;
God made man, man made money.
God made a nigger, made him in the night,
Made him in a hurry and forgot to paint him white.

Chorus:
Po' mo'nahs! You shall be free,
When the good Lord sets you free.

OLD DAN TUCKER

Martha McCulloch-Williams writes to the editor of the New York *Sun:*

"Here is a true and proper, if fragmentary, version of the ballad as chanted from my earliest youth, and derived, as is most immortal poesy, from North Carolina. Thence too comes the spurious initial stanza of the folk lore people:

"Ole Aunt Dinah she got drunk,
Felled in de fire and kicked up a chunk.
Red hot coal popped in her shoe—
Lordy a-mighty! How de water flew?

"Ole Dan Tucker was adjustable—you began singing it where you chose and could play both ends against the middle, or sing it backward, or forward, or improvise topical stanzas according to your mind and skill. It was a fine dancing tune, and the black fiddlers often sang it as they fiddled, the prompter meanwhile racking his wits to find new figures yet keep the proper rhythms.

"Let me say further the singing was commonly in negro dialect, but

[258]

not invariably so. That rested with the singers, who, singing for their own joy, neither knew nor cared if they sang in key, especially if they were roystering young blades riding home from a long dance around five o'clock in the morning. There were, as of most other dance songs, lawless and high colored versions for such tunes, versions which could not be given unexpurgated before ladies. But the sedatest could take no offence at the authorized ballad, which indeed was often used as a lullaby:

Rather fast

Ol' Dan Tuck - er clomb a tree, His Lord an' Marster for to see. De limb hit broke an' Dan got a fall, Never got to see his Lord at all!

CHORUS

Git out o' the way, Ol' Dan Tuck - er! Git out o' the way, Ol' Dan Tuck - er! Git out o' the way, Ol' Dan Tuck - er! You're too late to git your sup - per.

"Ole Dan'l Tucker clomb a tree,
His Lord and Marster for to see.
De limb hit broke and Dan got a fall—
Nuver got to see his Lord at all!

"Git out o' the way, Ole Dan Tucker!
Git out o' the way, Ole Dan Tucker!
Git out o' the way, Ole Dan Tucker!
You're too late to git your supper.

"Miss Tucker she went out one day,
To ride with Dan in a one horse sleigh.
De sleigh was broke, and de horse was blind—
Miss Tucker she got left behind.
Git out o' the way, etc.

"As I come down de new cut road,
I spied de peckerwood and de toad,
And every time de toad would jump
De peckerwood hopped upon de stump.
Git out o' the way, etc.

"And next upon de gravel road,
I met Br'er Tarypin and Br'er Toad.
And every time Br'er Toad would sing
Br'er Tarrypin cut de pigeon wing.
Git out o' the way, etc.

"Ole Dan and me we did fall out,
And what d'ye reckon it was about?
He trod on my corn and I kicked him on the shins;
That's jest the way this row begins.
Git out o' the way, etc.

[260]

"If Ole Dan he had corn to buy,
He'd mo'n and wipe his weepin' eye;
But when Ole Dan had corn to sell,
He was as sassy as all hell.
    Git out o' the way, etc."

But the North Carolina lady is wrong. The original six-stanza "Old Dan Tucker" was written by Dan Emmett, who was also the author of "Dixie" and many other popular songs. Not one of his stanzas is quoted by the writer. There are hundreds of spurious stanzas that yet survive.

I came to town de udder night,
I hear de noise, an' I saw de fight.
De watchman wuz a-runnin' roun'
Cryin' "Old Dan Tucker's come to town."

Chorus:

    So, git outa de way for old Dan Tucker,
    He's come too late to git his supper.
    Supper's over and breakfast cookin',
    Old Dan Tucker standin' lookin'.

Old Dan Tucker he went to de mill,
To git some meal to put in de swill;
The miller swo' by de point of his knife
He nebber had seed such a man in his life.

Dan Tucker and I we did fall out,
And what do you think it was about?
He tread upon corn; I kicked him on de chin,
An' dat's de way dis row begin.

Old Dan began in early life,
To play de banjo an' de fife;
He play de niggers all to sleep,
An' den into his bunk he creep.

Old Daniel Tucker wuz a mighty man,
He washed his face in a fryin' pan;
Combed his head wid a wagon wheel
And died wid de toofache in his heel.

And now Old Dan is a gone sucker,
And never can go home to supper.
Old Dan has had his las' ride,
An' de banjo's buried by his side.

COTTON–EYED JOE*

A Square Dance Song or Breakdown

If it had not-a been— for Cot-ton-eyed Joe,
Corn-stalk fid-dle and corn-stalk bow, I'm

I'd 'a' been— mar - - ried— for-ty years a - go.
gwine to beat hell out-a Cot-ton-eyed Joe.

If it had not 'a' been for Cotton-Eyed Joe,
I'd 'a' been married forty years ago.

Cornstalk fiddle and cornstalk bow
Gwine to beat hell out-a Cotton-Eyed Joe.

Gwine to go shootin' my forty-fo',
Won't be a nigger in a mile or mo'.

* In jigs of this type the fiddler sings a couplet and then plays indeterminately, with variations of the tune. Meanwhile the dance goes on.

[262]

Hain't seen ol' Joe since way last fall,
Say he's been sold down to Guines Hall.

Great long line and little short pole,
I'm on my way to the crawfish hole.

Oh, it makes dem ladies love me so
W'en I come round a-pickin' Cotton-Eyed Joe.

Hol' my fiddle an' hol' my bow,
Whilst I knock ol' Cotton-Eyed Joe.

Oh, law, ladies, pity my case,
For Ise got a jawbone in my face.

O Lawd, O Lawd, come pity my case,
For I'm gettin' old an' wrinkled in de face.

XII

BREAKDOWNS AND PLAY PARTIES

"They're all raisin' hell in Cumberland Gap."

The old folks in the mountains say it's the Devil makes their foot
pat, but the young bucks and the girls, they swing and don't care, while
the fiddler rhymes all night long to such breakdowns as "Old Joe
Clark," "Liza Jane," and "Sourwood Mountain." It is quite probable
that these tunes have their prototypes in English folk music, but even
so they have been made, by the "dee-iddle-ummings" of the fiddlers
and the denunciations of the revivalists, a more integral part of American culture than ever were the American versions of the Child Ballads.
And surely their imagery and grammar are those of the American
back country.

THE ARKANSAS TRAVELLER *

Some years of my teens were passed in the town of Salem, Columbiana County, Ohio. This was before any railroads passed through that country. . . . There were three taverns in Salem. . . . Each of the taverns, standing along the road, naturally exerted itself to present the greatest attractions to the traveller in order to secure the greatest amount of custom. The chief attraction in early times at the "Golden Fleece" was the music, the chef d'œuvre of which was considered to be the "Arkansas Traveller." The residents kept their attention upon any night when the play was likely to be enacted, and if it should get through town that this was to be given, that night would surely see the old barroom packed to the utmost. . . . One of the boys mounted upon a broken-backed or no-backed chair and commenced to play the first part of the tune. After playing it once or twice to familiarize the new members of his audience, he prefaced the performance with an explanation. . . .

The opening of the story presents this Arkansas squatter, just returned from a trip to New Orleans, and his first move is to get down his fiddle and attempt to reproduce the tune . . . he has heard for the first time . . . the "Arkansas Traveller." . . . He has already picked out the first part, but the second is too much for him and he fails in it. Therefore he is compelled to content himself by playing the first part only. While he is engaged in playing it over and over and over again, the "Arkansas Traveller" makes his appearance and the play begins. . . . One of the boys would play this tune in different keys and to different times, improvising right and left. . . . While thus engaged, his brother would enter the room dressed in

* Quoted in toto from *The Arkansas Traveller*, by Thomas Wilson, published in 1900 by the Press of Fred J. Heer, Columbus, Ohio. Mr. Wilson was then connected with the U. S. National Museum, Washington, D. C.

the guise of the Arkansas Traveller, and make his way up to the front part of the circle around the player, who would stop a little, maybe to tighten a string, . . . when the stranger asks him a question. Of course I do not remember the entire dialogue—I do not know if it was ever given twice the same way. It was a matter of improvisation, depending on the skill and ability of the players, the humor they were in, the time at their command, and the extent to which the audience could arouse them to enthusiasm. The first question was by the traveller:

TRAVELLER: How do you do, stranger?

SQUATTER: Do pretty much as I please, sir. (*Plays first part.*)

TRAVELLER: Stranger, do you live about here?

SQUATTER: I reckon I don't live anywheres else! (*Plays first part only.*)

TRAVELLER: Well, how long have you lived here?

SQUATTER: See that big tree there? Well, that was there when I come. (*Plays first part.*)

TRAVELLER: Well, you don't need to be so cross about it; I wasn't asking no improper questions at all!

SQUATTER: I reckon there's nobody cross here except yourself! (*Plays first part only.*)

TRAVELLER: How did your potatoes turn out here last year?

SQUATTER: They didn't turn out at all; we dug 'em out. (*Plays first part only.*)

TRAVELLER: Can I stay here all night?

SQUATTER: Yes, you kin stay right where you air, out en the road. (*Plays first part.*)

TRAVELLER: How far is it to the next tavern?

SQUATTER: I reckon it's upwards of some distance. (*Plays first part.*)

TRAVELLER: How long will it take to get there?

SQUATTER: You'll not git there at all, if ye stay here foolin' with me. (*Plays first part.*)

TRAVELLER: How far is it to the forks of the road?

SQUATTER: It ain't forked since I been here. (*Plays.*)

TRAVELLER: Where does this road go to?

SQUATTER: It ain't gone anywhere since I been here—jist stayed right here. (*Plays.*)

TRAVELLER: Why don't you put a new roof on your house?

SQUATTER: Because it's rainin' and I can't. (*Plays.*)

TRAVELLER: Why don't you do it when it is not raining?

SQUATTER: It don't leak then. (*Plays.*)

TRAVELLER: Can I get across the branch down here?

SQUATTER: I reckon you kin, the ducks cross whenever they want to. (*Plays.*)

TRAVELLER: Why don't you play the rest of the tune?

(*The player stops as quick as lightning.*)

SQUATTER: Gee, stranger, can you play the rest of that tune? I've been down to New Orleans and I heard it at the theatre, and I've been at work at it ever since I got back, trying to get the last part of it. If you can play the rest of that tune, you kin stay in this cabin for the rest of your natural life. Git right down, hitch your horse and come in! I don't keer if it is a-rainin'! I don't keer if the beds is all full! We'll make a shake-down on the floor and ye kin kiver with the door. We hain't got much to eat, but what we have, you're mighty welcome to it. Here, Sal, old woman, fly round and git some corn-dodgers and bacon for the gentleman,—he knows the last part of the tune! Don't you, stranger—didn't you say you did? . . . If you know it, you are a friend and a 'brother-come-to-me-arms'; if you don't, you've excited the tiger in my bosom and I'll have nothing short of your heart's blood! Git down, git down!

STRANGER: Yes, I can play it; there's no use of your getting mad. I'll play it for you as soon's I get something to eat.

SQUATTER: Fly 'round here, old woman, set the table, bring out the knives and forks.

(*Here the little boy was to put in his oar and say:* "Daddy, you know we haven't got any forks, and there ain't any knives to go 'round.")

SQUATTER: Like to know why there ain't! There's little butch and big butch, and short handle and cob handle, and no handle at all, and if that ain't knives enough to set any gentleman's table in this country, I would like to know! Git off'n your hoss, stranger, and come in and have someth'n, and then play the rest of that tune.

The result of it is that the stranger gets off, takes the seat of the squatter and the fiddle, and then starts in playing the last part of the tune, but refuses to play the first part.

Then the squatter becomes interested and begins plying questions to the stranger; . . . to all of which the stranger replies with as much imperturbability as is possible and in the same style as he was replied to when he came; that is, he gives answers as short as may be, and then ends the discussion by playing the tune, always and only in the second part.

I have known this to last for an hour, and I have never seen an audience go away from any entertainment better pleased than were the citizens of the town of Salem, were they guests, travellers or waggoners, when was played, in this simple and country style, the drama of "The Arkansas Traveller."

GROUN' HOG*

"This song belongs to an endless number of what may be termed fiddle and banjo songs. 'Groun' Hog' rises to epic heights, magnificently outdistancing 'Sir Lionel,' or 'Bangum and the Boar'! But in this case, the poor woodchuck is more sinned against than sinning, the mighty highland Nimrods being the aggressors. Sung by Tom Kelley and Dan Gibson, two singers and banjo pickers, at Hindman, Kentucky, 1915."—JOSIAH COMBS, Texas Christian University, Fort Worth, Texas.

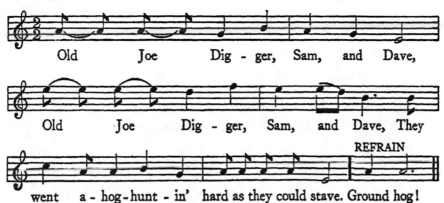

Old Joe Dig - ger, Sam, and Dave,
Old Joe Dig - ger, Sam, and Dave, They
went a - hog - hunt - in' hard as they could stave. Ground hog!

Old Joe Digger, Sam, and Dave, [Repeat]
They went a-hog-huntin' hard as they could stave.
    Ground hog!

Whistle up ye dog and loaden up ye gun,
Away to the hills to have some fun.

Too many rocks and too many logs,
Too many rocks to ketch groun' hogs.

* Tune from Volume II of Sharp's *English Folk-Songs from the Southern Appalachians.*

They picked up their guns and went to the brash,
By damn! Joe, here's the hog sign fraish.

One took a tree and it's one took a log,
Damn my soul if it ain't a groun' hog!

Git away, Sam, and le' me load my gun,
The groun' hog hunt has jist begun.

He's in here, boys, the hole's wore slick;
Run here, Sam, with yer forked stick!

Git down, Sam, and in there peep,
Fer I think I see him sound asleep.

Stand back, boys, and le's be wise,
Fer I think I see his beaded eyes.

Hold them dogs, boys, don't let 'em howl,
I thought I heerd the groun' hog growl.

Hello, Johnnie, cut a long pole,
To roust this groun' hog out of his hole.

Up jumped Sam with a ten-foot pole,
He roused it in that groun' hog's hole.

Work, boys, work jist as hard as ye can tear,
The meat'll do to eat and the hide'll do to wear.

Work, boys, work for all you earn,
Skin 'im atter dark and tan 'im in a churn.

Stand back, boys, le' me git my breath,
Ketchin' this groun' hog's might' nigh death.

I heerd 'im give a whistle and a wail,
I've wound my stick right in his tail.

[272]

Stand back, boys, and gi' me a little air,
I've got a little o' the groun' hog's hair.

Here he comes right in a whirl,
He's the biggest groun' hog in this worl'.

Sam cocked his gun and Dave pulled the trigger,
But the one killed the hog was old Joe Digger.

They took 'im by the tail and wagged 'im to a log,
And swore by gosh! he's a hell of a hog!

Up stepped Sal with a snigger and a grin:
"Whatcha goin' to do with the groun' hog skin?"

Scrapes 'im down to his head and feet,
By damn, Sam, here's a fine pile o' meat!

Carried him to the house and skinned 'im out to bile,
I bet forty dollars you could smell 'im fifty mile.

They put 'im in the pot and all begin to smile,
They eat that hog before he struck a bile.

Run here, man, hit's bilin'-hot,
Sam and Dave's both eatin' outn the pot.

Old Uncle Jack says, "I'll be damn!
If I can't git a foreleg I'll take a ham."

The children screamed and the children cried,
They love groun' hog cooked and fried.

Hello, mama, make Sam quit,
He's eatin' all the hog, I can't git a bit.

Hello, boys, ain't it a sin,
Watch that gravy run down Sam's chin!

Hello, mama, look at Sam,
He's eat all the hog 'n' a-soppin' out the pan!

Watch 'im, boys, he's about to fall,
He's eat till his pants won't button at all.

Hello, boys, what ye think o' that?
Sam's eat hog till he's right slick fat.

He eat that grease till it run to his nabel,
He'll eat no more hog until he's able.

CUMBERLAND GAP *

Lay down, boys, and take a lit - tle nap,
Lay down, boys, and take a lit - tle nap,

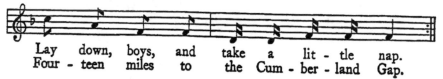

Lay down, boys, and take a lit - tle nap.
Four - teen miles to the Cum - ber - land Gap.

Lay down, boys, an' take a little nap,
Lay down, boys, an' take a little nap,
Lay down, boys, an' take a little nap,
They're all raisin' Hell in Cumberland Gap.

The first white man in Cumberland Gap,
Was Doctor Walker, an English chap.

* Stanzas from H. H. Fuson's *Ballads of the Kentucky Highlands*; stanzas and air from James Howard.

Daniel Boone on Pinnacle Rock,
He killed Indians with an old flintlock.

Cumberland Gap is a noted place,
Three kinds of water to wash your face.

Cumberland Gap with its cliff and rocks,
Home of the panther, bear, and fox.

September mornin' in Sixty-two,
Morgan's Yankees all withdrew.

They spiked Long Tom on the mountain top,
And over the cliffs they let him drop.

They burned the hay, the meal, and the meat,
And left the rebels nothing to eat.

Braxton Bragg with his rebel band,
He run George Morgan to the blue-grass land.

The rebels now will give a little yell,
They'll scare the niggers all to Hell.

Ol' Aunt Dinah, ef you don't keer,
Leave my little jug settin' right here.

Ef it's not here when I come back,
I'll raise Hell in Cumberland Gap.

Ol' Aunt Dinah took a little spell,
Broke my little jug all to Hell.

I've got a woman in Cumberland Gap,
She's got a boy that calls me "pap."

Me an' my wife an' my wife's gran'pap,
All raise Hell in Cumberland Gap.

Lay down, boys, an' take a little nap,
Lay down, boys, an' take a little nap,
Lay down, boys, an' take a little nap,
Fourteen miles to the Cumberland Gap.

SOURWOOD MOUNTAIN *

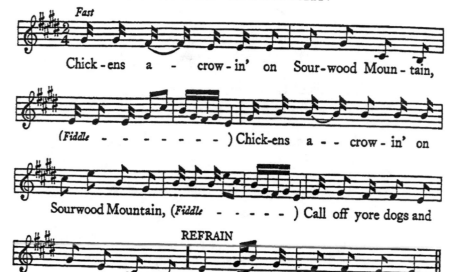

Chick-ens a - crow-in' on Sour-wood Moun-tain, (Fiddle - - - - - - -) Chick-ens a - - crow-in' on Sourwood Mountain, (Fiddle - - - - -) Call off yore dogs and let's go hunt-in', Hey-ho, dee-id-dle-um day.

Chickens a-crowin' on Sourwood Mountain,
Chickens a-crowin' on Sourwood Mountain,
Call up yore dogs and let's go a-huntin',
Hey-ho, dee-iddle-um-day.

My true love lives over the river,
A few more jumps and I'll be with her.

My true love is a blue-eyed daisy,
Ef I don' git her, I'll go crazy.

* From the singing of James Howard, Harlan, Kentucky. Additional stanzas are quoted from Jean Thomas's *Devil's Ditties*, Carl Sandburg's *American Songbag*, and H. H. Fuson's *Ballads of the Kentucky Highlands*.

My true-love lives at the head of the holler,
She won't come and I won't foller.

My true love lives over the ocean,
I'll go to see her, if I take a notion.

Say, old man, I want yore daughter,
To wash my clothes and carry my water.

Fifteen cents, a dollar and a quarter,
Say, young man, take her if you want her.

Ducks in the pond, geese in the ocean,
Devil's in the women if they take a notion.

OLD JOE CLARK*

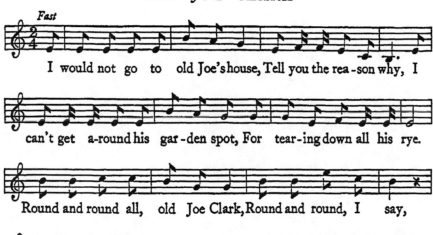

Fast

I would not go to old Joe's house, Tell you the rea-son why, I

can't get a-round his gar-den spot, For tear-ing down all his rye.

Round and round all, old Joe Clark, Round and round, I say,

He'll fol-ler me ten thou-sand miles, To hear my fid-dle play.

* James Howard of Harlan, Kentucky, sang this tune and some of the words. Other stanzas were contributed by H. H. Fuson, Esq., Harlan, Kentucky, Professor Josiah Combs of Fort Worth, Texas. Two stanzas are from Jean Thomas's *Devil's Ditties*.

I would not go to old Joe's house,
Tell you the reason why:
I can't get around his garden spot,
For tearing down all his rye.

Chorus:

   Round and round all, old Joe Clark,
   Round and round, I say,
   He'll foller me ten thousand miles,
   To hear my fiddle play.

Old Joe's got an old red cow,
I know her by the bell.
If she ever gits in my cornfield,
I'll shoot her shore as Hell.

Chorus:

   Round and round all, old Joe Clark,
   Round and round, I say,
   Round and round, old Joe Clark,
   I ain't got long to stay.

I went up to old Joe's house,
Old Joe wasn't at home;
I eat up all of his ham meat
And throwed away the bone.

Chorus:

   Fare you well, old Joe Clark,
   Good-by, Betty Brown,
   Fare you well, old Joe Clark,
   Fare you well, I'm gone.

I went down to old Joe Clark's,
Old Joe wasn't at home;

Jumped in bed with old Joe's wife
And broke her tucking comb.

I won't go down to old Joe's house,
I've told you here before;
He fed me in a hog-trough
And I won't go there any more.

———

Sixteen horses in my team,
And the leaders, they are blind;
And every time the sun goes down,
There's a pretty gal on my mind.

Eighteen miles of mountain road
And fifteen miles of sand;
If I ever travel this road again,
I'll be a married man.

Never got no money,
Got no place to stay,
Got no place to lay my head,
Chicken's a-crowin' for day.

I wish I was an apple
A-hanging on yonder's tree—
Ev'ry time a pretty gal passed
She'd take a bite of me.

Wish I was a sugar tree,
Standing in the middle of some town—
Ev'ry time a pretty gal passed,
I'd shake some sugar down.

Wish I had a nickel,
Wish I had a dime,
Wish I had a pretty lil gal,
For to kiss her an' call her mine.

Wish I was in Tennessee,
Settin' in a big armcheer,
One arm round my whisky jug,
The other round my dear.

I climbed up the oak tree,
She climbed up the gum;
Never saw a pretty lil gal,
But what I loved her some.

When I was a little girl
I used to play with toys;
But now I am a bigger girl
I'd rather play with boys.

When I was a little boy
I used want a knife;
But now I am a bigger boy
All I want is a wife.

THE GAL I LEFT BEHIND ME*

A popular soldier song; also used in play parties.

If ever I travel this road again,
And tears don't fall and blind me,
I'm going back to Tennessee
To the gal I left behind me.

* *Publications of the Texas Folk-Lore Society*, Vols. I and II.

Chorus:

 Oh, the pretty little gal, the sweet little gal,
 The gal I left behind me,
 With rosy cheeks and curly hair,
 The gal I left behind me.

If ever I travel this road again,
And the angels they don't blind me,
I'll reconcile and stay awhile
With the gal I left behind me.

I'll cross Red River one more time,
If the tears don't fall and drown me.
A-weeping for that pretty little gal,
The gal I left behind me.

I'll build my nest in a hollow tree,
Where the cuckoos they won't find me,
I'll go right back to see that gal,
The gal I left behind me.

THAT PRETTY LITTLE GAL

If ever I git off this warpath
And the Indians they don't find me,
I'll go right back to see that gal,
The gal I left behind me.

I could buy such girls as you
For fifteen cents a dozen,
But I'm going back tomorrow,
And marry my country cousin.

[281]

THE GAL I LEFT BEHIND ME

A Cowboy Version

I struck the trail in seventy-nine,
The herd strung out behind me.
As I jogged along my mind ran back
To the gal I left behind me.

Chorus:

> That sweet little gal, that true little gal,
> The gal I left behind me.

If ever I get off the trail
And the Indians they don't find me,
I'll make my way straight back again
To the gal I left behind me.

The wind did blow, the rain did fall,
The hail did fall and blind me;
I thought of that gal, that sweet little gal,
The gal I left behind me.

She wrote ahead to the place I said,
I was always glad to find it;
She says, "I'm true when you get through,
Ride back and you will find me."

When we sold out I took the train,
I knew where I would find her;
When I got back we had a smack
And that was no goldarned liar.

OL' MOTHER HARE

Popular square-dance tune of fifty years ago.

Ol' mo-ther Hare, What you do-in' dar?

Set-tin' in a cor-ner, Smok-in' my see-gar.

[283]

Ol' mother Hare,
What you doin' dar?
Settin' in corner,
Smokin' my seegar.

Ol' mother Hare,
What you doin' there?
Settin' on a butter plate
Pickin' out a hair.

Picked out one,
Picked out two,
Picked out one
And give it to you.

LIZA JANE *

When I go a-court-in', I'll go on the train.

When I go to mar-ry, I'll mar-ry Li-za Jane.

Oh, Law', Li-za, po' gal, Oh, Law', Li-za Jane,

Oh, Law', Li-za, po' gal, She died on the train.

* James Howard, blind, and one of the best of mountain fiddlers, furnished the tune; the stanzas have been taken from: Jean Thomas's *Devil's Ditties*, Harvey Fuson's *Ballads of the Kentucky Highlands*, Carl Sandburg's *American Songbag*, the manuscript of Dr. Josiah Combs, and the memories of people who have fiddled and danced into many a dawn to "Liza Jane."

When I go a-courtin',
I'll go on the train.
When I go to marry,
I'll marry Liza Jane.

Chorus:

  O Law', Liza, po' gal,
  O Law', Liza Jane,
  O Law', Liza, po' gal,
  She died on the train

The hardest work I ever did
Was a-brakin' on a train;
The easiest work I ever did
Was a-huggin' Liza Jane.

When I went to see her,
She met me at the door;
Her shoes and stockings in her hand,
And her feet all over the floor.

When I went to see her,
She wrung her hands and cried;
She swore I was the ugliest thing
That ever lived or died.

I ask little Liza to marry me—
What do you reckon she said?
Said she would not marry me,
If everybody else was dead.

Goin' up the mountain
To raise a patch of cane,
To make a barrel of sorghum
To sweeten up Liza Jane.

[285]

Whisky by the barrel,
Sugar by the pound,
A great big bowl to put it in,
And a spoon to stir it round.

I wish I had a needle and a thread
As fine as I could sew,
I would sew all the girls to my coat-tail,
And down the mountain I'd go.

———

Old corn likker's done made,
Still's tore out an' gone.
What will pore little Liza do,
When I'm took off an' gone?

Don't you weep, my darling,
Don't you weep nor cry;
I'll be back to see you
In the long old by-and-by.

You can climb the cherry tree,
And I will climb the rose;
How I love that pretty little gal,
God 'lmighty knows.

BLACK–EYED SUSIE

Another square-dance tune. The fiddler and the guitar player sing two lines and then play irregular intervals between couplets.

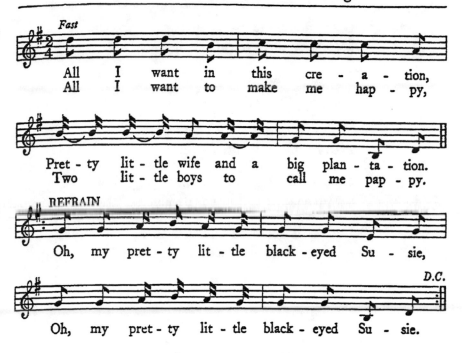

All I want in this creation,
Pretty little wife on a big plantation.

Chorus:

    Oh, my pretty little black-eyed Susie,
    Oh, my pretty little black-eyed Susie.*

Up Onion Creek and down Salt Water,
Some old man's goin' to lose his daughter.

All I want to make me happy,
Two little boys to call me pappy.

Black dog, white dog, little black nigger,
Good-by, boys, goin' to see the widow.

* May be repeated and prolonged indefinitely.

Goin' back home with a pocketful o' money,
Somebody there to call me honey.

If I stop and stumble in the water,
Some old man's goin' to lose his daughter.

Who's been here since I been gone?
Pretty little girl with a josey on.

Up dat oak and down dat ribber,
Two overseers and one little nigger.

Den we'll go to de Indian Nation,
A pretty little wife and a big plantation.

LOUISIANA GIRLS

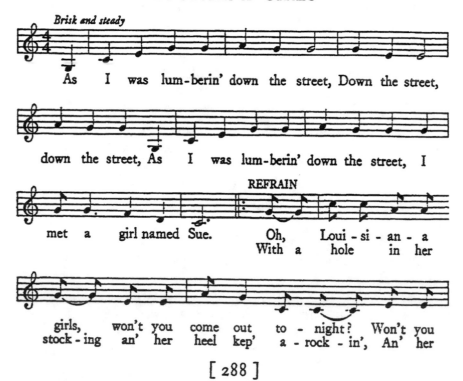

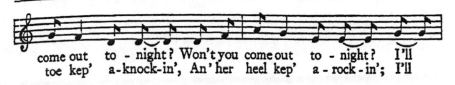

come out   to - night? Won't you come out   to - night?   I'll
toe kep'   a-knock-in', An' her   heel kep'   a - rock - in';   I'll

give you half   a   dol - lar   if you'll come out   to - night
dance   with   a   girl   with   a   hole   in   her stock - in',

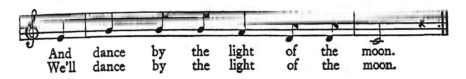

And   dance   by   the   light   of   the   moon.
We'll   dance   by   the   light   of   the   moon.

Chorus:

    O Louisiana girls, won't you come out tonight?
        Won't you come out tonight?
        Won't you come out tonight?
    I'll give you half a dollar if you'll come out tonight
        And dance by the light of the moon.
    With a hole in her stockin' an' her heel kep' a-rockin',
        An' her toe kep' a-knockin',
        An' her heel kep' a-rockin',
    I'll dance with a girl with a hole in her stockin',
        We'll dance by the light of the moon.

As I was lumberin' down the street,
    Down the street, down the street,
As I was lumberin' down the street
    I met a girl named Sue.

This handsome girl I chanced to meet,
    Chanced to meet, chanced to meet,
This handsome girl I chanced to meet,—
    Oh, she was fair to view.

I axed her would she have some talk,
  Have some talk, have some talk,
I axed her would she have some talk,
  And take a walk with me.

Her feet covered up the whole sidewalk,
  The whole sidewalk, the whole sidewalk,
Her feet covered up the whole sidewalk,
  As she stood close by me.

I axed her would she have a dance,
  Have a dance, have a dance;
I axed her would she have a dance—
  We both could make a stir.

I thought that I might get a chance,
  Get a chance, get a chance,
I thought that I might get a chance
  To shake a foot with her.

I'd like to make that girl my wife,
  Girl my wife, girl my wife,
I'd like to make that girl my wife
  To be happy all her life. (*Chorus.*)

WEEVILY WHEAT

In Appreciation of Miss Kate Thompson, Albany, New York

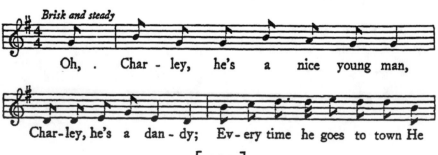

Oh, . Char-ley, he's a nice young man,
Char-ley, he's a dan-dy; Ev-ery time he goes to town He

brings them girls some can - dy.   Oh, I won't have none of your

wee - vi - ly wheat, I   won't have none of your bar - ley;   It'll

take some flour and a half an hour To bake a cake for Char-ley.

Oh, Charley he's a nice young man,
Charley he's a dandy;
Every time he goes to town
He brings them girls some candy.

Chorus:
Oh, I won't have none of your weevily wheat,
I won't have none of your barley,
It'll take some flour and a half an hour
To bake a cake for Charley.

Charley here and Charley there
And Charley over the ocean,
Charley he'll come back some day
If he doesn't change his notion.

Charley loves good wine and ale,
And Charley loves good brandy,
And Charley loves a pretty girl
As sweet as sugar candy. (*Chorus.*)

[291]

WEEVILY WHEAT (2)

Chorus:
> The higher up the cherry tree
> The riper grows the berry;
> The more you hug and kiss the girls
> The sooner they will marry.

Over the hill to feed my sheep
And over the river to Charley;
Over the river to feed my sheep
On buckwheat cake and barley.

How old are you, my pretty little Miss?
How old are you, my honey?
She answered me with a "Ha, ha" laugh,
"I'll be sixteen next Sunday."

Where do you live, my pretty little Miss?
Where do you live, my honey?
She answered me with a sweet to be,
"In the loom house with my mammy."

Run along, my pretty little Miss,
Run along home, my honey,
Run along home, my pretty little Miss,
I'll be right there next Sunday.

Papa's gone to New York town,
Mamma's gone to Dover,
Sister's wore her slippers out
A-kicking Charley over.

Take her by the lily-white hand,
And lead her like a pigeon;
Make her dance the Weevily Wheat
Till she loses her religion.

Come, my love, and trip with me,
'Tis Monday morning early;
First my hand and then my heart—
'Tis true I love you dearly.

Charley he is pretty and sweet,
Charley he's a dandy;
Charley he can kiss the girls
So complete and handy.

Over the water and over the lea,
And over the water to Charley.
Charley loves good wine and ale
And Charley loves apple brandy.

I have got a sweet little wife,
A wife of my own choosing;
Hug her neat and kiss her sweet
And go no more a-courting.

WAY OVER IN THE BLOOMING GARDEN

This game song, probably of English origin, is popular among the Negro school children of Texas. A teacher at Prairie View furnished words and music.

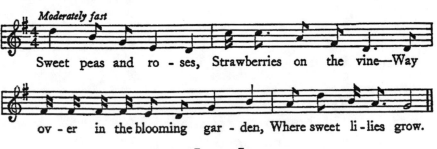

Sweet peas and ro - ses, Strawberries on the vine—Way ov - er in the blooming gar - den, Where sweet li - lies grow.

Sweet peas and roses, strawberries on the vine—
Way over in the blooming garden, where sweet lilies grow.

Choose you a partner, and choose him to your side,
Way over in the blooming garden, where sweet lilies grow.

Hug him so neatly and kiss him so sweetly,
Way over in the blooming garden, where sweet lilies grow.

Dere are sweet pinks an' roses, strawberries on de vine;
Rise up an' choose de one dat's suitable to yo' min'.

SKIP TO MY LOU

A Play Party Song

Lost my part-ner, skip to my Lou, Lost my part-ner, skip to my Lou, Lost my part-ner, skip to my Lou, Skip to my Lou, my dar-ling.

Chorus:
Lost my partner, skip to my Lou,
Lost my partner, skip to my Lou,
Lost my partner, skip to my Lou,
Skip to my Lou, my darling.

[294]

I'll get another one, purtier'n you,
I'll get another one, purtier'n you,
I'll get another one, purtier'n you,
Skip to my Lou, my darling.

Can't get a blue bird, jay bird'll do, etc.

Little red wagon, painted blue, etc.

Fly in the sugar bowl, shoo fly, shoo, etc.

The old gray mare has lost her shoe, etc.

Pretty brown eyes are looking at you, etc.

One old boot and a run-down shoe, etc.

My old shoe is torn in two.

Hair in the butter dish four feet long.

Hair in the biscuit six feet through.

Cows in the corn-field, two by two.

Rats in the bread-tray, how they chew!

You stole my partner, what'll I do?

I'll get another one, quicker'n you.

If I had a pistol, I'd shoot you, too.

SHOOT THE BUFFALO *

A Play Party Song

And it's la - dies to the cen - ter And it's
Chorus: And we'll shoot the buf - fa - lo — We'll —

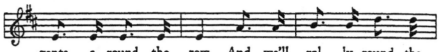

gents a - round the row, And we'll ral - ly round the
shoot the buf - fa - lo, We'll — ral - ly round the

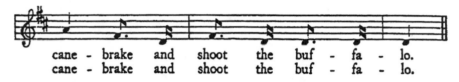

cane - brake and shoot the buf - fa - lo.
cane - brake and shoot the buf - fa - lo.

Rise you up, my dearest dear, present to me your hand,
I'll lead you in procession to a far and distant land.

Rise you up, my dearest dear, present to me your paw,
I'm sure you've got terbacker, I'd like to have a chaw.

Chorus:

And we'll shoot the buffalo, we'll shoot the buffalo,
We'll rally round the canebrake † and shoot the buffalo.

And it's ladies to the center and gents around the row,
And we'll rally round the canebrake and shoot the buffalo.

And we'll promenade, you know, and we'll promenade, you know,
And we'll all meet together and shoot the buffalo.

* A different musical setting in Sharp's *English Folk Songs from the Southern Appalachians*, Vol. II.
† "Cambric" is Appalachian Mountains. A good example of folk etymology.

The girls will sit and spin, the boys will sit and grin,
Rally round the barnyard and chase the old blue hen.

The girls will go to school, the boys will act the fool,
Rally round the barnyard and chase the old gray mule.

The girls will sew and patch, the boys will fight and scratch,
And we'll all meet together in the sweet potato patch.

Oh, the buffalo is dead, for I shot him in the head,
And we'll rally round the canebrake and shoot the buffalo.

Went down to low groun' to gather up my corn,
Raccoon set the dogs on me, possum blowed his ho'n.

Oh, the hawk shot the buzzard and the buzzard shot the crow,
And we'll rally round the canebrake and shoot the buffalo.

I'll buy my wife a horse and saddle she can ride,
And I'll buy me another one and ride by her side.

Went down to Raleigh, never been there befo',
White folks on the feather bed, niggers on the flo'.

GOING TO BOSTON

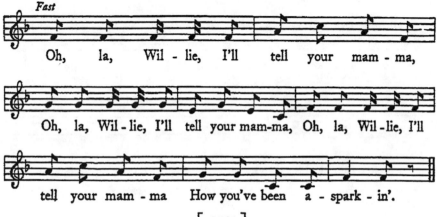

Oh, la, Wil-lie, I'll tell your mam-ma,
Oh, la, Wil-lie, I'll tell your mam-ma, Oh, la, Wil-lie, I'll
tell your mam-ma How you've been a-spark-in'.

[297]

Oh, la, Willie, I'll tell your mamma (three times)
How you've been a-sparking.

Fix up, girls, and let's go to Boston (three times)
To see this couple marry.

Saddle up, boys, and let's go with them (three times)
To see this couple marry.

Rocky road and we have to travel (three times)
To see this couple marry.

Court that girl an' then cain't git her (three times)
As we go up to Boston.

You'll swing your partner and then you'll git her,
Needle in the haystack.

SHOO, SHOO, SHOO–LYE *

Nebraska Version

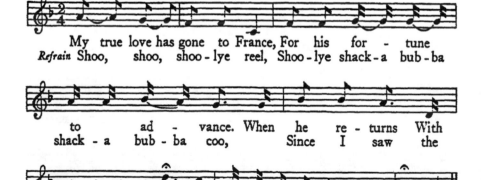

My true love has gone to France, For his for - tune
Refrain Shoo, shoo, shoo - lye reel, Shoo - lye shack - a bub - ba

to ad - vance. When he re - turns With
shack - a bub - ba coo, Since I saw the

him I'll dance, Ska - bib - ba la - la boo and a slo-o-ow reel.
sil - la bil - la hills, Ska - bib - ba la - la boo and a slo-o-ow reel.

* Words and music from John P. Hoover, San Mateo, California. Both versions are adapted to the tune printed below.

My true love has gone to France
For his fortune to advance.
When he returns, with him I'll dance,
    Ska-bibba-lala-boo and a slo-o-ow reel.

Chorus:

    Shoo, shoo, shoo-lye reel,
    Shoo-lye shacka-bubba shacka-bubba coo,
    Since I saw the silla-billa hills,
    Fikarl il doealala boo and a ala a ow ireal.

Colorado Version

I wish I were in Boston city,
Where all the girls they are so pretty;
If I didn't have a time 'twould be a pity,
    Dis cum pebble-and-a-boo so reel.

Chorus:

    Shoo, shoo, shoo-lye roo,
    Shoo-lye, shacka-lye, treat a barber cool;
    First time I saw a silla-billa eel,
        Dis cum pebble-and-a-boo so reel.

XIII

SONGS OF CHILDHOOD

When you wake you shall have
All the pretty little horses;
Blacks and bays, dapples and grays,
Coach and six-a little horses.

WHAT FOLKS ARE MADE OF

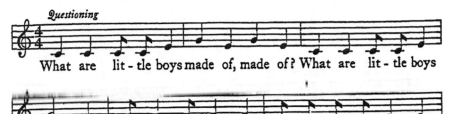

What are lit-tle boys made of, made of? What are lit-tle boys

made of? Pig-gins and pails and lit-tle pup-py tails,

That's what lit-tle boys are made of.

What are little boys made of, made of?
What are little boys made of?
Piggins and pails and little puppy tails,
That's what little boys are made of.

What are little girls made of? etc.
Sugar and spice and all things nice
And that's what little girls made of.

What's young men made of? etc.
Thorns and briars, they're all bad liars,
And that's what young men made of.

What's young women made of? etc.
Rings and jings and all fine things,
And that's what young women made of.

What's old men made of? etc.
Whisky and brandy and sugar and candy,
And that's what old men made of.

[303]

What's old women made of? etc.
Moans and groans in their old aching bones,
    And that's what old women made of.

What are little babies made of? etc.
Sugar and crumbs and all sweet things,
    And that's what little babies made of.

ALL THE PRETTY LITTLE HORSES

Dorothy Scarborough in her book, *On the Trail of Negro Folk-Songs*, says that this is one of the lullabies that the Negro mammies sang to their little white charges.

As a lullaby

Hush - a - by, Don't you cry, Go to sleep - y, lit - tle ba - by. When you wake, You shall have All the pret - ty lit - tle hors - es—Blacks and bays, Dapples and grays, Coach and six - a lit - tle hors - es. Hush - a - by, Don't you cry, Go to sleep - y, lit - tle ba - by.

Hushaby,
Don't you cry,

Go to sleepy, little baby.
When you wake,
You shall have
All the pretty little horses—
Blacks and bays,
Dapples and grays,
Coach and six-a little horses.
Hushaby,
Don't you cry,
Go to sleepy, little baby.

Hushaby,
Don't you cry,
Go to sleepy, little baby.
Way down yonder
In de medder
There's a po' lil lambie,
De bees an' de butterflies
Peckin' out its eyes,
De po' lil thing cried, "Mammy!"
Hushaby,
Don't you cry,
Go to sleepy, little baby.

THE OLD GRAY GOOSE

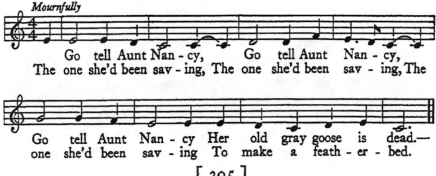

Go tell Aunt Nan-cy, Go tell Aunt Nan-cy,
The one she'd been sav-ing, The one she'd been sav-ing, The

Go tell Aunt Nan-cy Her old gray goose is dead.—
one she'd been sav-ing To make a feath-er-bed.

Go tell Aunt Nancy,
Go tell Aunt Nancy,
Go tell Aunt Nancy,
Her old gray goose is dead.

The one she'd been saving, (three times)
To make a feather bed.

She died last Friday, (three times)
With a pain in the back of her head.

Old gander's weeping, (three times)
Because his wife is dead.

The goslings are mourning, (three times)
Because their mother's dead.

LONG TIME AGO

Dedicated to Hugh Waters, Washington, D. C.

Once there was a lit-tle kit-ty, White as the snow.

She went out to hunt a mou-sie, Long time a-go.

Once there was a little kitty,
    White as the snow.
She went out to hunt a mousie,
    Long time ago.

Two black eyes had little kittie,
    Black as a crow,

[306]

And she spied a little mousie,
Long time ago.

Four soft paws had little kitty,
Soft as the snow,
And they caught the little mousie,
Long time ago.

Nine pearl teeth had little kitty,
All in a row,
And they bit the little mousie,
Long time ago.

When the kitty bit the mousie
Mousie cried out, "Oh!"
But she got away from kitty,
Long time ago.

THREE PIGS *

There was an old sow, she lived in a sty, And
three lit - tle pig - gies had she. She waddled a-round say - ing,

"Onk, Onk, Onk," While the lit - tle ones said, "Wee, Wee!"

There was an old sow, she lived in a sty,
And three little piggies had she.
She waddled around saying, "Onk, onk, onk,"
While the little ones said, "Wee wee!"

* As sung by Shirley Lomax Mansell and Bess Brown Lomax.

[307]

"My dear little brothers," said one of the brats,
"My dear little piggies," said he,
"Let us all in the future say, 'Onk, onk, onk.'
It's so childish to say, 'Wee wee!'"

Now these little piggies grew skinny and lean;
And lean they might very well be,
For somehow they couldn't say, "Onk, onk, onk,"
And they wouldn't say, "Wee wee, wee!"

Now these little piggies they up and died,
They died of the *Fee-lo-dee-zee*
From trying too hard to say "Onk, onk, onk!"
When they only should say, "Wee wee!"

A moral there is to this little tale,
A moral that's easy to see:
She waddled around saying, "Onk, onk, onk,"
For you only should say, "Wee-wee!"

TALE OF A LITTLE PIG *

There was an old wo-man and she had a lit-tle pig,
Oink - oink - oink, There was an old wo-man and she

* Words and tune from Shirley Lomax Mansell and Bess Brown Lomax.

had   a   lit - tle   pig,   Did - n't   cost   much   and   it

was - n't   ve - ry   big,   Oink - oink - oink.

There was an old woman and she had a little pig,
Oink-oink-oink,
There was an old woman and she had a little pig,
Didn't cost much and it wasn't very big,
Oink-oink-oink.

The little pig did a heap of harm,
Oink-oink-oink,
The little pig did a heap of harm,
A-rooting around that old man's farm,
Oink-oink-oink.

The little pig died for want of breath,
Oink-oink-oink,
The little pig died for want of breath.
Wasn't that an awful death!
Oink-oink-oink.

The little old woman, she sobbed and she sighed,
Oink-oink-oink,
The little old woman, she sobbed and she sighed,
Then she lay right down and died,
Oink-oink-oink.

The old man died for want of grief,
Oink-oink-oink,

The old man died for want of grief,
Wasn't that a great relief!
Oink-oink-oink.

There they lay all one, two, three,
Oink-oink-oink,
There they lay all one, two, three,
The man and the woman and the little piggee,
Oink-oink-oink.

There they laid all on a shelf,
Oink-oink-oink,
There they laid all on a shelf,
If you want any more, you can sing it yourself,
Oink-oink-oink.
Man and the woman, piggee!

FROG WENT A-COURTIN'

Moderately fast

Frog went a-court-in' an' he did ride, Unh-hunh,
Unh-hunh; Frog went a-court-in' an' he did ride,
Sword and pis-tol by his side, Unh-hunh, Unh-hunh.

Frog went a-courtin' and he did ride, unh-hunh,
Frog went a-courtin' and he did ride, unh-hunh,
Sword and pistol by his side, unh-hunh, unh-hunh,

Rode till he came to Miss Mousie's door, unh-hunh,
Rode till he came to Miss Mousie's door,
He gave three raps and a very loud roar, unh-hunh, unh-hunh.

He said, "Miss Mouse, are you within?" etc.
"Yes, I just sat down to spin."

He went right in and took her on his knee,
And he said, "Miss Mouse, will you marry me?"

Miss Mouse, she said, "I can't answer that
Until I see my Uncle Rat,

"Uncle Rat's in London Town,
And I don't know when he'll be down.

"Without my Uncle Rat's consent,
I wouldn't marry the President."

Uncle Rat came riding home;
"Who's been here since I've been gone?"

"A very worthy gentleman,
He said he'd marry me if he can."

When Uncle Rat gave his consent,
The weasel wrote the publishment.

"Where shall the wedding supper be?"
"Out in the woods in an old hollow tree."

"Who shall the wedding guests be?"
"A little lady bug and a bumblebee."

Mister Frog was dressed in a pea green,
Mistress Mouse she looked like a queen.

[311]

First that came was a little lady bug,
And she had whisky in her jug.

Next that came was a bumblebee
Dancing a jig with a two-legged flea.

"What shall the wedding supper be?"
"Two blue beans and a black-eyed pea."

First came in a little moth
For to lay the tablecloth.

Solemnly walked the Parson Rook,
Under his arm a very large book.

The owl did hoot, the birds, they sang,
And through the woods the music rang.

Next came in was a little red ant,
She always says, "I can't, I can't."

Next came in was a bumblebee,
She stung little Dickey on his knee.

Next came in was Doctor Fly,
He said that little Dick must die.

First came in was a little brown bug,
He drowned himself in the 'lasses jug.

Second came in was a little fly,
He ate so much he almost died.

Last came in was a little brown snake,
He coiled himself on the wedding cake.

The next came in was Mister Tick,
He ate so much till it made him sick.

The first came in was an old brown cow,
Tried to dance and didn't know how.

The next came in was an old gray mare,
Hip stuck out and shoulder bare.

The next came in was a little black dog,
Chased Miss Mousie in a hollow log.

The next came in was an old tomcat,
Swallowed Miss Mouse as slick as a rat.

Mr. Frog he went down to the lake,
And there he was swallowed by a big black snake.

Big black snake he swam to land,
And was killed by a Negro man.

Negro man he went to France,
And that's the end of my romance.

So here's the end of one, two, three,
The snake, the frog, and Miss Mousie.

There's bread and cheese upon the shelf,
If you want any, just help yourself.

CROWS IN THE GARDEN *

Crows in the gar - den pull - ing up corn,

Crows in the gar - den pull-ing up corn, Catch 'em, catch 'em,

string 'em up and stretch 'em. Plague up - on the whole con -

sarn. Gardener a - sleep in the shade of the barn,

Gardener a - sleep in the shade of the barn,

Wake him, wake him, tick - le him and shake him,

Eve - ry - thing will go to rack sure's you're born. Then

list - en to the mer - ry, mer - ry caw, caw, caw, For they've

* As sung by Shirley Lomax Mansell and Bess Brown Lomax.

gone a-way with a well filled craw; Then
list-en to the mer-ry, mer-ry caw, caw, caw, For they've
gone with a well filled craw-aw. This bus-y, bus-y
world is full of crows, Mo-ney is the corn and
sure to grow. Once they catch you nap-ping and a-
way it goes With a mer-ry, mer-ry haw, haw, haw.

Crows in the garden, pulling up corn,
Crows in the garden, pulling up corn,
Catch 'em, catch 'em, string 'em up and stretch 'em.
Plague upon the whole consarn.
Gardener asleep in the shade of the barn,
Gardener asleep in the shade of the barn,
Wake him, wake him, tickle him and shake him,
Everything will go to rack sure's you're born.
Then listen to the merry, merry caw, caw, caw,
For they've gone away with a well filled craw;

[315]

Then listen to the merry, merry caw, caw, caw,
For they've gone away with a well filled craw.

Chorus:
   This busy, busy world is full of crows,
   Money is the corn and sure to grow.
   Once they catch you napping and away it goes
   With a merry, merry haw, haw, haw.

Cattle of your neighbors break down your fence,
Cattle of your neighbors break down your fence.
Whale 'em, whale 'em, take a stick and frail 'em,
Send your neighbor word he must put 'em up in pens.
Lawyer come along, chock full of sense,
Lawyer come along, chock full of sense.
"Sue 'em, sue 'em, slap it to 'em, screw 'em,
Only get the evidence."
Then hark to him prate about the law, law, law,
Your neighbor's case not worth a straw,
But never, never let that law, law, law
Once get you in its claw-aw.

You must have a pretty watch and rings of gold,
You must have a pretty watch and rings of gold.
Some come hoaxing, some come coaxing
For the pretty chink you hold.
The weary, weary heart at length grows cold,
The weary, weary heart at length grows cold,
So much hurry, so much hurry
For the little chink you hold.
Then gentle music may your mind withdraw
From the toil and care of trade and law;
Then oh, how soothing is the fa, fa, fa
And the do, re, mi, sol, la-ah!

THE CONNECTICUT PEDDLER *

1

I'm a peddler, I'm a peddler,
I'm a peddler from Connecticut,
I'm a peddler, I'm a peddler,
And don't you want to buy?

2

Many goods have I in store,
So listen while I name them o'er,
So many goods you never saw before,
So very many goods you never saw before,
So listen while I name them o'er.

3

Here are pins,
Papers and needles and pins,
Tracts upon popular sins,
Any of which I will sell you.

4

And here are the seeds of asparagus,
Lettuce, beets, onions, and peppergrass
From the Limited Society,
Seeds of all kinds and variety,
Da, da, da, tiddle-dum, tiddle-dum,
Rum, tum tiddle-dum, tiddle-dee,
Rinktum, te-tiddle-dee, rinktum te-tiddle-dee, (*Repeat*)
Tiddle-dum, tiddle-dum, faddle whee.

* The music, words, and notes for this song were sent by Shirley Lomax Mansell and Bess Brown Lomax.

I'm a ped - dler, I'm a ped - dler, I'm a

ped - dler from Con - nect - i - cut, I'm a

ped - dler, I'm a ped - dler, And don't you want to buy?

Ma - ny goods have I in store, So lis - ten while I

name them o'er, So ma - ny goods you nev - er saw be -

fore, So ver - y ma - ny goods you nev - er saw be -

fore, So lis - ten while I name them o'er. Here are

pins, Pa - pers and need - les and pins, Tracts up - on pop - u - lar

sins,   An - y   of which I   will   sell   you. — And here
                                                                Da, da,

are   the   seeds   of   as - par - a - gus,   Let -
da,   tid - dle - dum,   tid - dle - dum,   Rum, tum,

tuce, beets,   on - ions   and   pep - per - grass   From
tid - dle - dum,   tid - dle - dee,   Rum, tum,   tid -

the   Lim - it - ed   So - ci - e - ty,
dle - dum   tid - dle - dee,   Rink - tum te tid - dle -

_D.C._

Seeds   of   all   kinds   and   va - ri - e - ty.
dee,   tid - dle - dum   tid - dle-dee   fad - dle   whee.

5

I'm a peddler, I'm a peddler,
I'm a peddler from Connecticut,
I'm a peddler, I'm a peddler,
Don't you want to buy?

1. This is probably the cry of the peddler as he comes up the road, to make the housewives notice his approach.

2. The second verse is to be sung all in one breath as steadily as possible, every note receiving the same amount of time. There are no pauses at all. The wily advertiser allows no one to get a word in edgewise.

4. The fourth verse is to be sung all in one breath, with the only pause after "variety." Take another breath for the "tiddle-dums," then make a long pause at the end of the stanza as an imaginary purchase goes on.

5. Repeat the first verse softly as the peddler passes from hearing.

BILLY BOY

Where have you been, Billy Boy, Billy Boy?
Where have you been, charming Billy?
I've been down the lane to see Miss Betsy Jane,
She's a young thing and cannot leave her mammy!

Where does she live, Billy Boy, Billy Boy?
Where does she live, charming Billy?
She lives on the hill, forty miles from the mill,
She's a young thing and cannot leave her mammy!

Did she ask you in, Billy Boy, Billy Boy?
Did she ask you in, charming Billy?
Yes, she asked me in with a dimple in her chin,
She's a young thing and cannot leave her mammy!

Did she take your hat, etc.?
Yes, she took my hat and she threw it at the cat, etc.

Did she set you a chair, etc.?
Yes, she set me a chair, but the bottom wasn't there, etc.

How old is she, etc.?
She's twice six, twice seven, three times twenty and eleven, etc.

How tall is she, etc.?
She's tall as a pine and straight as a vine, etc.

Can she fry a dish of meat, etc.?
Yes, she can fry a dish of meat as fast as you can eat, etc.

Can she make a loaf of bread, etc.?
She can make a loaf of bread with her nightcap on her head, etc.

Can she bake a cherry pie, etc.?
She can bake a cherry pie, in the twinkling of an eye, etc.

Can she bake a punkin well, etc.?
She can bake a punkin well, you can tell it by its smell, etc.

[321]

Can she sew and can she fell, etc.?
She can sew and she can fell, she can use her needle well, etc.

Can she make a pair of breeches, etc.?
She can make a pair of breeches fast as you can count the stitches, etc.

Can she make a feather bed, etc.?
She can make a feather bed that will rise above your head, etc.

Can she milk a muley cow, etc.?
She can milk a muley cow if her mammy shows her how, etc.

Is she fitted for your wife, etc.?
She's fitted for my wife as my pocket for my knife, etc.

Did she sit close to you, etc.?
Yes, she sat as close to me as the bark upon a tree, etc.

Did you ask her to wed, etc.?
Yes, I asked her to wed, and this is what she said, etc.

Can she milk a heifer calf, etc.?
Yes, and not miss the bucket more than half, etc.

Can she feed a sucking pig, etc.?
Yes, as fast as you can jig, etc.

Can she pull the sheet away, etc.?
No, that's a game my wife can't play, etc.

Are her eyes dark brown, etc.?
Yes, she was raised out of town, etc.

Is she very, very fair, etc.?
Oh, yes, she's fair, just touch her if you dare, etc.

PAPER OF PINS

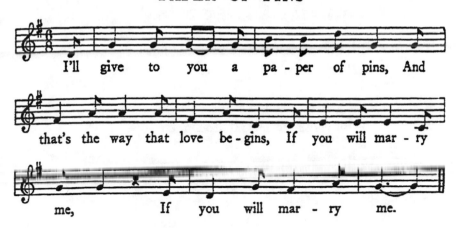

I'll give to you a paper of pins,
And that's the way that love begins,
    If you will marry me,
    If you will marry me.

I'll not accept a paper of pins,
If that's the way that love begins,
    And I won't marry you,
    And I won't marry you.

I'll give to you a coach and four,
That you may ride from door to door, etc.

I'll give to you a little lap dog,
To carry with you when you go abroad, etc.

I'll give to you a pacing horse,
That paced these hills from cross to cross, etc.

I'll give to you a coach and six
With every horse as black as pitch, etc.

I'll give to you a gown of green,
That you may shine as any queen, etc.

I'll give to you a dress of red,
All bound around with golden thread, etc.

I'll give to you a blue silk gown,
With golden tassels all around, etc.

I'll give to you my hand and heart,
That we may marry and never part, etc.

I'll give to you the keys of my chest,
That you may have gold at your request,
   If you will marry me,
   If you will marry me.

Oh, yes, I'll accept the key to your chest,
That I may have gold at my request,
   And I will marry you,
   And I will marry you.

And now I see that money is all,
And woman's love is nothing at all;
   So I'll not marry you,
   So I'll not marry you.

I'm determined to be an old maid,
Take my stool and live in the shade,
   And marry no one at all,
   And marry no one at all.

HARDLY THINK I WILL

To be sung with spirit; cheerfully.

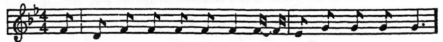

I'll tell you of a fel-low, Of a fel-low I have seen,
His name is not so scrumptious, In fact it's com-mon Bill,

He's nei-ther white nor yel-low, He's al-to-ge-ther green.
He wishes me to mar-ry him, But I hard-ly think I will.

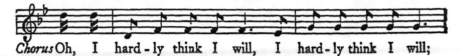

Chorus Oh, I hard-ly think I will, I hard-ly think I will;

He wish-es me to mar-ry him, But I hard-ly think I will.

I'll tell you of a fellow,
Of a fellow I have seen,
He's neither white nor yellow,
He's altogether green.
His name is not so scrumptious,
In fact it's common Bill.
He wishes me to marry him
But I hardly think I will.

Chorus:

Oh, I hardly think I will,
I hardly think I will;
He wishes me to marry him
But I hardly think I will.

[325]

He came one night to see me
And stayed so awfully late
I really thought the blockhead
Would never leave the gate.
He talked about the weather,
And tried so hard to please,
But when he saw he couldn't
He got down on his knees;
He begged and pleaded with me
Till his eyes began to fill,
He wishes me to marry him
But I hardly think I will. (*Chorus.*)

He said that if I'd marry him
He'd give me every limit,
But if I did not marry him
He'd die this very minute.
Now in the Holy Bible
It says, "Thou shalt not kill."
I thought the matter over,
And I guess I'll marry Bill.

Chorus:
> Oh, I guess I'll marry Bill,
> I guess I'll marry Bill;
> I thought the matter over,
> And I guess I'll marry Bill.

I LOVE LITTLE WILLIE*

I love little Willie, I do, Mama,
I love little Willie, tra, la, la, la, la.
I love little Willie, but don't tell Pa,
For he mightn't like it, Mama, Mama.

He told me he loved me, he did, Mama,
He told me he loved me, tra, la, la, la, la.
He told me he loved me, but don't tell Pa,
For he mightn't like it, Mama, Mama.

And now we are married, Mama, Mama,
And now we are married, tra, la, la, la, la,
And now we are married, now you can tell Pa,
For he's got to like it, Mama, Mama.

* Music and words from Bess Brown Lomax.

XIV

MISCELLANY

"Piggins and pails and little puppy tails."
"Rings and jings and all fine things."

THE FACTORY GIRL

Plaintively

No more shall I work in the fac - tory To

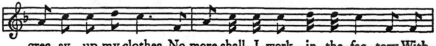

grea-sy up my clothes, No more shall I work in the fac-tory With

REFRAIN

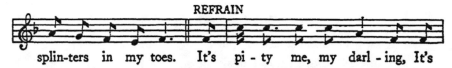

splin-ters in my toes. It's pi - ty me, my darl - ing, It's

pi - ty me, I say, It's pi - ty me,

my darl - ing, And car - ry me a - way.

Chorus:

It's pity me, my darling,
It's pity me, I say.
It's pity me, my darling,
And carry me away.

No more shall I work in the factory
To greasy up my clothes,

[331]

No more shall I work in the factory
With splinters in my toes.

It's pity me, my darling,
It's pity me, I say.
It's pity me, my darling,
And carry me away.

No more shall I hear the bosses say,
"Boys, you'd better daulf,"
No more shall I hear those bosses say,
"Spinners, you had better clean off."

No more shall I hear the drummer wheels
A-rolling over my head;
When factory girls are hard at work,
I'll be in my bed.

No more shall I hear the whistle blow
To call me up so soon;
No more shall I hear the whistle blow
To call me from my home.

No more shall I see the super come,
All dressed up so fine;
For I know I'll marry a country boy
Before the year is round.

No more shall I wear the old black dress,
Greasy all around;
No more shall I wear the old black bonnet,
With holes all in the crown.

HARD TIMES

Come listen awhile, and I'll sing you a song
Concerning the times (it will not be long)

When everybody is striving to buy,
And cheating each other, I cannot tell why—
And it's hard, hard times.

From father to mother, from sister to brother,
From cousin to cousin, they're cheating each other.
Since cheating has grown to be so much the fashion,
I believe to my soul it will run the whole nation—
And it's hard, hard times.

Now there is the talker, by talking he eats,
And so does the butcher by killing his meats.
He'll toss the steelyards, and weigh it right down,
And swear it's just right if it lacks forty pound—
And it's hard, hard times.

And there is the merchant, so honest, we're told.
Whatever he sells you, my friend, you are sold.
Believe what I tell you, and don't be surprised
To find yourself cheated half out of your eyes—
And it's hard, hard times.

And there is the lawyer, you plainly will see,
He will plead your case for a very large fee,
He'll law you and tell you the wrong side is right,
And make you believe that a black horse is white—
And it's hard, hard times.

And there is the doctor, I like to forgot,
I believe to my soul he's the worst of the lot.
He'll tell you he'll cure you for half you possess,
And when you're buried he'll take all the rest—
And it's hard, hard times.

And there's the old bachelor, all hated with scorn,
He's like an old garment all tattered and torn.
The girls and the widows all toss him a sigh,

And think it quite right, and so do I—
And it's hard, hard times.

And there's a young widow, coquettish and shy,
With a smile on her lips and a tear in her eye;
But when she gets married she'll cut quite a dash,
She'll give him the reins and she'll handle the cash—
And it's hard, hard times.

And there's the young lady I like to have missed,
And I believe to my soul she'd like to be kissed.
She'll tell you she loves you with all pretense
And ask you to call again some time hence—
And it's hard, hard times.

ON MEESH-E-GAN *

Frainch-man he don't lak to die in de fall,

When de mairsh she am so full of de game

An' de lee-tle bool-frog he's roll ver-ra fat

An' de lee-tle moosh-rat he's jus' de same.

* From Professor E. C. Beck, Central State Teachers College, Mount Pleasant, Michigan, as taken down from the singing of Newell B. Parsons, La Grange, Illinois.

Frainchman he don't lak to die in de fall,
    When de mairsh she am so full of de game
An' de leetle boolfrog he's roll verra fat
    An' de leetle mooshrat he's jus' de same.

Come, all you great beeg Canada man
    Who want fin' work on Meesh-e-gan,
Dere's beeg log drive all troo our lan',
    You sure fin' work on Meesh-e-gan.

When you come drive de beeg saw log,
    You have to jump jus' lak de frog.
De foreman come, he say go sak,
    You got in de watair all over your back.

P'rhaps you work on drive tree-four day,
    You fin' dat drive dat she don' pay,
You go to Sag-e-naw right away,
    Wait roun' tree-four day 'fore you get your pay.

Mebbe you stay in Sag-e-naw tree-four week,
    You get de ague, you feel damn seek,
One ounce quinine, two poun' cal-o-mel,
    You tak all dose 'fore you got well.

Now all you great beeg Canada man
    Who want fin' work on Meesh-e-gan,
Dere's great beeg snake all troo our lan',
    You sure get bit on Meesh-e-gan.

TEARIN' OUT–A WILDERNESS

A Cotton Chopping Song

De old gray hoss come tear-in' out-a wild-er-ness,

tear-in' out-a wild-er-ness, tear-in' out-a wild-er-ness. De

old gray hoss come tear-in' out-a wild-er-ness,

Down in A-la-bam'. *Refrain :*Hoe, boys, hoe! Hoe, boys, hoe!

> De old gray hoss come tearin' out-a wilderness,
> Tearin' out-a wilderness,
> Tearin' out-a wilderness,
> De old gray hoss come tearin' out-a wilderness,
> Down in Alabam'.

Chorus:

> Hoe, boys, hoe! Hoe, boys, hoe!
> Hoe, boys, hoe! Hoe, boys, hoe!

> A little black bull come down from de mountain,
> Down from de mountain,
> Down from de mountain,
> A little black bull come down from de mountain,
> Long time ago.

[336]

He stuck his horn through a white oak sapling,
     White oak sapling,
     White oak sapling,
He stuck his horn through a white oak sapling,
     Long time ago.

He threw dirt in de heifers' faces,
     Heifers' faces,
     Heifers' faces,
He threw dirt in de heifers' faces,
     Long time ago.

Twenty more black bull calves come that season,
     Come that season,
     Come that season,
Twenty more black bull calves come that season,
     Long time ago.

The words if not the tune of "The Old Gray Horse Came Tearin'
Out-a Wilderness" have been intermingled with a song mentioned in
Holman Day's *King Spruce* and referred to by Mrs. Fannie H. Eckstorm in her *Minstrelsy of Maine*: "The crazy prophet Eli has a
favorite song of which one stanza is given:

"Oh, the little brown bull came down from the mountain,
     Shang, ro-ango, whango-whey!
And as he was feeling salutatious
Chased old Pratt a mile, by gracious,
Licked old Shep and two dog Towsers,
Then marched back with old Pratt's trousers,
     Whang-whey."

Down in Texas my wife's father, who came from Virginia, sang to
a stirring note and for his children, repeating each couplet over and
over:

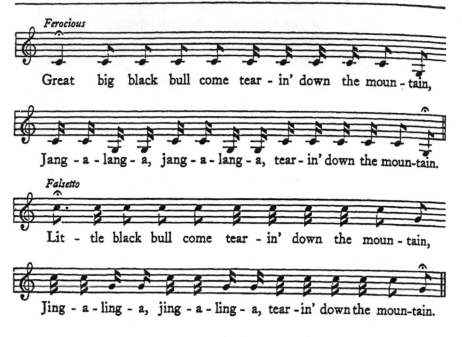

Ferocious

Great big black bull come tear - in' down the moun - tain,

Jang - a - lang - a, jang - a - lang - a, tear - in' down the moun-tain.

Falsetto

Lit - tle black bull come tear - in' down the moun - tain,

Jing - a - ling - a, jing - a - ling - a, tear - in' down the moun-tain.

"Great big, black bull came tearin' down the mountain,
Jang-a-lang-a, janga-lang-a, tearin' down the mountain.

"Little black bull came tearin' down the mountain,
Jing-a-ling-a, jing-a-ling-a, tearin' down the mountain, etc."

The "tearin'" of the big black bull was rendered in a deep bass voice, while the movements of the little bull were rendered in a high falsetto.

THE MAN ON THE FLYING TRAPEZE

This sentimental ballad of the nineteenth century, words and tune, comes from the memory of Mrs. Lowell Mellett of Washington, D. C., who recalls it as it was sung by her father and mother.

Oh, the girl that I loved she was handsome,
I tried all I knew her to please.
But I couldn't please her a quarter as well
As the man on the flying trapeze.

Chorus:
  Oh, he flies through the air with the greatest of ease,
  This daring young man on the flying trapeze.
  His figure is handsome, all girls he can please,
  And my love he purloined her away.

Last night as usual I went to her home.
There sat her old father and mother alone.
I asked for my love and they soon made it known
That she-e had flown away.

  Oh, he flies through the air, etc.

She packed up her box and eloped in the night,
To go-o with him at his ease.
He lowered her down from a four-story flight,
By means of his flying trapeze.

He took her to town and he dressed her in tights,
That he-e might live at his ease.
He ordered her up to the tent's awful height,
To appear on the flying trapeze.

Now she flies through the air with the greatest of ease,
This daring young girl on the flying trapeze.
Her figure is handsome, all men she can please,
And my love is purloinèd away.

Once I was happy, but now I'm forlorn,
Like an old coat that is tattered and torn,
Left to this wide world to fret and to mourn,
Betrayed by a maid in her teens.

YE BALLADE OF IVAN PETROFSKY SKEVAR*

The sons of the pro-phet are val-iant and bold, And are

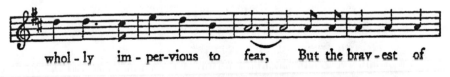

whol-ly im-per-vious to fear, But the brav-est of

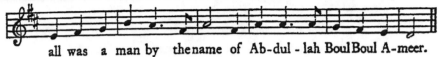

all was a man by the name of Ab-dul-lah Boul Boul A-meer.

The sons of the prophet are valiant and bold,
    And are wholly impervious to fear,
But the bravest of all was a man by the name
    Of Abdullah Boul Boul Ameer.

If you wanted a man to encourage the van,
    Or to harass the foe from the rear,
Or to storm a redoubt, you had only to shout
    For Abdullah Boul Boul Ameer.

This son of the desert in battle aroused
    Could spit twenty men on his spear,
A terrible creature, sober or soused,
    Was Abdullah Boul Boul Ameer.

There are brave men in plenty, and well known to fame,
    In the army that's run by the Czar,
But the bravest of all was a man by the name
    Of Ivan Petrofsky Skevar.

*Text furnished by Paul B. Camp and John W. Loveland, Jr.

He could imitate Irving, tell fortunes by cards,
    And play on the Spanish guitar.
In fact quite the cream of the Muscovite team
    Was Ivan Petrofsky Skevar.

The ladies all loved him, his rivals were few,
    He could drink them all under the bar.
As gallant or tank there was no one to rank
    With Ivan Petrofsky Skevar.

One day that bold Russian he shouldered his gun,
    And with his most cynical sneer
Was going down town, when he came right upon
    Brave Abdullah Boul Boul Ameer.

"Young man," said Boul Boul, "is existence so dull,
    That you hanker to end your career?
For, infidel, know, you have trod on the toe
    Of Abdullah Boul Boul Ameer.

"So take your last look upon sky, sea, brook,
    And send your regrets to the Czar,
For by this I imply that you're going to die,
    Oh, you Ivan Petrofsky Skevar."

"But your murderous threats are to me but a joke,
    For my pleasure and pastime is war,
And I'll tread on your toes whene'er I may choose,"
    Quoth Ivan Petrofsky Skevar.

Then that brave Mameluke drew his trusty chabook,
    Crying "Allah il Allah Akbar,"
And with murder intent, he ferociously went
    At Ivan Petrofsky Skevar.

But the Russian gave back not a step at th' attack,
    For Ivan had never known fear,
And with quickly aimed gun, put a stop to the fun,
    Of Abdullah Boul Boul Ameer.

Yet the whistling chabook did like lightning descend,
    And caught Ivan right over the ear.
But the bayonet of Ivan pressed right through the heart
    Of Abdullah Boul Boul Ameer.

The Russian commander spurred thither in haste,
    To seek for his favorite Hussar.
Lo, pierced through the snoot from the fatal chabook,
    Lay Ivan Petrofsky Skevar.

The Sultan rode up the disturbance to quell,
    Or to give to the victor a cheer,
But he arrived just in time to take hasty farewell
    Of Abdullah Boul Boul Ameer.

Then Gotchikoff, Skabeloff, Menchikoff too,
    Drove up in the Emperor's car,
But only in time to bid rapid adieu
    To Ivan Petrofsky Skevar.

There lieth a stone where the Danube doth roll,
    And on it in characters clear
Is, "Stranger, remember to pray for the soul
    Of Abdullah Boul Boul Ameer."

The Muscovite maiden her sad vigil keeps
    In her home by the cold Northern star,
And the name that she murmurs so oft in her sleep
    Is Ivan Petrofsky Skevar.

BEAUTIFUL

"During the years 1919–21," writes Joseph W. Clokey, Pomona College, California, "I was on the faculty of Western College for Women. The girls there sang this song incessantly and vociferously."

Ain't it fierce to be so beau - ti - ful, beau - ti - ful, So
Ain't it fierce to be so brain - y, brain - y, So

rar - in', tear - in' beau - ti - ful, beau - ti - ful!
rar - in', tear - in' brain - y, brain - y!

I ain't got no peace of mind, ——
I ain't got no peace of mind, The

Ev - 'ry - bod - y is so aw - full - y kind. Out -
profs they are so aw - full - y kind. Out -

side of my door they stand, stand,
side of their doors they stand, stand,

Wait - in' for my heart and hand, hand,
Wait - in' for to shake my hand, hand,

(Spoken in a high-pitched baby voice)

Al - most ev - 'ry sin - gle hour, Some one's sure to
Al - most ev - 'ry sin - gle day, Some one's sure to

send me flowers. Ain't it fierce to be so beau - ti - ful!
give me "A." Ain't it fierce to be so brain - y!

Ain't it fierce to be so beautiful, beautiful,
So rarin', tearin' beautiful, beautiful!
I ain't got no peace of mind,
Ev'rybody is so awfully kind.
Outside of my door they stand, stand,
Waitin' for my heart and hand, hand,
Almost ev'ry single hour,
Some one's sure to send me flowers.
Ain't it fierce to be so beautiful!

Ain't it fierce to be so brainy, brainy,
So rarin', tearin' brainy, brainy!
I ain't got no peace of mind,
The profs they are so awfully kind.
Outside of their doors they stand, stand,
Waitin' for to shake my hand, hand,
Almost ev'ry single day,
Some one's sure to give me "A."
Ain't it fierce to be so brainy!

THE HIGHLY EDUCATED MAN *

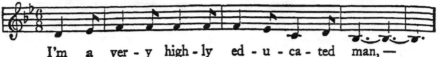

I'm a ver-y high-ly ed-u-ca-ted man,—

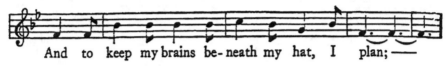

And to keep my brains be-neath my hat, I plan;—

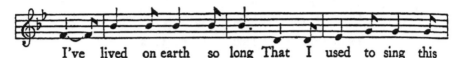

I've lived on earth so long That I used to sing this

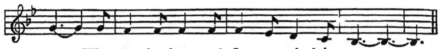

song When A-bra-ham and Is-aac rushed the can.—

I'm a very highly educated man—
And to keep my brains beneath my hat, I plan;
 I've lived on earth so long
 That I used to sing this song
When Abraham and Isaac rushed the can.

I was born about ten thousand years ago—
And there's hardly anything that I don't know;
 For I saw old Pharaoh's daughter,
 Picking Moses from the water—
I can lick the man who says it isn't so.

I was there when Gabriel searched the garden o'er,
I met Eve and Adam flying from the door.
 When the apple they were eating,
 I was round the corner peeping—
I can prove that I'm the man that ate the core.

* Text provided by Paul B. Camp and John W. Loveland, Jr.

[346]

I saw Cain and Abel playing in the glade,
And I'm sure that it was poker that they played;
    But here's the little rub,
    Did he hit him with a Club?
I'm sure it was a Diamond or a Spade.

I was there when Noah built his famous ark,
And I crawled in through a window after dark.
    I saw Jonah eat the whale,
    Daniel twist the lion's tail,
And I crossed the land of Canaan on a lark.

I saw Solomon and all his wives so fair,
I saw Absalom left hanging by the hair.
    And when I saved King David's life,
    And he offered me a wife,
I said, "Now you're talking business, have a chair."

I saw Pharaoh being pestered by the fleas,
I helped Brigham Young invent Limburger cheese,
    And when sailing down the bay
    With Methuselah one day
I saved his flowing whiskers in the breeze.

I was there when Alexander crossed the sea,
And I always cheered him on to victory—
    And when King Darius died,
    I was fighting by his side,
So he gave his horse and chariot to me.

Oh, I'm the man who built the Parthenon,
At which Euripides said, "Well, I swan!"
    And I used to serve pink teas,
    For my friend Praxiteles—
While Pilate served us from his demijohn.

Oh, I used to whittle toothpicks for King Saul,
And I clubbed the big Goliath with a maul.
    Though the son of Priam swore,
    And the Trojan host got sore,
I Bostoned with fair Helen on the wall.

I was there when John Baptist lost his head,
And I heard the very words Salome said;
    When they brought the bloody charger,
    Both his eyes were growing larger,
My gosh! A dance like that would raise the dead.

Oh, I sailed with Cleopatra on the Nile,
And thus she whispered to me with a smile:
    "Now, as for poor old Tony,
    I always thought him phony,
But I certainly am struck on *you* a pile."

I was present at the battle of the Nile,
And did the bullets fly, well I should smile.
    And when Pharaoh hit the King,
    With a cutlass on the wing,
I was lying at the bottom of the pile.

I was present when they sopped up Caesar's gore,
When the Senators went skating round the floor;
    It was I who swiped the crown,
    That he foolishly turned down,
And I hocked it with a Jew in Baltimore.

I was there when Cincinnatus left the plow,
And the Roman thus addressed me with a bow,
    "Now if *you* would only go,
    I would surely be de trop,
And could stay at home and milk my Jersey cow."

I saw Nero fiddling when he burned up Rome,
I told him it looked like his future home.
When he had the nerve to swear,
I dragged him from his chair,
And broke a Pilsner bottle on his dome.

I remember when the country had a king.
I saw Mrs. Harvard pawn her wedding ring.
I set the flags a-flying,
When George Washington quit lying.
I heard Patti when she first began to sing.

I sold spearheads in the Neolithic Age,
And I trained a Dinosaurus for the stage.
But when I made a fire,
And a wheel without a tire,
My cave received a lot of patronage.

Oh, I have trained some actresses most rare,
'Twas I showed Anna Held the way to wear
Those marvelous creations
That provoke the mirth of nations,
'Twas I taught Eva Tanguay not to care.

I saw Caesar stand upon the Senate floor,
And the Romans crowded round him three or four;
All at once he said, "You Brute,
You have struck me in the snoot!"
As he fell, he kicked a panel from the door.

I was present at the siege of La Rochelle,
When a cannon ball demolished our hotel;
And King Henry of Navarre,
When he felt the awful jar,
Said, "They certainly are raising merry hell!"

Oh, I made a face at Empress Josephine,
And regret to state the fact that I was seen;
    So I fought at break of day,
    With Napoleon, and say,
I shot him through the goozle with a bean.

I was present when King Alfred burned the cake,
And 'twas lucky, for 'twould make his stomach ache;
    And when Robert watched the spider,
    As he sat there drinking cider,
I convinced him Christian Science was a fake.

I was the bard of Avon's closest chum,
I could tell a story that would make things hum—
    For when Shakespeare wrote his plays,
    He was always in a daze,
From the influence of Spearmint chewing gum.

Queen Victoria was dead in love with me—
We were married in Milwaukee secretly—
    But soon I was up and shook her
    And was off with General Hooker,
Fighting skeeters down in sunny Tennessee.

DARKY SUNDAY SCHOOL*

Jo - nah was an im - mi-grant, so runs the Bi - ble tale, He took a steer - age pas - sage in a trans - at - lan - tic whale; Now Jo - nah in the bel - ly of the whale was quite com - pressed, So Jo - nah pressed the but - ton, and the whale he did the rest. —

Jonah was an immigrant, so runs the Bible tale,
He took a steerage passage in a transatlantic whale;
Now, Jonah in the belly of the whale was quite compressed,
So Jonah pressed the button, and the whale he did the rest.

Chorus:

Young folks, old folks, everybody come,
Join our darky Sunday School, and make yourself to hum,

* Text furnished by Paul B. Camp and John W. Loveland, Jr.

[351]

There's a place to check your chewing gum and razors at the
  door,
And hear such Bible stories as you never heard before.

Adam was the first man that ever was invented,
  He lived all his life and he never was contented;
He was made out of mud in the days gone by
  And hung on the fence in the sun to get him dry.

The good book says Cain killed his brother Abel,
  He hit him on the head with a leg of a table.
Then along came Jonah in the belly of the whale,
  The first submarine boat that ever did sail.

Esau was a cowboy of the wild and woolly make,
  Half the farm belonged to him and half to Brother Jake;
Now, Esau thought his title to the farm was none too clear,
  So he sold it to his brother for a sandwich and a beer.

Noah was a mariner who sailed around the sea,
  With half a dozen wives and a big menagerie;
He failed the first season when it rained for forty days,
  For in that sort of weather no circus ever pays.

Elijah was a prophet who attended country fairs,
  He advertised his business with a pair of dancing bears;
He held a sale of prophecies most every afternoon,
  And went up in the evening in a painted fire balloon.

Then down came Peter, the Keeper of the Gates,
  He came down cheap on excursion rates.
Then along came Noah a-stumblin' in the dark,
  He found a hatchet and some nails and built himself an ark.

[352]

David was a shepherd and a scrappy little cuss,
   Along came Goliath, just a-spoilin' for a muss;
Now, David didn't want to fight, but thought he must or bust,
   So he cotched up a cobblestone and busted in his crust.

Ahab had a wife, and her name was Jezebel;
   She went out in the vineyard to hang the clothes and fell.
She's gone to the dogs, the people told the king,
   Ahab said he'd never heard of such an awful thing.

Samson was a strong man of the John L. Sullivan school,
   He slew ten thousand Philistines with the jawbone of a mule.
But Delilah captured him and filled him full of gin,
   Slashed off his hair, and the coppers run him in.

Samson was a husky guy as every one should know,
   He used to lift five hundred pounds as strong man in his show.
One week the bill was rotten, all the actors had a souse,
   But the strong-man act of Samson's, it just brought down
         the house.

Salome was a chorus girl who had a winning way,
   She was the star attraction in King Herod's Cabaret.
Although you can hardly say discretion was her rule,
   She's the favorite Bible figure in the Gertrude Hoffman school.

There are plenty of these Bible tales. I'll tell you one tomorrow
   How Lot, his wife and family fled from Sodom and Gomorrah;
But his wife she turned to rubber and got stuck upon the spot,
   And became a salty monument and missed a happy Lot.

Now Joey was unhappy in the bowels of the soil,
   He lost his pretty rainbow coat because he wouldn't toil.
He hollered, howled, and bellowed until far into the night,
   But of course you couldn't see him, for he was out of sight.

[353]

It happened that a caravan was passing by the place,
Laden down with frankincense and imitation lace.
They heard the Sheeney yelling and pulled him from the well
If this ain't a proper ending, then you can go to Harvard.

THE OLD BACHELOR *

I am a stern old bachelor,
My age is forty-four;
I do declare I'll never live
With women any more.

Little sod shanty,
Sod shanty give to me,

* A song of the Middle West, from the collection of Professor E. F. Piper, University of Iowa.

[354]

For I'm a stern old bachelor
From matrimony free.

I live upon a homestead claim,
From women I am hid;
I do not have to dress a wife
Or take care of a kid.

I have a stove that's worth five cents,
A table worth fifteen;
I cook my meals in an oyster can,
And always keep it clean.

I go to bed whene'er I please,
And get up jest the same;
I change my socks three times a year
With no one to complain.

I go to church on Sunday morn
Without a wife to storm;
My latest paper not rolled up
To beautify her form.

And when I die and go to heaven
As all good bachelors do,
I will not have to fret for fear
My wife won't get there, too.

RATTLE SNAKE *

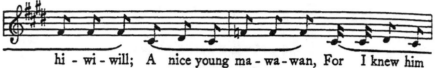

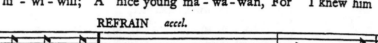

A nice young ma-wa-wan
Lived on a hi-wi-will;
A nice young ma-wa-wan,
For I knew him we-we-well.

Refrain:
     To my rattle, to my roo-rah-ree!

This nice young ma-wa-wan
Went out to mo-wo-wow
To see if he-we-we
Could make a sho-wo-wow.

He scarce had mo-wo-wowed
Half round the fie-we-wield
Till up jumped—come a rattle, come a sna-wa-wake,
And bit him on the he-we-weel.

* Words and tune from Dr. L. W. Payne, University of Texas. This song is usually printed under the title "Springfield Mountain." See Pound's *American Ballads and Songs*.

He laid right dow-wo-wown
Upon the gro-wo-wound
And shut his ey-wy-wyes
And looked all aro-wo-wound.

"O pappy da-wa-wad,
Go tell my ga-wa-wal,
That I'm a-goin' ter di-wi-wie,
For I know I sha-wa-wall.

"O pappy da-wa-wad,
Go spread the ne-wu-wus;
And here come Sa-wa-wall
Without her sho-woo-woos."

"O John, O Joh-wa-wahn,
Why did you go-wo-wo
Way down in the mead-we-we-dow
So far to mo-wo-mow?"

"O Sal, O Sa-wa-wal,
Why don't you kno-wo-wow
When the grass gets ri-wi-wipe,
It must be mo-wo-wowed?"

Come all young gir-wi-wirls
And shed a tea-we-wear
For this young ma-wa-wan
That died right he-we-were.

Come all young me-we-wen
And warning ta-wa-wake
And don't get bi-wi-wit
By a rattle sna-wa-wake.

[357]

XV
VAQUEROS OF THE SOUTHWEST

"Between the Nueces River and the Rio Grande . . . the brush country is still a cow country, and brush hands, mostly Mexicans, still 'kill up' their horses running wild cattle. . . . Here the mesquite is just one among many thorned growths, most of them known to the people of the region only by their Mexican names. They give the land a character as singular as that afforded to Corsica by the *maquis* or to Florida by the everglades. . . .

In running in this brush a vaquero rides not so much on the back of his horse as under and alongside. He just hangs on, dodging limbs as if he were dodging bullets, back, forward, over, under, half of the time trusting his horse to course right on this or that side of a bush or tree. If he shuts his eyes to dodge, he is lost. Whether he shuts tnem or no, he will, if he runs true to form, get his head rammed or raked. Patches of the brush hand's bandana hanging on thorns and stobs sometimes mark his trail. The bandana of red is his emblem. . . . Unseen and unapplauded, he has never been pictured on canvas or in print. An 'observer' might hear him breaking limbs; that is all. When he does his most daring and dangerous work, he is out of sight down in a thicket."

—J. FRANK DOBIE, *A Vaquero of the Brush Country*, Dallas, Texas, 1929.

ALLÁ EN EL RANCHO GRANDE *

Composer and Author Silvano R. Ramos

Moderately slow

A - llá en el rancho gran - de, a - llá don - de vi -
ví - a, ha - bía una ran - che - ri - ta, que a -
le - gre me de - cí - a: "Voy a ha - cer - te unos cal -
zo - nes, co - mo los que usa el ran - che - ro, Te, los co -
mien - zo de la - na y los a - ca - bo de cue - ro."

Allá en el rancho grande, allá donde vivía,
Había una rancherita, que alegre me decía:

"Voy a hacerte unos calzones
Como los que usa el ranchero.
Te los comienzo de lana
Y los acabo de cuero."

* *Publications of the Texas Folk-Lore Society.*

DOWN ON THE BIG RANCH

Down on the big ranch, down there where I lived,
There was a rancherita, who merrily said to me:
"I'm going to make you a pair of breeches
Like those that the ranchero wears.
I'll begin making them of wool
And I'll finish them in leather."

EL AMOR QUE TE TENÍA *

Publications of Texas Folk-Lore Society.

Vi - no un fuer - te re - mo - li - no, mi bien,

ra - ma y a - mor se lle - vó.

El amor que te tenía, mi bien,
En un ramo quedó.
El amor que te tenía, mi bien,
En un ramo quedó.
Vino un fuerte remolino, mi bien,
Rama y amor se llevó.
Vino un fuerte remolino, mi bien,
Rama y amor se llevó.

Mañana me voy pa' San Diego, mi bien,
A sembrar frijol y arroz.
Mañana me voy pa' San Diego, mi bien,
A sembrar frijol y arroz.
Y de allá te mando decir, mi bien,
Como se mancuernan dos.
Y de allá te mando decir, mi bien,
Como se mancuernan dos.

No me busques por vereda, mi bien,
Búscame de atravesía.
No me busques por vereda, mi bien,
Búscame de atravesía.
Y allá me hallaras cantando, mi bien,
Del amor que te tenía.
Y allá me hallaras cantando, mi bien,
Del amor que te tenía.

THE LOVE THAT I HAD

The love that I had for you, my dear,
Hanging from a branch remained.
The love that I had for you, my dear,
Hanging from a branch remained.
A strong whirlwind came along, my dear,
And branch and love took away.
A strong whirlwind came along, my dear,
And branch and love took away.

Tomorrow I'm going to San Diego, my dear,
To sow beans and rice.
Tomorrow I'm going to San Diego, my dear,
To sow beans and rice.
From there I'll write to you, my dear,
About how to couple two.
From there I'll write to you, my dear,
About how to couple two.

Do not look for me along the path, my dear,
Look for me along the short cut.
Do not look for me along the path, my dear,
Look for me along the short cut.
There you shall find me singing, my dear,
About the love I had for you.
There you shall find me singing, my dear,
About the love I had for you.

EL ABANDONADO (THE ABANDONED ONE)

"The love song is by far the most common of all Mexican folk-songs. During the trail driving days many of the cowboys who drove herds from Southern Texas to Kansas and beyond were Mexicans. I have often asked old trail drivers if the vaqueros had any such songs as the Texas cowboys had. Invariably the answer has been that the vaqueros sang little else but love songs." *

Me abandonastes, mujer, porque soy muy pobre
Y la desgracia es ser hombre apasionado.
Pues ¿qué he de hacer, si yo soy el abandonado?
Pues, qué he de hacer, será por el amor de Dios.

* Frank Dobie, in "Verses of the Texas Vaqueros" (*Publications of the Texas Folk-Lore Society*).

Tres vicios tengo, los tres tengo adoptados:
El ser borracho, jugador, y enamorado.
Pues ¿qué he de hacer, si soy el abandonado?
Pues, qué he de hacer, será por el amor de Dios.

Pero ando ingrato si con mi amor no quedo;
Tal vez otro hombre con su amor se habrá jugado.
Pues ¿qué he de hacer, si soy el abandonado?
Pues, qué he de hacer, será por el amor de Dios.

Translation

You abandon me, woman, because I am very poor; the misfortune is to be a man of passionate devotion. Then, what am I to do if I am the abandoned one? Well, whatever I am to do will be done by the will of God.

Three vices I have cultivated: gambling, drunkenness, and love. Then what am I to do if I am the abandoned one? Well, whatever I am to do will be done by the will of God.

But I go unhappy, if with my love I cannot remain. Perhaps another man has toyed with her love. Then what am I to do if I am the abandoned one? Well, whatever I am to do, will be done by the will of God.

CUATRO PALOMITAS BLANCAS *

Cua - tro   pa - lo - mi - tas blan - cas,   cua - tro

pa - lo - mi - tas blan - cas,   cua - tro   pa - lo -

* Publications of the Texas Folk-Lore Society.

mi - tas blan - cas, sen - ta - das en un al - e -
ro, sen - ta - das en un al - e - ro.

Cuatro palomitas blancas,
Cuatro palomitas blancas,
Cuatro palomitas blancas,
Sentadas en un alero,
Sentadas en un alero.

Unas a las otras dicen, (3)
"No hay amor como el primero." (2)

Me gusta el pan con queso, (3)
Cuando se vive en el rancho. (2)

Pero mas me gusta un beso, (3)
Debajo de un sombrero ancho. (2)

Translation

Four little white doves,
Four little white doves,
Four little white doves,
Perched on a gable end,
Perched on a gable end.

They say to each other, (3)
"There is no love like the first." (2)

[367]

I like bread with cheese, (3)
When I live on a ranch. (2)

But I like a kiss much better, (3)
Under a broad-brimmed sombrero. (2)

TRAGEDIA DE HERACLIO BERNAL

"The majority of the population of Mexico is today in the grip of a social system little, if materially at all, differing from that of the Middle Ages in Europe. . . . The peon wears shoes instead of sandals on feast-days, whereas his grandfather wore homemade brogans; but modernity has come no nearer home to him than this. His culture, aspirations, and life, those of the days of Robin Hood and the Cid . . . have served to produce there the 'tragedia,' a form of ballad which is purely medieval in atmosphere and inspiration. . . . The 'tragedia' is a product of the people themselves. It is rarely ever printed or even reduced to writing. Its verses are composed orally and are preserved in the memory of the . . . strolling guitar or harp players who are the counterpart of the medieval 'juglar.' . . . One of the most popular, and also one of the most typical of the bandit ballads is the extremely fragmentary one that follows. It celebrates the deeds of one Heraclio Bernal, a bandit who was active in Northwestern Mexico during the eighties and early nineties, and who was the cause of considerable embarrassment to the Mexican government before he was finally killed near Mazatlán. Every singer in Northwestern Mexico knows fragments of this ballad, though no one seems to possess it entire. . . . Bernal, in the mouth of the improviser of the ballads, takes on all the attributes of the popular hero of the Robin Hood type, robbing the rich to give to the poor, and defying tyrannical authority in a truly medieval fashion." *

* W. A. Whatley in the *Publications of the Texas Folk-Lore Society.*

A - ño de no - ven - ta y cuatro en la
ciu - dad de Ma - zat - lán por pri - me - ra
vez se can - ta la tra-ge - di - a de Ber - nal.

Translation

Año de noventa y cuatro
en la ciudad de Mazatlán
por primera vez se canta
la tragedia de Bernal.

In the year of ninety-four, in
the city of Mazatlán, this, the song
of Bernal, is sung for the first
time.

Heraclio Bernal decía
cuando iba para Saucillos
que en la bolsa traía platas
y en la cintura casquillos.

Heraclio Bernal, when he visited Saucillos, was wont to declare
that he carried silver in his pocket
and cartridges at his waist.

Refrain:
Vuela, vuela, palomita,
encarámate a aquel nopal:
di que diez mil pesos ofrecen
por la vida de Bernal.

Fly, little dove, and perch upon
yonder cactus; and proclaim that
ten thousand pesos are offered for
the head of Bernal.

Una familia en la sierra
ʹstaba muy arruinada;
y les dió quinientos pesos
para que se remediaran.

A family in the mountains was
in dire poverty; and he gave them
five hundred pesos to mend their
fortunes.

[369]

Heraclio Bernal decía
cuando encontraba a un arriero
que él no robaba pobres,
antes les daba dinero.

Heraclio Bernal would say,
when he met a muleteer, that he
did not rob the poor, but rather
gave them money.

En la sierra de Durango
mató a diez gachupines
y mandó curtir los cueros
para lucirlos en botines.

In the mountains of Durango
he killed ten Spaniards, and had
their skins tanned to make boots
withal.

Decía doña Bernardina
la querida de Bernal:
"Mas que la vida me cueste
yo lo mando a retratar."

Doña Bernardina, the mistress
of Bernal, said: "I will have a
portrait made of him, though it
cost me my life."

Y lo retrató entonces
en su caballo oscuro
que en medio de la acordada *
se estaba fumando un puro.

And she had his portrait painted,
riding upon his bay horse, and
smoking a cigar in the midst of a
troop of mounted police.

Desde Torreón de Coahuila
hasta las aguas del mar,
todito aquello andaba
no lo osaban molestar.

From Torreón in Coahuila to
the waters of the sea, he wandered
at will, and none dared to molest
him.

En una vez en la sierra
de sorpresa lo tomaron;
a él y a Fabián el indixo
en una playa los cercaron.

On a time in the mountains,
they took him by surprise; he and
Fabián the Indian were besieged
in a narrow valley.

Y Heraclio Bernal decía,
en su caballo alazán:
"¡Pues ahora rompemos el sitio
y entramos a Mazatlán!"

And Heraclio Bernal, mounted
on his sorrel horse, said to him:
"Now we will break the siege and
enter Mazatlán."

* The *acordada* is a troop of Mexican mounted rural police.

[370]

Y de siete de los Rochas
que a prenderlos vinieron
buenos y sanos a sus casas
solamente tres volvieron.

And of the seven Rochas who
came to apprehend them, safe and
well to their homes only three
returned.

Decía don Crispín García,
el jefe de Mazatlán:
"Vénganme dos acordadas
y la Guardia Nacional."

Said Don Crispín García, the
mayor of Mazatlán: "Let me have
two troops of mounted police and
the National Guard."

Y en Mazatlán lo mataron,
por traición y por detrás
porque ese don Crispín García
era bueno para entregar.

And in Mazatlán he was killed,
by treason and from behind, for
that Don Crispín García was skill-
ful in treason.

Todavía despues de muerto
cuando en la caja lo tenían,
la acordada y los soldados
mucho miedo le tenían.

And even after he was dead, as
he lay in his coffin, the mounted
police and the soldiers feared him
greatly.

. . . .

¡Ay, ricos de la costa!
¡ya no morirán de susto!
ya mataron a Bernal,
ahora dormirán a gusto.

O rich men of the coast! No
longer will you die of fear; now
they have killed Bernal, now you
may sleep at your ease.

Y lloran todas las muchachas
del mineral de Mapimí:
"Ya mataron a Bernal,
ya no lo verán aquí."

And all of the girls of the mines
of Mapimí weep and say: "Now
they have killed Bernal, never will
he return."

Y aquí termino mi canto
pues así tuvieron final
la vida y los hechos
del gran Heraclio Bernal.

And here I end my song, for
thus ended the deeds and the life
of the great Heraclio Bernal.

XVI

COWBOY SONGS

"The higher you git's too low for me."—Cowboy to a bucking bronco.

FROM THE CHUCK WAGON

Oh, the cow-puncher loves the whistle of his rope,
As he races over the plains,
And the stage-driver loves the popper of his whip,
And the rattle of his Concord chains;
And I pray the Lord we'll all be saved
And we'll keep the golden rule;
But I'd rather be at home with the girl I love
Than to monkey with this goddam mule.

COWBOYS' GETTIN'–UP HOLLER

A common call in Far-West camp life.

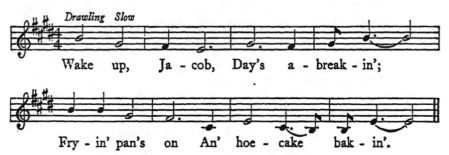

Wake up, Ja - cob, Day's a - break - in';

Fry - in' pan's on An' hoe - cake bak - in'.

Wake up, Jacob, day's a-breakin',
Fryin' pan's on an' hoe-cake bakin'.

Bacon in the pan, coffee in the pot;
Git up now and git it while it's hot.

[375]

THE OLD CHIZZUM TRAIL*

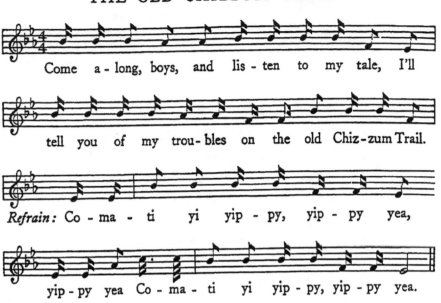

Come a-long, boys, and lis-ten to my tale, I'll

tell you of my trou-bles on the old Chiz-zum Trail.

Refrain: Co-ma-ti yi yip-py, yip-py yea,

yip-py yea Co-ma-ti yi yip-py, yip-py yea.

Come along, boys, and listen to my tale,
I'll tell you of my experience on the Old Chizzum Trail.

Chorus:

    Coma-ti yi yippy, yippy yea, yippy yea,
    Coma-ti yi yippy, yippy yea.

I was born in Texas in the year '89,
I can ride anything this side the state line.

Went down to San Antone and went to workin' cattle,
And here come the sheep men and we had a battle.

There ain't no better territory in the United States,
But she shore is hotter than hell's own gates.

---

* Additional stanzas to those printed in *Cowboy Songs* (New York: The Macmillan Company)
There remain hundreds of unprintable stanzas.

It's I an' Bill Jones was good old cronies,
We was always together on our sore-backed ponies.

We left Nelson Ranch on June twenty-third,
With a drove of Texas cattle, two thousand in the herd.

We whooped them through Gonzales, night was drawin' nigh,
We bedded them down on a hill close by.

Foot in the stirrup, my seat in the saddle,
Best little cowboy that ever rode a-straddle.

Slicker in the wagon and pouring down hail,
Goin' round the herd with a dogie by the tail.

It's rainin' like hell and it's gittin' mighty cold,
And the long-horned sons-a-guns are gittin' mighty hard to hold.

Saddle up, boys, and saddle up well,
For I think these cattle have scattered to hell.

Me and old Blue Dog arrived on the spot,
And we put them to milling like the boiling of a pot.

I'm on my best horse and I am goin' on a run,
I'm the quickest-shootin' cowboy that ever pulled a gun.

I flushed them left, couldn't get 'em to stop,
I can run as long as an eight-day clock.

My seat in my saddle, and I gave a little shout,
The lead cattle broke an' the herd went about.

My quirt in my hand, my slicker on my saddle,
I hung and rattled with them goddam cattle.

Some of 'em we captured without half tryin',
They was so damned scared they didn't need hog-tyin'.

[377]

We strung 'em out next mornin', and the boss made a count
And he said, "Boys, we are just a few out.

"Make a circle, boys, and don't lose no time,
I am sure they will be easy to find."

It was over the hillside and over the draws,
And we soon brought in the old Two Bars.*

I hit my little pony and he give a little rack,
And damned big luck if we ever get back.

I'm headed south just whoopin' and a-yellin',
If I don't find a steer, I'll take a heifer yearling.

Jumped in the saddle and hit him with my quirt,
The hind cinch busted and the saddle hit the dirt.

With my blankets and my gun and a rawhide rope,
I'm a-slidin' down the trail in a long keen lope.

I'll chew my tobacco and I'll squirt my juice,
I'm goin' down to town to see the old Blue Goose.

I went to the bar and struck on a bell,
Here comes a bunch of niggers running like hell.

Pulled out my gun, brought it on the level,
And them damn niggers run like the devil.

And they got me by the foreleg and put me in jail,
And I couldn't find a damn soul to go my bail.

Boss come around with a whip in his hand
And he swore, by God, I wasn't worth a damn.

* The road brand burned on the sides of the cattle.

I sold my horse and I sold my saddle,
You can go to hell with your longhorn cattle.

I'm goin' back home, I'm not jokin' or lyin',
I'm goin' back home, just a-yellin' and a-flyin'.

I hunted up the boss to draw my roll,
He stepped in the bank and he paid me in gold.

I'm goin' downtown to get a little dope
'Cause my back's all broke from the draggin' of the rope.

Jumped on the train and gave such a yell,
The goose-back broke and the train went to hell.

When I thought of my gal I nearly would cry,
I'll quit herding cows in the sweet by and by.

I hadn't been at home but some days two or three
When I put off my gal for to see.

"If you've made up your mind to quit the cowboy life,
I have fully decided to be your little wife."

Farewell, old Blue Dog, I wish you no harm,
I've done quit the business to go on the farm.

No more a cow-puncher to sleep at my ease,
'Mid the crawlin' of the lice and the bitin' of the fleas.

WHEN I WAS A COWBOY

Lead Belly, prisoner at Angola, the State Farm of Louisiana, sings his saga of cowboy life and of his purely imaginary adventures in the West.

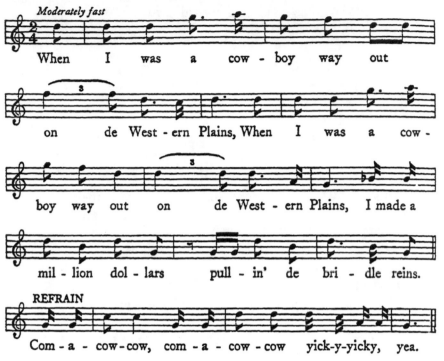

When I was a cowboy, way out on de Western Plains,
When I was a cowboy, way out on de Western Plains,
I made a million dollars pullin' de bridle reins.

Refrain:
      Coma-cow-cow, coma-cow-cow, yicky-yicky-yea.

Oh, de hardes' battle was ever on a Bunker Hill,
When we an' a bunch o' cowboys run into Buffalo Bill.

Oh, de hardes' battle was ever on-a Western plains,
When me an' a bunch o' cowboys run into Jesse James.

When me an' a bunch o' cowboys run into Jesse James,
De bullets was a-fallin' jes' like a shower rain.

      Coma-cow-cow, coma-cow-cow, yicky-yicky-yea.

COWBOY TO PITCHING BRONCO

A practice, once common in Texas, called for boasting talk from the probably scared cowboy as the wild horse, ridden for the first time, began his frantic pitching to dislodge his rider. Each line of the chant measures the period while the horse is in the air. The chant goes on indefinitely, other verses being added or the first being repeated, until the final exclamation when the horse suddenly stops to breathe.

To be declaimed, not sung

Born on the Col - o - ra - do, Sired by an al - li - ga - tor, I'm a bold, bad man from Crip - ple Creek, Col - o - ra - do. When I get back there'll be a tor - na - do. Git high - er, Git high - er, The high - er you git's too low for me. Want to git my po - ny back and throw my nig - gers through the crack; I'm tell - in' you, flam - doo - zle - dum.

The above rote and time values can but poorly, approximately, and arbitrarily reproduce the cowboy's *chant*; its freedom of motion, unusual disposition of accent, and rising and falling of the voice are never twice the same.

Born on the Colorado,
Sired by an alligator,
I'm a bold, bad man
From Cripple Creek, Colorado.
When I git back
There'll be a tornado!

Git higher, git higher,
The higher you git's
      Too low for me.
Want to git my pony back
And throw niggers through the crack;
I'm tellin' you,
      Flamdoozledum!

OTHER COWBOY BOASTING CHANTS

I'm wild and woolly
And full of fleas;
Ain't never been curried
Below the knees.

I'm a wild she wolf
From Bitter Creek,
And it's my time
To h-o-w-l, whoop-i-e-e-ee.

Horse and man talk as horse pitches—
            "I want ye!"
            "You cain't git me!"
            "I want ye!"
    · "You'll have to throw me first."
            "I want ye!"
            "Ah, you done got me!"

⌈ 382 ⌉

Wasp nests and yaller jackets,
The higher you pitch, the sweeter my navy tastes.
Born on the Gaudalupe,
Ten miles below Duck Pond,
Raised in the Rocky Mountains.
Hang one spur where the collar works
And the other where the crupper works.

Four rows of jaw teeth
And holes punched for more;
Steel ribs and iron backbone,
And tail put on with screws,
Double dew-clawed,
Knock-kneed and bandy-shanked,
Nine rows of teeth,
And holes punched for more.

GOOD–BY, OLD PAINT

Boothe Merrill, a friend of college days, gave me this song in 1910, in Cheyenne, Wyoming, where we were attending the great Frontier Days celebration. Accidentally I had met him just as he was coming out of the saloon. He expressed astonishment at finding a former Y.M.C.A. leader going into a saloon, and I equal surprise at discovering him coming *out* of a saloon. While settling the controversy in one of the private back rooms of this place, Boothe sang "Old Paint," which he said was popular at times in western Oklahoma. For the last dance all other music is stopped, and the revelers, as they dance to a slow waltz time, sing "Good-by, Old Paint." The song is yet used in remote western communities until the fiddler comes.

[383]

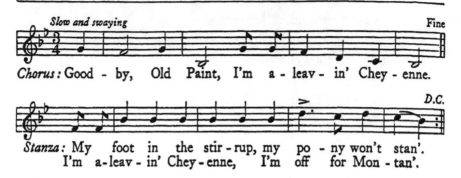

Chorus: Good - by, Old Paint, I'm a - leav - in' Chey - enne.

Stanza: My foot in the stir - rup, my po - ny won't stan'.
I'm a - leav - in' Chey - enne, I'm off for Mon - tan'.

My foot in the stirrup, my pony won't stan',
I'm a-leavin' Cheyenne, I'm off for Montan'.

Chorus:

Good-by, old Paint, I'm a-leavin' Cheyenne,
Good-by, old Paint, I'm a-leavin' Cheyenne.*

I'm a-ridin' old Paint, I'm a-leadin' old Fan,
Good-by, little Annie, I'm off for Cheyenne.

Old Paint's a good pony, he paces when he can,
Good morning, young lady, my hosses won't stand.

Oh, hitch up your hosses and feed 'em some hay,
And seat yourself by me, as long as you stay.

My hosses ain't hungry, they'll not eat your hay,
My wagon is loaded and rolling away.

I am a-riding old Paint, I am a-leading old Dan,
I'm goin' to Montan' for to throw the hoolihan.

They feed in the coulees, they water in the draw,
Their tails are all matted, their backs are all raw.

* To be repeated until one thinks of more words or the waltz stops.

Old Bill Jones had two daughters and a song:
One went to Denver, and the other went wrong.

His wife she died in a pool-room fight,
And still he sings from morning to night.

Oh, when I die, take my saddle from the wall,
Put it on my pony, lead him from the stall.

Tie my bones to his back, turn our faces to the west,
And we'll ride the prairie that we love the best.

GIT ALONG, LITTLE DOGIES*

As I was a-walk-ing one morn-ing for plea-sure, I
spied a cow-punch-er all rid-ing a-long; His
hat was throwed back and his spurs was a-jin-glin', As
he ap-proached me a-sing-in' this song: Whoopee
ti yi yo git a-long, lit-tle do-gies, It's

* Reprinted from *Cowboy Songs* (New York: The Macmillan Company, 1910).

your mis - for - tune and none of my own, Whoopee

ti yi yo, git a - long, lit - tle do - gies, For you

know Wy - om - ing will be your new home.

YODELS

Very slow

1. Hoo - - - - - - - - Hoo - Hoo - Hoo.

2. Hoo - - - - - - - Hoo - Hoo - Hoo. —

3. He - oo - He - oo - oo - He - oo - oo - oo - oo

Hoo - - - - - - - - - - Hoo - Hoo - Hoo.

Yodels, sung by cowboy, ad. lib., between verses of above and at its conclusion.

Not fast

As I walked out one morn - ing for plea - sure, I

met a cow-punch-er a - jog - ging a - long. His

hat was thrown back and his spurs they was jin-glin', And

as he ad-vanced he was sing-ing this song, Sing-ing

Whoop - li - o get a - long, my lit - tle doughies, For Wy-

om - ing shall be your new home. And it's

driv - ing and damn-ing and curs - ing those dough-ies to

our mis - for - tune but none of their own.

As I walked out one morning for pleasure,
I spied a cow-puncher come all riding alone;
His hat was throwed back and his spurs was a-jingling,
As he approached me a-singin' this song,

Chorus:

Whoopie ti yi yo, git along, little dogies,†
It's your misfortune, and none of my own.
Whoopee ti yi yo, git along, little dogies,
For you know Wyoming will be your new home.

† Pronounced with the *o* long and the *g* hard.—"A big-bellied calf with no mammy. Nothin' in his guts but dough. An orphant calf which has lost his mammy and his pappy has run away with an other cow."

Early in the spring we round up the dogies,
Mark 'em and brand 'em and bob off their tails;
Drive up our horses, load up the chuck-wagon,
Then throw the dogies out on the trail.

It's whoopin' and yellin' and a-drivin' them dogies;
Oh, how I wish that you would go on;
It's a-whoopin' and punchin' and go on-a, little dogies,
For you know Wyoming is to be your new home.

Some boys goes up the trail for pleasure,
But that's where you get it most awfully wrong;
For you haven't any idea the trouble they give us
While we go driving them along.

When the night comes on and we hold them on the bed-ground,
These little dogies that roll on so slow;
Round up the herd and cut out the strays,
And roll the little dogies that never rolled before.

Your mother she was raised way down in Texas,
Where the jimson weed and sand-burrs grow;
Now we'll fix you up on prickly pear and cholla
Till you're ready for the trail to Idaho.

Oh, you'll be beef for Uncle Sam's Injuns;
"It's beef, heap beef," I hear them cry.
Git along, git along, git along-a, little dogies,
You're gonna be beef steers by and by.

Following a talk I made at Bryn Mawr in November, 1932, Owen Wister related an incident in his own experience which he incorporated subsequently in a letter:

"Here is that second verse of the 'Little Doughies':

"In the morn*ing* we throw off the bedground,
Aiming to graze *them* an hour or two,
When they are full you think you can drive them
On to the trail, *but* be damned if you do.
        Singing Hoop-li-ô
Get along my little doughies,
For Wyoming will be your new hôme.
And it's driving and damning and cursing those doughies
To our misfor*tune* but none of their own.

"It took me about half an hour to make sure of the capricious melody. We sat under a live oak in McCulloch County, Texas, some twenty miles from Brady City, in March, 1893. I made the boy sing it until I had taken the notes down with the words under them. He sang in 6/8 time, andante, dwelling according to whim on certain unexpected syllables: Those I have either underlined (for a short hold) or marked with a circumflex accent indicating a note often prolonged through several measures.

"The music resembles very slightly the tune you sing, and nothing else at all that I know. It's altogether the wildest I have met in print or in open air; and whatever it was originally, the open air and the plains and the night have played their part in giving it the shape I succeeded in capturing. It may well be that the young fellow had music in his soul, and that what he gave me had touches of his own."

Mr. Wister adds a note on the manuscript of the music:

"Just from habit I write 'doughies.' Remember that the above melody varies so much according to the caprice of the singer (not in intervals but in holding a note when he feels like it) that writing it down has to be approximate." Mr. Wister's tune is the second example as printed on pp. 386–7.

THE BUFFALO SKINNERS*

In honor of Miss Dora Kittredge

'Twas in the town of Jacks - bo - ro, In eigh-teen eigh - ty - three, When a man by the name of Cre - go Came step-ping up to me; Say - ing, "How do you do, young fel - low, And how would you like to go And spend one sum - mer sea - son On the range of the buf - fa - lo?"

Come all you jolly cowboys and listen to my song,
There are not many verses, it will not detain you long;
It's concerning some young fellows who did agree to go
And spend one summer pleasantly on the range of the buffalo.

*In Bulletin No. 7 of the Folk Songs Society of the Northeast, a brother or possibly the parent of this song is shown to be a Maine lumberjack song, "Canaday I-O."

It happened in Jacksboro in the spring of seventy-three,
A man by the name of Crego came stepping up to me,
Saying, "How do you do, young fellow, and how would you like to go
And spend one summer pleasantly on the range of the buffalo?"

"It's me being out of employment," this to Crego I did say,
"This going out on the buffalo range depends upon the pay.
But if you will pay good wages and transportation too,
I think, sir, I will go with you to the range of the buffalo."

"Yes, I will pay good wages, give transportation too,
Provided you will go with me and stay the summer through;
But if you should grow homesick, come back to Jacksboro,
I won't pay transportation from the range of the buffalo."

It's now our outfit was complete—seven able-bodied men,
With navy six and needle gun—our troubles did begin;
Our way it was a pleasant one, the route we had to go,
Until we crossed Pease River on the range of the buffalo.

It's now we've crossed Pease River, our troubles have begun.
The first damned tail I went to rip, Christ! how I cut my thumb!
While skinning the damned old stinkers our lives wasn't a show,
For the Indians watched to pick us off while skinning the buffalo.

He fed us on such sorry chuck I wished myself most dead,
It was old jerked beef, croton coffee, and sour bread.
Pease River's salty as hell fire, the water I could never go—
Oh, God! I wished I'd never come to the range of the buffalo.

Our meat it was buffalo rump and iron wedge bread,
And all we had to sleep on was a buffalo robe for a bed;
The fleas and graybacks worked on us, oh, boys, it was not slow,
I'll tell you there's no worse hell on earth than the range of the buffalo.

Our hearts were cased with buffalo hocks, our souls were cased with
   steel,
And the hardships of that summer would nearly make us reel,
While skinning the damned old stinkers, our lives they had no show,
For the Indians waited to pick us off on the hills of Mexico.

The season being near over, old Crego he did say
The crowd had been extravagant, was in debt to him that day.
We coaxed him and we begged him, and still it was no go—
We left his damned old bones to bleach on the range of the buffalo.

Oh, it's now we've crossed Pease River and homeward we are bound,
No more in that hell-fired country shall ever we be found.
Go home to our wives and sweethearts, tell others not to go,
For God's forsaken the buffalo range and the damned old buffalo.

THE STAMPEDE *

When the hot sun smiles on the endless miles
   That lead to the distant mart,
And the cattle wail down the well-worn trail,
   And moan till it grips the heart,
And they gasp for air in the dust clouds there,
   As they jostle their way along
With uplifted ear so that they may hear
   The cow-puncher's evening song.

Far up at the head rode old "Texas Red"—
   A man of determined face—
And his keen gray eye took in earth and sky
   As he rode with a centaur's grace.
On the left was Joe on his white pinto;
   Jim Smith patrolled on the right.

* First published in *Wild West Weekly* (Street and Smith, 79 Seventh Ave., New York).

[392]

And the other tricks took an even six,
  And we needed them all that night.

And to quench our thirst we had dared the worst
  And fought for a nester's well;
But he had a girl with a witching curl,
  And she cast a golden spell.
So our shots went wide from the sinner's hide
  As he faded from our view,
And the charming miss blew old Red a kiss
  And smiled as his pony flew.

'Twas a pretty play, but he spurred away,
  His face like a prairie blaze.
And he hit the dirt as he plied his quirt
  Till lost in the friendly haze,
While the bawling shrilled as the cattle milled,
  And their eyes grew shot with fear—
For they knew right well that a merry hell
  Lurked in the gathering smear.

In the north black clouds like funeral shrouds
  Rolled down with an icy breath,
And we faced a fight on a brutal night
  With odds on the side of death;
For a trailing herd when it's rightly stirred
  Is a thing for a man to shun,
And no coward band ever holds command
  When the norther's on the run.

In the ghostly hush that precedes the rush
  Of the wild wind-driven flood,
We made our dash to the thunder's crash,
  Spurs set till they drew the blood;

But the Storm King struck to our bitter luck,
  We rode in the lightning's glare,
And the north wind whirled through a watery world,
  And laughed at our puny dare.

Then the cattle swerved as a mob unnerved
  And shrank from a raging thing,
And they drifted back on the beaten track,
  Tail to the norther's sting.
We fought like men, but 'twas useless then—
  They plunged down the backward track.
Theirs a single creed—'twas the dread stampede—
  Straight at the nester's shack!

There was death at stake, and 'twas make or break
  In the rush of that frenzied mob;
But we'd risked our lives in a hundred drives,
  And we figured to know our job.
Then a sudden hail on the whistling gale
  And a horse went slithering by—
'Twas old Texas Red, and we knew he sped
  To the girl of the flashing eye.

With a wicked grip on his biting whip,
  He smoked down on the heaving ranks,
And his searching eye set to do or die
  As he fanned at his pony's flanks;
And we gazed aghast when we saw at last—
  Old Tex at the head of the ruck,
And we made a prayer for the rider there,
  Just a wish for a hero's luck.

Straight she stood and still, at the storm's wild will,
  Close by the nester's well,

And her eyes were kissed by the driving mist
    As she faced that living hell;
But when Texas Red, 'crost his pony's head,
    Erect in his stirrups rose,
Like a sprite she sprung—to his shoulder clung—
    A rod from the leader's nose.

MUSTANG GRAY *

There was a no-ble ran-ger, They called him Mus-tang Gray;

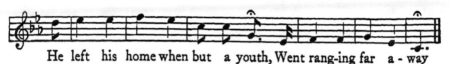

He left his home when but a youth, Went rang-ing far a-way

There was a noble ranger,
They called him Mustang Gray;
He left his home when but a youth,
Went ranging far away.

Chorus:

But he'll go no more a-ranging
The savage to affright;
He's heard his last war whoop
And fought his last fight.

He ne'er would sleep within a tent
No comforts would he know;
But like a brave old Tex-i-an
A-ranging he would go.

* Frank Dobie in *Publications of the Texas Folk-Lore Society*, Vol. X.

When Texas was invaded
By a mighty tyrant foe,
He mounted his noble war horse
And a-ranging he did go.

Once he was taken prisoner,
Bound in chains upon the way;
He wore the yoke of bondage
Through the streets of Monterey.

A señorita loved him
And followed by his side;
She opened the gates and gave to him
Her father's steed to ride.

God bless the señorita,
The belle of Monterey;
She opened wide the prison door
And let him ride away.

And when this veteran's life was spent,
It was his last command,
To bury him on Texas soil
On the banks of the Rio Grande.

And there the lonely traveler,
When passing by his grave,
Will shed a farewell tear
O'er the bravest of the brave.

Now he'll go no more a-ranging,
The savage to affright;
He's heard his last war whoop
And fought his last fight.

HELL IN TEXAS

Oh, the Dev - il in Hell they say he was chained, And
there for a thous - and years he re - mained; He
nei - ther com - plained nor did he groan, But de -
cid - ed he'd start up a hell of his own, Where
he could tor - ment the souls of men with - out
be - ing shut in a pris - on pen, So he
asked the Lord if he had an - y sand Left
o - ver from mak - ing this great land.

Oh, the Devil in hell they say he was chained,
And there for a thousand years he remained;

He neither complained nor did he groan,
But decided he'd start up a hell of his own,
Where he could torment the souls of men
Without being shut in a prison pen;
So he asked the Lord if He had any sand
Left over from making this great land.

The Lord He said, "Yes, I have plenty on hand,
But it's away down south on the Rio Grande,
And, to tell you the truth, the stuff is so poor
I doubt if 'twill do for hell any more."
The Devil went down and looked over the truck,
And he said if it came as a gift he was stuck,
For when he'd examined it carefully and well
He decided the place was too dry for a hell.

But the Lord just to get the stuff off His hands
He promised the Devil He'd water the land,
For he had some old water that was of no use,
A regular bog hole that stunk like the deuce.
So the grant it was made and the deed it was given;
The Lord He returned to His place up in heaven.
The Devil soon saw he had everything needed
To make up a hell and so he proceeded.

He scattered tarantulas over the roads,
Put thorns on the cactus and horns on the toads,
He sprinkled the sands with millions of ants
So the man that sits down must wear soles on his pants.
He lengthened the horns of the Texas steer,
And added an inch to the jack rabbit's ear;
He put water puppies * in all of the lakes,
And under the rocks he put rattlesnakes.

* The word that went here was a corrupt form of *ajalote*—Texas-Mexican for that wondrous and hideous form of aquatic salamander, so common in the tanks and troughs of West Texas, known as water dog or water puppy.

He hung thorns and brambles on all of the trees,
He mixed up the dust with jiggers and fleas;
The rattlesnake bites you, the scorpion stings,
The mosquito delights you by buzzing his wings.
The heat in the summer's a hundred and ten,
Too hot for the Devil and too hot for men;
And all who remained in that climate soon bore
Cuts, bites, stings, and scratches, and blisters galore.

He quickened the buck of the bronco steed,
And poisoned the feet of the centipede;
The wild boar roams in the black chaparral;
It's a hell of a place that we've got for a hell.
He planted red pepper beside of the brooks;
The Mexicans use them in all that they cook.
Just dine with a Greaser and then you will shout,
"I've hell on the inside as well as the out!"

Concerning this song George E. Hastings, Professor of English in the University of Arkansas, writes: *

"Between 1904 and 1909, while living in Pittsburgh, Pennsylvania, I frequently attended dinners and smokers given by the Princeton Club.

"At one of these reunions, held in 1908 or 1909, I heard for the first time a song delineating in spirited style the creation of the arid regions of the Southwest. My recollection is that the singer called the song 'Arizona.'

"Among my friends in the Princeton Club there were four young men, Lloyd Smith, '08, William S. Houston, '08, Alfred C. Boswell, '05, and John J. Heard, '04, who so much enjoyed singing that they not only made a joyful noise at the smokers, but frequently met in private session for the purpose of holding 'song services.' I am not sure who it was that sang 'Arizona' on the occasion mentioned above, but I know that it was one of these four. Whoever the singer may have

* *Publications of the Texas Folk-Lore Society*, Vol. IX (1931).

been, I was so pleased with the song that I later took down the words from his dictation, and since that time I have always been willing to sing it myself if sufficiently urged to do so. Later when Mr. John A. Lomax published his collection, *Cowboy Songs,* I found in it 'Hell in Texas,' which proved to be a different and somewhat longer version of the song I had learned in Pittsburgh. All scholars know that popular ballads grow by accretion. This truth I soon exemplified by adding to the version that I already knew sixteen lines from that found in *Cowboy Songs.*

"To this hybrid version, Professor Lawrence Powell, of the University of Arkansas, obligingly set down the tune in musical notation.

"I wanted to find out as much as I could about the history of the version that I learned more than twenty years ago. As Mr. Alfred C. Boswell is a trained musician, I first consulted him. I located him at Châlet Windspillen, Gstaad, Canton Bern. On receiving my letter, he replied that he remembers the tune of 'Hell in Texas,' but cannot recall the words. He has an impression that he first heard the song sung by Jack Heard or Bill Houston.

"Next I wrote these gentlemen, who still live in Pittsburgh. Bill Houston got the copy he sent to me from Lloyd Smith. None of my friends in Pittsburgh knows the song as 'Hell in Texas'; Jack Heard calls it 'The Devil in Hell,' and Bill Houston 'The Founding of New Mexico.' * Alfred Boswell in his letter says that he does not know who imported this robust song 'into the anæmic atmosphere of Western Pennsylvania,' but Bill Houston and Lloyd Smith are able to supply this information. They learned the song from Alexander Milne, Jr., Princeton, '09, who lives in Pittsburgh. He learned it in 1907 at a summer camp in Maine, from a young man named Scott who had been a cowboy in New Mexico and learned the song there.

"If the tune is not exactly the same as that sung by my friends, the fault is mine. . . . Of the words, the fifth and sixth lines of the first stanza, the fifth and sixth lines of the second stanza, all of the fifth stanza and the last of the sixth stanza are derived from Mr. Lomax's

* N. Howard Thorp, an old-time range man of New Mexico and compiler of *Songs of the Cowboys,* prefaces "Hell in Texas" with the remark that "this song was originally entitled 'The Birth of New Mexico.' "

version; the rest of the lines make up the song as I first learned it.

"Once when I sang the song in the open air auditorium at the University of Arkansas, a lady from the 'Magic Valley' [the lower Rio Grande district of Texas] arose and denounced the maker of the song as a slanderer."

The text of "Hell in Texas" printed in *Cowboy Songs* came from the proprietor of the Buckhorn Saloon in San Antonio, Texas, a famous resort for the thirsty, yet operated as a soft-drink place. When he handed me the printed broadside, the proprietor of the Buckhorn told me that he had given away more than 100,000 printed copies. John R. Steele, of the United States Signal Corps, stationed at Brownsville in early frontier days, is said to have written the song. Others claimed it. General W. T. Sherman, once stationed in Texas, was suggested as the author by a Texas newspaper. The claim grew out of a report that Sherman had said that if he owned both Texas and hell he would rent out Texas and live in hell. Whereupon a Texan is said to have retorted: "Well, damn a man who won't stand up for his own country."

"Hell in Texas" had a forerunner or follower in Arizona, where the keeper of a gambling saloon in Tucson was moved to write what follows. "Arizona," said a fervid orator, "needs only water and climate to make it a Paradise." "Yes," retorted an unsympathetic hearer. "That's all hell needs."

ARIZONA

How It Was Made and Who Made It

The Devil was given permission one day
To select him a land for his own special sway;
So he hunted around for a month or more,
And fussed and fumed and terribly swore,
But at last was delighted a country to view
Where the prickly pear and the mesquite grew.
With a survey brief, without further excuse,
He stood on the bank of the Santa Cruz.

He saw there were some improvements to make,
For he felt his own reputation at stake.
An idea struck him, and he swore by his horns
To make a complete vegetation of thorns.
He studded the land with the prickly pear,
And scattered the cactus everywhere;
The Spanish dagger, sharp-pointed and tall,
And at last the chollas to outstick them all.

He imported the Apaches direct from hell,
With a legion of skunks, with a loud, loud smell
To perfume the country he loved so well.
And then for his life he couldn't see why
The river needed any more water supply,
And he swore if he gave it another drop
You might have his head and horns for a mop.

He filled the river with sand till 'twas almost dry,
And poisoned the land with alkali;
And promised himself on its slimy brink
To control all who from it should drink.
He saw there was one improvement to make,
So he imported the scorpion, tarantula, and snake,
That all that might come to this country to dwell
Would be sure to think it was almost hell.

He fixed the heat at a hundred and 'leven,
And banished forever the moisture from heaven;
And remarked as he heard his furnaces roar
That the heat might reach five hundred more.
And after he fixed things so thorny and well
He said, 'I'll be damned if this don't beat hell.'
Then he flapped his wings and away he flew
And vanished from earth in a blaze of blue.

THE KILLER *

Dobe Bill, he came a-riding from the canyon, in the glow
Of a quiet Sunday morning from the town of Angelo;
Ridin' easy on the pinto that he dearly loved to straddle,
With a six-gun and sombrero that was wider than his saddle.
And he's hummin' as he's ridin' of a simple little song
That's a-rumblin' through the cactus as he's gallopin' along:

"Oh, I've rid from San Antony through the mesquite and the sand,
I'm a r'arin', flarin' bucko, not afraid to play my hand.
I'm a hootin', shootin' demon and I has my little fun
With my pinto called Apache and Adolphus—that's my gun."

Straight to Santa Fe he drifted, and he mills around the town,
Sorta gittin' of his bearin's while he pours his liquor down.
But he's watchin'—always watchin'—every hombre in the place,
Like he's mebbe sorta lookin' for some certain hombre's face.

Then one night he saunters careless to the place of "Monte Sam,"
And he does a bit of playin' like he doesn't give a damn.
All at once it's still and quiet, like a calm before a blow,
And the crowd is tense and nervous, and the playin's stopped and slow.

At the bar a man is standin' sneerin' as his glances lay.
Like a challenge did he fling 'em, darin' 'em to make a play.
"Two-Gun" Blake, the Pecos killer, hated, feared wherever known,
Stood and drank his glass of mescal with assurance all his own.

Then the eyes of Blake, the killer, caught the glance of Dobe Bill,
And they held each one the other with the steel of looks that kill.

* Source unknown. First published in *Wild West* Weekly (Street & Smith, 29 Seventh Ave., New York City).

Then the tones of Blake came slowly, with a sneer in every word:
"Well, you've found me!" But the other gave no sign he saw or heard.

Walkin' calmly toward the speaker, he advanced with steady pace.
Then he grinned and, quick as lightnin', slapped him squarely in the
face.
"Shoot, you snake!" he whispered hoarsely. "Shoot, you lily-livered
cur!
Draw! You're always strong for killin'; now I'm here to shoot for
her!"

Some there was that claimed they saw it, as the killer tried to draw—
But there's no one knows for certain just exactly what they saw.
I'll agree the shootin' started quick as Blake had made his start—
Then a brace of bullets hit him fair and certain through the heart.

As he fell, his hand was graspin' of the gun he'd got too late,
With the notches on it showin' like the vagaries of fate.
And the man who stood there lookin' at the killer as he lay,
Murmured: "Nell, I've kept my promise. I have made the scoundrel
pay!"

Dobe Bill, he went a-ridin' from the town of Santa Fe
On a quiet Sunday morning, goin' happy on his way,
Ridin' happy on that pinto that he dearly loved to straddle,
With his six-gun and sombrero that was wider than his saddle.
And he's hummin' as he's goin' of a simple little song
That's a-boomin' through the cactus as he's gallopin' along:

"Oh, I'm goin' down the valley, through the mesquite and the sand.
I'm a r'arin', flarin' bucko, not afraid to play my hand.
I'm a hootin', shootin' demon and I has my little fun
With my bronco called Apache and Adolphus—that's my gun."

SNAGTOOTH SAL *

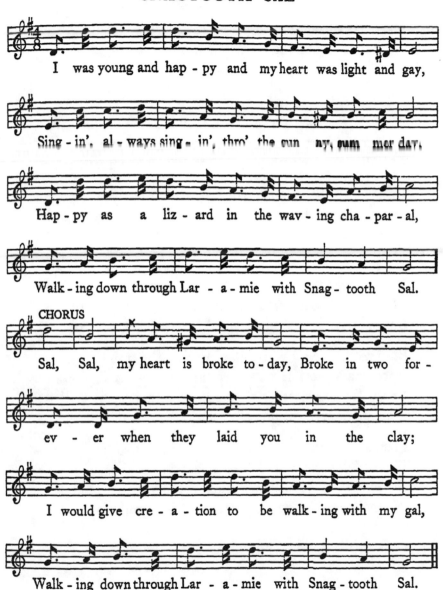

I was young and hap - py and my heart was light and gay,

Sing - in', al - ways sing - in', thro' the sun - ny, sum - mer day,

Hap - py as a liz - ard in the wav - ing cha - par - al,

Walk - ing down through Lar - a - mie with Snag - tooth Sal.

CHORUS

Sal, Sal, my heart is broke to - day, Broke in two for -

ev - er when they laid you in the clay;

I would give cre - a - tion to be walk - ing with my gal,

Walk - ing down through Lar - a - mie with Snag - tooth Sal.

* Lowell O. Reese published a fragment of "Snagtooth Sal" fifteen years ago in the *Saturday Evening Post*. The tune comes from Frank Shay's *Drawn from the Wood* (New York: Macaulay Co.).

I was young and happy and my heart was light and gay,
Singin', always singin', through the sunny, summer day;
Happy as a lizard in the waving chaparral,
Walking down through Laramie with Snagtooth Sal.

Chorus:
　　Sal, Sal, my heart is broke today,
　　Broke in two forever when they laid you in the clay;
　　I would give creation to be walking with my gal,
　　Walking down through Laramie with Snagtooth Sal.

I met her in the evening, when the stars where shining bright.
We walked and talked and billed and cooed till twelve o'clock
　　　at night.

She told me that she loved me, she swore she'd be my pal,
But she turned me down completely, did my Snagtooth Sal.
I thought I had her safely in my aching heart's corral,
But she died and left me longin' for my Snagtooth Sal.

Bury me tomorrow where the lily blossoms spring,
Underneath the willows where the little robins sing.
You will yearn to see me—but ah, nevermore you shall—
Walking down through Laramie with Snagtooth Sal.

Plant a little stone above the little mound of sod;
Write: "Here lies a lovin' an' a busted heart, begod!"
Nevermore you'll see him walkin' proudly with his gal—
Walkin' down through Laramie with Snagtooth Sal.

TYING A KNOT IN THE DEVIL'S TAIL

"One night when I had been in Arizona only a short while, I went
on a moonlight picnic. There is no moon in the world like the Arizona
moon—and that night it came up slowly between two prongs of a

cactus—full, startling gold against the blackness of the cactus, and not so damnably cold as other moons.

"Miles we rode up the river-bed, and it was so cold—that satisfying, sensuous cold—it came through my rough-neck sweater and chaps and I revelled in it.

"Later on there was a huge fire and broiled steaks—and afterwards I sat on the edge of a tree which was thrown clear through the fire, and listened to the cowboy who was sitting next to me, sing. Song after song he sang—cowboy ballads which I had not heard before, as well as those with which I was familiar. One I shall never forget. It seemed my cowboy burned the fringe of his chaps as he sang to me, and there was a parody to that song made up afterwards. . . ." *

Way high up in the Syree Peaks
　　Where the yellow pines grow tall,
Old Sandy Bob and Buster Jiggs
　　Had a round-up camp last fall.

They took their horses and their runnin' irons
　　And maybe a dog or two;
And they 'lowed they'd brand all the long-eared calves
　　That came within their view.

Many a long-eared dogie
　　That didn't hush up by day
Had his long ears whittled and his old hide scorched
　　In a most artistic way.

One fine day, says Buster Jiggs
　　As he throwed his cigo down,
"I'm tired o' cow-piography
　　And I 'lows I'm goin' to town."

* Contributed to the collection of Dr. Hazard by Helen Becker of Mills College.

So they saddles up and they hits a lope,
    Fer it wa'n't no sight of a ride,
And them was the days that a good cow-punch'
    Could ile up his inside.

They started her in at the Kentucky Bar
    At the head of Whisky Row
And ends her up at the Depot House,
    Some forty drinks below.

They sets her up and they turns around
    And goes her the other way;
An' to tell the God-forsaken truth
    Them boys got tight that day.

When they were on their way to camp
    A-packin' a pretty good load,
Who should they meet but the Devil hisself
    Come a-prancin' down the road.

Says he, "Ye ornery cowboy skunks,
    Ye'd better hunt for your holes,
'Cause I've come up from hell's rim-rock
    To gather in your souls."

Says Buster Jiggs: "The Devil be damned!
    We boys are feelin' kinda tight,
But you don't gather any cowboy souls
    Unless you want a fight."

So he punches a hole in his old cigo
    And he throws her straight and true
An' he loops it over the Devil's horns
    An' he takes his dallies true.

Old Sandy Bob was a riata-man
With his gut-line coiled up neat,
But he shakes her out an' he builds a loop
An' he ropes the Devil's hind feet.

They stretches him out and they tails him down,
An' while their irons were gettin' hot
They cropped and swallow-forked his ears
An' branded him up a lot.

They prunes him up with a dehorning saw
An' they knotted his tail for a joke;
An' then they rode off an' left him there
Tied up to a lilac-jack oak.

Now when you're way up high in the Syree Peaks
An' you hear one hell of a wail,
It's only the Devil a-bellerin' round
About those knots in his tail.

SUSAN VAN DUSAN*

Oh, Susan Van Dusan,
The gal of my choosin',
She sticks to my bosom
Like glue.

Oh, Susan Van Dusan,
Oh, I will quit usin'
Tobacco and boozin'
For you.

* Contributed to the collection of Dr. Hazard, Mills College, California, by Helen-Ruth Nelson. who writes: "This song was sung to me by my brother after he had spent a summer with cowboys on a ranch in the vicinity of Salmon, Idaho."

Oh, Susan Van Dusan,
What gum are you usin'
That sticks to my bosom
Like you?

THE COWBOY'S DREAM *

Tune: "Bring Back My Bonnie to Me"

When I think of the last great round-up
On the eve of eternity's dawn,
I think of the host of cowboys
That have been with us here and have gone.

Chorus:

Roll on, roll on,
Roll on, little dogies, roll on, roll on,
Roll on, roll on,
Roll on, little dogies, roll on.

I think of those big-hearted fellows,
Who'll divide with you blanket and bread,
With a piece of stray beef well roasted,
And charge for it never a red.

I wonder if any will greet me,
On the sands of that evergreen shore,
With a hearty "God bless you, old fellow,"
That I've met so often before.

And I often look upward and wonder
If the green fields will seem half so fair,
If any the wrong trail have taken
And will fail to be over there.

* From an article entitled "Ballads and Songs of the Frontier Folk," by J. Frank Dobie, in *Texas Folk-Lore Publications*, No. VI.

The trail that leads down to perdition
Is paved all the way with good deeds;
But in the great round-up of ages,
Dear boys, this won't answer your needs.

The trail to green pastures, though narrow,
Leads straight to the home in the sky,
To the headquarters ranch of the Father
In the land of the sweet by and by.

The Inspector will stand at the gateway,
Where the herd, one and all, must go by,
And the round-up by the angels in judgment
Must pass 'neath His all-searching eye.

No maverick or slick will be tallied
In that great book of life in His home,
For he knows all the brands and the earmarks
That down through all ages have come.

But, along with the strays and the sleepers,
The tailings must turn from the gate;
No road brand to give them admission.
But that awful sad cry: "Too late!"

But I trust in that last great round-up
When the Rider shall cut the big herd,
That the cowboy will be represented
In the earmark and brand of the Lord.

To be shipped to that bright, mystic region,
Over there in green pastures to lie,
And be led by the crystal still waters
To the home in the sweet by and by.

RED RIVER SHORE*

At the foot of yon mountain, where the fountain doth flow,
The greatest creation, where the soft wind doth blow,
There lived a fair maiden; she's the one I adore,
She's the one I would marry on Red River shore.

I spoke to her kindly, saying, "Will you marry me?
My fortune's not great." "No matter," said she.
"Your beauty's a plenty, you're the one I adore;
You're the one I would marry on Red River shore."

I asked her old father, would he give her to me.
"No, sir, she shan't marry no cowboy," said he.
So I jumped on my bronco and away I did ride
And left my true love on Red River side.

She wrote me a letter, and she wrote it so kind,
And in this letter, these words you could find:
"Come back to me, darling. You're the one I adore,
You're the one I would marry on Red River shore."

So I jumped on my bronco and away I did ride
To marry my true love on Red River side.
But her dad knew the secret, and with twenty and four
Came to fight this young cowboy on Red River shore.

I drew my six-shooter, shooting round after round,
Till six men were wounded and seven were down.
No use for an army of twenty and four;
I'm bound for my true love on Red River shore.

At the foot of yon mountain, where the fountain doth flow,
The greatest creation, where the soft wind doth blow,
There lives a fair maiden; she's the one I adore;
She's the one I will marry on Red River shore.

*Words from Slim Critchlow, Utah Buckaroos, Salt Lake City, Utah.

ROY BEAN*

Known as "The Law West of the Pecos."

Cowboys, come and hear the story of Roy Bean in all his glory.
"The law west of Pecos," read his sign.
We must let our ponies take us to a town on lower Pecos
Where the high bridge spans the canyon thin and fine.

He was born one day in Toyah, where he learned to be a lawyer,
A teacher and a barber and the mayor.
He was cook and old-shoe mender, sometimes preacher and bartender,
And it cost two bits to have him cut your hair.

He was right smart of a hustler and considerable a rustler,
And at mixing up an eggnog he was grand;
He was clever, he was merry, he could drink a Tom and Jerry,
On occasion at a round-up took a hand.

Though the story isn't funny, there was once Roy had no money,
Which for him was not so very strange or rare;
So he went to help Pop Wyndid, but he got so absent-minded
That he put his RB brand on old Pap's steer.

As old Pap got right smart angry, Roy Bean went down to Langtry,
Where he opened up an office and a store.
There he'd sell you drinks or buttons or another rancher's muttons,
Though the latter made the other feller sore.

Once there came from Austin City a young dude reported witty,
And out of Bean he sorta guessed he'd take a rise;
So he got unusual frisky as he up and called for whisky
Sayin', "Bean, now hurry up, gol durn your eyes."

* From Slim Critchlow, Utah Buckaroos, Salt Lake City, Utah.

[413]

Then down he threw ten dollars, which the same Roy quickly collars,
And the same Roy holds to nine and hands back one;
Then the dude he gave a holler, when he saw that single dollar,
And right then began the merriment and fun.

The dude he slammed the table just as hard as he was able,
The price of whisky was too high, he swore.
Said Roy Bean, "For all your fussin' and your most outrageous cussin'
You are fined the other dollar by the law.

"On this place I own a lease. I'm the Justice of the Peace,
And the law west of the Pecos all is here,
And you've acted very badly." Then the dude he went off sadly
While down his lily cheek there rolled a tear.

One fine day they found a dead man who in life had been a red man,
Though it's doubtless he was nothing else than bad.
They called Bean to view the body. First he took a drink of toddy,
Then he listed all the things the dead man had.

For a red man he was tony, for he had a pretty pony
And a dandy bit and saddle and a rope;
He'd a very fine Navajo rug and a quart within his jug
And a pony that was dandy on the lope.

So the find it was quite rare-o, for he'd been a cocinero
And his pay day hadn't been so far away.
He'd a brand-new fine white Stetson and a silver Smith and Wesson,
While a purse of forty dollars jingled gay.

Said Roy Bean: "You'll learn a lesson, for you have a Smith and Wesson
And to carry implements of war is wrong.
Forty dollars I will fine you, for we couldn't well confine you,
As already you've been layin' around too long."

Now, you boys have heard the story of Roy Bean in all his glory;
He's the man who was the justice and the law,
He was handy with his hooks, and he was ornery in his looks,
And just now I ain't gonna tell you any more.

AN IDAHO COWBOY DANCE*

Git yo' little sage hens ready, trot 'em out upon the floor;
Line up there, you cusses; steady, lively now, one couple more.
Shorty, shed that old sombrero; Bronco, douse that cigarette;
Stop that cussin', Casimero, 'fore the ladies. Now all set!

S'lute your ladies all together, ladies opposite the same;
Hit the lumber with your leathers, balance all an' swing your dame.
Bunch the heifers to the middle, circle stags and do-se-do;
Pay attention to the fiddle, swing her round and off you go!

First four forward, back to your places; second follow, shuffle back;
Now you've got it down to cases, swing 'em till your trotters crack.
Gents all right, a-heel-and-toeing. Swing 'em, kiss 'em if you kin;
On to next and keep a-goin' till you hit your pards again!

Gents to center, ladies round 'em; form a circle, balance all.
Whirl your gals to where you found 'em, promenade around the hall.
Balance to your pards and trot 'em round the circle double quick,
Grab and kiss 'em while you've got 'em, hold 'em to it if they kick!

Ladies, left hand to your sonnies, alamain, grand right and left;
Balance all and swing your honeys, pick 'em up and feel their heft.
Promenade like skeery cattle, balance all and swing your sweets;
Shake yer spurs and make 'em rattle. Kino! Promenade to seats!

* *Old Dad's Scrap Book*, clipping.

[415]

IN TOWN

Whee—oop! Whoop—eee!
Does any one find any flies on me?
Say! I am the king of the cow-puncher clan,
A sizable sort of a fightin' man,
With my lungs full of air, an' my pockets of cash,
Achin' an' longin' to make it flash,
Ready for anythin', wise or rash;
Come on, you fellers, the round's on me!
Whee—oop! Whoop—eee!

Here's all my wad, an' I'm blowin' it free!
Fruit of six months on the lonely old plains—
Usin' it simply to addle my brains;
Gamblers an' women an' barkeeps will take—
Send me back broke to the round-up—but then
That is their business, so—fill 'em again!
I came into town for a helluva spree,
An' I'm havin' it, ain't I?
Whee—oop! Whoop—eee!

Whee—oop! Whoop—eee!
I know I'm a fool, an' a fool I will be
Till a nice little girlie says, "Billy, be wise,"
An' I gather some wisdom from readin' her eyes.
But there ain't any girl of that sort who's my friend,
An' the other kind tell me to "Spend, Billy, spend!"
So I'm havin' my fun in the best way I know;
The dollars come hard, an' it's easy they go—
Well, fill 'em up, partners, the drinks are on me!
Whee—oop! Whoop—eee!

BUCKING BRONCO*

My love is a rider, wild broncos he breaks,
Though he's promised to quit it, just for my sake.
He ties up one foot, the saddle puts on,
With a swing and a jump he's mounted and gone.
[Or For he found him a horse and it suited him so
He vowed he'd ne'er ride any other bronco.]

The first time I met him, 'twas early one spring,
Riding a bronco, a high-headed thing.
He tipped me a wink as he gaily did go;
For he wished me to look at his bucking bronco.

The next time I saw him 'twas late in the fall,
Swinging the girls at Tomlinson's ball.
He laughed and he talked as we danced to and fro,
Promised never to ride on another bronco.

He made me some presents, among them a ring;
The return that I made him was a far better thing;
. . . .
He's won it by riding his bucking bronco.

My love has a gun, and that gun he can use,
But he's quit his gun fighting as well as the booze;
And he's sold him his saddle, his spurs and his rope,
And there's no more cow-punching, and that's what I hope.

My love has a gun that has gone to the bad,
Which makes poor old Jimmy feel pretty damn sad;
For the gun it shoots high and the gun it shoots low,
And it wabbles about like a bucking bronco.

* From *Cowboy Songs*.

[417]

Now, all you young maidens, where'er you reside,
Beware of the cowboy who swings the rawhide;
He'll court you and pet you and leave you and go
In the spring up the trail on his bucking bronco.

POOR LONESOME COWBOY *

I ain't got no father,
I ain't got no father,
I ain't got no father,
To buy the clothes I wear.

I'm a poor lonesome cowboy,
I'm a poor lonesome cowboy,
I'm a poor lonesome cowboy,
And a long ways from home.

I ain't got no mother,
To mend the clothes I wear.

I ain't got no sister,
To go and play with me.

I ain't got no brother,
To drive the steers with me.

I ain't got no sweetheart,
To sit and talk with me.

I'm a poor lonesome cowboy,
I'm a poor lonesome cowboy,
I'm a poor lonesome cowboy,
And a long ways from home.

² From *Cowboy Songs.*

XVII

SONGS OF THE OVERLANDERS

Brave old Mackenzie long has laid him down
To rest beside the trail that bears his name.
A granite makes his monument.
The Northers moaning o'er the low divide
Go gently by his long deserted camps.

JOE BOWERS*

Many years ago a correspondent from Idaho sent in a song called "Joe Bowers," which he said he had heard sung by a thousand miners after a hard day's work, as they loitered about the mouth of a mine before separating for the night. In 1912 I read this ballad at a smoker of the Modern Language Association at Cornell University presided over by Professor Olmsted, now of the University of Minnesota. Later Cony Sturgis came to me and said that he had seen the same song written on the walls of an old tavern not many miles from Ithaca. Since that time I have discovered that "Joe Bowers" was one of the popular songs among the Confederate soldiers of the Civil War. I have run upon men who knew it in Wyoming, in Texas, and in other Western and Southern states.

Its author, according to Judge T. J. C. Flagg, writing in the *Pike County*, Missouri, *News*, June 27, 1899, was a Pennsylvanian named Johnson, a song writer and comic singer. The song is to be found in the second edition of *Johnson's Original Comic Songs*, San Francisco, 1860. He was a famous performer and comic singer in the low theaters and "dance houses" of the early days, but finally lost his reason and ended his days in a lunatic asylum.

The St. Louis *Republic* of May 27, 1900, tells us that there was a Joe Bowers and he did have a brother Ike, a sweetheart named Sally, and he joined the Argonauts and went gold-hunting in California. Joe was born on Salt River, Pike County, Missouri, in 1829.

On the long overland way out to California as a bull driver, Joe had a lot of time to think of Sally. He told his troubles to some of his friends. According to one account his fellow traveller, Frank W.

*Words from *Johnson's Original Comic Songs*, San Francisco, 1860. Tune from J. H. Cox's *Ballads of the South* (Cambridge, Mass.: Harvard University Press).

Smith, wrote the poem. Immediately it was sung by his companions. "Soon it was sung in every state in the Union, and even in England."

Yet another story is that Frank Smith wrote "Joe Bowers" as a joke on Joe, who was himself fond of joking. Later it got into print and then became a song. Joe never came back from California to dear old Pike County. And more about Sally no one knows.

My name it is Joe Bow - ers, I've got a broth-er Ike; I

came from old Mis-sou - ri, Just all the way from Pike; I'll

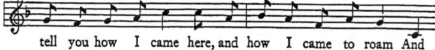

tell you how I came here, and how I came to roam And

leave my poor old ma - ma so far a - way from home.

My name it is Joe Bowers, I've got a brother Ike,
I came from old Missouri, yes, all the way from Pike;
I'll tell you why I left thar and how I came to roam,
And leave my poor old mammy so far away from home.

I used to love a gal thar, they called her Sally Black;
I axed her for to marry me, she said it was a whack;
"But," says she to me, "Joe Bowers, before we hitch for life,
You'd orter have a little home to keep your little wife."

Says I, "My dearest Sally, oh, Sally, for your sake,
I'll go to Californy and try to raise a stake."

Says she to me: "Joe Bowers, oh, you are the chap to win.
Give me a kiss to seal the bargain." And she threw a dozen in.

I shall ne'er forgit my feelin's when I bid adieu to all.
Sally cotched me round the neck, then I began to bawl.
When I sot in they all commenced, you ne'er did hear the like,
How they all took on and cried the day I left old Pike.

When I got to this 'ere country, I hadn't nary red;
I had sich wolfish feelin's, I wished myself most dead,
But the thoughts of my dear Sally soon made these feelin's git,
And whispered hopes to Bowers, Lord! I wish I had 'em yit.

At length I went to minin', put in my biggest licks,
Come down upon the bowlders jist like a thousand bricks;
I worked both late and early, in rain, and sun and snow,
But I was workin' for my Sally, so 'twas all the same to Joe.

I made a very lucky strike, as the gold itself did tell,
And saved it for my Sally, the gal I loved so well,
I saved it for my Sally, that I might pour it at her feet,
That she might kiss and hug me and call me something sweet.

But one day I got a letter from my dear, kind brother Ike,
It came from old Missouri, sent all the way from Pike;
It brought me the gol-darndest news as ever you did hear,
My heart is almost busted, so pray excuse this tear.

It said my Sal was fickle, that her love for me had fled,
That she'd married with a butcher, whose hair was awful red;
It told me more than that—oh, it's enough to make one swear!
It said Sally had a baby, and the baby had red hair.

Now I've told you all that I could tell about the sad affa'r,
'Bout Sally marryin' the butcher, and the butcher had red ha'r.
Whether it was a boy or gal child, the letter never said,
It only said its cussed hair was inclinèd to be a red.

[423]

SWEET BETSY FROM PIKE

Did you ev - er hear tell of Sweet Bet - sy from

Pike, Who crossed the wide 'prai - ries with

her lov - er Ike? With two yoke of

cat - tle and one spot - ted hog, A tall

Shang - hai roost - er and an old yal - ler dog.

Sing too - ral - i - oo - ral - i oo - ral i - ay,

Sing too - rall - i - oo - ral - i - oo - ral - i - ay.

Did you ever hear tell of sweet Betsy from Pike,
Who crossed the wide prairies with her lover Ike,
With two yoke of cattle and one spotted hog,
A tall shanghai rooster and an old yaller dog?

Chorus:
    Sing-too-rall-i-oo-ral-i-oo-ral-i-ay,
    Sing-too-rall-i-oo-ral-oo-ral-i-ay.

One evening quite early they camped on the Platte,
'Twas near by the road on a green shady flat;
Where Betsy, quite tired, lay down to repose,
While with wonder Ike gazed on his Pike County rose.

They swam the wide rivers and crossed the tall peaks,
And camped on the prairie for weeks upon weeks.
Starvation and cholera and hard work and slaughter,
They reached California spite of hell and high water.

Out on the prairie one bright starry night
They broke the whisky and Betsy got tight,
She sang and she shouted and danced o'er the plain,
And showed her bare arse to the whole wagon train.

The Injuns came down in a wild yelling horde,
And Betsy was skeered they would scalp her adored;
Behind the front wagon wheel Betsy did crawl,
And there she fought the Injuns with musket and ball.

The alkali desert was burning and bare,
And Isaac's soul shrank from the death that lurked there:
"Dear old Pike County, I'll go back to you."
Says Betsy, "You'll go by yourself if you do."

They soon reached the desert, where Betsy gave out,
And down in the sand she lay rolling about;
While Ike in great terror looked on in surprise,
Saying, "Betsy, get up, you'll get sand in your eyes."

Sweet Betsy got up in a great deal of pain
And declared she'd go back to Pike County again;
Then Ike heaved a sigh and they fondly embraced,
And she traveled along with his arm round her waist.

They went to Salt Lake to inquire the way,
And Brigham declared that sweet Betsy should stay;
But Betsy got frightened and ran like a deer,
While Brigham stood pawing the earth like a steer.

The wagon tipped over with a terrible crash,
And out on the prairie rolled all sorts of trash;
A few little baby clothes done up with care
Looked rather suspicious, but it was all on the square.

One morning they climbed a very high hill,
And with wonder looked down on old Placerville;
Ike shouted and said, as he cast his eyes down,
"Sweet Betsy, my darling, we've got to Hangtown."

Long Ike and sweet Betsy attended a dance,
Where Ike wore a pair of his Pike County pants;
Sweet Betsy was covered with ribbons and rings,
Said Ike, "You're an angel, but where are your wings?"

A miner said, "Betsy, will you dance with me?"
"I will that, old hoss, if you don't make too free;
But don't dance me hard. Do you want to know why?
Doggone ye, I'm chock-full of strong alkali."

Long Ike and sweet Betsy got married of course,
But Ike, getting jealous, obtained a divorce;
And Betsy, well satisfied, said with a shout,
"Good-by, you big lummox, I'm glad you backed out."

CROSSING THE PLAINS *

(Air: "Caroline of Edinburgh")

Come, all you Californians, I pray ope wide your ears,
If you are going across the plains, with snotty mules and steers;
Remember beans before you start, likewise dried beef and ham;
Beware of ven'son, damn the stuff, it's oftentimes a ram.

You must buy two revolvers, a bowie knife and belt,
Says you, "Old feller, now stand off, or I will have your pelt."
The greenhorn looks around about, but not a soul can see,
Says he, "There's not a man in town but what's afraid of me."

You shouldn't shave, but cultivate your down, and let it grow,
So when you do return, 'twill be as soft and white as snow;
Your lovely Jane will be surprised, your ma'll begin to cook;
The greenhorn to his mother'll say, "How savage I must look!"

"How do you like it overland?" his mother she will say.
"All right, excepting cooking, then the devil is to pay;
For some won't cook, and others can't, and then it's curse and damn,
The coffee pot's begun to leak, so has the frying pan."

It's always jaw about the teams, and how we ought to do,
All hands get mad, and each one says, "I own as much as you."
One of them says, "I'll buy or sell, I'm damned if I care which."
Another says, "Let's buy him out, the lousy son of a bitch."

You calculate on sixty days to take you over the Plains,
But there you lack for bread and meat, for coffee and for brains;
Your sixty days are a hundred or more, your grub you've got to divide,
Your steers and mules are alkalied, so foot it—you cannot ride.

* Put's Original California Songster (1855), p. 13.

[427]

You have to stand a watch at night, to keep the Indians off,
About sundown some heads will ache, and some begin to cough;
To be deprived of health we know is always very hard,
Though every night some one is sick, to get rid of standing guard.

Your canteens, they should be well filled, with poison alkali,
So when you get tired of traveling, you can cramp all up and die;
The best thing in the world to keep your bowels loose and free,
Is fight and quarrel among yourselves, and seldom if ever agree.

There's not a log to make a seat, along the river Platte,
So when you eat, you've got to stand, or sit down square and flat;
It's fun to cook with buffalo wood, take some that's newly born,
If I knew once what I know now, I'd 'a' gone around the Horn!

The desert's nearly death on corns, while walking in the sand,
And drive a jackass by the tail, it's damn this overland;
I'd rather ride a raft at sea, and then at once be lost.
Says Bill, "Let's leave this poor old mule, we can't get him across."

The ladies have the hardest time, that emigrate by land,
For when they cook with buffalo wood, they often burn a hand;
And then they jaw their husbands round, get mad and spill the tea,
Wish to the Lord they'd be taken down with a turn of the di-a-ree.

When you arrive at Placerville, or Sacramento City,
You've nothing in the world to eat, no money—what a pity!
Your striped pants are all worn out, which causes people to laugh,
When they see you gaping round the town like a great big brindle calf.

You're lazy, poor, and all broke down, such hardships you endure;
The post office at Sacramento all such men will cure;
You'll find a line from ma and pa, and one from lovely Sal,
If that don't physic you every mail, you never will get well.

COMING AROUND THE HORN*

(Air: "Dearest May")

Now, miners, if you'll listen, I'll tell you quite a tale,
About the voyage around Cape Horn, they call a pleasant sail;
We bought a ship, and had her stowed with houses, tools and grub,
But cursed the day we ever sailed in the poor old rotten tub.

Chorus:
Oh, I remember well, the lies they used to tell,
Of gold so bright, it hurt the sight, and made the miners yell.

We left old New York City, with the weather very thick,
The second day we puked up boots, oh, wusn't we all seasick!
I swallowed pork tied to a string, which made a dreadful shout,
I felt it strike the bottom, but I could not pull it out.

We all were owners in the ship, and soon began to growl,
Because we hadn't ham and eggs, and now and then a fowl;
We told the captain what to do, as him we had to pay,
The captain swore that he was boss, and we should him obey.

We lived like hogs, penned up to fat, our vessel was so small,
We had a "duff" but once a month, and twice a day a squall;
A meeting now and then we held, which kicked up quite a stink,
The captain damned us fore and aft, and wished the box would sink.

Off Cape Horn, where we lay becalmed, kind Providence seemed
    to frown,
We had to stand up night and day, none of us dared sit down;
For some had half a dozen boils, 'twas awful, sure's you're born,
But some would try it on the sly, and got pricked by the Horn.

* *Put's Original California Songster,* p. 37.

We stopped at Valparaiso, where the women are so loose,
And all got drunk as usual, got shoved in the calaboose;
Our ragged, rotten sails were patched, the ship made ready for sea,
But every man, except the cook, was up town on a spree.

We sobered off, set sail again, on short allowance, of course,
With water thick as castor-oil, and stinking beef much worse;
We had the scurvy and the itch, and any amount of lice,
The medicine chest went overboard, with blue mass, cards and dice.

We arrived at San Francisco, and all went to the mines,
We left an agent back to sell our goods of various kinds;
A friend wrote up to let us know our agent, Mr. Gates,
Had sold the ship and cargo, sent the money to the States.

THE BULL-WHACKER *

I'm a lonely bull-whacker
On the Red-Cloud line,
I can lick any son-of-a-gun
That will yoke an ox of mine.
And if I can catch him,
You bet I will or try,
I'll lick him with an oxbow—
Root hog or die.

It's out on the road
With a very heavy load,
With a very awkward team
And a very muddy road,
You may whip and you may holler,
But if you cuss it's on the sly;
Then whack the cattle on, boys—
Root hog or die.

* Text from *Cowboy Songs* (New York: The Macmillan Company, 1910).

It's out on the road
These sights are to be seen,
The antelope and buffalo,
The prairie all so green—
The antelope and buffalo,
The rabbit jumps so high;
It's whack the cattle on, boys—
Root hog or die.

It's every day at twelve
There's something for to do;
And if there's nothing else,
There's a pony for to shoe;
I'll throw him down,
And still I'll make him lie;
Little pig, big pig,
Root hog or die.

Now perhaps you'd like to know
What we have to eat,
A little piece of bread
And a little dirty meat,
A little black coffee,
And whisky on the sly;
It's whack the cattle on, boys—
Root hog or die.

There's hard times on Bitter Creek
That never can be beat,
It was root hog or die
Under every wagon sheet;
We cleaned up all the Indians,
Drank all the alkali.
And it's whack the cattle on, boys—
Root hog or die.

There was good old times in Salt Lake *
That never can pass by,
It was there I first spied
My China girl called Wi,
She could smile, she could chuckle,
She could roll her hog eye;
Then it's whack the cattle on, boys—
Root hog or die.

Oh, I'm going home *
Bull-whacking for to spurn,
I ain't got a nickel,
And I don't give a durn.
'Tis when I meet a pretty girl,
You bet I will or try,
I'll make her my little wife—
Root hog or die.

BRIGHAM YOUNG †

Now Brigham Young is a Mormon bold,
And a leader of the roaring rams,
And shepherd of a lot of fine tub sheep
And a lot of pretty little lambs.
Oh, he lives with his five and forty wives,
In the city of the Great Salt Lake,
Where they breed and swarm like hens on a farm
And cackle like ducks to a drake.

* Necessarily emended.
† From *Cowboy Songs*.

Oh, Brigham, Brigham Young,
It's a miracle how you survive,
With your roaring rams and your pretty little lambs
And your five and forty wives.

Number forty-five is about sixteen,
Number one is sixty and three;
And they make such a riot, how he keeps them quiet
Is a downright mystery to me
For they clatter and they claw and they jaw, jaw, jaw,
And each has a different desire;
It would aid the renown of the best shop in town
To supply them half what they desire.

Now, Brigham Young was a stout man once,
And now he is thin and old;
And I am sorry to relate he is bald on the pate,
Which once had a covering of gold.
For his oldest wives won't have white wool,
And his young ones won't have red,
So, with tearing it out, and taking turn about,
They have torn all the hair off his head.

Now, the oldest wives sing songs all day,
And the young ones all sing songs;
And amongst the crowd he has it pretty loud—
They're as noisy as Chinese gongs.
And when they advance for a Mormon dance
He is filled with the direst alarms;
For they are sure to end the night in a tabernacle fight
To see who has the fairest charms.

GREER COUNTY *

Tom Hight is my name, an old bachelor I am,
You'll find me out West in the county of fame,
You'll find me out West on an elegant plain,
And starving to death on my government claim.

Hurrah for Greer County! The land of the free,
The land of the bedbug, grasshopper, and flea;
I'll sing of its praises, I'll tell of its fame,
While starving to death on my government claim.

How happy am I when I crawl into bed—
A rattlesnake hisses a tune at my head,
A gay little centipede, all without fear,
Crawls over my pillow and into my ear.

My clothes is all ragged as my language is rough,
My bread is corn-dodgers, both solid and tough;
But yet I am happy, and live at my ease
On sorghum molasses, bacon, and cheese.

Good-by to Greer County where blizzards arise,
Where the sun never sinks and a flea never dies,
And the wind never ceases but always remains
Till it starves us to death on our government claims.

Farewell to Greer County, farewell to the West,
I'll travel back East to the girl I love best,
I'll travel back to Texas and marry me a wife,
And quit cornbread for the rest of my life.

* Text from *Cowboy Songs.*

XVIII
THE MINER

THE HARD WORKING MINER

James Howard, blind fiddler of Harlan, Kentucky, sang this doleful ditty most dolefully through the nose.

The hard-work-ing mi - ner, his dan - gers are great, So
Chorus: He's on - ly a mi - ner, been killed un - der-ground, He's

ma - ny while mi - ning have met their sad fate, While
on - ly a mi - ner and one more is gone, Killed

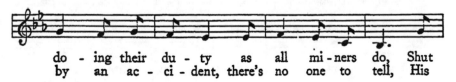

do - ing their du - ty as all mi - ners do, Shut
by an ac - ci - dent, there's no one to tell, His

out from the day - light and dar - ling ones too.
mi - ning's all o - ver, poor mi - ner fare - well.

The hard-working miner, his dangers are great,
So many while mining have met their sad fate,
While doing their duty as all miners do,
Shut out from the daylight and darling ones too.

[437]

Chorus:

He's only a miner, been killed underground,
He's only a miner and one more is gone,
Killed by an accident, there's no one to tell,
His mining's all over, poor miner farewell.

He left his dear wife and little ones too,
To win them a living as all miners do;
But while he was working for those whom he loved,
He met a sad fate from a bowlder above.

A miner is gone; we'll see him no more.
May God be with the miner wherever he may go.
God pity the miner, protect him as well,
Shield him from danger while down in the ground.

THE DREARY BLACK HILLS *

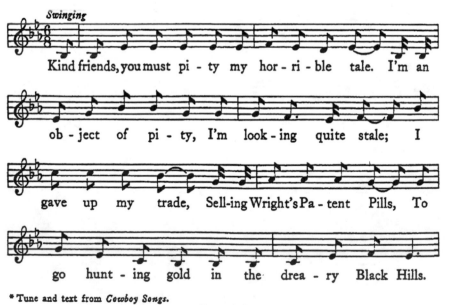

Kind friends, you must pi-ty my hor-ri-ble tale. I'm an
ob-ject of pi-ty, I'm look-ing quite stale; I
gave up my trade, Sell-ing Wright's Pa-tent Pills, To
go hunt-ing gold in the drea-ry Black Hills.

* Tune and text from *Cowboy Songs.*

[438]

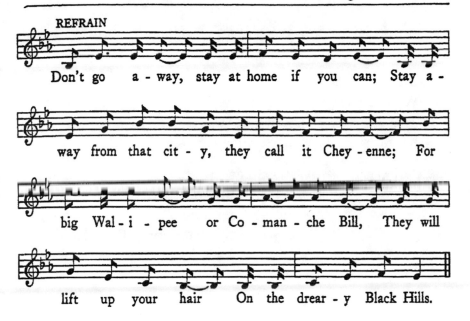

REFRAIN

Don't go a - way, stay at home if you can; Stay a -
way from that cit - y, they call it Chey - enne; For
big Wal - i - pee or Co - man - che Bill, They will
lift up your hair On the drear - y Black Hills.

Kind friends, you must pity my horrible tale,
An object of pity, I'm looking quite stale,
I gave up my trade selling Wright's Patent Pills
To go hunting gold in the dreary Black Hills.

Don't go away, stay at home if you can,
Stay away from that city, they call it Cheyenne,
For big Wallipe or Comanche Bill
They will lift up your hair on the dreary Black Hills.

The roundhouse at Cheyenne is filled every night
With loafers and bummers of most every plight;
On their backs is no clothes, in their pockets no bills,
Each day they keep starting for the dreary Black Hills.

I got to Cheyenne, no gold could I find,
I thought of the lunch route I'd left far behind;

Through rain, hail, and snow, froze plumb to the gills—
They call me the orphan of the dreary Black Hills.

Oh, I wish the man who started this sell
Was a captive, and Crazy Horse had him in hell.
There's no use in groaning or swearing like pitch,
But the man who would stay here is a son of a bitch.

Don't go away, stay at home if you can,
Stay away from that city, they call it Cheyenne,
For old Sitting Bull or Comanche Bill
They will take off your scalp on the dreary Black Hills.

JUST FROM DAWSON *

(Tune, "Bingen on the Rhine")

A Dawson City mining man lay dying in the ice,
He didn't have a woman nurse, he didn't have the price;
But a comrade knelt beside him as the sun sank in repose
To listen to his dying words and watch him while he froze.

The dying man propped up his head above four rods of snow,
And said: "I never saw it thaw at 98 below.
Take this little pinhead nugget that I swiped from Jason Dills
And send it home to Deadwood, to Deadwood on the hills.

"Tell the fellows in the home land to remain and have a cinch,
That the price of patent pork-chops here is 80 cents per inch.
And I speak as one that's been here scratching around to find the gold
And at 10 per cent of discount now could not buy up a cold.

* From F. A. and Edith H. Brewer.

"Tell my sweetheart not to mourn for me with sorrow too intense,
For I'm going to a warmer and far more cheerful hence.
Oh, the air is growing thicker, and the breezes give me chills,
Gee! I wish I was in Deadwood, in Deadwood on the hills.

"Tell my friends and tell my enemies, if you ever reach the East,
That the Dawson City region is no place for man or beast;
That the land's too elevated and the wind too awful cold,
And the hills of South Dakota yield as good a grade of gold.

"Now, so long," he faintly whispered. "I have told you what to do."
And he closed his weary eyelids and froze solid P.D.Q.
We procured an organ box and C.O.D.'d the bills
And sent the miner home that night to Deadwood on the hills.

XIX

THE SHANTY-BOY

"A peavy hook it is my pride,
An ax I well can handle."

THE LOST JIMMIE WHALEN *

This is an American fragment of a Canadian ballad that has to do
with the death of a young lumberjack, Jimmie Whalen.

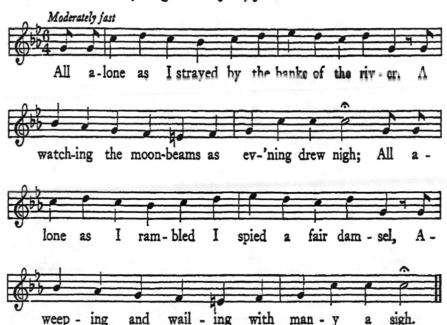

Moderately fast

All a-lone as I strayed by the banks of the riv - er, A
watch-ing the moon-beams as ev-'ning drew nigh; All a -
lone as I ram-bled I spied a fair dam - sel, A-
weep - ing and wail - ing with man - y a sigh.

All alone as I strayed by the banks of the river,
A-watching the moonbeams as the evening drew nigh;
All alone as I rambled I spied a fair damsel,
A-weeping and wailing with many a sigh.

A-weeping for one who is now lying lowly,
A-mourning for one who no mortal can save,
As the foaming dark waters flow sadly about him,
As onward they speed over young Jimmie's grave.

* From Franz L. Rickaby's *Ballads and Songs of the Shanty-Boy* (Cambridge, Mass.: Harvard University Press).

"O Jimmie, can't you tarry here with me,
Not leave me alone distracted in pain?
But since death is the dagger that has cut us asunder,
And wide is the gulf, love, between you and I . . ."

THE SHANTY-BOY AND THE FARMER'S SON *

As I walked out one eve - ning just as the sun went
down, I care - less - ly did ram - ble till I
came to Tren - ton town. I heard two maids con -
vers - ing as slow - ly I passed by; One said she loved a
farm - er's son, the oth - er a shan - ty - boy.

As I walked out one evening just as the sun went down,
I carelessly did ramble till I came to Trenton town.
I heard two maids conversing as slowly I passed by.
One said she loved a farmer's son, the other a shanty-boy.

* From Rickaby's *Ballads and Songs of the Shanty-Boy* (Cambridge, Mass.: Harvard University Press).

[446]

The one that loved her farmer's son, these words I heard her say:
"The reason that I love him, at home with me he'll stay.
He'll stay at home in winter, to the shanties he will not go,
And when the spring it doth come, his land he'll plow and sow."

"All for to plow and sow your land," the other girl did say.
"If the crops should prove a failure, your debts you couldn't pay.
If the crops should prove a failure and the grain market be low,
The sheriff he will sell you out to pay the debts you own."

"All for the sheriff selling us out, it doth not me alarm.
You have no need to be in debt when you're on a good farm.
You raise your bread all on your farm; you don't work through storms
    of rain,
While your shanty-boy must work each day his family to maintain."

"Oh, how you praise your shanty-boy, who off to the woods must go!
He's ordered out before daylight to work through storms and snow,
Whilst happy and contented my farmer's son doth lie,
And tell to me some tales of love while the cold winds whistle by."

"That's the reason I praise the shanty-boy. He goes up early in the fall.
He is both stout and hearty, and fit to stand the squall.
It's with pleasure I'll receive him in the spring when he comes down,
And his money quite free he'll spend with me when your farmers' sons
    have none.

"I could not stand those silly words your farmer's son would say.
They are so green the cows oft-times have taken them for hay.
How easy it is to know them when they come into town!
Small boys will run up to them sayin' 'Mossback, are ye down?'"

"What I said about your shanty-boy, I hope you'll excuse me,
And of my ignorant farmer's son I hope I do get free.
Then if ever I do get a chance, with a shanty-boy I'll go,
And I'll leave poor mossback stay at home his buckwheat for to sow."

GERRY'S ROCKS *

Come all you jolly fellows, wherever you may be,
I hope you'll pay attention and listen unto me.
It's all about some shanty-boys, so manly and so brave.
'Twas on the jam on Gerry's rock they met their watery grave.

'Twas on one Sunday morning as you shall quickly hear,
Our logs were piled up mountain-high, we could not keep them clear,
"Turn out, brave boys," the foreman cried, with a voice devoid of fear,
"And we'll break up the jam on Gerry's rock and for Eagletown we'll
    steer."

* From Franz L. Rickaby's *Ballads and Songs of the Shanty-Boy.*

[448]

Some of the shanty-boys were willing, while others they hung back,
For to work on Sunday, they thought it was not right.
But six American shanty-boys did volunteer to go
To break the jam on Gerry's rock with their foreman, young Monroe.

They had not rolled off many logs before the boss to them did say,
"I would you all to be on your guard, for the jam will soon give way."
He had no more than spoke those words before the jam did break
    and go,
And carried away those six brave youths with their foreman, young
    Monroe.

As soon as the news got into camp and attorneys came to hear,
In search of their mangled bodies the river we did steer,
And one of their dead bodies found, to our great grief and woe,
All bruised and mangled on the beach lay the corpse of young Monroe.

We took him from the water, smoothed back his raven-black hair,
There was one fair form amongst them whose cries did rend the air,
There was one fair form amongst them, a girl from Saginaw town,
Whose mournful cries did rend the skies for her lover that was
    drowned.

We buried him quite decently. 'Twas on the twelfth of May,
Come all you jolly shanty-boys, and for your comrade pray.
We engraved upon a hemlock tree that near his grave did grow—
The name, the age, the drownding date of the foreman, young Mon-
    roe.

His mother was a widow living down by the river side.
Miss Clark she was a noble girl, this young man's promised bride.   .
The wages of true love the firm to her did pay,
And liberal subscription she received from the shanty-boys that day.

She received their presents kindly and thanked them every one,
Though she did not survive him long, as you shall understand;

Scarcely three weeks after, and she was called to go,
And her last request was to be laid by her lover, young Monroe.

Come all you brave shanty-boys, I'd have you call and see
Two green graves by the river side where grows the hemlock tree;
The shanty-boys cut off the wood where lay those lovers low—
'Tis the handsome Clara Clark and her true love, brave Monroe.

BUNG YER EYE *

I am a jolly shanty-boy,
As you will soon discover;
To all the dodges I am fly,
A hustling pine-woods rover.
A peavy hook it is my pride,
An ax I well can handle;
To fell a tree or punch a bull,
Get rattling Danny Randall.

Bung yer eye: bung yer eye.

I love a girl in Saginaw,
She lives with her mother;
I defy all Michigan,
To find such another.
She's tall and fat, her hair is red,
Her face is plump and pretty;
She's my daisy Sunday best-day girl,
And her front name stands for Kitty.

Bung yer eye: bung yer eye.

I took her to a dance one night,
A mossback gave the bidding,
Silver Jack bossed the shebang,

* Words sent by Stewart Edward White in 1909.

[450]

And Big Dan played the fiddle.
We danced and drank the livelong night,
With fights between the dancing—
Till Silver Jack cleaned out the ranch,
And sent the mossbacks prancing.

Bung yer eye: bung yer eye.

THE BANKS OF THE PAMANAW *

While strolling out one evening
  In the latter part of June,
The sun had sunk far in the west
  And brightly shone the moon,

I strolled away from camp, my boys,
  To view the scenery round;
'Twas there I spied this Indian maid
  A-sitting on the ground.

As I advanced up towards her,
  She did not seem afraid.
I boldly stepped up to her
  And unto her I said:

"You do surprise me very much
  Although you're but a squaw,
To see you here so lonely on
  The banks of the Pamanaw."

"Draw nigh to me, young man," she said,
  "And I will tell you all,
The truth I will unfold to you,
  And the cause of my downfall.

* This ballad was taken from the reciting of an old lumberjack, William McBride of Isabella City, Michigan, 1931. Sent by Professor E. C. Beck, Central State Teachers College, Mount Pleasant, Michigan

[451]

"My brother and my sister died,
  Likewise my pa and ma;
They left me here so lonely on
  The banks of the Pamanaw.

"And that's not all, young man," she said;
  "A lover once was mine.
He was a true, bold Indian scout
  On the British bounty line.

"He courted me and he flattered me,
  Called me his lovely squaw;
But now he's gone and left me on
  The banks of the Pamanaw."

Said I, "My pretty, fair maiden,
  Come go along with me;
I'll take you to a better land,
  To a pale-face countree.

"I'll dress you up in costly robes,
  The likes you never saw;
No more you need to ramble on
  The banks of the Pamanaw.

"Oh, no! Oh, no! young man," she said.
  "This you may very well know,
For I have taken, oh, my oath
  To live with the red deer and doe.

"For the white folks may break their oaths;
  Though I am but a squaw,
I'll live and die and keep my vows
  On the banks of the Pamanaw."

XX

THE ERIE CANAL

"Fifteen years on the Erie Canal,
She aimed for Heaven but she went to Hell."
—WALTER D. EDMONDS, in *Rome Haul*.

The Introduction (page xxix) contains the story of how the first version of the Erie Canal ballad, as herein printed, was put together. The words demand music, and undoubtedly the song was sung. At one time the tune was recorded for me by a former towpath boy, William D. Totten of Seattle, Washington, though, unfortunately, on wax which has since crumbled. Twenty years was too long to wait. Recently I spent some time in Albany, Syracuse, and Buffalo in the effort to unearth the original melody. All the mule drivers are long gone, but the search did result in uncovering some scraps of old canal songs that seem to deserve perpetuation.

Canal-boat mule drivers (the towpath boys) sang for precisely the same reason that cowboys yodeled and sang when riding around the sleeping herds at night. The canal boats also moved on at night. The singers made music in order to keep awake and secure entertainment out of their monotonous duties. In Albany I found a complaint filed in 1835 against singing at night by canallers. Evidently the complainers lived near the banks of the canal.

BALLAD OF THE ERIE CANAL

The following song was picked up in six different states: Texas, Illinois, Washington, Montana, New York, and Pennsylvania—each state contributing a stanza or more not found in the others (see Introduction).

I am all the way from Buffalo,
Upon the good boat *Danger*,
A long, long trip we had, my boys,
I feel just like a stranger.
Petty fogs, artful storms,
Forget them I never shall;
I am every inch a sailor, boys,
On the Erie Canal.

Chorus:

So haul in yer bowlines,
Stand by the saddle mule;
Low bridge, boys, dodge yer head,
Don't stand up like a fool;
For the Erie is a-risin'
An' the whisky's gittin' low;
I hardly think we'll get a drink
Till we git to Buffalo.

We left Albany harbor
About the break of day;
If rightly I remember,
'Twas the second day of May.
We trusted to our driver;

Although he was but small,
Yet he knew all the windings
Of that raging Canawl.

Early every morning
Ye can hear the flunkies call,
Come aft and git your lime juice,
Come aft, one and all;
Come aft and git your lime juice,
And don't bring any back;
Before you git to Syracuse
Ye's goin' to get the sack.

Three days out from Albany
A pirate we did spy;
The black flag with the skull and bones
Was a-wavin' up on high;
We signaled to the driver
To h'ist the flag o' truce,
When we found it was the *Mary Jane*
Just out o' Syracuse.

Two days out from Syracuse
The vessel struck a shoal,
And we like to all been foundered
On a chunk of Lackawanna coal.
We hollered to the captain
On the towpath treadin' dirt;
He jumped on board and stopped the leak
With his old red flannel shirt.

The cook she was a kind soul,
She had a ragged dress;
We h'isted her upon a pole
As a signal of distress;

The winds began to whistle
And the waves began to roll,
And we had to reef our royal
On the raging Canawl.

When we got to Syracuse
The off mule he was dead,
The nigh mule got blind staggers
And we cracked him on the head;
The captain he got married,
The cook she went to jail,
And I was the only son of a bitch
That's left to tell the tale.

Four long days we sailed the Hudson,
Sal and I and Hank;
We greased ourselves with tallow fat
And slid out on a plank;
The crew are in the poorhouse,
The captain he's in jail,
And I'm the sole survivin' man
That's left to tell the tale.

THE ERIE CANAL

From Rev. Charles A. Richmond, Washington, D. C.

I've got a mule, her name is Sal,
Fifteen miles on the Erie Canal;
She's a good old worker and a good old pal,
Fifteen miles on the Erie Canal.
We've hauled some barges in our day,
Filled with lumber, coal, and hay,

[457]

And we know ev'ry inch of the way
From Albany to Buffalo.

Refrain:

Low bridge, ev'rybody down!
Low bridge, for we're going through a town;
And you'll always know your neighbor,
You'll always know your pal,
If you ever navigated on the Erie Canal.

We better get along on our way, old gal,
Fifteen miles on the Erie Canal,
'Cause you bet your life I'd never part with Sal,
Fifteen miles on the Erie Canal.
Git up there, mule, here comes a lock,
We'll make Rome 'bout six o'clock.
One more trip and back we'll go,
Right back home to Buffalo.

The stanzas that follow were unearthed as a result of advertising in Albany, Syracuse, and Buffalo.

May 23, 1933. From Mrs. G. W. Tillapough, Mexico, New York:

Sandy Dan he had red hair,
He looked six ways for Sunday.
He peddled clams the whole week through,
And every day was Sunday.
    Sunday night he went
    To see red-headed Sal,
And took her to his clamboat
Way down on the Erie Canal.

"The other six verses the same except 'Every day was Monday' in the second verse, 'Tuesday' in the third verse and so on."
Sandy Dan, it would seem, had company every night.

THE ERIE CANAL BALLAD

From Professor J. V. Denney, Head of the English Department, Ohio State University, Columbus, Ohio. Sung to the tune of "Old Black Joe."

Once I was a brakeman on the E-r-i-e Canal;
I fell in love with the cook, a cross-eyed gal named Sal,
She shook me for the driver, a red-headed son of a gun
And left me here as you may see—a poor old bum.

Chorus:

I'm going, I'm going, for I know my time has come!
And to the workhouse I must go, a poor old bum.
As a free-lunch destroyer, I'm the terror of the route,
I can wrastle with the sausage or a plate of sauerkraut
And when I get a plate of beans, oh, don't I make them
   hum!
They're such a solid comfort to a poor old bum.

From E. R. Herriman, Syracuse, New York, about May 1, 1933:

I've just come down from Buffalo
Upon the great boat *Danger;*
Had a long trip on the Erie
And I feel just like a stranger.

Chorus:

Haul in your bowlines,
Stand by your saddle mules,
Don't dodge your head for low bridges,
Don't act so like a fool!
Keep up your courage, boys,
We'll land you safely in,
And when we get to Buffalo, boys,
We'll roll in barrels of gin.

[459]

From "An old Buffalo girl," May 10, 1933:

A light on the Erie Canal,
The water was three feet deep,
The pollywog swallowed his tail
And the tears rolled down his cheeks.

From N. E. Bugbee, Cortland, New York, May 13, 1933:

I've traveled all around this world and Tonawanda, too,
Was cast on desert islands, was beaten black and blue,
Was shot and cut at Bull's Run, I've wandered since a boy;
But I'll ne'er forget the trip I drove from Buffalo to Troy.

Chorus:

For it was tramp, tramp and tighten up your lines,
And watch the playful horse flies 'round the mules they climb,
For it was cuss, kick, and swish, forget it I never shall
When I drove a team of sorrel mules on the Erie Canal.

The cook we had on board that boat stood six feet in her sock,
Her hand was like an elephant's ear, her breath would open a lock;
A maiden of sixty summers was she, she slept upon the floor,
And when at night she'd get to sleep, phew! Sufferin'! How she'd
    snore!

From D. Gillispie, Buffalo, New York, May 13, 1933. "Sung by
Johnny Bartley in the eighties, at the Alhambra Varieties on Commercial Street near the Erie Canal."

I've traveled all around this world and Tonawanda too.
I've been cast on desert islands and beaten black and blue.
I fought and bled at Bull's Run and wandered since a boy—
But I'll never forget the trip I took from Buffalo to Troy.
Whoa! Back! Get up! Forget it I never shall,
When I drove a team of spavin mules on the Erie Canal.

The cook we had on board the deck stood six feet in her socks—
Her hand was like an elephant's ear and her breath would open the
    locks.

A maid of fifty summers was she, the most of her body was on the
floor,
And when at night she went to bed, oh, sufferin', how she'd snore!

Whoa! Back! Get up! and tighten up your line—
And watch the playful flies as on the mules they climb.
Whoa! Back, duck your nut, forget it I never shall,
When I drove a team of spavin mules on the Erie Canal.

Sung by Henry "Kip" Conway, Morrisburg, Ontario:

The Erie's raging and the gin is going low,
We'll never get another drink till we get to Buffalo.
The cook I had on deck stood six foot in her sock,
Had a hoof like an elephant and her breath would open a lock;
She could kick, smile, or dance—forget I never shall
When I drove the team of mules on the Erie-I Canal.

Chorus:
  Hit 'er, shove 'er, go up in the juber-ju;
  Give her a line and let her go, ol' Kip'll pull her through.

I had a second cousin on the towpath treading dirt,
Git aboard, you son of a gun, with your lousy undershirt.
Hit 'er, shove 'er, go up in the juber-ju;
Give her a line and let her go, ol' Kip'll pull her through.

Three nights out of Hudson
We struck a rock of coal,
Which gave the boat a h—l of a shock (fearful shock)
And stove in quite a hole.

I hollered to my driver on the towpath treading dirt;
And he jumped aboard and stopped the leak
With his lousy undershirt.

One night on the Erie I couldn't sleep a wink,
The crew they all bore down on me

[461]

Because I refused to drink.
Fearful storms and heavy fogs, forget 'em I never shall,
For I'm every inch a sailor boy upon the Erie Canal.

When we arrived at Buffalo,
With Sally, Jack, and Hank,
We greased ourselves in tallow fat
And slid off on a plank;
Sally's in the poorhouse,
The rest of the crew's in jail,
And I'm the only ("son ——") bugger afloat
That's left to tell the tale.

From R. G. Summers, Buffalo, New York, May 11, 1933:
"As requested by the *News* of the 10th I'm enclosing what I know of one old Erie Canal song. If Mr. Lomax can use it, O.K. If not, O.K. The Canal is my old love so as to speak. Only I never saw any animal-drawn boats on it. I am by profession an engineer both Marine and Stationary and at present at Jacob Dold Packing Company. But when I see anything about the Canal I read *all* of it. I was up and down it for five summers without a stop. I don't know the name of the enclosed and don't know if there is more of it or not. But you sure are welcome to what I enclose."

You yacht on the Hudson,
You ride on the lake,
But a trip on the Erie,
You bet takes the cake;
Where the beefsteak is tough
As a fighting dog's neck,
And the cook she plays tag
With the flies out on deck.

Our cook she's a daisy,
And dead stuck on me;
Has fiery red hair
And she's sweet sixty-three;

Though sunburned and freckled,
A daisy you bet,
And we use her at night
For a headlight on deck.

So haul in your tow line
And take in your slack,
Take a reef in your breeches
And straighten your back;
Through sunshine and storm
Down the towpath we'll walk,
And we'll touch up the mules
When they kick and they balk.

A verse sung by Cork Leg Jonny Bartley, in Bonnys Theatre, Commercial Street, about 1877. From E. S. Franke, Buffalo, New York, May 17, 1933:

The cook we had upon the deck
Stood six feet in her socks;
Her hand was like an elephant's ear,
Her breath would open the locks.
A maid of sixty summers was she,
As handsome as a pig,
And every time she'd go to sleep
Oh, suffering, how she'd snore!

Chorus:

Then it's tramp-tramp-tramp,
And tighten up your lines;
And watch the playful horse flies,
As o'er the mules they climb.
Gidap, gidap, whoa!
Forget it I never shall,
When I drove a pair
Of spavined mules
On the Erie Canal.

[463]

ERIE CANAL

From Daniel J. Martin, Kenmore, New York, about May 1, 1933:

It was a long, long trip on the Erie
On the good ship called *The Danger*.
A short way out from Buffalo
They took me for a stranger.
A long way out we struck a rock
Of Lackawanna coal;
It gave the boat such a hell of a shock
It stowed it quite a hole.
I hollered to my shipmate,
"Put out your flag of truce."
We're every inch a sailor
And we're bound for Syracuse.

So haul in your bowline,
Stand by your Sire Mule;
Low bridge, dodge your head,
Don't stand there like a fool;
For the Erie it is raging
And the gin is getting low,
And I hardly think we'll get a drink
Till we reach old Buffalo.

From *Harper's New Monthly Magazine*, December, 1873:

Come, sail-i-ors, landsmen, one and all,
And I'll sing to you the dan-ge-ors of the ra-gi-ing canawl;
For I've been at the mer-ci-e of the win-di-as and waves,
And I'm one of the many fellows what expects a watery grave—

We left Al-bi-any a-bout the break of day;
As near as I can remember 'twas the second day of May;
We depen-di-ed on our driver, though he was very small,
Although we knew the dan-ge-ors of the ra-gi-ing canawl.

From A. A., Auburn, New York:
"There used to be a company that ran a chain of barns on the line of the canal and furnished boatmen for towing boats. At Weedsport, the line barn was taken care of by Ezekiel Radford, who made and sold horse liniment.

"There was a song about Zeke and his liniment that I would like to see in print if any of your readers know it. It started like this:

"Ezekiel he came out
And began to howl and shout,
    Saying: 'Captain, are your horses galded any?
I've a liniment here to sell
That will cure them right up well;
    I don't think that I have ever sold you any.'

"Following is the song previously asked for."

A TRIP ON THE ERIE

You may talk about pleasures
    And trips on the lake;
But a trip on the Erie,
    You bet, takes the cake.
With the beefsteak as tough
    As a fighting dog's neck
And the flies playing tag
    With the cook on the deck.

The cook, she's a daisy;
    She's dead gone on me.
She has fiery red hair;
    And she's sweet twenty-three.
She's cross-eyed and freckled;
    She's a darling and a pet.
And we use her for a headlight
    At night on the deck.

[465]

So haul in your tow line
    And pull in your slack;
Take a reef in your trousers,
    And straighten your back.
And mind what I say,
    Driver, never forget
To touch the mules gently
    When the cook's on the deck.

From *Rome Haul*, by Walter D. Edmonds (Little, Brown & Co.):

Schenectady, Schenectady
Is halfway up to Uticy.

*   *   *

Drop a tear for big-foot Sal,
The best damn cook on the Erie Canal,
She aimed for Heaven but she went to Hell,
Fifteen years on the Erie Canal.
The missioner said she died in sin,
Hennery said it was too much gin,
There weren't no bar where she hadn't been
        From Albany to Buffalo.

Low bridge! Everybody down!
Low bridge! We're coming to a town!
You'll always know your neighbor, you'll always know your pal,
If you ever navigated the Erie Canal.

LOW BRIDGE, EVERYBODY DOWN
OR
FIFTEEN YEARS ON THE ERIE CANAL *

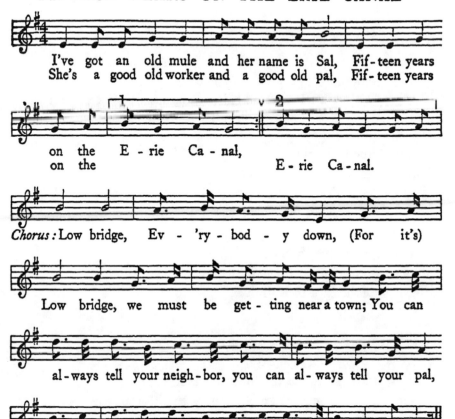

I've got an old mule and her name is Sal, Fif-teen years
She's a good old worker and a good old pal, Fif-teen years

on the E - rie Ca - nal,
on the E - rie Ca - nal.

Chorus: Low bridge, Ev - 'ry - bod - y down, (For it's)

Low bridge, we must be get - ting near a town; You can

al - ways tell your neigh - bor, you can al - ways tell your pal,

If you've ev - er na - vi - ga - ted on the E - rie Ca - nal.

I've got an old mule and her name is Sal,
Fifteen years on the Erie Canal,
She's a good old worker and a good old pal,
Fifteen years on the Erie Canal.
We've hauled some barges in our day,

* Words and music by William S. Allen (F. B. Haviland Publishing Co., New York City).
Reprinted by special permission of the copyright owners.

Filled with lumber, coal and hay—
And every inch of the way I know
From Albany to Buffalo.

Chorus:
    Low bridge, everybody down,
    Low bridge! We're coming to a town!
    You can always tell your neighbor, you can always tell your pal,
    If you've ever navigated on the Erie Canal.

We'd better look around for a job, Old Gal,
Fifteen years on the Erie Canal,
You bet your life I wouldn't part with Sal,
Fifteen years on the Erie Canal.
Giddap there, Gal, we've passed that lock,
We'll make Rome 'fore six o'clock—
So one more trip and then we'll go
Right straight back to Buffalo.

Chorus:
    Low bridge, everybody down;
    Low bridge, I've got the finest mule in town.
    Once a man named Mike McGintey tried to put over Sal,
    Now he's way down at the bottom of the Erie Canal.

Oh! where would I be if I lost my pal?
Fifteen years on the Erie Canal,
Oh, I'd like to see a mule as good as Sal,
Fifteen years on the Erie Canal.
A friend of mine once got her sore,
Now he's got a broken jaw,
'Cause she let fly with her iron toe
And kicked him in to Buffalo.

Chorus:

Low bridge, everybody down;
Low bridge, I've got the finest mule in town.
If you're looking for trouble, better stay away,
She's the only fighting donkey on the Erie Canal.

I don't have to call when I want my Sal,
Fifteen years on the Erie Canal,
She trots from the stall like a good old gal,
Fifteen years on the Erie Canal.
I eat my meals with Sal each day,
I eat beef and she eats hay,
She ain't so slow if you want to know,
She put the "Buff" in Buffalo.

Chorus:

Low bridge, everybody down,
Low bridge, I've got the finest mule in town.
Eats a bale of hay for dinner, and on top of that my Sal
Tries to drink up all the water in the Erie Canal.

You'll soon hear them sing all about my gal,
Fifteen years on the Erie Canal,
It's a darned fine ditty 'bout my darn fool Sal,
Fifteen years on the Erie Canal.
Oh, any band will play it soon,
Darned fool words and darned fool tune;
You'll hear it sung everywhere you go,
From Mexico to Buffalo.

Chorus:

Low bridge, everybody down,
Low bridge, I've got the finest mule in town.
She's a perfect, perfect lady, and she blushes like a gal
If she hears you sing about her and the Erie Canal.

[469]

THE E–RI–E *

Moderately fast

We were for - ty miles from Al - ba - ny, For -

get it I nev - er shall, What a ter - ri - ble storm we

had one night On the E - ri - e Ca - nal.

REFRAIN

Oh, the E - ri - e was a - ris - ing, The

gin was get - ting low, And I scarce - ly think We'll

get a drink Till we get to Buf - fa -

lo — — Till we get to Buf - fa - lo.

We were forty miles from Albany,
Forget it I never shall,
What a terrible storm we had one night
On the E-ri-e Canal.

* Words and music from Carl Sandburg's *American Songbag*.

Refrain:
> Oh, the E-ri-e was a-rising,
> The gin * was getting low,
> And I scarcely think
> We'll get a drink
> Till we get to Buffalo,
> Till we get to Buffalo.

We were loaded down with burley,
We were chock-up full of rye;
And the captain he looked down at me
With his goddam wicked eye.

Oh, the girls are in the *Police Gazette*,
The crew are all in jail;
I'm the only living sea cook's son
That's left to tell the tale.

THE RAGING CAN-ALL †

Come list to me, ye heroes, ye nobles, and ye braves,
For I've been at the mercy of the winds and the waves;
I'll tell you of the hardships to me that did befall
While going on a voyage up the Erie can-all;

From out of this fam'd harbor we sailed without fear,
Our helm was put hard up, and for Albany did steer;
We spoke full fifty craft, without any accident at all,
Until we passed into that 'ere raging can-all.

It seemed as if the Devil had work in hand that night,
For our oil was all out, and our lamps they gave no light;

---

* In Walter D. Edmonds's *Rome Haul*, "strap."
† From *Negro Forget-Me-Not Songster, Containing all the negro songs ever published with a choice collection of ballad songs, now sung in concerts* (Cincinnati: Bratton & Barnard, 1848).

The clouds began to gather, and the rain began to fall,
And I wished myself off and safe from the raging can-all.

With hearts chock-full of love, we thought of our sweethearts dear,
And straight for Utica our gallant bark did steer;
But when in sight of that 'ere town, there came on a white squall,
Which carried away our mizzenmast, on the raging can-all.

The winds came roaring on, just like a wild-cat scream;
Our little vessel pitched and tost, straining every beam,
The cook she dropt the bucket and let the ladle fall,
And the waves ran mountains-high on the raging can-all.

Our boat did mind the helm, just like a thing of life;
Our mate he offered prayers for the safety of his wife:
We threw our provisions overboard, butter, cheese, and all,
And was put on short allowance, on the raging can-all.

Now the weather being foggy we couldn't see the track,
We made our driver come on board, and hitched a lantern on his back;
We told him to be fearless, and then it blew a gale,
To jump up and knock down a horse, that's taking in a sail.

The captain bid the driver to hurry with all speed,
His orders were obeyed, for he soon cracked up his lead;
With that 'ere kind of towing, he allowed, by twelve o'clock,
We should have the old critter right bang agin the dock.

But sad was the fate of our poor devoted bark,
For the rain kept pouring faster, and the night it grew dark:
The horses gave a stumble, and the driver gave a squall,
And they tumbled head and heels into the raging can-all.

The captain cried out, with a voice so clear and sound,
"Cut them horses loose, my boys, or else we will be drowned";

The driver paddled to the shore, although he was but small,
While the horses sunk to rise no more in the raging can-all.

The cook she wrung her hands, and then she came on deck,
Saying, "Alas! what will become of us? Our vessel is a wreck."
The steersman knocked her over, for he was a man of sense,
And the helmsman jumpt ashore and lashed her to a fence.

We had a load of Dutch, and we crowed 'em in the hole,
And the varmint weren't the least concerned for the welfare of their
    souls;
The captain he went down to them, implored them for to pray,
But all the answer that he got was "due deutsch sproken nix come
    arouse ex for shtae."

The captain trembled for his money, likewise for his wife,
But to muster courage up, he whittled with a knife:
He said to us with a faltering voice, while tears began to fall,
"Prepare to meet your death this night, on the raging can-all."

The passengers to save their souls, wouldn't part with any money;
The bar-keeper went on his knees, then took some peach and honey;
A lady took some brandy, she'd have it neat or not at all,
Kase there was lots of water in the raging can-all.

The captain came on deck, with spyglass in his hand,
But the fog it was so 'tarnal thick he couldn't spy the land;
He put his trumpet to his mouth, as loud as he could bawl,
He hailed for assistance from the raging can-all.

The sky was rent asunder, the lightning it did flash,
The thunder rattled above, just like eternal smash;
The clouds were all upsot, and the rigging it did fall,
And we scudded under bare poles on that raging can-all.

A mighty sea rolled on astern, and then it swept our deck,
And soon our gallant little craft was but a floating wreck;
All hands sprung forward, aft the mainsheet for to haul,
And slap dash! went chicken coop into the raging can-all.

We took the old cook's petticoat, for want of a better dress,
And rigged it out upon a pole, a signal of distress;
We pledged ourselves hand to hand, aboard the boat to bide,
And not to quit the deck while a plank hung to her side.

At length that horrid night cut dirt from the sky,
The storm it did abate, and a boat came passing by,
She soon espied our signal, while each on his knees did fall,
Thankful we escaped a grave on the raging can-all.

We each of us took a nip, and sighed the pledge anew,
And wonderful as danger ceased, how up our courage grew,
The craft in sight bore down on us, and quickly was 'longside,
And we all jumped aboard and for Buffalo did ride.

And if I live a thousand years, the horrors of that night
Will ever in my memory be a spot most burning bright;
There's naught in this varsel world, can ever raise my gall,
As the thought of my voyage on the raging can-all.

And now, my boys, I'll tell you how to manage wind and weather,
In a storm hug the towpath, and lay feather to feather,
And when the weather gets bad, and rain begins to fall,
Jump right ashore, and streak it from the raging can-all.

The yarn is rather long, my boys, so I will let it drop,
You can get the whole particulars in Kearney's bookshop,
At two hundred seventy-two Pearl Street, you've only got to call,
And you'll get an extra dose of the raging can-all.

XXI

THE GREAT LAKES

"But I—I fed the fishes,
I gave them my best wishes—
I fed the fishes clear to old St. Joe."

From *Ben King's Poems.*

RED IRON ORE *

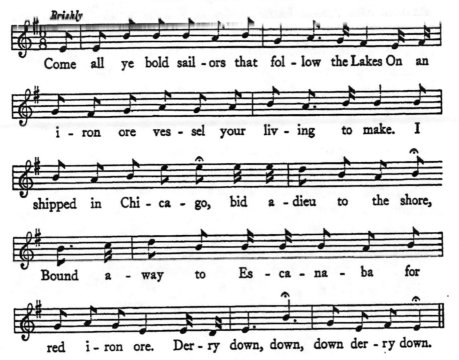

Come all ye bold sail - ors that fol - low the Lakes On an i - ron ore ves - sel your liv - ing to make. I shipped in Chi - ca - go, bid a - dieu to the shore, Bound a - way to Es - ca - na - ba for red i - ron ore. Der - ry down, down, down der - ry down.

Come all you bold sailors that follow the Lakes
On an iron-ore vessel your living to make.
I shipped in Chicago, bid adieu to the shore,
Bound away to Escanaba for red iron ore.

Chorus:
    Derry down, derry down, derry down.

* From Frank L. Rickaby's *Ballads and Songs of the Shanty-Boy.*

[477]

In the month of September, the seventeenth day,
Two dollars and a quarter is all they would pay,
And on Monday morning the *Bridgeport* did take
The *E. C. Roberts* out in the lake.

The wind from the south'ard sprang up a fresh breeze,
And away through Lake Michigan the *Roberts* did roar,
And on Friday morning we passed through death's door.

This packet she howled across the mouth of Green Bay,
And before her cutwater she dashed the white spray.
We rounded the sand point, our anchor let go,
We furled in our canvas, and the watch went below.

Next morning we hove alongside the exile,
And soon was made fast to an iron-ore pile,
They lowered their chutes and like thunder did roar,
They spouted into us that red iron ore.

Some sailors took shovels while others got spades,
And some took wheelbarrows—each man to his trade.
We looked like red devils, our fingers got sore,
We cursed Escanaba and that damned iron ore.

The tug *Escanaba* she towed out of the Minch,
The *Roberts* she thought she had left in a pinch,
And as she passed us by she bid us good-by,
Saying, "We'll meet you in Cleveland next Fourth of July."

Through Louse Island it blew a fresh breeze;
We made the Foxes, the Beavers, the Skillagees;
We flew by the Minch for to show her the way,
And she never hove in sight till we were off Thunder Bay.

Across Saginaw Bay the *Roberts* did ride
With dark and deep water rolling over her side.
And now for Port Huron the *Roberts* must go,
Where the tug *Kate Williams* took us in tow.

We went through North Passage—O Lord, how it blew!
And all round the Dummy a large fleet there came too.
The night being dark, Old Nick it would scare.
We hove up next morning and for Cleveland did steer.

Now the *Roberts* in Cleveland, made fast stem and stern,
And over the bottle we'll spin a big yarn.
But Captain Harvey Shannon had ought to stand treat,
For getting to Cleveland ahead of the fleet.

Now my song is ended, I hope you won't laugh.
Our dunnage is packed and all hands are paid off.
Here's health to the *Roberts*, she's stanch, strong, and true;
Not forgotten the bold boys that comprise her crew.

Derry down, down, down, derry down.

XXII

SAILORS AND SEA FIGHTS

"She's a deep-water ship an' a deep-water crew.
Ye can keep to the coast, but we're damned if we do."

JOHNNY COME DOWN TO HILO *

"Shanties which were originated by the Negro stevedores in the Gulf ports form a large class. . . . These songs were developed as an aid in stowing cotton, the bales being rammed tightly into the ship's hold. . . . As the shanties proved useful, either for hauling or for the windlass, they were picked up by the ships' crews and became part of the shantyman's repertoire. . . .

"There can be no doubt of the Negro origin of the next shanty; as to how, when or where, there is no trace. The lines are a mixture taken from other shanties; scarcely one is peculiar to this shanty alone, although the melody is distinctive enough. Bullen says that it 'brings to my mind most vividly a dewy morning in Garden Reach where we lay just off the King of Oudh's palace waiting our permit to moor. I was before the mast in one of Berat's ships, the *Herat*, and when the order came at dawn to man the windlass I raised this shanty and my shipmates sang the chorus as I never heard it sung before or since. There was a big ship called the *Martin Scott* lying inshore of us and her crew were all gathered on deck at their coffee when the order came to 'Vast Heaving,' the cable was short. And that listening crew, as soon as we ceased singing, gave us a stentorian cheer, an unprecedented honor. I have never heard that noble shanty sung since, but sometimes even now I can in fancy hear its mellow notes reverberating amid the fantastic buildings of the palace and see the great flocks of pigeons rising and falling as the strange sounds disturbed them."

* The descriptive paragraphs and the shanty are quoted from Joanna Colcord's *Roll and Go* (Indianapolis: Bobbs-Merrill Co.).

SHANTY-MAN

I neber see de like since I been born,
When a big buck nigger wid his sea boots on,

CHORUS

Says: "Johnny come down to Hilo,
Poor old man!
Oh, wake her, oh, shake her,
Oh, wake dat gal wid de blue dress on!
When Johnny comes down to Hilo,
Poor old man!"

I lub a little gal across de sea;
She's a 'Badian beauty, and she says to me:

"Oh, was you ebber down in Mobile Bay,
Where dey screws cotton on a summer day?

"Did you ebber see de old plantation boss,
And de long-tail filly and de big black hoss?"

HEAVE AWAY *

Heave a - way, heave a - way! I'd

ra - ther court a yel - low gal than work for Hen - ry Clay.

Heave a - way, heave a - way! — — Yel - low

gal, I want to go, I'd ra - ther court a yel - low

gal than work for Hen - ry Clay. Heave a -

way! Yel - low gal, I want to go.

* From Allen, Ware, and Garrison's *Slave Songs of the United States* (New York: Peter Smith).

Heave away, heave away!
I'd rather court a yellow gal than work for Henry Clay.
Heave away, heave away!
Yellow gal, I want to go,
I'd rather court a yellow gal than work for Henry Clay.
Heave away!
Yellow gal, I want to go!

WHISKY JOHNNY *

As we sailed on the wa-ter blue, Whis-ky John-ny! A good long pull and a strong one too, Whis-ky for my John-ny!

As we sailed on the water blue,
Whisky Johnny!
A good long pull and a strong one too,
Whisky for my Johnny!

Whisky killed my brother Tom,
Whisky Johnny!
I drink whisky all day long,
Whisky for my Johnny!

Whisky made me pawn my clothes,
Whisky Johnny!

* We are indebted for words and air to Carl Sandburg and through him to Robert Frost. Three
stanzas are quoted from the *Post Statesman* of San Francisco.

Whisky gave me this red nose,
Whisky for my Johnny!

Whisky is the life of man,
Whisky Johnny!
I'll drink my whisky while I can,
Whisky for my Johnny!

Oh, whisky straight and whisky strong,
Whisky Johnny!
Give me whisky and I'll sing you a song,
Whisky for my Johnny!

Whisky killed my poor old dad,
Whisky Johnny!
Whisky druv my mother mad,
Whisky for my Johnny!

I drink whisky, my wife drinks gin,
Whisky Johnny!
And the way she drinks it is a sin,
Whisky for my Johnny!

I and my wife cannot agree,
Whisky Johnny!
For she drinks whisky in her tea,
Whisky for my Johnny!

I had a girl, her name was Lize,
Whisky Johnny!
She puts whisky in her pies,
Whisky for my Johnny!

Whisky stole my brains away,
Whisky Johnny!
The bos'n pipes and I'll belay,
Whisky for my Johnny!

THE RIO GRANDE *

SOLO

Oh, John - ny came o - ver the o - ther day,

CHORUS   SOLO

Way, Ri - o! Oh, John - ny came o - ver the

CHORUS

o - ther day, For we're bound for the Ri - o Grande!

CHORUS

Way, Ri - o! Way, Ri - o! Sing fare you well, my

bon - ny brown gal, For we're bound for the Ri - o Grande!

Oh, Johnny came over the other day,
    Way, Rio!
Oh, Johnny came over the other day,
    For we're bound for the Rio Grande!

Chorus:
    Way, Rio!
    Way, Rio!
    Sing fare you well, my bonny brown gal,
    For we're bound for the Rio Grande!

*The tune and the first three stanzas are quoted from *Ballads and Sea Songs from Nova Scotia*, by Roy W. Mackenzie (Cambridge, Mass.: Harvard University Press); the final three stanzas, from *Capstan Bars*, by David W. Bone (New York: Harcourt, Brace and Co.).

"Now give me your hand, my dear lily-white;
Way, Rio!
If you'll accept me, I'll make you my wife."
For we're bound for the Rio Grande!

"Now, Johnny, I love you and don't want you to go,
Way, Rio!
And if you stay I'll love you so so."
For we're bound for the Rio Grande!

Additional couplets

She's a deep-water ship, an' a deep-water crew.
Ye can keep to the coast, but we're damned if we do.

We was sick of the beach when our money was gone,
And signed in this packet to drive her along.

Oh, blow ye winds steadily; fair may ye blow.
She's a starvation packet, good God, let 'er go!

THE BLACK BALL LINE *

". . . celebrates the first and most famous line of American packet ships to run between New York and Liverpool. Started in 1816, these little ships of 300 to 500 tons furnished for many years the only means of regular communication between this continent and Europe, sailing regularly from New York on the first and sixteenth of each month. In order to keep up their average time of three weeks out and six weeks home, the ships were driven unmercifully, and acquired a bad name among sailors for the iron discipline maintained on board. The Black Ball liners carried a crimson swallowtail flag with a black ball in the center. . . ."

* The paragraph and the song are quoted from Joanna Colcord's *Roll and Go* (Indianapolis: Bobbs-Merrill Co.).

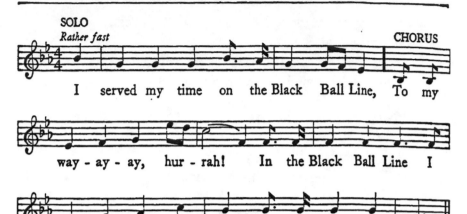

SOLO
Rather fast   CHORUS

I served my time on the Black Ball Line, To my

way - ay - ay, hur - rah! In the Black Ball Line I

served my time, Hur - rah for the Black Ball Line!

SHANTY-MAN

I served my time on the Black Ball Line,

CHORUS

To my way-ay-ay, hurrah!

SHANTY-MAN

In the Black Ball Line I served my time,

CHORUS

Hurrah for the Black Ball Line!

Once there was a Black Ball ship
That fourteen knots an hour could clip.

You will surely find a rich gold mine;
Just take a trip in the Black Ball Line.

Just take a trip to Liverpool,
To Liverpool, that Yankee school.

The Yankee sailors you'll see there,
With red-top boots and short-cut hair.

[490]

BLOW THE MAN DOWN *

As I was a-walkin' down Paradise Street,
To me aye, aye—blow the man down!
A saucy young p'liceman I chanced for to meet;
Blow the man down, to me aye, aye, blow the man down!
Whether he's white man or black man or brown,
Give me some time to blow the man down,

* From Carl Sandburg's *The American Songbag* (New York: Harcourt, Brace and Co.).

Give me some time to blow the man down,
Blow the man down! bullies!

"You're off some clipper that flies the Black Ball,"
To me aye, aye—blow the man down!
"You've robbed some poor Dutchman of coats, boots, and all."
Blow the man down, etc.

"P'liceman, p'liceman, you do me much wrong,"
To me aye, aye—blow the man down!
"I'm a peace party sailor just home from Hongkong."
Blow the man down, etc.

They gave me six months in the Ledington jail,
To me aye, aye—blow the man down!
For kickin' an' fightin' and knockin' 'em down;
Blow the man down, etc.

Other versions of "Blow the Man Down," the first quoted from
the collection of William Doerflinger:

As I was walkin' down Paradise Street,
To my aye, aye—blow the man down!
A handsome young damsel I chanced for to meet,
Blow the man down, etc.

I came alongside her and took her in tow,
To my aye, aye—blow the man down!
And broadside to broadside away we did go,
Blow the man down, etc.

* * *

Bryan O'Lynn had no breeches to wear,
To my aye, aye—blow the man down!
So we bought a sheepskin and made him a pair,
Blow the man down, etc.

With the skinny side out and the woolly side in,
To my aye, aye—blow the man down!

A fine pair of breeches had Bryan O'Lynn,
Blow the man down, etc.

GET UP, JACK! JOHN, SIT DOWN! *

Oh, the ships will come and the ships will go,
As long as the waves do roll:
The sailor lad, likewise his dad,
He loves the flowing bowl:
A lass ashore we do adore,
One that is plump and round, round, round.
When the money is gone, it's the same old song,
Get up, Jack! John, sit down!

Chorus:

Singing, Hey! laddie, ho! laddie,
Swing the capstan 'round, 'round, 'round
When the money is gone it's the same old song,
Get up, Jack! John, sit down!

[I] go and take a trip in a man-o'-war
To China or Japan,
In Asia, there are ladies *fair*
Who love the sailorman.
When Jack and Joe palavers, O,
And buy the girls a gown, gown, gown.
When the money is gone it's the same old song,
Get up, Jack! John, sit down!

When Jack is ashore he beats his way
Towards some boarding-house:
He's welcome in with his rum and gin,
And he's fed with pork and s[c]ouse:

* This song was sung and written down by John Thomas, a Welsh sailor on the *Philadelphian*, in
1896.

For he'll spend and spend and never offend,
But he'll lay drunk on the ground, ground, ground:
When my money is gone it's the same old song:
Get up, Jack! John, sit down!

When Jack is old and weatherbeat,
Too old to roustabout,
In some rum-shop they'll let him stop,
At eight bells he's turned out.
Then he cries, he cries up to the skies:
"I'll soon be homeward bound, bound, bound."
When my money is gone it's the same old song:
Get up, Jack! John, sit down!

JACK WRACK *

"Frank Vickery, mate of the four-masted cargo schooner *Avon Queen*, whose home port is on the Mirimichi River in New Brunswick, began during a lonely anchor watch one night to relate some of his experiences with well-known boarding-house masters during the great days of sail. These memories brought to his mind the rare forecastle ballad of 'Jack Wrack'—how Jack lost his money on the famous Barbary Coast in Frisco, and was shipped off to sea again in a whaler bound to the Bering grounds, for a long voyage which may have lasted two or three years.

" 'Shanghai' Brown is among that coterie of more notorious boarding-house masters who were known to nearly every sailorman. His place stood on Battery Street in San Francisco in the days when ship-masters must pay head money for their crews and when men before the mast were the prey of land sharks who took their money and their advances and then hustled them into the forecastles of outward-bounders. I have heard the song under the title 'Ben Breezer,' also, while the lines of a variant called 'Dixie Brown' are to be found in Mackenzie's *Ballads and Sea Songs from Nova Scotia*."

* From William Doerflinger, New York City.

1. The first time I went to Fris - co, I went up-on a
spree. My money at last I spent it fast, Got
drunk as drunk could be; I was ful - ly in - clined, made
up my mind, I'd go to sea no more!

2. That night I slept with An - ge-line, too drunk for to turn in
bed. My clothes were new and my mon-ey was too; Next
mor-ning with them she fled! And as dai - ly I walked the
streets a - round you'd hear the peo - ple roar, "Oh, there

Rit.

goes Jack Wrack. Poor sail - or lad, he must go to sea once more!"

[495]

The first time I went to Frisco, I went upon a spree.
My money at last I spent it fast, got drunk as drunk could be;
I was fully inclined, made up my mind, to go to sea no more!
That night I slept with Angeline, too drunk for to turn in bed.

My clothes was new, and my money was too;
Next morning with them she fled!
And as daily I walked the streets around you'd hear the people roar,
"Oh, there goes Jack Wrack! Poor sailor lad, he must go to sea once more!"

The first one that I came to was a son-of-a-gun called Brown.
I asked him for to take me in; he looked on me with a frown.
He says, "Last time you were paid off, with me you chalked no score,
But I'll take your advance and I'll give you a chance to go to sea once more!"

He shipped me on board of a whaler, bound for the Arctic seas.
The wintry wind from the west-nor'west Jamaica rum would freeze!
With a twenty-foot oar in each man's hand we pulled the livelong day;
It was then I swore when once on shore I'd go to sea no more!

Come all you young seafaring men that's listening to my song!
I hope in what I've said to you that there is nothing wrong.
Take my advice and don't drink strong drinks, or go sleeping on the shore,
But get married, my boys, and have all night in, and go to sea no more!

THE BOSTON COME–ALL–YE *

OR

THE FISHES

"We have the testimony of Kipling in *Captains Courageous* that it was a favorite within recent years of the Banks fishermen."

* From Joanna Colcord's *Roll and Go* (Indianapolis: Bobbs-Merrill Co.).

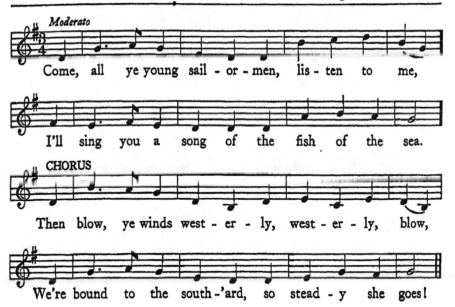

Come, all ye young sail-or-men, lis-ten to me,

I'll sing you a song of the fish of the sea.

CHORUS

Then blow, ye winds west-er-ly, west-er-ly, blow,

We're bound to the south-'ard, so stead-y she goes!

Come, all ye young sailormen, listen to me,
I'll sing you a song of the fish of the sea.

Chorus:

Then blow ye winds westerly, westerly blow,
We're bound to the south'ard, so steady she goes!

Oh, first come the whale, the biggest of all;
He clumb up aloft and let every sail fall.

And next come the mack'rel with his striped back;
He hauled aft the sheets and boarded each tack.

Then come the porpoise with his short snout;
He went to the wheel, calling "Ready! About!"

Then come the smelt, the smallest of all;
He jumped to the poop and sung out "Topsail, haul!"

The herring come saying, "I'm the king of the seas,
If you want any wind, why, I'll blow you a breeze."

Next come the cod with his chucklehead;
He went to the main-chains to heave at the lead.

Next come the flounder as flat as the ground;
Says, "Damn your eyes, chucklehead, mind how you sound!"

THE WONDERFUL CROCODILE

H. E. Greenough writes from Dartmouth, Nova Scotia (January 26, 1921):

"I have known this song since a boy . . . one of those that used to be roared out in the back rooms of the taverns frequented by seamen forty or so years ago."

Come list ye lands-men all to me, To
Ship-wrecked I was one sap-py rouse And

tell the truth I'm bound— What happened to me by
cast all on the shore, So I re-solved to

going to sea And the won-ders that I found.
take a cruise The coun-try to ex-plore. To

my ri tol looral loo a li do, Ri tol loo-ral lay, To my

ri tol lol fol, lid-dle lol de fol, To my tol loo ral lay.

Come list ye, landsmen, all to me,
To tell the truth I'm bound—
What happened to me by going to sea
And the wonders that I found.
Shipwrecked I was one sappy rouse
And cast all on the shore,
So I resolved to take a cruise,
The country to explore.

Chorus:

To my ri tol looral loralido,
Ritol looral lay,
To my ri tol lol fol liddle lol de fol,
To my tol looral lay.

Oh, I had not long scurried out,
When close alongside the ocean,
'Twas there that I saw something move,
Like all the earth in motion.
While steering close up alongside
I saw it was a crocodile;
From the end of his nose to the tip of his tail
It measured five hundred mile.

This crocodile I could plainly see
Was none of the common race,
For I had to climb a very high tree
Before I could see his face.
And when he lifted up his jaw,
Perhaps you may think it a lie,
But his back was three miles through the clouds
And his nose near touched the sky.

Oh, up aloft the wind was high,
It blew a hard gale from the south;

I lost my hold and away I flew
Right into the crocodile's mouth.
He quickly closed his jaws on me,
He thought to nab a victim;
But I slipped down his throat, d'ye see,
And that's the way I tricked 'im.

I traveled on for a year or two
Till I got into his maw,
And there were rum kegs not a few
And a thousand bullocks in store.
Through life I banished all my care
For on grub I was not stinted;
And in this crocodile lived ten years,
Very well contented.

This crocodile being very old,
One day at last he died;
He was three years in catching cold,
He was so long and wide.
His skin was three miles thick, I'm sure,
Or very near about;
For I was full six months or more
In making a hole to get out.

So now I'm safe on earth once more,
Resolved no more to roam.
In a ship that passed I got a berth,
So now I'm safe at home.
But, if my story you should doubt,
Did you ever cross the Nile—
'Twas there he fell—you'll find the shell
Of this wonderful crocodile.

CAPTAIN ROBERT KIDD

You captains bold and brave, hear our cries, hear our cries,
You captains bold and brave, hear our cries,
You captains brave and bold, though you seem uncontrolled,
Don't for the sake of gold lose your souls, lose your souls.
Don't for the sake of gold lose your souls.

My name was Robert Kidd, when I sailed, when I sailed,
My name was Robert Kidd, when I sailed,
My name was Robert Kidd, God's laws I did forbid,
And so wickedly I did, when I sailed.

My parents taught me well, when I sailed, when I sailed,
My parents taught me well, when I sailed,
My parents taught me well to shun the gates of hell,
But against them I rebelled when I sailed.

I cursed my father dear when I sailed, when I sailed,
I cursed my father dear when I sailed,
I cursed my father dear and her that did me bear,
And so wickedly did swear when I sailed.

I made a solemn vow when I sailed, when I sailed,
I made a solemn vow when I sailed,
I made a solemn vow to God I would not bow,
Nor myself one prayer allow, as I sailed.

I'd a Bible in my hand when I sailed, when I sailed,
I'd a Bible in my hand when I sailed,
I'd a Bible in my hand by my father's great command,
And sunk it in the sand when I sailed.

I murdered William Moore, as I sailed, as I sailed,
I murdered William Moore, as I sailed,

I murdered William Moore, and left him in his gore,
Not many leagues from shore, as I sailed.

And being cruel still, as I sailed, as I sailed,
And being cruel still, as I sailed,
And being cruel still, my gunner I did kill,
And his precious blood did spill, as I sailed.

My mate was sick and died, as I sailed, as I sailed,
My mate was sick and died as I sailed,
My mate was sick and died, which me much terrified,
When he called me to his bedside, as I sailed,

And unto me did say, "See me die, see me die,"
And unto me did say, "See me die,"
And unto me did say, "Take warning now by me,
There comes a reckoning day, you must die.

"You cannot then withstand, when you die, when you die,
You cannot then withstand when you die,
You cannot then withstand the judgment of God's hand,
But bound then in iron bands you must die."

I was sick and nigh to death, as I sailed, as I sailed,
I was sick and nigh to death, as I sailed,
I was sick and nigh to death, and I vowed at every breath,
To walk in wisdom's ways as I sailed.

I thought I was undone, as I sailed, as I sailed,
I thought I was undone as I sailed,
I thought I was undone and my wicked glass had run,
But health did soon return, as I sailed.

My repentance lasted not, as I sailed, as I sailed,
My repentance lasted not, as I sailed,

My repentance lasted not, my vows I soon forgot,
Damnation's my just lot, as I sailed.

I steered from sound to sound, as I sailed, as I sailed,
I steered from sound to sound, as I sailed,
I steered from sound to sound, and many ships I found,
And most of them I burned, as I sailed.

I spied three ships from France as I sailed, as I sailed,
I spied three ships from France, as I sailed,
I spied three ships from France, to them I did advance,
I took them all by chance, as I sailed.

I spied three ships of Spain as I sailed, as I sailed,
I spied three ships of Spain, as I sailed,
I spied three ships of Spain, I fixed on them amain,
Till most of them were slain, as I sailed.

I'd ninety bars of gold as I sailed, as I sailed,
I'd ninety bars of gold as I sailed,
I'd ninety bars of gold and dollars manifold,
With riches uncontrolled, as I sailed.

Then fourteen ships I saw, as I sailed, as I sailed,
Then fourteen ships I saw, as I sailed,
Then fourteen ships I saw, and brave men they were,
Ah! they were too much for me, as I sailed.

Thus being o'ertaken at last, I must die, I must die,
Thus being o'ertaken at last, I must die,
Thus being o'ertaken at last, and into prison cast,
And sentence being passed, I must die.

Farewell, the raging sea, I must die, I must die,
Farewell, the raging sea, I must die,

Farewell, the raging main, to Turkey, France, and Spain,
I ne'er shall see you again, I must die.

To Newgate now I'm cast, and must die, and must die,
To Newgate now I'm cast, and must die,
To Newgate now I'm cast, with a sad and heavy heart,
To receive my just desert, I must die.

To Execution Dock I must go, must go,
To Execution Dock I must go,
To Execution Dock will many thousands flock,
But I must bear the shock, I must die.

Come all you young and old, see me die, see me die,
Come all you young and old, see me die,
Come all you young and old, you're welcome to my gold,
For by it I've lost my soul, and must die.

Take warning now by me, for I must die, for I must die,
Take warning now by me, for I must die,
Take warning now by me, and shun bad company,
Lest you come to hell with me, for I must die,
Lest you come to hell with me, for I must die.

THE FLYING CLOUD *

My name is Gil - bert How - eld - ing, as
you may un - der - stand. I was born in the town of

* The correspondent in Missouri who sends this, wishing his name not to be published, writes: "My father, from whom I learned the ballad, had forgotten the last verse." The air is from Shay's *More Drunken Friends and Pious Companions* (New York: Macaulay Company).

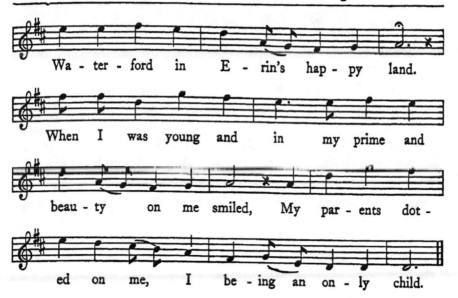

Wa - ter - ford in E - rin's hap - py land.

When I was young and in my prime and

beau - ty on me smiled, My par - ents dot -

ed on me, I be - ing an on - ly child.

My name is Gilbert Howelding, as you may understand.
I was born in the town of Waterford in Erin's happy land.
When I was young and in my prime and beauty on me smiled,
My parents doted on me, I being an only child.

My parents bound me to a trade near Waterford's own town,
They bound me to a cooper there whose name was William Brown.
I served him true and faithful for eighteen months or more,
When I shipped on board the *Ocean Queen* bound for Belfrasia's shore.

When I reached Belfrasia I fell in with Captain Moore,
Commander of the *Flying Cloud*, belonging to Try More.
He asked me if I would consent on a sailing voyage to go
To the burning shores of Africa where the sugar cane does grow.

The *Flying Cloud* was a Spanish ship, five hundred tons she bore,
She could easily sail around any ship going out of Baltimore,
Her sails they were as white as snow, on them there was no stain,
And eight nine-pounder big brass guns she carried abaft her main.

So in a short while after we reached the African shore,
And eighteen hundred of those poor men from their native home
    we bore,
We crowded them upon the deck and stored them all below
With eighteen inches to the man, was all they had to go.

We set sail shortly after with our cargo of slaves.
'Twas better then for those poor souls if they had seen their graves—
The plague and fever came on board and swept them half away;
We dragged their bodies on the deck and throwed them on the waves.

'Twas in a short time after we reached the Cuban shore,
And sold them to the planters there to be slaves for evermore,
Where the tea and coffee fields do grow beneath the burning sun,
To lead a long and wretched life till their long career is done.

Well, when our money was spent we struck out for sea again,
And Captain Moore he came on board and said to us, his men,
"There's gold and silver to be had if with me you'll remain,
We'll hoist the Haughty Pirate's flag and scour the Spanish Main."

At last we all consented, excepting five young men,
Two of them were Boston boys, two more from Newfoundland,
The other was an Irish lad belonging to Try More—
I wish to God I'd joined those men and staid with them on shore.

We robbed and plundered many a ship along the Spanish Main,
Left many a widow and orphan in sorrow to remain.
Their crews, we made them walk the plank, gave them a watery grave,
For the saying of our captain was that dead men tell no tales.

We were chased it was full many a time by lines and frigates too.
Full many a time across our bows their burning shells they threw,
Full many a time astern of us their cannon roared loud,
But 'twas vain for them who'd ever try to catch the *Flying Cloud*.

A man-of-war, an English ship, from the navy hove in view
And fired a shot across our bow for a signal to heave to.
We paid no heed to answer back but made haste with the wind,
When a chance shot struck our mainmast, and we were forced to heave
    to then.

We cleared our deck for action as she came up alongside,
And soon across our quarter deck there ran the crimson tide.
We fought till Captain Moore was killed with eighteen of our men.
When a bombshell set our ship on fire, we were forced to surrender
    then.

CONSTITUTION AND GUERRIÈRE*

Oft - times it has been told How the
Brit - ish sea - men bold Could flog the tars of
France so neat and han - dy, oh! And they nev - er found their
match Till the Yank - ees did 'em catch — Oh, the
Yank - ee boys for fight-ing are the dan - dy, oh!

*Tune is from Joana Colcord's *Roll and Go* (Indianapolis: Bobbs-Merill Co.).

Oft-times it has been told
How the British seamen bold
Could flog the tars of France
So neat and handy, oh!

And they never found their match
Till the Yankees did 'em catch—
Oh, the Yankee boys, for fighting
Are the dandy, oh!

The *Guerrière*, a frigate bold,
On the foamy ocean rolled,
Commanded by proud Dacres—
The grandee, oh!

With as choice a British crew
As a rammer ever drew—
They could flog the Frenchmen
Two to one, so handy, oh!

When the *Constitution* hove in view,
Says proud Dacres to his crew,
"Come, clear the ship for action,
And be handy, oh!

"To the weather gage now get her,
And to make our men fight better,
Give them to drink gunpowder,
Mixed with brandy, oh!"

Now, the British shot flew hot,
Which the Yankees answered not,
Till they got within the distance
They called handy, oh!

Then the first broadside we poured
Carried their mainmast by the board—
Which made their lofty frigate
Look abandoned, oh!

Our second told so well
That their fore and mizzen fell,
Which downed the royal ensign
So handy, oh!

Then proud Dacres came on board
To deliver up his sword—
Loath was he to part with it,
'Twas so handy, oh!

"Oh, keep your sword," says Hull,
"If it only makes you dull,—
Come! cheer up, and let us have
A little brandy, oh!"

Then fill your glasses full
And we'll drink to Captain Hull,
And merrily we'll push about
The brandy, oh!

John Bull may toast his fill,
Let the world say what it will,
But the Yankee boys for fighting
Are the dandy, oh!

SIEGE OF PLATTSBURG *

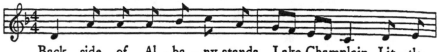

Back side of Al - ba - ny stands Lake Champlain, Lit - tle

pond, two - thirds full of wa - ter. Platts - burg there too,

close up - on the main, Lit - tle town she'll grow big - ger,

though, here - af - ter. On Lake Cham-plain Un - cle

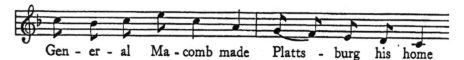

Sam set his boats, And Cap-tain Mc-Don-ough to sail 'em, While

Gen - er - al Ma - comb made Platts - burg his home

With the ar - my whose cou - rage nev - er fails 'em.

Back side Albany stan' Lake Champlain—
Little pond, half full of water.
Platt'burg dere too, close upon de main,
Town small—he grow bigger, do, hereafter.

* Sent by R. W. G. Vail, Ithaca, N. Y. Copied from an old newspaper, *Brother Jonathan*, published by Wilson and Company, New York, July 4, 1845, to tune of "Boyne Water." This version is as sung in the theater at Albany in the character of a Negro sailor.

On Lake Champlain
Uncle Sam set he boat,
And Massa M'Donough to sail 'em,
While General Macomb
Make Platt'burg he home
Wid de army, who courage neber fail 'em.

On 'lebenteenth day of Sep-tem-ber
In eighteen hund'ed and fourteen,
Gubbener Probose, and he British sojer,
Come to Plat-te-burg, a tea-party courtin';
And he boat come too
Arter Uncle Sam boat.
Massa Donough do look sharp out de winder.
Den General Macomb
(Ah, he always a-home)
Catch fire, too, jis' like a tinder.

Bang! bang! bang! den de cannons 'gin to roar
In Platt'burg and all 'bout dat quarter.
Gubbener Probose try he hand upon de shore,
While he boat take he luck 'pon de water,
But Massa M'Donough
Knock de boat in de head,
Break he heart, broke he shin, 'tove he caff in,
And Gen'ral Macomb
Start old Probose home.
Tot me soul, den, I mos' die a-laffin'.

Probose scare so, he lef' all behin'—
Powder, ball, cannon, teapot, an' kittle.
Some say he catch a col', trouble in he min'
'Cause he eat so much col' and raw victual'.
Uncle Sam berry sorry
To be sure for he pain,

Wish he nuss heself up well and hearty
For Gen'ral Macomb
And Massa Donough home,
When he notion for anudder tea-party.

THE BUCCANEERS *

"THE DEAD MAN'S CHEST"

Fifteen men on the Dead Man's Chest,
   Yo-ho-ho and a bottle of rum!
Drink and the devil had done for the rest,
   Yo-ho-ho and a bottle of rum!
The mate was fixed by the bo'sun's pike,
An' the bo'sun brained by a marlinspike,
And the cookie's throat was marked belike;
It had been clutched by fingers ten,
And there they lay, all good, dead men,
Like break o' day in a boozin' ken—
   Yo-ho-ho and a bottle of rum!

Fifteen men of a whole ship's list,
   Yo-ho-ho and a bottle of rum!
Dead and bedamned and their souls gone whist,
   Yo-ho-ho and a bottle of rum!
The skipper lay with his nob in gore
Where the scullion's ax his cheek had shore,
And the scullion he was stabbed times four;
And there they lay, and the soggy skies
Dripped ceaselessly in upstaring eyes,
By murk sunset and by foul sunrise—
   Yo-ho-ho and a bottle of rum!

Fifteen men of 'em stiff and stark,
   Yo-ho-ho and a bottle of rum!

* From *Seven Seas*, September, 1915. Author unknown.

Ten of the crew bore the murder mark,
    Yo-ho-ho and a bottle of rum!
'Twas a cutlass swipe or an ounce of lead,
Or a gaping hole in a battered head,
And the scuppers' glut of a rotting red;
And there they lay, ay, damn my eyes,
Their lookouts clapped on Paradise,
Their souls gone just the contrawise—
    Yo-ho-ho and a bottle of rum!

Fifteen men of 'em good and true,
    Yo-ho-ho and a bottle of rum!
Every man Jack could 'a' sailed with Old Pew,
    Yo-ho-ho and a bottle of rum!
There was chest on chest of Spanish gold
And a ton of plate in the middle hold,
And the cabin's riot of loot untold—
And there they lay that had took the plum,
With sightless eyes and with lips struck dumb,
And we shared all by rule o' thumb—
    Yo-ho-ho and a bottle of rum!

More was seen through the stern light's screen,
    Yo-ho-ho and a bottle of rum!
Chartings undoubt where a woman had been,
    Yo-ho-ho and a bottle of rum!
A flimsy shift on a bunker cot
With a dirk slit sheer through the bosom spot
And the lace stiff dry in a purplish rot—
Or was she wench or shuddering maid,
She dared the knife and she took the blade—
Faith, there was stuff for a plucky jade!
    Yo-ho-ho and a bottle of rum!

[513]

Fifteen men on the Dead Man's Chest,
Yo-ho-ho and a bottle of rum!
Drink and the devil had done for the rest,
Yo-ho-ho and a bottle of rum!
We wrapped 'em all in a mainsail tight
With twice ten turns of a hawser's bight,
And we heaved 'em over and out of sight,
With a yo-heave-ho and a fare-ye-well,
And a sullen plunge in a sullen swell,
Ten fathoms along on the road to hell—
Yo-ho-ho and a bottle of rum!

DESTROYER LIFE*

This song was shouted out at mess by the officers and crew aboard
U. S. Destroyer *Murray*, on foreign service, 1917 to 1919.

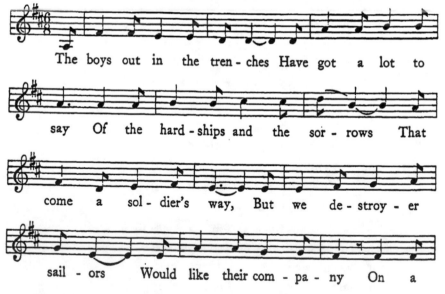

The boys out in the tren-ches Have got a lot to
say Of the hard-ships and the sor-rows That
come a sol-dier's way, But we de-stroy-er
sail-ors Would like their com-pa-ny On a

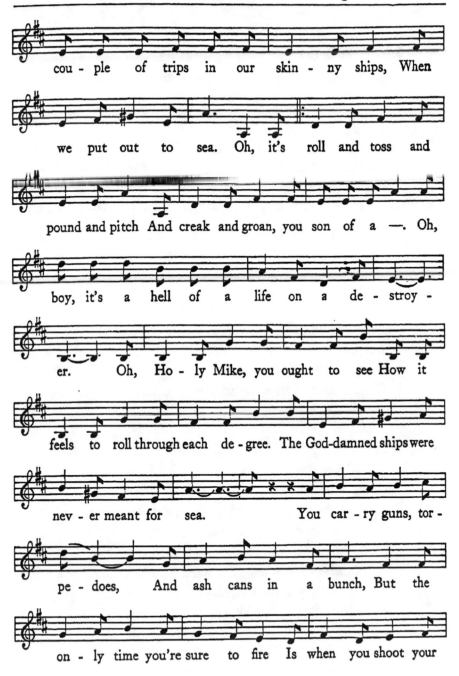

cou - ple of trips in our skin - ny ships, When

we put out to sea. Oh, it's roll and toss and

pound and pitch And creak and groan, you son of a —. Oh,

boy, it's a hell of a life on a de - stroy -

er. Oh, Ho - ly Mike, you ought to see How it

feels to roll through each de - gree. The God-damned ships were

nev - er meant for sea. You car - ry guns, tor -

pe - does, And ash cans in a bunch, But the

on - ly time you're sure to fire Is when you shoot your

lunch. Your food it is the na - vy bean, You hunt the slim - y

sub - ma - rine It's a son of a — — of a

life on a de - stroy - - er. Oh, it's - er.

The boys out in the trenches
Have got a lot to say
Of the hardships and the sorrows
That come the soldier's way.
But we destroyer sailors
Would like their company
On a couple of trips in our skinny ships,
When we put out to sea.

Chorus:

Oh, it's roll and pitch
And creak and groan, you son of a bitch.
Oh, boy, it's a hell of a life on a destroyer.
Oh, Holy Mike, you ought to see
How it feels to roll through each degree.
The God-damned ships were never meant for sea.
You carry guns, torpedoes,
And ash-cans in a bunch,
But the only time you're sure to fire
Is when you shoot your lunch.
Your food it is the navy bean,

You hunt the slimy submarine.
It's a son-of-a-bitch of a life on a destroyer.

We've heard of muddy dug-outs,
Of shell holes filled with slime,
Of cootie hunts and other things,
That fill a soldier's time.
But believe me, bo, that's nothing,
To what it's like at sea,
When the barometer drops
And the clinometer hops,
And the wind blows dismally.

XXIII

WARS AND SOLDIERS

"Yankee Doodle had a mind
    To whip the Southern Traitors."

"Those lyin', thievin' Yankees,
    I hate 'em wuss an' wuss."

YANKEE DOODLE

In the concluding paragraph of a seventy-eight-page article on the story of "Yankee Doodle" (not including a number of pages of musical variants) Oscar G. T. Sonneck, formerly chief of the Division of Music in the Library of Congress, has this to say of its authorship: "Thus to sum up, Dr. Richard Shuckburgh's connection with 'Yankee Doodle' remains as mysterious as ever." *

In another connection Mr. Sonneck writes: " 'Dixie' is more generally popular than 'Yankee Doodle' in America, though the words [of 'Dixie'] are seldom sung." He then quotes:

> " 'Yankee Doodle' is the tune
> Americans delight in;
> 'Twill do to whistle, sing, or play
> And just the thing for fightin'."

Fa - ther and I went down to camp, A-
long with Cap - tain Good - ing, And there we saw the
men and boys, As thick as has - ty pud - ding.

REFRAIN

Yan - kee doo - dle, keep it up, Yan - kee doo - dle dan - dy;
Mind the mu - sic and the step, and with the girls be han - dy.

* Dr. Shuckburgh is generally known as the author of "Yankee Doodle."

Father and I went down to camp,
Along with Captain Gooding;
And there we saw the men and boys,
As thick as hasty pudding.

Yankee doodle, keep it up,
Yankee doodle dandy;
Mind the music and the step,
And with the girls be handy.

There was Captain Washington
Upon a slapping stallion,
A-giving orders to his men,
I guess there was a million.

And then the feathers on his hat,
They looked so 'tarnal fin-a,
I wanted pockily to get
To give to my Jemima.

And then we saw a swamping gun,
Large as a log of maple;
Upon a deucèd little cart,
A load for father's cattle.

And every time they shoot it off,
It takes a horn of powder;
It makes a noise like father's gun,
Only a nation louder.

I went as nigh to one myself,
As 'Siah's underpinning;
And father went as nigh ag'in,
I thought the deuce was in him.

We saw a little barrel, too,
The heads were made of leather;
They knocked upon it with little clubs,
And called the folks together.

And there they'd fife away like fun,
And play on cornstalk fiddles,
And some had ribbons red as blood,
All bound around their middles.

The troopers, too, would gallop up
And fire right in our faces;
It scared me almost to death
To see them run such races.

Uncle Sam came there to change
Some pancakes and some onions,
For 'lasses cake to carry home
To give his wife and young ones.

But I can't tell half I see,
They kept up such a smother;
So I took my hat off, made a bow,
And scampered home to mother.

Cousin Simon grew so bold,
I thought he would have cocked it;
It scared me so I streaked it off,
And hung by father's pocket.

And there I saw a pumpkin shell,
As big as mother's basin;
And every time they touched it off,
They scampered like the nation.

Yankee doodle, keep it up,
Yankee doodle dandy;
Mind the music and the step,
And with the girls be handy.

In searching for the lost words and tune of "Henrietta Lee," we had the aid of F. E. Peyton, Greenwich, Connecticut, ballad enthusiast, and sales manager for the Condé Nast Press, who quoted from the Providence *Journal* as follows:

"Although a careful search of the records fails to reveal any poetic appreciation of the paddle-boat in Narragansett Bay, numerous rhymesters have sung the praises of the clam. One bit of doggerel, to be sung to the tune of 'Yankee Doodle,' to the accompaniment of kettle-drum and Jew's-harp, dates from the time when the bay steamers and the clambakes entered whole-heartedly into their felicitous partnership."

It seems worthy of quotation here.

Let gouty monarchs share their shams
'Neath silken-wove pavilions;
But give us Narragansett clams—
The banquet for the millions.
    Yankee Doodle, etc.

Along the Narragansett shore,
Polite in their salams, sir,
Sat copper-colored kings of yore
And feasted on their clams, sir.
    Yankee Doodle, etc.

Successor to these doughty kings
Sits now the Yankee nation,
And every jolly Yankee sings
His clam-orous collation.
    Yankee Doodle, etc.

But how each valiant Yankee crams
We surely need not tell, sir,
If only you bring on the clams
All smoking in the shell, sir.
              Yankee Doodle, etc.

A Civil War fragment from the South:

    Yankee Doodle had a mind
To whip the Southern traitors,
Just because they did not choose to live
On codfish and potatoes.
Yankee Doodle, fa, so, la,
Yankee Doodle dandy,
And so to keep his courage up
He took a drink of brandy.

Yankee Doodle drew his sword
And practiced all his passes;
Come, boys, we'll take another drink
When we get to Manassas.
Yankee Doodle, fa, so, la,
Yankee Doodle dandy
Never got to Manassas plain
And never drank his brandy.

Yankee Doodle, all for shame;
You're always intermeddling.
Leave guns alone, they're dangerous things;
You'd better stick to peddling.
Yankee Doodle, fa, so, la,
Yankee Doodle dandy,
When you get to Bully Run
You'll throw away your brandy.

Two stanzas I have sung from childhood.

Yankee Doodle went to town,
He rode a little pony;
He stuck a feather in his hat
And called it macaroni.*

Yankee Doodle rode to town
To buy a pair of trousers; †
He swore he could not see the town
For so many houses.

Chorus:
Yankee Doodle, fa, so, la,
Yankee Doodle dandy;
Yankee Doodle, fa, so, la,
Buttermilk and brandy.

BRADDOCK'S DEFEAT

It was our hard general's false treachery,
Which caused our destruction in that great day.
Oh, he is a traitor, his conduct does show;
He was seen in the French fort, six hours ago.

And to be marked by the French, I am sure,
There round his hat, a white handkerchief he wore,
And one of our bold soldiers he stood by a tree,
And there he slew many till him he did see.

* This stanza shows our indebtedness to England. In Texas the cowboy did not stick the feather "in his hat."
† Or, All dressed up in his blouses.

"Would you be like an Indian, to stand by a tree?"
And with his broadsword, cut him down instantly.
His brother stood by him, and saw he was slain,
His passion grew on him, he could not refrain.

"Although you're a general, brave Braddock," said he,
"Revenged for the death of my brother I'll be."
When Washington saw that, he quickly drew nigh,
Said, "O my bold soldier, I'd have you forbear."

"No, I will take his life, if it ruins us all."
And Washington turned round to not see him fall.
He up with his musket, and there shot him down.
Then Braddock replied, "I received a wound.

"If here is this place, my life I should yield,
Pray carry your general, boys, out of the field."

. . . .

Then General Gatefore, he took the command,
And fought like a hero for old Eng-i-land.
He fled through the ranks, like a cat to her game,
But alas, and alack, he was short-i-ly slain.

Then General Gates, he took the command,
And fought like a hero for old Eng-i-land.
He wished that the river had never been crossed
And so many Englishmen shamefully lost.

We had for to cross, it was at the very last,
And cross over the river, they killed us so fast.
Men fell in the river till they stopped up the flood
And the streams of that river ran red down with blood.

JOHN BROWN'S BODY

John Brown's bod - y lies a-mould'ring in the grave,

John Brown's bod - y lies a-mould-'ring in the grave,

John Brown's bod - y lies a-mould-'ring in the grave; His

soul is march - ing on. Glo - ry, glo - ry, hal - le -

lu - jah! Glo - ry, glo - ry, hal - le - lu - jah!

Glo - ry, glo - ry, hal - le - lu - jah! His soul is marching on!

John Brown's body lies a-mold'ring in the grave,
John Brown's body lies a-mold'ring in the grave,
John Brown's body lies a-mold'ring in the grave,
His soul is marching on.

Chorus:
Glory, glory, hallelujah!
Glory, glory, hallelujah!
Glory, glory, hallelujah!
His soul is marching on!

[528]

The stars of heaven are looking kindly down,
   On the grave of old John Brown.

He's gone to be a soldier in the army of the Lord,
   His soul is marching on.

John Brown died that the slave might be free,
   But his soul goes marching on.

He captured Harper's Ferry with his nineteen men so true,
And he frightened old Virginia till she trembled through
      and through;
They hung him for a traitor, themselves the traitor crew,
   But his soul goes marching on.

John Brown's knapsack is strapped to his back,
   His soul is marching on.

His pet lambs will meet on the way,
   And they'll go marching on.

They will hang Jeff Davis on a sour apple tree,
   As they go marching on.

Now has come the glorious jubilee,
   When all mankind are free.

HOLD ON, ABRAHAM *

We're going down to Dixie, to Dixie, to Dixie,
We're going down to Dixie, to Dixie, to fight for the dear Old Flag,
And should we fall in Dixie, in Dixie, in Dixie,
And should we fall in Dixie, we'll die for the dear Old Flag.

* From Songs of the Civil War in Harris Collection, Brown University.

Chorus:

Hold on, Abraham, never say die to your Uncle Sam,
Uncle Sam's boys are coming right along, six hundred thousand
   strong.

Our flag shall float o'er Dixie, o'er Dixie, o'er Dixie,
Our flag shall float o'er Dixie, the Red, the White, the Blue,
We'll ne'er give up till Dixie, till Dixie, till Dixie,
We'll ne'er give up till Dixie sings "Yankee Doodle Doo."

General Grant he's in Dixie, in Dixie, in Dixie,
General Grant he's in Dixie and ready for the foe.
Do you think he'll give up in Dixie, in Dixie?
Do you think he'll give up Dixie? Oh, no, no, no, no, no, no, NO!

Our friends have gone to Dixie, to Dixie, to Dixie,
Our friends have gone to Dixie to fight for the dear Old Flag.
And we're all going to Dixie, to Dixie, to Dixie,
And we're all going to Dixie to stand by the dear Old Flag.

Our Halleck's bound for Dixie, for Dixie, for Dixie, with a million
   boys or two.
He'll never give up old Dixie till she's back in the Union true.
Bold Kenney fell in Dixie, in Dixie, in Dixie, while fighting for us all.
And there is General Burnside, our Burnside, old Burnside,
He will avenge his fall.

And where is General Butler, our Butler, old Butler,
And where is Picayune Butler? He's gone to Dixie town.
And there he keeps a-stirring, a-stirring, a-stirring,
And there he keeps a-stirring the Secesh up and down.

Brave comrades have come from Dixie, from Dixie, from Dixie,
Brave comrades have come from Dixie to speed the Cause along.
They're going back to Dixie, to Dixie, to Dixie,
They're going back to Dixie, with a brigade full and strong.

DIXIE   *Daniel Decatur Emmett*

I wish I was in the land of cot - ton,

'Sim - mon seed and san - dy bot-tom; Look a - way, look a -

way, look a-way, Dix-ie land.   In Dix - ie land   whar

I was born in, Ear - ly on a fros - ty morn-in',

Look a - way, look a - way, look a - way, Dix - ie land.

REFRAIN

Den   I wish I was in Dix - ie; hoo - ray, hoo -

ray! In Dix - ie land we'll take our stand to

lib and die in Dix - ie. A - way, a -

way, a - way down South in Dix - ie, A -

way, a - way, a - way down South in Dix - ie.

Dis world was made in jis' six days,
An' finished up in various ways.
Look away! look away! look away! Dixie land!
Dey den make Dixie trim and nice,
And Adam called it "Paradise."
Look away! look away! look away! Dixie land!

Chorus:

Den I wish I was in Dixie; hooray, hooray!
In Dixie land we'll take our stand,
To lib and die in Dixie.
Away, away, away down south in Dixie;
Away, away, away down south in Dixie.

I wish I was in the land of cotton,
'Simmon * seed and sandy bottom;
Look away, look away, look away, Dixie land.
In Dixie land, whar I was born in,
Early on a frosty mornin';
Look away, look away, look away, Dixie land.

Old missus marry "Will de Weaber";
William was a gay deceiber;
Look away, look away, look away, Dixie land.
When he put his arm around 'er
He smiled as fierce as a forty-pounder;
Look away, look away, look away, Dixie land.

His face was sharp as a butcher's cleaber,
But dat did not seem to grieb her;
Look away, look away, look away, Dixie land.

* Often written, and usually sung, in the South, "cinnamon."

Old missus acted de foolish part,
And died fer de man dat broke her heart;
Look away, look away, look away, Dixie land.

Now here's a health to the nex' old missus
And all de gals dat want to kiss us;
Look away, look away, look away, Dixie land.
But if you want to drive away sorrow,
Come and hear dis song tomorrow;
Look away, look away, look away, Dixie land.

Dar's buckwheat cakes and Injun batter,
Makes you fat er a little fatter;
Look away, look away, look away, Dixie land.
Den hoe it down an' scratch your grabbel,
To Dixie's land I'm bound to trabbel;
Look away, look away, look away, Dixie land.

Another stanza popular with Confederate soldiers:

Way down South in the fields of cotton,
Cinnamon seed and sandy bottom,
    Look away! look away!
Then way down in the fields of cotton,
Vinegar shoes and paper stockin's,
    Look away in Dixie land.

WAR SONG*

Come all you jol - ly sol - diers, I will sing to you a song, I'll try to be brief, I will not de - tain you long— Con - cern - ing all my trou - bles and how they did ad - vance, And how I got a-round them and what a nar - row chance.

Come all you jolly soldiers, I will sing to you a song,
I'll try to be brief, I'll not detain you long,
Concerning all my troubles and how they did advance
And how I got around them and what a narrow chance.

With a bottle of good whisky I put the guard to sleep;
Then down upon my knees so slyly I did creep,
And when I had gone around them and found I had got through
I set down upon a little rock and there put on my shoe.

* From Jean Thomas' *Devil's Ditties* (Chicago: W. W. Hatfield).

The ferriage it was guarded and I had nary horse.
I cast my eyes around a little raft I spied;
I thought by good judgment I could get to the other side.
I jumped upon my little raft, so gently sailed across.

Not thanking them for ferriage nor eitherwise a horse
I struck out up old Lickin, I set my head for home,
To see my wife and children all that was my intent,
To see my wife and children that I had left at home.

When I come to find them I found them all asleep.
I told my wife I had been a prisoner and now on my retreat;
She gave to me my supper, a blanket in my hand,
Told me to leave this country and go to Dixie's land.

GOOD OLD REBEL

In memory of Carey Page

Collier's Weekly, April 4, 1914, devoted a column to this famous
song of Reconstruction days. It was written by Major Innes Randolph,
a member of the staff of General J. E. B. Stuart, and a native of
Virginia. Richard N. Brooke of Washington, D. C., suggests that
the song is "a bit of fun not supposed to reflect Major Randolph's own
sentiments but to illustrate the irreconcilable spirit of the illiterate
element in some sections."

Herbert Quick, who wrote the story for *Collier's,* added that millions sang the song who had never heard of Major Randolph. When
the Duchess of Manchester sang it before the Prince of Wales on one
occasion, he repeatedly encored "that fine American song with the cuss
words in it." Laura Lee Davidson of Baltimore says that the song
was sung "in many a Southern parlor in the bitter days of Reconstruction; and to have heard the author himself sing it is a joy to be

remembered." The accepted version *B*, and *A*, a Texas composite, follow. Some unknown person has added one stanza. The author of the music is unknown.

Miss Carey Page, daughter of Ralph Page and granddaughter of Walter H. Page, gave me tune *A* following a talk I had made to a group of Bryn Mawr students in November, 1932. At that time she was a member of the freshman class. The song is published in memory of her beautiful life.—J. A. L.

A

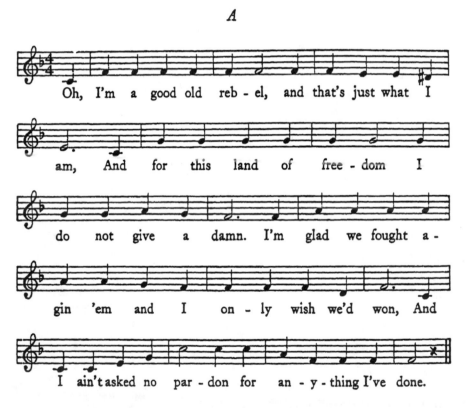

Oh, I'm a good old reb - el, and that's just what I am, And for this land of free - dom I do not give a damn. I'm glad we fought a - gin 'em and I on - ly wish we'd won, And I ain't asked no par - don for an - y - thing I've done.

Oh, I'm a good old rebel, that's what I am,
And for this land of freedom, I don't give a damn;
I'm glad I fought agin her, I only wish we'd won,
And I ain't axed any pardon for anything I've done.

I fought with old Bob Lee for three years about,
Got wounded in four places and starved at Point Lookout.
I caught the rheumatism a-campin' in the snow,
But I killed a chance of Yankees and I wish I'd killed some mo'!

Three hundred thousand Yankees is dead in Southern dust,
We got three hundred thousand before they conquered us;
They died of Southern fever, of Southern steel and shot—
I wish they was three million instead of what we got.

I hate the Constitution, this great republic, too;
I hate the nasty eagle, and the uniform so blue;
I hate their glorious banner, and all their flags and fuss.
Those lying, thieving Yankees, I hate 'em wuss and wuss.

I hate the Yankee nation and everything they do;
I hate the Declaration of Independence, too;
I hate the glorious Union, 'tis dripping with our blood;
I hate the striped banner, I fought it all I could.

I won't be reconstructed! I'm better now than them;
And for a carpetbagger, I don't give a damn;
So I'm off for the frontier, soon as I can go,
I'll prepare me a weapon and start for Mexico.

I can't take up my musket and fight them now no mo',
But I'm not goin' to love 'em and that is certain sho';
And I don't want no pardon for what I was or am,
I won't be reconstructed and I don't give a damn.

B *

An un - re - con - struct - ed reb - el, and that is what I am, For this great land of free - dom I do not give a damn. I'm glad we fought a - gin 'em, I'm sor - ry that they won; and I do not ask your par - don for an - y - thing I done.

Oh, I'm a good old Rebel,
Now that's just what I am;
For this "fair land of Freedom"
I do not care a damn.
I'm glad I fit against it—
I only wish we'd won.
And I don't want no pardon
For anything I've done.

I hates the Constitution,
This great Republic too;

* Tune from Mrs. Harriett Wyckoff, Washington, D. C., niece of the author of the song, and John
T. Vance, Law Librarian, Library of Congress.

I hates the Freedmen's Bureau,
In uniforms of blue.
I hates the nasty eagle,
With all his brag and fuss;
But the lyin', thievin' Yankees,
I hates 'em wuss and wuss.

I hates the Yankee nation,
And everything they do;
I hates the Declaration
Of Independence too.
I hates the glorious Union,
'Tis dripping with our blood;
And I hates the striped banner—
I fit it all I could.

I followed old Marse Robert
For four years, near about.
Got wounded in three places,
And starved at Point Lookout.
I cotch the roomatism
A-campin' in the snow,
But I killed a chance of Yankees—
And I'd like to kill some mo'.

Three hundred thousand Yankees
Is stiff Southern dust;
We got three hundred thousand
Befo' they conquered us.
They died of Southern fever
And Southern steel and shot;
And I wish it was three million
Instead of what we got.

[539]

I can't take up my musket
And fight 'em now no mo',
But I ain't a-goin' to love 'em,
Now that is sartin sho';
And I don't want no pardon
For what I was and am;
And I won't be reconstructed,
And I don't care a damn.

BENNY HAVENS, OH! *

"It is more than a century since Benny Havens first sold cakes and ale to the cadets at West Point, and over half a century since he went to his last sleep in the Highland Union Cemetery on the banks of the Hudson; but his spirit lives on in that matchless song which originated one winter evening around the convivial bowl in his tavern by the river. Generations of cadets sang it at Benny's and carried it with them from the Everglades to the Yellowstone; and today it has become an enduring and inseparable part of those old traditions which unite the corps of the present with the long gray line of the past.

"For some years prior to 1832, Benny Havens, who had served as first lieutenant of the Highland Falls company in the War of 1812, occupied a one-story cottage a short distance west of the old cadet hospital. It was here that Edgar Allan Poe, who often remarked that Benny was the 'sole congenial soul in the entire God-forsaken place,' became devoted to him. At first Benny sold only ale, cider, and buckwheat cakes, but subsequently he dispensed a more potent beverage. As a result, in 1832, he was expelled from the military reservation.

"Shortly after his expulsion, Benny Havens opened a tavern on the river's edge below the cliffs of Highland Falls, about a mile and a half from cadet barracks. To this tavern, after taps and against regula-

* From the *West Point Scrap Book, 1871* (New York: D. Van Nostrand) through Major Isaac Spalding, Office Chief of Staff, Washington, D. C.

tions, came many cadets whose names were later to be written on their country's roll of honor. Many of our famous generals of the last century were fond of recalling the cold winter nights when they had slipped out of barracks and skated down the river to partake of the good cheer at Benny's. It is even recorded that Cadet Jefferson Davis, in attempting to evade some officers who had descended upon Benny's tavern, once fell over a cliff and was nearly killed.

"I suspect that not many of Benny's young visitors during his early days in Highland Falls knew that their host was something of a churchman; yet he left proof of this fact in an old legal document which he signed in 1836 as a trustee of the First Presbyterian Church of Highland Falls.

"The song that has perpetuated Benny's fame was originally composed by Lieutenant O'Brien of the Eighth Infantry. He had been an assistant surgeon in the army, but had just been commissioned in the infantry when, in 1838, he visited his friend Ripley A. Arnold of the First Class. Together they made many visits to Benny's, where O'Brien composed the first few stanzas of the song and sang them to the tune of 'The Wearing of the Green.' O'Brien died in a Florida campaign a few years later. For many years after his death each class added a verse to the song. Of the nine given here, the first, fifth, and sixth are those generally sung.

"During the Civil War the song was widely sung in the army, and many army verses were improvised. During the summer of 1865 when boatloads of returning soldiers were daily passing Benny's, the bands would strike up 'Benny Havens, Oh!' while hundreds of voices joined in the song.

"From Nevada's hoary ridges, from stormy coasts of Maine,
From lava beds and Yellowstone the story never waned;
Wherever duty called, they went, their steps were never slow,
With 'Alma Mater' on their lips and 'Benny Havens, Oh.'

"When this life's troubled sea is o'er and our last battle's through.
If God permits us mortals there his blest domain to view,

Then we shall see in glory crowned, in proud celestial row,
The friends we've known and loved so well at Benny Havens', oh!

"On May 29, 1877, in his ninetieth year, Benny Havens died. A few years later the building of the West Shore Railroad necessitated moving the Benny Havens tavern. It was carefully taken apart and carted about five miles back into the hills to a point near Long Pond Mountain, where it was reërected. There it stands today, but little changed from the days when Benny Havens was its genial host."

Come, fill your glasses, fellows, and stand up in a row,
To singing sentimentally we're going for to go;
In the army there's sobriety, promotion's very slow,
So we'll sing our reminiscences of Benny Havens, oh!

Chorus:
    Oh! Benny Havens, oh! Oh! Benny Havens, oh!
    We'll sing our reminiscences of Benny Havens, oh!

Let us toast our foster-father, the Republic, as you know,
Who in the paths of science taught us upward for to go;
And the maidens of our native land, whose cheeks like roses glow,
They're oft remembered in our cups at Benny Havens', oh!

To the ladies of our Army our cups shall ever flow,
Companions in our exile and our shield 'gainst every woe;
May they see their husbands generals, with double pay also,
And join us in our choruses at Benny Havens', oh!

Come fill up to our generals, God bless the brave heroes.
They're an honor to their country, and a terror to their foes;
May they long rest on their laurels, and troubles never know,
But live to see a thousand years at Benny Havens', oh!

To our kind old Alma Mater, our rock-bound Highland home,
We'll cast back many a fond regret as o'er life's sea we roam;

Until on our last battle-field the lights of heaven shall glow,
We'll never fail to drink to her and Benny Havens, oh!

May the Army be augmented, promotion be less slow,
May our country in the hour of need be ready for the foe;
May we find a soldier's resting-place beneath a soldier's blow,
With room enough beside our graves for Benny Havens, oh!

And if amid the battle shock our honor e'er should trail,
And hearts that beat beneath its folds should turn or basely quail;
Then may some son of Benny's, with quick avenging blow,
Lift up the flag we loved so well at Benny Havens', oh!

To our comrades who have fallen, one cup before we go,
They poured their life-blood freely out pro bono publico.
No marble points the stranger to where they rest below;
They lie neglected far away from Benny Havens', oh!

When you and I and Benny, and all the others, too,
Are called before the "final board" our course in life to view,
May we never "fess" on any point, but straight be told to go,
And join the army of the blest at Benny Havens', oh!

THE WILD MIZ–ZOU–RYE *

(Old Cavalry Song)

"The history of this well-known and widely sung song, like that of so many others, is an illusive and tantalizing will-o'-the-wisp. One follows a promising clue only to find that the end of one trail is but the beginning of another. The song has been sung in different forms as a soldier song and as a sea chantey. Captain W. B. Whall, in his *Ships, Songs, and Shanties*, concludes that it was originally a song, not a sea chantey, and ascribes its probable origin to American

* Words and tune from Major Isaac Spalding, Office Chief of Staff, Washington, D. C.

and Canadian voyageurs. He gives a version of the song in which a white trader courts the daughter of Chief Shenandoah and carries her away across the 'wide Missouri.' Joanna C. Colcord, in *Roll and Go*, has a version called 'Shenandoah,' which was used on ships after the Civil War. In *The American Songbag*, Carl Sandburg has 'The Wide Mizzoura,' some stanzas of which are very similar to those given here.

"The cavalry jealously claims this song for its very own, having acquired it, no doubt, during the frontier days. Sometimes the 'would not have me for a lover' stanza is followed by one beginning, 'Because I was a wagon soldier'; but the cavalry claims this to be a field artillery intrusion and an attempt to steal its song.

"In some versions, too, we learn that after Nancy reached Kansas City, 'then she had a nigger baby'; and in the Philippines I once heard of a group that, being as mellow with liquor as the song is with age, ascribed the parentage of Nancy's baby to various individuals present—with disastrous results to the singers."

For sev - en long years I court - ed Nan - cy,

Hi! Ho! the roll - ing ri - ver! For

sev - en long years I court - ed Nan - cy,

Ha! Ha! I'm bound a - way for the wild Miz - zou - rye!

For seven long years I courted Nancy—
Hi! Oh! The rolling river!
For seven long years I courted Nancy—
Ha! Ha! I'm bound away for the wild Miz-zou-rýe.

She would not have me for a lover—
Hi! Oh! The rolling river!
She would not have me for a lover—
Ha! Ha! I'm bound away for the wild Miz-zou-rýe.

And so she took my fifteen dollars—
Hi! Oh! The rolling river!
And so she took my fifteen dollars—
Ha! Ha! I'm bound away for the wild Miz-zou-rýe.

And then she went to Kansas City—
Hi! Oh! The rolling river!
And then she went to Kansas City—
Ha! Ha! I'm bound away for the wild Miz-zou-rýe.

And there she had a little sh-sh-baby— *
Hi! Oh! The rolling river!
And there she had a little sh-sh-baby— *
Ha! Ha! I'm bound away for the wild Miz-zou-rýe.

She must have had another lover—
Hi! Oh! The rolling river!
She must have had another lover—
Ha! Ha! I'm bound away for the wild Miz-zou-rýe.

He must have been a ——th Cavalry Soldier—
Hi! Oh! The rolling river!
He must have been a ——th Cavalry Soldier—
Ha! Ha! I'm bound away for the wild Miz-zou-rýe.

* When this is sung by a group of army men, the chorus sings "sh-sh" while one lone man breaks
out irrepressibly with "baby."

[545]

I'm drinkin' of rum and chawin' tobacco—
Hi! Oh! The rolling river!
I'm drinkin' of rum and chawin' tobacco—
Ha! Ha! I'm bound away for the wild Miz-zou-rýe.

I learned this song from Tommy Tompkins—
Hi! Oh! The rolling river!
I learned this song from Tommy Tompkins—
Ha! Ha! I'm bound away for the wild Miz-zou-rýe.

SHENANDOAH *

Missouri she's a mighty river,
Away-ay, you rolling river.
The Indians camp along its borders,
Aha, I'm bound away
'Cross the wide Missouri.

The white man loved an Indian maiden,
With notions his canoe was laden.

O Shenandoah, I love your daughter,
I've crossed for her the rolling water.

The chief, he made an awful holler,
He turned away the trader's dollars.

Along there came a Yankee skipper,
He winked at her and tipped his flipper.

He sold the chief some fire water,
He got him drunk and stole his daughter.

O Shenandoah, I long to hear you,
Come back across the rolling water.

(Each verse carries the same refrain as the first.)

* Sent by Captain A. E. Dingle, Cove Cottage, West Bermuda. Tune identical with "The Wild Miz-zou-rye."

DAMN THE FILIPINOS

"This song became current among the officers and soldiers in the early Philippine campaign, and at the same time so obnoxious to the 'friendly' natives that the singing of it was forbidden by the general officer in command." *

In that land of do - py dreams, hap - py

peace-ful Phil - ip-pines, Where the bo - lo man is hik - ing

night and day; Where Ta - ga - los steal and lie, where A -

mer - i - ca - nos die, There you hear the sol - diers sing this

eve - ning lay: Damn, damn, damn the Fil - i - pi - nos,

cross - eyed ka - ki - ack la - drones, Un - der -

neath our star - ry flag, civ - i - lize 'em with a Krag,

And re - turn us to our own be - lov - ed homes.

* *Harper's Weekly*, March 5, 1910.

In that land of dopy dreams, happy peaceful Philippines,
   Where the bolo-man is hiking night and day;
Where Tagalos steal and lie, where Americanos die,
   There you hear the soldiers sing this evening lay:

Chorus:

   Damn, damn, damn the Filipinos, cross-eyed kakiack ladrones
   Underneath our starry flag civilize 'em with a Krag,
   And return us to our own beloved homes.

Underneath the nipa thatch, where the skinny chickens scratch,
   Only refuge after hiking all day long,
When I lay me down to sleep, slimy lizards o'er me creep,
   Then you hear the soldiers sing this evening song:

   Damn, damn, damn the Filipinos, etc.

Social customs there are few, all the ladies smoke and chew.
   And the men do things the padres say are wrong.
But the padres cut no ice—for they live on fish and rice—
   Where you hear the soldiers sing this evening song:

   Damn, damn, damn the Filipinos, etc.

A ROOKIE'S LAMENT *

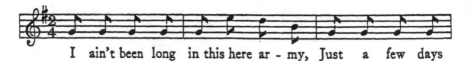

I   ain't been long   in this here ar - my,   Just   a   few   days

* Selected as typical by Major Isaac Spalding, Office Chief of Staff, Washington, D C. Another one
of the interminables.

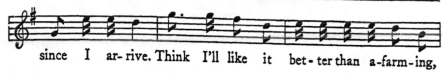

since I ar-rive. Think I'll like it bet-ter than a-farm-ing,

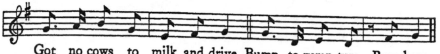

Got no cows to milk and drive, Bump-to-rump-tum Bum-bum.

I ain't been long in this here army,
Just a few days since I arrive.
Think I'll like it better than a-farmin'—
Got no cows to milk and drive.
    Bump-ta-rump-tum. Bum. Bum.

The very first thing in the morning,
A feller with a horn makes a lot of noise.
Then another feller they calls the Sergeant
Says: "Get up, now. Turn out, boys."

Then they take you to the bathroom,
Place like that, I never seen before.
Water comes in through a hole in the ceiling,
Runs right out through a hole in the floor.

They teach you about this soldier business,
How to march and turn around.
Put a gun upon your shoulder,
"One, two, three," and you put it on the ground.

They teach you about the signal business,
A feller waves a flag at a feller far away.
But one thing, I can't get on to:
How does he know what he's trying to say?

[549]

You form in line and write on a paper,
A feller up there gives you your pay.
Take it to the squad room. Put it on a blanket,
A feller hollers, "Craps," and takes it all away.

Then they take you out a-hiking,
Over roads of rock and sand.
I think what the Colonel wants to know is—
Can his horse outhike a man?

Then I transferred to the Cavalry,
Thought it'd be nice to have a horse to ride.
Now I find that the place that I ride on,
Have to use "New Skin" for hide.

You form in line and march to the stable,
With your brush and currycomb.
Groom your horse as long as you're able.
Fall in again, and march back home.

They gave me a horse that looked like Dobbin,
The horse I used to ride on the farm.
Before I could stop that horse from runnin',
I wish I'd had Jack Johnson's arm.

I finally got him back to the stable,
I said to the Cap'n, "I stopped her, Bill."
The Cap'n said to the First Sergeant,
"Take this bird, and throw him in the Mill."

Then if you should get your leg broke,
Doctor won't charge you one red cent.
"C.C." pills is all you need—
Your leg ain't broke—just badly bent.

Went downtown to see a moving picture,
Stepped outside to get a glass of beer.
Missed the last car, and when I seen the Sergeant,
Had to go out and dig another "rear."

And so on ad infinitum.

THE COMPANY COOK

The company cook had a greasy look,
A nasty galoot was he;
His only shirt was stiff with dirt,
And his breeches a sight to see.

Chorus:

> The cook, the cook, the company cook,
> An autocrat was he;
> With his pots and pans, and bottles and cans,
> And his household crockery.

The fact of it is that the cooking biz
In the army grades downhill;
And the stuff we got to put in the pot
Was too often fit for swill.

And a man with a bit of Yankee grit
Would rather dodge the place;
Who held the berth was no good on earth,
Everlastingly in disgrace.

The one we had was a regular cad
With a witless sort of look;
A cross betwixt a mule and a 'tarnal fool,
He was born for a company cook.

[551]

A beastly tramp, yet he ruled the camp
With a battered iron spoon;
He made us wait, he ever was late,
And we were ever too soon.

He'd beat any bird you ever heard,
He'd warble and whistle and trill;
And many a note came out of his throat.

. . . .

He'd whinny and neigh in a natural way,
Why, he'd fool all the horses in camp;
And the measly mules, like a lot of darned fools,
Was just stuck on the musical tramp.

Well, along in the fall he stopped whistling at all,
Just sozzled around and cried;
And first thing we knows, he had turned up his toes,
I'll be darned if he hadn't died.

So we dug him a hole by the side of a knoll,
By the side of a little brook;
Each man wore a grin as we lowered him in—
This typical company cook.

His mortal coil went under the soil,
He had gone to be a spook;
As we said farewell, the devil in hell
Was roasting the company cook.

WE'VE DONE OUR HITCH IN HELL *

I'm sitting here a-thinking
Of the things I left behind,

* From C. E. Anson, Wyoming.

[552]

And I hate to put in writing
What's running through my mind.
We've dug a million trenches
And cleared ten miles of ground,
And a tougher place this side of hell
I know is yet unfound.
But there's still one consolation,
Gather, comrades, while I tell:
When we die, we're bound for heaven,
For we've done our hitch in hell.

We've built a hundred kitchens
For our cooks to stew our beans;
We've stood a hundred guard mounts,
And kept tab on all the scenes;
We've washed a million mess kits,
And peeled a million spuds;
We've rolled a million blankets,
And washed a million duds.
The number of parades we've made
Is surely hard to tell,
But we'll now parade in heaven,
For we've done our hitch in hell.

We've killed a million rattlesnakes
That tried to take our cots;
We've shook a million centipedes
From out our army socks;
We've marched a hundred thousand miles,
And made a thousand camps;
We've pulled a million cactus thorns
From out our army pants.
But when our work on earth is done,

Our friends on earth will tell
That we were true-blue soldiers,
And have done our hitch in hell.

When the final taps are sounded
And we lay aside life's cares;
When we do the last parade, boys,
Upon the golden stairs;
When the angels bid us welcome,
And with the harps begin to play;
'Tis then we'll hear the bugle calling
To that great and happy day.
Then St. Peter 'll tell the angels
How we charged and how we fell;
"Give a front seat to Third Wyoming,
For they've done their hitch in hell."

IF YOU WANT TO KNOW WHERE THE PRIVATES ARE *

"There is a lot more truth in this song than one is likely to suspect,
official reports of Army Operations to the contrary notwithstanding."

If you want to know where the pri - vates are, I'll

tell you where they are, I'll tell you where they are, Yes, I'll

* Reprinted by permission of the copyright owners from *Songs My Mother Never Taught Me*,
by John J. "Jack" Niles, Douglas S. "Doug" Moore, and A. A. "Wally" Wallgren, published
and copyrighted 1929 by The Macaulay Company.

tell you where they are, · If you want to know where the pri - vates are, I'll tell you where they are: Up to their ears in mud. I saw them, I saw them Up to their ears in mud and slime. If you want to know where the pri - vates are, I'll tell you where they are: Up to their ears in mud.

If you want to know where the privates are,
I'll tell you where they are,
I'll tell you where they are,
Yes, I'll tell you where they are.
If you want to know where the privates are—
I'll tell you where they are,
Up to their ears in mud.
I saw them, I saw them—
Up to their ears in mud and slime.
If you want to know where the privates are,

I'll tell where they are—
Up to their ears in mud.

If you want to know where the sergeants are,
Etc., etc.,
Clipping the old barbed wire.

If you want to know where the captains are,
Etc., etc.,
Drinking the privates' rum.

If you want to know where the officers are,
Etc., etc.,
Down in their deep dug-out.

If you want to know where the generals are,
Etc., etc.,
Back in gay Paree.

THE HEARSE SONG *

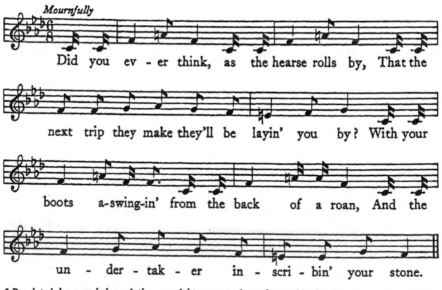

Mournfully

Did you ev-er think, as the hearse rolls by, That the next trip they make they'll be layin' you by? With your boots a-swing-in' from the back of a roan, And the un-der-tak-er in-scri-bin' your stone.

Did you ever think as the hearse rolls by
That the next trip they take they'll be layin' you by,
With your boots a-swingin' from the back of a roan
And the undertaker inscribin' your stone'?

When the old motor hearse goes rollin' by,
You don't know whether to laugh or cry.
For the grave diggers may get you too,
Then the hearse's next load may consist of you.

They'll take you over to Field Thirteen,*
Where the sun is shinin' and the grass is green,
And they'll throw in dirt and they'll throw in rocks,
And they don't give a damn if they break your pine box.

Oh, the bugs crawl in and the bugs crawl out,
They do right dress and they turn about,
Then each one takes a bite or two,
Out of what the war office used to call you.

Oh, your eyes drop out and your teeth fall in,
And the worms crawl over your mouth and chin,
They invite their friends and their friends' friends too,
And you're chewed all to hell when they're through with you.

HINKY DINKY, PARLEY-VOO?

"In the beginning she was a ma'm'selle from Armentières, a daughter fair with lily-white skin and golden hair; and there, in 1915, some British soldier met her, loved her, and sang her praises. Long before the war was ended she hailed from many a town in France, and the ballad that Tommy had made for her had been adopted and greatly lengthened by his American cousins. It had become a vehicle for com-

* The cemetery of the Aviation Corps.

ment not only on the beauty and generosity of the ma'm'selle herself, but on everything else from the rarity of French customs to the activities of the Y.M.C.A. and the courage of the commanding generals." *

The following version of the famous "Hinky-Dinky" is a composite of verses from *Sound Off*, Sandburg's *American Songbag*, and Niles and Moore's *Songs My Mother Never Taught Me*. There is in print a private, not mailable, collection of more than six hundred stanzas concerning the famous mademoiselle.

Oh, land-lord, have you a daugh-ter fair, par-ley-voo? Oh, land-lord, have you a daughter fair, par-ley-voo? Oh, land-lord, have you a daughter fair, To wash a sol - - dier's un - der - wear? Hin - ky - din - ky, par - ley - voo?

Oh, landlord, have you a daughter fair, parley-voo?
Oh, landlord, have you a daughter fair, parley-voo?
Oh, landlord, have you a daughter fair,
To wash a soldier's underwear?
Hinky-dinky, parley-voo!

* From Edward Arthur Dolph, in *Sound Off*.

Oh, yes, I have a daughter fair,
With lily-white hands and golden hair.

Mademoiselle from Armentières,
She hadn't been kissed in forty years.

She might have been young for all we knew,
When Napoleon flopped at Waterloo.

She never could hold the love of a man,
For she took her baths in a talcum can.

Mademoiselle from Armentières,
Mademoiselle from Armentières,
You'll never get your Croix de Guerre,
If you never wash your underwear.

Mademoiselle from Orléans,
She made me sell my Liberty Bonds.

The French, they are a funny race,
They fight with their feet and save their face.

The cootie is the national bug of France,
The cootie's found all over France,
No matter where you hang your pants.

Our grease-ball * is a goddam dirty bum,
He bails out swill and makes the slum.

Oh, the seventy-seventh went over the top,
A sous lieutenant, a Jew, and a Wop.

The medical corps, they held the line,
With C.C. pills and iodine.

* Grease-ball = cook.

[559]

The officers get all the steak,
And all we get is the belly-ache.

The general got a Croix de Guerre,
The son-of-a-gun was never there.

An American soldier on the Rhine,
He kissed the women and drunk the wine.

The little marine fell in love with his nurse,
He's taken her now for better or worse.

My Froggie girl was true to me,
She was true to me, she was true to you,
She was true to the whole damn army, too.

The *Pretoria* passed a ship today,
For the ship was going the other way.

Where are the girls that used to swarm,
About me in my uniform?

You might forget the gas and shell,
But you'll never forget the mademoiselle.

There's many and many a married man,
Wants to go back to France again.

'Twas a hell of a war as we recall,
But still 'twas better than none at all.

XXIV

WHITE SPIRITUALS

"I am bound for the Promised Land."

"Spontaneous song became a marked characteristic of the camp meetings. Rough and irregular couplets or stanzas were concocted out of Scripture phrases and everyday speech, with liberal interspersing of hallelujahs and refrains. Such ejaculatory hymns were frequently started by an excited auditor during the preaching, and taken up by the throng until the meeting dissolved into a 'singing-ecstasy' culminating in a general handshaking. Sometimes they were given forth by a preacher, who had a sense of rhythm, under the excitement of his preaching and the agitation of his audience. . . . Many of these rude songs perished in the using, some were written down, passing from hand to hand. The camp-meeting song books which began to appear in the first decade of the nineteenth century doubtless contain such of these as proved effective and popular." *

* From *White Spirituals of the Southern Uplands*, by George Pullen Jackson, who quotes from *The English Hymn*, by Louis F. Benson.

BEAR THE NEWS, MARY

G. D. Vowel, who sat on his front porch in Harlan, Kentucky, and sang this spiritual into our microphone, heard it over forty years ago in Knoxville, Tennessee, at a revival meeting.

Bear the news, Ma - ry, Bear the news, Ma - ry, Bear the news, Ma - ry, I'm on my way to glo - ry. If you git there be - fore I do, I'm a-hunting a home to go to, Just tell them all I'm a-com - ing too, I'm a-hunt - ing a home to go to.

Bear the news, Mary,
Bear the news, Mary,
Bear the news, Mary,
I'm on my way to glory.

If you git there before I do,
I'm a-hunting a home to go to,
Just tell them all I'm a-coming too,
I'm a-hunting a home to go to.

[563]

Bear the news, Mary,
Bear the news, Mary,
Bear the news, Mary,
I'm on my way to glory.

PARTING FRIENDS *

Fare - well, my friends, I'm bound for Ca - naan,
Your com - pa - ny has been de - light - ful,

I'm trav - 'ling through the wil - der - ness.
You who doth leave my mind dis - tressed.

I go a - way, be - hind to leave you,

Per - haps nev - er to meet a - gain;

But if we nev - er have this pleas - ure,

I hope we'll meet on Ca - naan's land.

* From Professor George Pullen Jackson's *White Spirituals of the Southern Uplands.* "Under the title 'Parting Friends,' McCurry (editor of the *Social Harp*) gives the following song with the note: 'The author, when eight years old, learned the air of this tune from Mrs. Catherine Penn. That was, therefore, in the year 1829.'"

Farewell, my friends, I'm bound for Canaan,
I'm trav'ling through the wilderness,
Your company has been delightful,
You who doth leave my mind distressed.
I go away, behind to leave you,
Perhaps never to meet again;
But if we ever have this pleasure,
I hope we'll meet on Canaan's shore.

BURGES *

Moderately slow

I'm glad that I am born to die,
From grief and woe my soul shall fly,
And we'll all shout to-geth-er in that morn-ing,
In that morn-ing, in that morn-ing,
And we'll all shout to-geth-er in that morn-ing.

I'm glad that I am born to die,
From grief and woe my soul shall fly,
And we'll all shout together in that morning,
In that morning, in that morning,
And we'll all shout together in that morning.

* From Professor George Pullen Jackson's *White Spirituals of the Southern Uplands*, reprinted from the *Social Harp*.

FEW DAYS *

I pitch my tent on this camp ground, few days, few days,
And give old Satan another round,
And I am going home.
I can't stay in these diggings, few days, few days,
I can't stay in these diggings,
I am going home.

* From George Pullen Jackson's *White Spirituals of the Southern Uplands* (University of North Carolina Press). Professor Jackson reprinted the song from the *Social Harp*.

WEDLOCK *

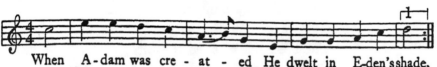

When A-dam was cre - at - ed He dwelt in E-den's shade,
As Mo-ses has re - lat - ed, Be-fore a bride was

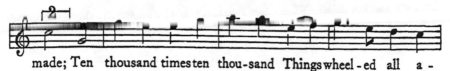

made; Ten thousand times ten thou-sand Things wheel-ed all a -

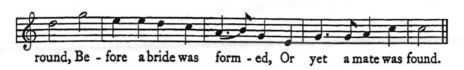

round, Be - fore a bride was form - ed, Or yet a mate was found.

When Adam was created,
He dwelt in Eden's shade,
As Moses has related,
Before a bride was made;
Ten thousand times ten thousand
Things wheelèd all around,
Before a bride was formèd,
Or yet a mate was found.

He had no consolation,
But seemed as one alone,
Till, to his admiration,
He found he'd lost a bone.
This woman was not taken
From Adam's head, we know;
And she must not rule o'er him,
It's evidently so.

* From George Pullen Jackson's *White Spirituals of the Southern Uplands.*

This woman she was taken
From near to Adam's heart,
By which we are directed
That they should never part.
The book that's called the Bible,
Be sure you don't neglect;
For in every sense of duty,
It will you both direct.

The woman is commanded
To do her husband's will,
In everything that's lawful,
Her duty to fulfill.
Great was his exultation,
To see her by his side;
Great was his elevation,
To have a loving bride.

This woman she was taken
From under Adam's arm;
And she must be protected
From injury and harm.
This woman was not taken
From Adam's feet, we see;
And she must not be abusèd,
The meaning seems to be.

The husband is commanded
To love his loving bride;
And live as does a Christian,
And for his house provide.
The woman is commanded
Her husband to obey,

In everything that's lawful,
Until her dying day.

Avoiding all offenses,
Not sow the seeds of strife—
These are the solemn duties
Of every man and wife.

WICKED POLLY *

Young peo - ple who de - light in sin, I'll tell you what has late - ly been, A wo - man who was young and fair Died in sin and deep de - spair.

Young people who delight in sin, I'll tell you what has lately been:
A woman who was young and fair died in sin and deep despair.

She went to frolics, dances and play, in spite of all her friends could
say.
"I'll turn to God when I get old, and He will then receive my soul."

On Friday morning she took sick, her stubborn heart began to break.
She called her mother to her bed, her eyes were rolling in her head.

* From *White Spirituals of the Southern Uplands*, by George Pullen Jackson (University of North
Carolina Press, publishers).

"O mother, mother, fare you well, your wicked Polly's doomed to
hell,
The tears air lost you shed for me; my soul is lost, I plainly see.

"My earthly father, fare ye well; your wicked Polly's doomed to hell.
The flaming wrath begins to roll; I'm a lost and ruined soul.

"Your counsels I have slipted all, my carnal appetite to fill.
When I am dead, remember well, your wicked Polly groans in hell."

She gnawed her tongue before she died; she rolled, she groaned, she
screamed and cried:
"Oh, must I burn forevermore till a thousand, thousand years are
o'er?"

It almost broke her mother's heart to see her child in hell depart:
"Oh, is my daughter gone to hell? My grief so great no tongue can
tell."

She wrung her hands and groaned and cried and gnawed her tongue
before she died;
Her nails turned black, her voice did fail, she died and left this lower
vale.

Young people, let this be your case, oh, turn to God and trust His
grace.
Down on your knees for mercy cry, lest you in sin like Polly die.

NOW OUR MEETING'S OVER *

"One of the songs used to close a camp meeting."

Now, fathers, now our meeting's over, fathers, we must part,
And if on earth we meet no more, I love you in my heart.
Then we'll land on that shore, then we'll land on that shore.
Then we'll land on that shore and we'll shout forever more!

To continue, substitute "mothers," brothers," etc., for "fathers."

* Sent in by Sam P. Bayard of Pennsylvania, one of the youngest and most successful collectors of our indigenous folk songs.

THE OTHER SHORE *

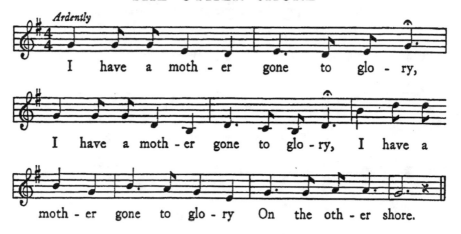

I have a moth-er gone to glo-ry,

I have a moth-er gone to glo-ry, I have a

moth-er gone to glo-ry On the oth-er shore.

I have a mother gone to glory,
I have a mother gone to glory,
I have a mother gone to glory
On the other shore.

By and by I'll go to meet her,
(Repeat as in stanza one.)

Won't that be a happy meetin'?
(Repeat as before.)

There we'll shout and sing forever,
(Repeat as before.)

There we'll meet our good old neighbors,
(Repeat as before.)

There we'll see our blessed Saviour,
(Repeat as before.)

And so on ad infinitum, including father, brother, sister, neighbors, etc.

* "Calling the mourners" song widely sung at "brush arbor" camp meetings by Texas circuit riders fifty years ago.

AMAZING GRACE *

A - maz - ing grace, how sweet the sound, That saved a wretch like me! I once was lost, but now I'm found; Was blind, but now I see. Oh, you must be a lov - er of the Lord, — — Oh, you must be a lov - er of the Lord, Oh, you must be a lov - er of the Lord, — — Or you can't go to heav'n when you die.

Amazing grace, how sweet the sound,
That saved a wretch like me!

* The three stanzas sung to "common meter," are printed in many of the old hymn books under the title of "Warwick." The entire song, sung to the music herewith printed, was very popular in Texas. It was often sung enthusiastically at camp meetings when "mourners" were being called to the altar.

[573]

I once was lost, but now am found;
Was blind, but now I see.

Refrain:

Oh, you must be a lover of the Lord,
Oh, you must be a lover of the Lord,
Oh, you must be a lover of the Lord,
Or you can't go to heav'n when you die.

Through many dangers, toils, and snares,
I have already come;
'Tis grace that brought me safe this far,
And grace will lead me home.

'Twas grace that taught my heart to fear,
And grace my fears relieved;
How precious did that grace appear,
The hour I first believed!

XXV

NEGRO SPIRITUALS

"I want to cross over in a ca'm time."

"I'm so glad God fixed it so
Dat de rich mus' die as well as de po'."

"What melody would stop him [an American] on the street if he were in a strange land, and make the home feeling well up within him, no matter how hardened he might be, or how wretchedly the tune were played? . . . The most potent, as well as the most beautiful among them [the melodies], according to my estimation, are certain of the so-called plantation melodies and slave songs, all of which are distinguished by unusual and subtle harmonies, the thing which I have found in no other songs but those of Scotland and Ireland."—ANTON DVORAK, in *Century Magazine*, February, 1895.

"The songs [of the Southern Negro] are folksongs in the truest sense; that is, they are songs of the folk, created by a folk, giving voice to the emotional life of a folk; for which life America is responsible. They are beautiful songs. . . . Musicians have never been so conscious as now of the value of folksong elements. Music is seeking new vehicles of expression, and is seeking them where they are most sure to be found—in the field of the folksong. We have such a field; it is rich and should be cultivated."—H. E. KREHBIEL, in *Afro-American Folksongs*, 1914.

MANY T'OUSAND GO *

"A song to which the rebellion has actually given rise. This wa:
composed by nobody knows whom . . . and has been sung in secret.
. . . The peck of corn and the pint of salt were slavery rations."

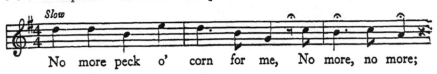

No more peck o' corn for me, No more, no more;

No more peck o' corn for me, Man-y t'ou-sand go.

No more peck of corn for me, no more, no more;
No more peck of corn for me, many t'ousand go.

No more driver's lash for me, etc.

No more pint of salt for me, etc.

No more hundred lash for me, etc.

No more mistress call for me, etc.

LAY DIS BODY DOWN †

O grave-yard, O grave-yard, I'm

walk-in' t'rough de grave-yard; Lay dis bod-y down.

* This song is reprinted with the words and music and note from *Slave Songs of the United States*,
by W. F. Allen, C. P. Ware, and L. M. Garrison (New York: Peter Smith).
† This spiritual from the days of slavery is reprinted from *Slave Songs of the United States*.

[577]

O graveyard,
O graveyard,
I'm walkin' t'rough de graveyard;
Lay dis body down.

I know moonlight,
I know starlight,
I'm walkin' t'rough de starlight;
Lay dis body down.

I lay in de grave
An' stretch out my arms,
I'm layin' in de graveyard;
Lay dis body down.

MONE, MEMBER, MONE

A Negro sermon in song, with the congregation as chorus.

Tell-a me who dat had a rod?
Mone, member, mone!
Hit was Moses, chil' of God.
Mone, member, mone!
Who dat hit dat mighty rock?
Mone, member, mone!
Moses strike one, heaven clock.
Mone, member, mone!
Struck it one an' struck it two.
Mone, member, mone!
Watch out, Moses, what you do!
Mone, member, mone!

Struck it three times, ring-a ring.
Mone, member, mone!
Watch dem healin' waters spring.
Mone, member, mone!
Come ye now and squench yo' thirst.
Mone, member, mone!
Yes, de preacher an' de elder first.
Mone, member, mone!
Den de leader an' de member nex',
Mone, member, mone!
Bringin' wid 'em a gospel tex'.
Mone, member, mone!
Sinner-man, is you gwineter stay,
Mone, member, mone!
Way behin' on de blessed day?
Mone, member, mone!
Hypocrite, you got no room,
Mone, member, mone!
To repent dis side in de tomb.
Mone, member, mone!

MOANIN'

The backwoods congregations of the South, both Negro and white, before they were rich or stable enough to buy hymn books and when few, if any, of the members could read, used to be led in singing by their ministers. These men would "line out" several phrases from the Bible or, perhaps, from Watts's hymnal, and the congregations would take them up and repeat them in a singsong fashion. Long after the white churches had abandoned this mode of singing, the Negro congregations kept it up, and on Victor record No. 20810 the

Reverend Mr. Gates and his congregation have shown what a remarkable thing the Negroes have made of it.

De trum - pet sounds it in my soul

De - - - - - - - trum - - -

pet - - - - - sounds - - - -

it - - - - - in - - - my — —

soul - - - I ain't got long to stay here.

PREACHER

De trumpet sounds it in my soul,

CONGREGATION

De trumpet sounds it in my soul,

PREACHER

I ain' got long to stay here,

CONGREGATION

I ain' got long to stay here.

[580]

HEALIN' WATERS

In a certain country Baptist church a little old woman "from slavery times" would, when she got happy in the Lord, go about through the congregation shaking hands and singing "Healin' Waters." The song was recorded by a student at Prairie View Normal in Texas.

Heal - in' wa - ters done move, Heal - in' wa - ters done move,

What's de mat - ter now? Come to Je - sus.

Healin' waters done move,
Healin' waters done move,

What's de matter now?

Healin' waters done move,
Healin' waters done move,

Come to Jesus!

Healin' waters done move,
Healin' waters done move,

Soul gittin' happy now,

Healin' waters done move,
Healin' waters done move,

Hallelujah!

Healin' waters done move,
Healin' waters done move.

[581]

'LIGION SO SWEET

A Negro Baptizing

My friend John B. Jones, now of Los Angeles, California, sent me from Houston, Texas, this song which he once took down at a Negro baptizing. My friend wrote:

"The minister in charge was a solemn-faced, deep-voiced, white-haired old man. Taking a long stick to guide his footing and to locate a firm bottom to the pool, he waded slowly into the water, carefully feeling his way. Finally, he turned and motioned to his deacons on the bank to lead in the candidates for baptism. As they stepped down into the water, the crowd sang:

" 'Le's go down to Jurdon, le's go down to Jurdon;
De clear ribber Jurdon is mighty deep,
Le's go down to Jurdon;
De ol' ribber Jurdon is mighty deep,
But 'ligion is so sweet.'

"Just before each person was baptized, again the congregation sang:

" 'Missionary Baptist is my name, missionary Baptist is my name.
Missionary Baptist is my name, 'ligion is so sweet.
De Lord said baptism it mus' be, for 'ligion is so sweet;
De Lord said baptism it mus' be, we gwine 'bey his will;
De Lord said baptism it mus' be, for 'ligion is so sweet.
What kind o' manner o' man is he? All things dey obey his will.
What kind o' manner o' man is he? He spoke to de sea an' de sea
was still.
De Lord said baptism it mus' be,
De lil babe in de manger,
What kind o' manner o' man is he?
He walk on de land and he walk on de sea,
An' 'ligion is so sweet.'

"As each baptized person was led out of the water, shouting with joy, some in their ecstasy even trying to fly away from the earth, the crowd sang with splendid effect:

" 'Newbawn, newbaw-awn,
Newbawn chil', newbawn chil',
Like a little babe in de manger.
De ol' ribber Jurdon was mighty deep,
But 'ligion was so sweet.'

"Again, after the ceremony was finished, the entire congregation stood around the baptized persons singing:

" 'De ol' ribber Jurdon was so deep,
An' now our brother in Christ we greet.
De ol' ribber Jurdon was so deep,
But 'ligion was so sweet.
He said baptism it mus' be,
If he from sin 'll set us free;
And all things here obey his will.
Spoke to de sea an' de sea was still,
For 'ligion was so sweet.'

"The crowd trooped away still singing, and the baptizing was over."

DIVES AND LAZ'US

[A Fragment]

Wo' his purple an' linen, too,
    Ring dat big bell;
Don't keer what sort-a rags fer you,
    Ring dat big bell;
Dine sumptious ev'y day,
    Ring dat big bell;
Tell Laz'us go away.

[583]

Chorus:

Ring-a dat big bell,
Dat bigges' big one!
Tell-a me whut he done done
Way down in hell!

Laz'us lay outside,
.Ring-a dat big bell;
Dogs lick his so' side,
Ring-a dat big bell;
But when he bof die,
Ring-a dat big bell,
'Laz'us he even up-high.

Rich man I hears folks tell,
Ring-a dat big bell,
Dropped into lownes' hell,
Ring-a dat big bell;
Laz'us lay close an' fast,
Ring-a dat big bell,
In Ab'ham's breas' at last.

SET DOWN, SERVANT *

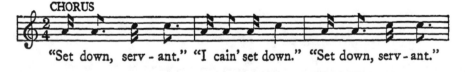

"Set down, serv - ant." "I cain' set down." "Set down, serv-ant."

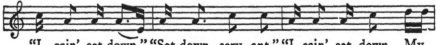

"I cain' set down." "Set down, serv-ant." "I cain' set down, My

* Sung by Eadie Corbin and Ed Frison.

FINE

soul's so hap-py dat I cain' set down. My Lawd, you know,

That you promised me, Prom-ised me a long white robe

An' a pair of shoes." "Go yon - der, an - gel,

Fetch me a pair of shoes, Place dem on - a my

ser - vant's feet. Now, ser - vant, please set down."

Chorus:

"Set down, servant."
"I cain' set down."
"Set down, servant."
"I cain' set down."
"Set down, servant."
"I cain' set down.
My soul's so happy,
Dat I cain' set down."

"My Lawd, you know
Dat you promise me,
Promise me a long white robe
An' a pair of shoes."
"Go yonder, angel,

[585]

Fetch me a pair of shoes,
Place them on-a my servant's feet. . . .
Now, servant, please set down."

"My Lawd, you know
That you promise me,
Promise me a long white robe
An' a starry crown."
"Go yonder, angel,
Fetch me a starry crown,
Place it on-a my servant's head. . . .
Now, servant, you set down."

"My Lawd, you know
That you promise me,
Promise me a long white robe
An' a golden waistband."
"Go yonder, ángel,
An' fetch me a golden waistband,
Place it 'round my servant's waist. . . .
Now, servant, you set down."

OH, LAWD, HOW LONG?

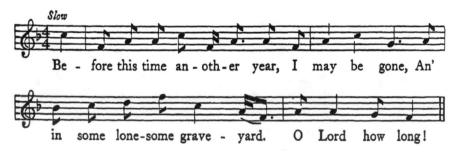

Be - fore this time an - oth-er year, I may be gone, An'
in some lone-some grave - yard. O Lord how long!

Before this time another year I may be gone,
And in some lonesome graveyard, oh, Lawd, how long?

Jes' so de tree fall, jes' so it lie,
Jes' so de sinner live, jes' so he die.

My mother's broke the ice an' gone—oh, Lawd, how long?
An' soon she'll sing dat heavenly song—oh, Lord, how long?

NEVER SAID A MUMBALIN' WORD

With pathos

Oh, dey whupped him up de hill, up de
hill, up de hill, Oh, dey whupped him up de
hill an' he nev - er said a mum - ba - lin'
ward, Oh, dey whupped him up de hill an' he
nev - er said a mum - ba - lin' word, He jes'
hung down his head an' he cried.

The huge and genial Negro blacksmith on Camp C of the Louisiana State Farm at Angola furnished the words and air for this spiritual, which is known throughout Texas, Mississippi, and Tennessee.

Oh, dey whupped him up de hill, up de hill, up de hill,
Oh, dey whupped him up de hill, an' he never said a mumbalin' word,
Oh, dey whupped him up de hill, an' he never said a mumbalin' word,
He jes' hung down his head, an' he cried.

Oh, dey crowned him wid a thorny crown, thorny crown, thorny crown,
Oh, dey crowned him wid a thorny crown, an' he never said a mumbalin' word,
Oh, dey crowned him wid a thorny crown, an' he never said a mumbalin' word,
He jes' hung down his head, an' he cried.

Well, dey nailed him to de cross, to de cross, to de cross,
Well, dey nailed him to de cross, an' he never said a mumbalin' word,
Well, dey nailed him to de cross, an' he never said a mumbalin' word,
He jes' hung down his head, an' he cried.

Well, dey pierced him in de side, in de side, in de side,
Well, dey pierced him in de side, an' de blood come a-twinklin' down,
Well, dey pierced him in de side, an' de blood come a-twinklin' down,
Den he hung down his head, an' he died.

HELL AND HEAVEN *

With spirit

I been 'buked an' I been scorned, Chil-drens, I been

* Sung in part at Parchman, Mississippi, by an enthusiastic group. The spelling varies because some stanzas were obtained elsewhere.

[588]

'buked and   I been scorned, Chil-drens, I   been 'buked and   I   been

scorned,   I been talked   a - bout sure as you born.

Chorus:

> I been 'buked an' I been scorned,
> Childrens, I been 'buked an' I been scorned,
> Childrens, I been 'buked an' I been scorned,
> I been talked 'bout sure as you're born.

I met ol'. Satan on the way,
I met ol' Satan on the way,
I met ol' Satan on the way,
He says, "Young man, you're too young to pray."

Ef you want to see ol' Satan run,
Jes' fire off dat gospel gun.

Ol' Satan wears a mighty big shoe,
Ef you don' watch, gwine slip it on you.

Ol' Satan's like a snake in de grass,
Always in some Christian's pass.

What's ol' Satan grumblin' about,
He's in hell an' he cain' get out.

Ol' Satan's mad, an' I am glad,
He missed de soul he thought he had.

Ol' Satan's like an ol' greyhoun',
Runnin' dem sinners roun' an' roun'.

Ol' Satan's a-settin' on a red-hot seat,
A-coolin' of his head an' a-warmin' of his feet.

I rather pray myself away,
Dan live an' burn in hell one day.

Oh, hell is deep an' hell is wide,
Oh, hell ain' got no bottom or side.

. . . .

Two milk-white hosses, side by side,
Me an' my Jesus gwineter take a ride.

King Jesus give me a little broom,
Jes' fer to sweep my heart clean.

What kin' o' shoes does de angels wear?
Don' wear none, case dey walks on de air.

One o' dese mornin's bright an' fair,
Gwineter hitch on my wings an' try de air.

When I gits to heaven, got nothin' to do
But fly aroun' an' sing hallelu.

Away up in heaven where I'm gwineter shout,
Nobody dere to put me out.

I haven' been to heaven, but I've been tol',
De streets in heaven are paved in gol'.

I want to go to heaven at my own expense,
Ef I cain' git through the gate, I'll jump de fence.

When I go to heaven, I want to go right,
I want to go to heaven all dressed in white.

When I git to heaven, gwineter take my stan',
Gwineter wrastle wid my Lawd like a nachul man.

When I git to heaven, gwineter sit an' tell,
Tell dem angels ring dem bells.

When I git to heaven, gwineter be at ease,
Me an' my God's gwineter do as we please!

MAN GOIN' ROUND *

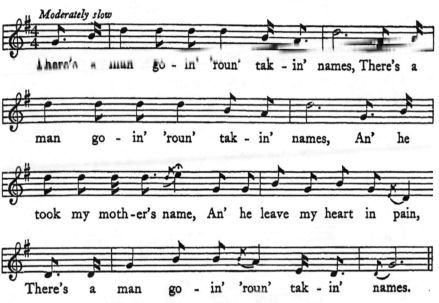

Moderately slow

There's a man go - in' 'roun' tak - in' names, There's a
man go - in' 'roun' tak - in' names, An' he
took my moth-er's name, An' he leave my heart in pain,
There's a man go - in' 'roun' tak - in' names.

There's a man goin' 'roun' takin' names,
There's a man goin' 'roun' takin' names,
An' he took my mother's name,
An' he leave my heart in pain,
There's a man goin' 'roun' takin' names.

There's a man goin' 'roun' takin' names,
There's a man goin' 'roun' takin' names,
An' he took my father's name,
An' he leave my heart in pain,
There's a man goin' 'roun' takin' names.

(Sister, brother, etc.)

* From Carl Sandburg's *American Songbag* (New York: Harcourt, Brace and Co.).

GOOD-BY, MOTHER

This semi-spiritual very probably had its origin in one of the little "ballits" that the wandering "musickaners" and "songsters" sometimes print and sell on their road up and down through the South. Quite often, when a Negro buys one of these cheaply printed slips of red or pink or green paper on which such songs are printed, he has a very vague idea, if any at all, of the air that is intended for the song; but, if this is the case, the stanzas soon acquire a tune. A Negro woman somewhere in the neighborhood of Richmond sang this rather extravagant lament.

Rather fast

Good - by, Mother, good - by, Your voice I shall
hear it no mo', Death done flamished yo' body,
An' de grave is nailed over yo' do'.

Refrain:

> Good-by, mother, good-by,
> Your voice I shall hear it no mo',
> Death done flamished * yo' body,
> An' de grave is nailed over yo' do'.

Oh, how it made me wonder—
I fold up my arms an' I scream,
When I went down to dat lonesome graveyard,
An' I heerd my mother callin' me.

* A possible corruption of "vanquished" or "vanished."

If I had a dear mother—
There's the wrong one in my house—
But ever since my mother been dead,
I been goin' from pillar to pos'.

My heart overwells in trouble,
My eyes drip down in tears,
I got to go to heaven,
'Cause I know it's diffunt from here.

THIS TRAIN *

*This spiritual was sung for us by William McDonald, "Tight-Eye," of the Mississippi State Farm at Parchman.

This train is bound for glory, this train,
This train is bound for glory, this train,
This train is bound for glory,
If you ride it, you must be holy, this train.

This train don' pull no extras, this train,
Don' pull nothin' but de Midnight Special.

This train don' pull no sleepers, this train,
Don' pull nothin' but the righteous people, this train.

This train don' pull no jokers, this train,
Neither don' pull no cigar smokers, this train.

This train is boun' for glory, this train,
If you ride it, you mus' be holy, this train.

Wha————a-hoo————wha-awha-a-hoo————

DEEP RIVER

Deep riv - er, Deep riv - er, Lawd, Deep

riv - er, Lawd, I want to cross o - ver in a

ca'm time. I want to meet death smil - in', I

want   to   meet death   smil - in', Lawd, I   want   to   meet death

smilin',   I want to cross   o - ver   in   a   ca'm time.

Chorus:
> Deep river,
> Deep river, Lawd,
> Deep river, Lawd,
> I want to cross over in a ca'm time.

I'm gonna meet death smilin',
I'm gonna meet death smilin', Lawd,
I'm gonna meet death smilin', Lawd,
I want to cross over in a ca'm time.

My mother's done crossed over,
My mother's done crossed over, Lawd,
My mother's done crossed over, Lawd,
She's done crossed over in a ca'm time.

And sometimes, it seems, one's father "has done crossed over," and one's sister, brother, aunty, and cousins, along with the elders and the deacons of the church.

BLIN' MAN STOOD ON DE WAY
AN' CRIED

This spiritual is known and much sung in the country Negro churches throughout South and East Texas.

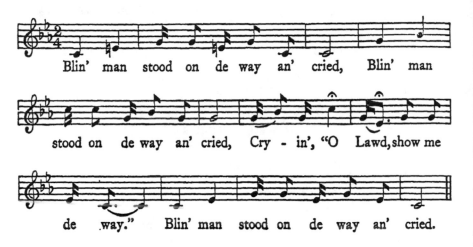

Blin' man stood on de way an' cried, Blin' man stood on de way an' cried, Cry - in', "O Lawd, show me de way." Blin' man stood on de way an' cried.

Blin' man stood on de way an' cried,
Blin' man stood on de way an' cried,
Cryin', "O Lawd, show me de way."
Blin' man stood on de way an' cried.

Cryin', "Help me, O Lawd, if you please,"
Cryin', "Help me, O Lawd, if you please,"
Cryin', "O Lawd, show me de way."
Blin' man stood on de way an' cried.

When I was a sinner I stood on de way an' cried,
When I was a sinner I stood on de way an' cried,
Cryin', "O Lawd, show me de way."
Blin' man stood on de way an' cried.

[596]

DESE BONES GWINE TO RISE AGAIN*

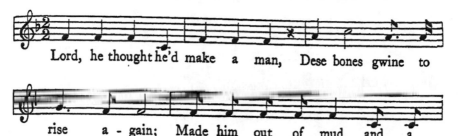

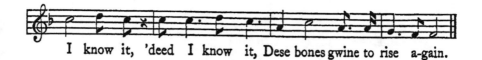

De Lord he thought he'd make a man—
Dese bones gwine to rise again;
Made him out-a dirt an' a little bit o' sand—
Dese bones gwine to rise again.

Refrain:
    I know it, 'deed I know it,
    Dese bones gwine to rise again.

Adam was de fust he made—
Dese bones gwine to rise again.
He put him on de bank and lay him in de shade—
Dese bones gwine to rise again.

*Words principally from Professor Wauchope of the University of South Carolina; the tune and a few stanzas from Carl Sandburg's *American Songbag*.

Thought He'd make a 'ooman, too—
Dese bones gwine to rise again.
Didn't know 'xactly what to do—
Dese bones gwine to rise again.

Took a rib from Adam's side—
Dese bones gwine to rise again.
Made Miss Eve for to be his bride—
Dese bones gwine to rise again.

Put 'em in a gyarden, rich and fair—
Dese bones gwine to rise again.
Tol' 'em dey might eat whatever wuz dere—
Dese bones gwine to rise again.

But to one tree dey mus' not go—
Dese bones gwine to rise again.
Mus' leave de apples dere to grow—
Dese bones gwine to rise again.

Ol' Miss Eve come walkin' roun'—
Dese bones gwine to rise again.
Spied a tree all loaded down—
Dese bones gwine to rise again.

Sarpint quoiled around-a chunk—
Dese bones gwine to rise again.
At Miss Eve his eye he wunk—
Dese bones gwine to rise again.

Firs' she took a little pull—
Dese bones gwine to rise again.
Den she fill her apron full—
Dese bones gwine to rise again.

[598]

Den Adam took a little slice—
Dese bones gwine to rise again.
Smack his lips an' say 'twas nice—
Dese bones gwine to rise again.

De Lord he come a-wanderin' roun'—
Dese bones gwine to rise again.
Spied dem peelin's on de groun'—
Dese bones gwine to rise again.

De Lord he speaks wid a ponstrus voice—
Dese bones gwine to rise again.
Shuck dis ol' worl' to its ve'y joists—
Dese bones gwine to rise again.

"Adam, Adam, where art thou?"
Dese bones gwine to rise again.
"Heah, Marse Lord, Ise a-comin' now."
Dese bones gwine to rise again.

"Stole my apples, I believe?"
Dese bones gwine to rise again.
"No, Marse Lord, but I spec' it wuz Eve."
Dese bones gwine to rise again.

De Lord he riz up in his wrath—
Dese bones gwine to rise again.
Told 'em, "Yo' beat it down de path."
Dese bones gwine to rise again.

"Out o' dis gyarden you mus' git."
Dese bones gwine to rise again.
"Earn yo' living by yo' sweat."
Dese bones gwine to rise again.

[599]

He put an angel at de do'—
Dese bones gwine to rise again.
Tol' 'em not to never come dere no mo'—
Dese bones gwine to rise again.

Ob dis tale dere ain' no mo'—
Dese bones gwine to rise again.
Eve eat de apple, gib Adam de co'—
Dese bones gwine to rise again.

HARD TRIALS *

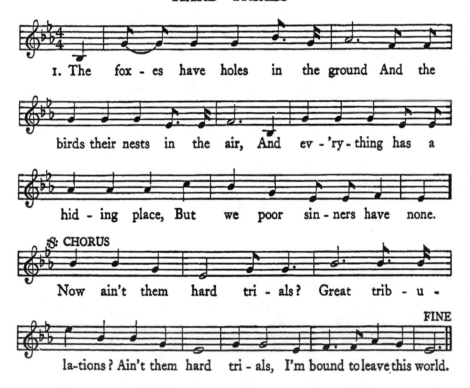

1. The fox-es have holes in the ground And the

birds their nests in the air, And ev-'ry-thing has a

hid-ing place, But we poor sin-ners have none.

CHORUS

Now ain't them hard tri-als? Great trib-u-

FINE

la-tions? Ain't them hard tri-als, I'm bound to leave this world.

* Stanzas four and five were contributed by Virginia Lee Comer, who writes that they were sung on her great-grandfather's plantation in Augusta, Georgia. The last two stanzas were contributed by Judge John M. Green, Yoakum, Texas.

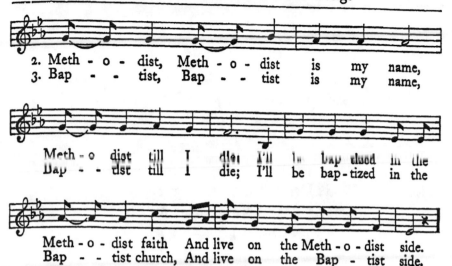

2. Meth - o - dist, Meth - o - dist   is   my   name,
3. Bap - - tist, Bap - - tist   is   my   name,

Meth - o - dist till I die, I'll be bap - tized in the
Bap - - tist till I die; I'll be bap - tized in the

Meth - o - dist faith And live on the Meth - o - dist side.
Bap - - tist church, And live on the Bap - tist side.

De foxes have holes in de groun'
An' de birds have nests in de air,
An' ev'rything have a hiding place,
But we poor sinners have none.

Chorus:

    Now ain't dat hard trials—triberlations?
    Now ain't dat hard trials—triberlations?
    Ise bound to leave this world.

Methodist, Methodist is my name,
Methodist till I die;
I'll be baptized in de Methodist faith
And live on the Methodist side.

Baptist, Baptist is my name,
Baptist till I die;
I'll be baptized in de Baptist faith
And live on the Baptist side.

You may go this-a-way, you may go that-a-way,
You may go from do' to do',

[601]

But if you haven't got de grace of God in your heart
De debil will get you sho'.

Some say John was a Methodist,
And some says John was a Jew;
But de Holy Bible tells us
Dat John was a preacher, too.

Up stepped old Satan,
Wid a black Bible under his arm;
Says he, "My Lord, give me justice,
Den some ob dese people is mine."

Sinner man lay sick in bed,
Death come a-knockin' at de do';
Says he, "Go 'way, Death, come in, Doctor.
I ain't ready to go."

Christian man lay sick in bed,
Death come a-knockin' at de do';
Says he, "Come in, Death, go 'way, Doctor.
Ise ready to go."

DAT LONESOME STREAM

Rat, Tight-Eye, Double Head, along with a chorus of other convicts at Camp D, Parchman, Mississippi, sang this fine spiritual.

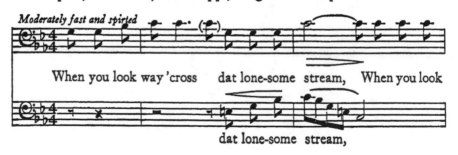

Moderately fast and spirited

When you look way 'cross   dat lone-some stream,   When you look

dat lone-some stream,

way 'cross   dat lone-some stream, Way to   Zi - on

way 'cross   dat lone-some stream,   Zi - on

Lawd, Lawd, Lawd, When you look way down   dat lone-some stream.

ritard.

Lawd, Lawd, Lawd,   way down   dat lone-some stream.

When you look way 'cross dat lonesome stream,
When you look way 'cross dat lonesome stream,
Way to Zion, Lawd, Lawd, Lawd,
When you look way 'cross dat lonesome stream—

When you look way down dat lonesome road,
When you look way down dat lonesome road,
Way to Zion, Lawd, Lawd, Lawd,
When you look way down dat lonesome road—

I got a mother dead an' gone,
I got a mother dead an' gone,
Way to Zion, Lawd, Lawd, Lawd,
I got a mother dead an' gone.

She lef' me here to weep an' mo'n,
She lef' me here to weep an' mo'n,
Way to Zion, Lawd, Lawd, Lawd,
She lef' me here to weep an' mo'n.

[603]

Dark cloud risin' in de eas',
Dark cloud risin' in de eas',
Way to Zion, Lawd, Lawd, Lawd,
Look like it gonna be a storm.

When I look way 'cross dat lonesome stream,
When I look way 'cross dat lonesome stream,
Way to Zion, Lawd, Lawd, Lawd,
When I look way 'cross dat lonesome stream—

WOE BE UNTO YOU*

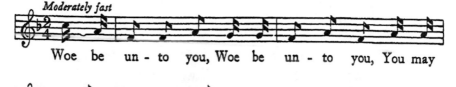

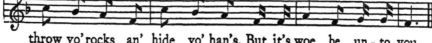

Woe be unto you,
Woe be unto you,
You may throw yo' rocks an' hide yo' hands,
But it's woe be unto you.

Well, it's woe be unto you,
Well, it's woe be unto you,
You may dip yo' snuff an' hide yo' box,
But it's woe be unto you.

* Ruthie May Bevil, summer student in Prairie View Normal School for Negroes, gave us this spiritual.

Well, it's woe be unto you,
It's woe be unto you,
You may dig yo' grave an' hide yo' spade,
But it's woe be unto you.

TONE DE BELL EASY *

When you hear dat Ise a - dy - in', I don' want no - bo - dy to moan. All I want my frien's to do Is give dat bell a tone, Well, well, well, tone de bell eas - y, Well, well, well, tone de bell eas - y, Well, well, well, tone de bell eas - y, Je - sus gon - na make up my dy - in' bed.

* Some words from article of Martha Emmons in *Publications of Texas Folk-Lore Society*, Vol. X.

When you hear dat Ise a-dyin',
I don' want nobody to mo'n.
All I want my frien's to do
Is give dat bell a tone.

Chorus:

   Well, well, well, tone de bell easy,
   Well, well, well, tone de bell easy,
   Well, well, well, tone de bell easy,
   Jesus gonna make up my dyin' bed.

Mary was a-grievin';
Martha said, "He isn' los' "—
But late dat Friday evenin'
He was hangin' to de cross.

Well, well, well, he was hangin' in mis'ry,
Well, well, well, he was hangin' in mis'ry,
Well, well, well, he was hangin' in mis'ry,
Jesus gonna make up my dyin' bed.

Jesus said to his disciples,
"I can see you are afraid;
But if you keep my commandments,
I'm gonna make up yo' dyin' bed."

Well, well, well, he's my dyin'-bed maker,
Well, well, well, he's my dyin'-bed maker,
Well, well, well, he's my dyin'-bed maker,
Jesus gonna make up my dyin' bed.

When you see me dyin',
I don't want you to make no alarms;
For I can see King Jesus comin'
To fol' my dyin' arms.

Well, well, well, he's my soul's 'mancipator,
Well, well, well, he's my soul's 'mancipator,
Well, well, well, he's my soul's 'mancipator,
Jesus gonna make up my dyin' bed.

When you hear dat I'm a-dyin',
I don't want you to be afraid;
All I want my frien's to do
Is take de pillow from under my head.

Well, well, well, so I can die easy, etc.

Mother on her dyin' bed,
Children roun' her bed, cryin'.
"Go 'way, children, don' worry my min',
'Cause you know Ise born to die."

Well, well, well, I don' min' dyin', etc.

When I had a mother,
I had somewhere to go;
But, since my mother's been dead and gone,
I been wand'rin' frum do' to do'.

Well, well, well, I got good religion, etc.

Ever since me an' Jesus been married
We haven' been a minute apart;
He put the receiver in my han'
An' de Holy Ghos' in my heart.

Well, well, well, so I kin call up Jesus, etc.

Oh, meet me, Jesus, meet me,
Meet me in de middle o' de air,

So's if my wings should fail me,
Please meet me wid another pair.

Well, well, well, so I kin fly to Jesus, etc.

When you hear I'm dyin'
Some one'll say I'm los';
But jes' come down to de Jerdon
An' ask de ferryman did I cross.

Well, well, well, I'll be done cross over, etc.

When you hear I'm dyin',
I don' want you to mo'n;
All I want my frien's to do
Is give dat bell a tone.

Well, well, well, tone de bell easy, etc.

SWING LOW, SWEET CHARIOT*

This version of the most widely popular of all Negro spirituals was sent in by Archie A. Searcy, Houston, Texas. The spelling is his.

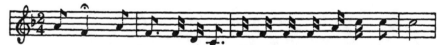

Swing low, sweet char - i - ot,   Com-ing for to car-ry   me home.

Swing low, sweet char - i - ot,   Com-ing for to car - ry me home.

* Music from *The Story of the Jubilee Singers of Fisk University, Nashville, Tennessee.*

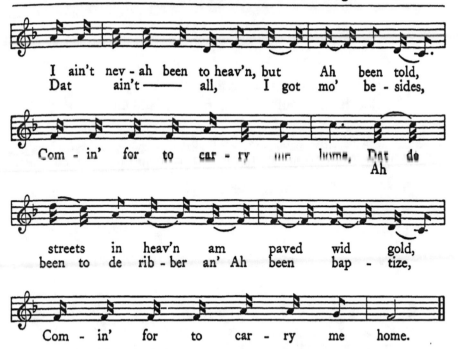

I ain't never been to heaven but Ah been told,
    Comin' fuh to carry me home,
Dat de streets in heaben am paved with gold,
    Comin' fuh to carry me home.

Chorus:

        Swing low, sweet chariot,
        Comin' fuh to carry me home,
        Swing low, sweet chariot,
        Comin' fuh to carry me home.

Dat ain't all, I got mo' besides—
Ah been tuh de ribber an' Ah been baptize'.

Lemme tell yuh whut's a mattah o' fac',
Ef yuh evah leaves de debbil, yuh nevah go back.

[609]

Yuh see dem sisters dress so fine?
Well, dey ain't got Jesus on dey min'.

Ef salvation wuz a thing money could buy,
Den de rich would live an' de po' would die.

But Ah'm so glad God fix it so,
Dat de rich mus' die jes' as well as de po'!

WHEN MY BLOOD RUNS CHILLY AND COL'

Intense

When-a my blood runs chill-y an' col', Ise got to go,

Ise got to go, Ise got to go. Oh,

when-a my blood runs chill-y an' col', Ise got to go

way be-yond de moon. Do, Lord, Do, Lord,

Do re-mem-ber me, Oh, do, Lord, do, Lord,

do re - mem - ber me, Oh, do, Lord, do, Lord,

do re - mem - ber me, oh, do, Lord, re - mem - ber him

Oh, when-a my blood runs chilly an' col', Ise got to go,
  Ise got to go, Ise got to go;
Oh, when-a my blood runs chilly an' col', Ise got to go,
  Way beyond de moon.

Chorus:

  Do, Lord, do, Lord, do remember me,
  Oh, do, Lord, do, Lord, do remember me,
  Oh, do, Lord, do, Lord, do remember me,
  Oh, do, Lord, remember me.

Ef you cain't bear no crosses, you cain't wear no crown,
  Ef you cain't bear no crosses, you cain't wear no crown,
Ef you cain't bear no crosses, you cain't wear no crown,
  Way beyond de moon.

Ise got a mother * in de Beulah land, she's callin' me,
  She's callin' me, she's callin' me,
Ise got a mother in de Beulah land, she's callin' me,
  Way beyon' de sun.

De harder yo' crosses, de brighter yo' crown,†
  De harder yo' crosses, de brighter yo' crown,
De harder yo' crosses, de brighter yo' crown,
  Way beyon' de moon.

* Sung also for father, brother, sister, etc.
† Or, Right under your cross, there lies your crown.

Hit rains, hit hails,
Different sorts o' wedder,
Hit rains, hit hails,
Wusser de better.
Steal up to de back do',
Den on to de bed,
Lawsy, Lawsy, mister,
Da's 'nough said.

BIBLIOGRAPHY

A bibliography of American folksongs, compiled by Harold W. Thompson for his class in American Folk-Literature at the New York State College for Teachers and presented with his compliments to John A. Lomax, with New York's greetings to Texas and a loud shout for Professor George Lyman Kittredge of Harvard.

ALLEN, W. F., WARE, C. P., AND GARRISON, L. MoK., *Slave Songs of the United States*. New York: Peter Smith, 1929.
The original edition was published in 1867 by A. Simpson and Co., New York. Important.

BALLANTA-TAYLOR, N. G. J., *St. Helena Island Spirituals*. New York: G. Schirmer, 1925.

BARBEAU, C. M., AND SAPIR, E., *Folksongs of French Canada*. New Haven: Yale University Press, 1925.

BARBEAU, M., ENGLAND, P., AND WILLAN, H., *Chansons Canadiennes*. 2 vols. London and Boston: Frederick Harris Co. and Boston Music Co., 1929.

BARNES, NELLIE, *American Indian Love Lyrics and Other Verse*. New York: The Macmillan Co., 1925.

BARRY, P., ECKSTORM, F. H., AND SMYTH, M. W., *British Ballads from Maine*. New Haven: Yale University Press, 1929.
Important.

BARTHOLOMEW, M., *Yale Glee Club Series*. New York: G. Schirmer, 1927– .
Some of the best chanteys and spirituals arranged for choral use with men's voices.

BINGHAM, SETH (composer), *Five Cowboy Songs*. New York: H. W. Gray Co., 1930.
Solos with elaborate accompaniments; also choral arrangements for men's voices.

BONE, D. W., *Capstan Bars*. New York: Harcourt, Brace & Co., 1932.
Chanteys and sketches about their use.

Bulletin of the Folksong Society of the Northeast, 1930–

Bibliography

BURLEIGH, H. T. (composer), *Four Negro Folksongs*. New York: Ricordi, 1921.
Not spirituals.

BURLEIGH, H. T., *Negro Spirituals*. New York, 1917– .
Many of the most beautiful spirituals arranged for solo voice with rather elaborate accompaniments; also arrangements for choral use.

BURLIN, MRS. N. C. (NATALIE CURTIS), *Hampton Series of Negro Folk-Songs*. 4 vols., 8vo. New York: G. Schirmer, 1918–1919.
Very careful recording of Negro harmonizations.

BURLIN, N. C. (NATALIE CURTIS), *The Indian's Book*. New York: Harper & Brothers, 1907.

CAMPBELL, O., AND SHARP, C. J., *English Folk Songs from the Southern Appalachians*. New York: G. P. Putnam's Sons, 1917.
See also Sharp, C. J.

COLCORD, JOANNA, *Roll and Go*. Indianapolis: Bobbs-Merrill Co., 1924.
Chanteys. Out of print, but best American collection.

COX, J. H., *Folk-Songs of the South*. Cambridge, Mass.: Harvard University Press, 1925.
Important collection of the West Virginia Folklore Society.

CRONYN, G. W., *The Path on the Rainbow*. New York: Boni & Liveright, 1918.
Anthology of songs and chants from the Indians of North America; words only.

DANN, H., AND LOOMIS, H. W., *Fifty-eight Spirituals for Choral Use*. Boston: C. C. Birchard Co., 1924.

DAUGHTERS OF UTAH PIONEERS, *Pioneer Songs*. Salt Lake City, Utah: Daughters of Utah Pioneers, 1932.
By no means all of these are genuine folksongs. The arrangements are by A. M. Durham.

DAVIS, A. K., JR., *Traditional Ballads of Virginia*. Cambridge, Mass.: Harvard University Press, 1929.
Important collection of the Virginia Folklore Society.

DENSMORE, FRANCES, *The American Indians and Their Music*. New York: Woman's Press of the Y.W.C.A., 1926.
Popular presentation by a recognized authority on the Indian.

DENSMORE, FRANCES, *Indian Action Songs*. Boston: C. C. Birchard, 1921.

DENSMORE, FRANCES. An important series of bulletins of the Bureau of American Ethnology, including: No. 80, *Mandan and Hidatsa Music* (1923); No. 90, *Papago Music* (1929); No. 93, *Pawnee Music* (1929); No. 102,

Bibliography

Menominee Music (1932); and No. 110, *Yuman and Yaqui Music* (1932).
See also, if possible, Bulletins Nos. 45, 53, 61, 75—all out of print. Washington, D. C.: Smithsonian Institution.

DETT, R. N., *Listen to the Lambs.* New York: G. Schirmer, 1923.
The most famous adaptation of a spiritual for choral use, as an anthem in eight parts.

DETT, R. N., *Negro Spirituals.* Cincinnati: John Church Co., 1919.
Some of the finest adaptations of spirituals as art-songs for solo voices; also choral arrangements.

DETT, R. N., *Religious Folk-Songs of the Negro as Sung on the Plantations.* Hampton, Va., and New York: Hampton Institute and G. Schirmer, 1926.

DITON, C., *Thirty-six South Carolina Spirituals.* New York: G. Schirmer, 1928.
Simply harmonized in four parts.

DOLPH, E. A., *Sound Off: Soldier Songs.* New York: Cosmopolitan Book Corporation, 1927.

ECKSTORM, F. H., AND SMYTH, M. W., *Minstrelsy of Maine.* Boston: Houghton Mifflin Co., 1927.
Important.

FARWELL, ARTHUR, *Folk-Songs of the West and South.* Newton Center, Mass.: Wa-Wan Press, 1905.
One of a series of publications marking the rise of interest in our folk-songs on the part of American composers.

FINGER, C. J., *Frontier Ballads.* New York: Doubleday, Doran & Co., 1927.

FISHER, W. A., *Seventy Negro Spirituals.* Boston: Oliver Ditson Co., 1926.
For solo voice, with admirable introductions and with accompaniments by leading composers.

FISHER, W. A., *Ye Olde New-England Psalm-Tunes, 1620–1820.* Boston: Oliver Ditson Co., 1930.

FLANDERS, H. H., AND BROWN, GEORGE, *Vermont Folk-Songs and Ballads.* Brattleboro, Vt.: Stephen Daye Press, 1931.
Important collection by Vermont Folklore Society.

FLETCHER, A. C., *Indian Games and Dances with Native Songs.* Boston: C. C. Birchard Co., 1915.

Folk-Say. Published annually since 1929 by the University of Oklahoma.

FUSON, H. H., *Ballads of the Kentucky Highlands.* London: Mitre Press, 1931.

GAUL, H. B., *Nine Negro Spirituals.* New York: H. W. Gray Co., 1918.
In octavo volume, paper cover. Some of the most attractive of the art-song arrangements for solo voice.

Bibliography

GIBBON, J. M., *Canadian Folk Songs.* New York: E. P. Dutton & Co., 1927.

GORDON, R. W., "The Folk-Songs of America": a series of 18 articles in the Sunday Magazine of the *New York Times*, beginning 2 January, 1927.
Popular articles by a scholar; important.

GORDON, R. W., "Old Songs That Men Have Sung": a department in *Adventure Magazine* from 10 July, 1923, to November, 1927.
Very important; edited by one of the leading collectors.

GRAY, R. P., *Songs and Ballads of the Maine Lumberjacks.* Cambridge, Mass.: Harvard University Press, 1924.

GREENLEAF, E. B., AND MANSFIELD, G. Y., *Ballads and Sea Songs of Newfoundland.* Cambridge, Mass.: Harvard University Press, 1933.

HAGUE, E., "Spanish-American Folk-Songs." In *Memoirs of the American Folklore Society*, Vol. X, 1917.

HALLOWELL, E., *Calhoun Plantation Songs*, 2nd ed. Boston: C. W. Thompson Co., 1907.

HANDY, W. C., *Blues.* New York: A. & C. Boni, 1926.

HOWARD, J. T., *Our American Music.* New York: T. Y. Crowell Co., 1931.
Note especially Chapter XV on "Our Folk-Music," and also the Bibliographies.

HUDSON, A. P., *Specimens of Mississippi Folk-Lore.* Ann Arbor, Mich. (mimeographed), and University of Mississippi, 1928. Mimeographed for the editor and on sale in well-bound copies.
Important collection of the Mississippi Folklore Society.

HULBERT, A. B., *Forty-niners.* Boston: Little, Brown and Co., 1932.
Contains migration songs and tells of the circumstances under which they were sung.

JACKSON, G. P., *White Spirituals in the Southern Uplands.* Chapel Hill, N. C.: University of North Carolina Press, 1933.
Pioneer work; important also for the history of the Negro spiritual.

JACKSON, G. S., *Early Songs of Uncle Sam.* Introduction by K. B. Murdock. Boston: B. Humphries, 1933.

JOHNSON, GUY B., *Folk Culture on St. Helena Island, South Carolina.* Chapel Hill, N. C.: University of North Carolina Press, 1930.
Important; should be read in connection with Mr. Ballanta-Taylor's book listed above.

JOHNSON, GUY B., *John Henry.* Chapel Hill, N. C.; University of North Carolina Press, 1929.

Bibliography

JOHNSON, J. R., *Utica Jubilee Singers Spirituals*. Boston: Oliver Ditson Co., 1930.

For male voices in harmony. An important Introduction by C. W. Hyne contains a valuable classification of Negro folksongs.

JOHNSON, J. W. AND J. R., *The Book of American Negro Spirituals* and *The Second Book of American Negro Spirituals*. New York: Viking Press, 1925, 1926.

Journal of American Folk-Lore. 1888– .

There is an Index to Vol. I–XL, covering the years 1888–1927, published as Volume XIV of the *Memoirs of the American Folk-Lore Society* and distributed by G. E. Stechert and Co., New York, in 1930. In Vol. XLI of the *Journal*, pp. 1–60, will be found an important "Bibliography of American Folklore, 1915–28," compiled by Alexander Lesser. The *Journal* is the most important publication named in the present Bibliography.

KENNEDY, R. E., *Black Cameos*. New York: A. & C. Boni, 1924.

Sketches and songs.

KENNEDY, R. E., *Mellows*. New York: A. & C. Boni, 1925.

Negro work songs, street cries, and spirituals.

KENNEDY, R. E., *More Mellows*. New York: Dodd, Mead & Co., 1931.

Accompaniments free but not difficult. Entertaining descriptions of the singers.

KORSON, G. G., *Songs and Ballads of the Anthracite Miner*. New York: Frederick H. Hitchcock, The Grafton Press, 1927.

KREHBIEL, H. E., *Afro-American Folk Songs*. New York: G. Schirmer, 1914.

Pioneer work by distinguished critic of music.

LARKIN, M., AND BLACK, H., *Singing Cowboy*. New York: Alfred Knopf, 1931.

Simple accompaniments.

LOMAX, JOHN A., *Cowboy Songs and Other Frontier Ballads*. New York: The Macmillan Co., 1910.

Revised with additions, 1916; several reprints.

LOMAX, JOHN A., *Songs of the Cattle Trail and Cow Camp*. New York: The Macmillan Co., 1919.

LUCE, ALLENA, *Canciones Populares*. New York: Silver, Burdett & Co., 1921.

Contains many songs and children's games from Puerto Rico, Cuba, and Mexico.

LUMMIS, C. F., *The Land of Poco Tiempo*. New York: Charles Scribner's Sons, 1906.

McGILL, J., *Folk-Songs of the Kentucky Mountains.* New York and London: Boosey & Co., 1917.

MACKENZIE, W. R., *Ballads and Sea Songs from Nova Scotia.* Cambridge, Mass.: Harvard University Press, 1928.

MACKENZIE, W. R., *The Quest of the Ballad.* Princeton, N. J.: Princeton University Press, 1919.

MATTFELD, J., *The Folk-Music of the Western Hemisphere: A List of References in the New York Public Library.* New York Public Library, 1925. Out of print; important.

METFESSEL, M. F., *Phonophotography in Folk Music.* Chapel Hill, N.C.: University of North Carolina Press, 1929.

MICHELSON, THOMAS, Important series of studies of Indian rituals, published in bulletins of the Bureau of American Ethnology, including: No. 87, *Notes on the Buffalo-Head Dance of the Thunder Gens of the Fox Indians* (1928); No. 89, *Observations on the Thunder Dance of the Bear Gens of the Fox Indians* (1929); No. 95, *Contributions to Fox Ethnology* [Buffalo Dance and Great Sacred Pack] (1930); No. 105, *Notes on the Fox Wâpanōwiweni* (1932). Washington, D. C.: Smithsonian Institution.

MONROE, MINA, AND SCHINDLER, K., *Bayou Ballads, Twelve Folk-Songs from Louisiana.* New York: G. Schirmer, 1921.

NEWELL, W. W., *Games and Songs of American Children.* New York: Harper & Brothers, 1883. Out of print; still the standard work.

NILES, J. J., *Singing Soldiers.* New York: Charles Scribner's Sons, 1927.

ODUM, H. W., *Rainbow Round My Shoulder.* Indianapolis: Bobbs-Merrill Co., 1928.

ODUM, H. W., AND JOHNSON, G. B., *The Negro and His Songs.* Chapel Hill, N. C.: University of North Carolina Press, 1925.

ODUM, H. W., AND JOHNSON, G. B., *Negro Workaday Songs.* Chapel Hill, N. C.: University of North Carolina Press, 1926. Important.

PASKMAN, D., AND SPAETH, S., *Gentlemen, Be Seated.* New York: Doubleday, Doran & Co., 1928. Minstrel shows and minstrels.

PETERSON, C. G., *Creole Songs from New Orleans in the Negro Dialect.* New Orleans: L. Gruenewald and Co., 1902. Revised, 1909.

POUND, LOUISE, *American Ballads and Songs.* New York: Charles Scribner's Sons, 1922. Songs of whites only. Admirable introduction and notes.

Bibliography

Publications of the Texas Folk-Lore Society, 1916– .
First volume out of print. Admirably written to entertain as well as to inform; contributions from such important collectors as the present editor, J. Frank Dobie. Volume X, for 1932, entitled *Tone the Bell Easy*, is a good example of the great interest of the series.

RANDOLPH, VANCE, *Ozark Mountain Folks*. New York: Vanguard Press, 1932.

RANDOLPH, VANCE, *The Ozarks*. New York: Vanguard Press, 1931.

RICHARDSON, E. P., AND SPAETH, S., *American Mountain Songs*. New York: Greenberg, Publisher, 1927.
Simple accompaniments.

RICKABY, FRANZ, *Ballads and Songs of the Shanty-Boy*. Cambridge, Mass.: Harvard University Press, 1926.

SANDBURG, CARL, *The American Songbag*. New York: Harcourt, Brace & Co., 1927. Two editions—the second much lower in price than the first.
Words and music, with delightful comments; a very important book, avowedly borrowing from Messrs. Gordon, Lomax, and other leading collectors. Some of the musical settings are much too elaborate and "modern."

SARGENT, H. C., AND KITTREDGE, G. L., *English and Scottish Popular Ballads*. Boston and New York: Houghton Mifflin Company, 1904.
Edited from the great Child Collection. Indispensable for an appreciation of ballads; very important Introduction by Professor Kittredge.

SCARBOROUGH, DOROTHY, *On the Trail of Negro Folk-Songs*. Cambridge, Mass.: Harvard University Press, 1925.

SHARP, C. J., *American-English Folk Songs*. New York: G. Schirmer, 1918.

SHARP, C. J., *Nursery Songs from the Appalachian Mountains*. London and New York: Novello & Co., 1921–1923.

SHARP, C. J., AND CAMPBELL, O., *English Folk Songs from the Southern Appalachians*. New York: G. P. Putnam's Sons, 1917.
The enlarged edition of this work published in two volumes by the Oxford University Press in 1932 is the most important of the contributions to the subject of American folk-song made by the greatest English collector. The editor of the new edition is M. Karpeles.

SHAY, FRANK, *Iron Men and Wooden Ships*. New York: Doubleday, Doran & Co., 1925.
Sailor songs and chanteys.

SHAY, FRANK, *My Pious Friends and Drunken Companions*. New York: Macaulay Co., 1927.
Songs and ballads of conviviality.

Bibliography

SHAY, FRANK, *More Pious Friends and Drunken Companions.* New York: Macaulay Co., 1928.

SHERWIN, S., KATZMAN, L., AND MOORE, B., *Songs of the Gold Miners.* New York: Carl Fischer & Son, 1932.

SHOEMAKER, H. W., *Mountain Minstrelsy of Pennsylvania.* Philadelphia: McGirr, 1931.

SIRES, INA, AND REPPER, C., *Songs of the Open Range.* Boston: C. C. Birchard Co., 1928.

SMITH, N. C., *New Plantation Melodies as Sung by the Tuskegee Students.* Tuskegee, Ala.: Tuskegee Press, 1909.

SMITH, REED, *South Carolina Ballads.* Cambridge, Mass.: Harvard University Press, 1928.

Important collection of South Carolina Folklore Society; lucid and interesting discussions by the editor, forming an excellent introduction to the whole subject of the American ballad.

SMYTHE, A. T., AND OTHERS, *The Carolina Low-Country.* New York: The Macmillan Company, 1932.

Handsome and important volume containing forty-nine Negro songs and several valuable essays, including R. W. Gordon's chapter on "The Negro Spiritual."

SPAETH, S. G., *Read 'Em and Weep.* New York: Doubleday, Doran & Co., 1927.

SPAETH, S. G., *The Songs You Forgot to Remember.* New York: Doubleday, Doran & Co., 1927.

SPAETH, S. G., *Weep Some More, My Lady.* New York: Doubleday, Doran & Co., 1927.

SPECK, F. G., *Ceremonial Songs of the Creek and Yuchi Indians.* Philadelphia: University of Pennsylvania Museum, Anthropological Publications, Vol. I, Number II, 1911.

STURGIS, E. B., AND HUGHES, R., *Songs from the Hills of Vermont.* New York: G. Schirmer, 1919.

Texts important; accompaniments too elaborate.

TALLEY, T. W., *Negro Folk Rhymes.* New York: The Macmillan Co., 1922.

Some of these rhymes are probably of white origin.

TERRY, R. R., *The Shanty Book.* 2 parts. London: J. Curwen & Sons (Germantown, Philadelphia: Curwen, Inc.), 1921, 1926.

Inasmuch as chanteys are usually common property of British and Ameri-

[620]

Bibliography

can sailors, the best of English collections, arranged for solo voice with piano-
forte accompaniments, deserves mention.

THOMAS, JEAN, *Devil's Ditties*. Chicago: W. Wilbur Hatfield, 1931.

THORPE, N. H., *Songs of the Cowboys*. Boston: Houghton Mifflin Co., 1921.

TURNER, HARRIET, *Folk Songs of the American Negro*. Boston: Boston Music Co., 1925.

VAN STONE, M. R., *Spanish Folk Songs of New Mexico*. Chicago: R. F. Sey-
mour, 1926.

WHITE, N. C., *Negro Folk Melodies*. Philadelphia: Presser, 1927.

WHITE, N. I., *American Negro Folk-Songs*. Cambridge, Mass.: Harvard
University Press, 1928.
    Important. Extensive bibliography.

WHITEMAN, P., AND MCBRIDE, M. M., *Jazz*. New York: J. H. Sears
and Co., 1926.

WHITNEY, A. W., AND BULLOCK, C. C., *Folk-Lore from Maryland*.
Vol. XVIII of the *Memoirs of the American Folk-Lore Society*. New York:
G. E. Stechert and Co., Agents, 1925.
    Contains words of songs.

WOLFORD, L. J., *The Play-Party in Indiana: A Collection of Folksongs and
Games*. Indianapolis: Indiana Historical Commission, 1916.

WORK, J. W., *Folk Song of the American Negro*. Nashville, Tenn.: Fisk
University Press, 1915.

WYMAN, LORAINE, AND BROCKWAY, HOWARD, *Lonesome Tunes: Folk Songs
from the Kentucky Mountains*. New York: H. W. Gray Co., 1916.
    Accompaniments elaborate; a volume popular among professional singers,
and a pioneer work in arousing interest.

WYMAN, LORAINE, AND BROCKWAY, HOWARD, *Twenty Kentucky Mountain
Songs*. Boston: Oliver Ditson Co., 1920.

INDEX

[623]

Index

[624]

Index